Romantic Passion

✻ *Romantic Passion* ✻

A UNIVERSAL EXPERIENCE?

WILLIAM JANKOWIAK

EDITOR

new york   columbia university press

Columbia University Press
New York   Chichester, West Sussex
Copyright © 1995 Columbia University Press

Library of Congress Cataloging-in-Publication Data

Romantic passion: a universal experience? / William Jankowiak,
  editor.
     p.   cm.
Includes bibliographical references and index.
  ISBN 978-0-231-09686-7 (cloth)   ISBN 978-0-231-09687-4 (paper)
    1. Love. 2. Love——Cross-cultural studies.   I. Jankowiak,
William R.
BF575.L8R66   1995
306.7——dc20
                                        95-6954
                                        CIP

Casebound editions of Columbia University Press books are
printed on permanent and durable acid-free paper.

Printed in the United States of America

Beginnings have blunted our shovels;
now eroded forms echo in powdery clay.
Something else in the pottery lies broken
against my best mind, yet there in our best effort
to escape or shape it.
  • THOMAS PALADINO, *Presences,* 1983

Contents

Romantic Passion

Introduction

WILLIAM JANKOWIAK

After being in the field for less than sixty days, I received a letter from my girlfriend explaining that she could not visit me in Inner Mongolia. Stunned, I turned to my Chinese companion for sympathy and advice. I reviewed the ins and outs of our relationship and asked how I could change her mind. Surprised at the nature of my request, he blurted out, "My God, you love her. I thought all you Americans ever wanted from a woman was sexual pleasure."

The study of romantic passion (or romantic love) as it is experienced in non-Western cultures is virtually nonexistent. Why bother to explore what is, according to historical conception, supposedly not there? After all it is a given that romantic passion and its companion, affection, are unique to Euro-American culture (Aries 1962; Rougement 1974). For many historians romantic love never existed outside of Europe. For others it occurs in non-Western nations-states among only the cultural elite, those individuals lucky enough (or unlucky, if you will) to have the necessary sophistication and leisure time to cultivate an aesthetic appreciation for such a subjective experience (Grant 1976; Stone 1988). In brief, a rare experience for the rarest of individuals. It has long been taken for granted that romantic love is the fruit of cultural refinements and not an experience readily available or accessible

2   to non-Westerners in general. Indeed it has become axiomatic among Western literati that the experience of romantic passion is a mark of cultural refinement, if not obvious superiority, and that the less cultured "masses" are incapable of such refinement: desire and lust, yes; romance and love, no. The hidden inference of this assumption may be that romantic love is the prize or reward of true culture.

Reinterpretation of the work of the previous generation has led to a challenge of the notion of an "affectionless" past. Accordingly, physiological detachment and socially prescribed customs of disengagement may not have been inherent in the preindustrial European modes of courtship (Gillis 1988; MacDonald 1981; MacFarlane 1987; Pollock 1983). This revisionist work, however, continues to view romantic passion as the mere precursor to, or embryo of, premarital and extramarital affairs but not substantial in and of itself to warrant comprehensive investigation (see Stearns and Stearns 1985). Consequently, little has been done to alter the persistent notion that romantic passion is a European contribution to world culture.

The premise of much of this research is apparent: cultural traditions center the individual emotionally and psychologically in an intricate web of social dependency with others, thereby rechanneling or defusing the possibility and thus intensity of an individual's private emotional experience. This web of dependency, with its many attendant demands and expectations, in turn undermines the individual's proclivity to fantasize about a lover or fully explore the subjective realm of the erotic. From these and countless related studies it has often been inferred that the non-Western cultures are, by their very nature, incapable of romantic passion or are too closed off to feelings and desires independent of the social context or customary expectation. By this logic the social context circumscribes an individual's experience and a simplistic one-to-one correspondence of circumscription to experience is assumed, implying that the internal life of the non-Westerner is one dimensional, temperamentally inhibited, and heavily dependent on societal values (Averill 1980; Coppinger and Rosenblatt 1968; Rougement 1974; Dion and Dion 1988; Endleman 1989; Rosenblatt 1966, 1967).

Unlike social historians who examine the impact of institutional shifts in the social order, attachment theorists seek the origins of behavioral patterns and propensities in early childhood development (Bowlby 1951; Shaver, Hazan, and Bradshaw 1988). They theorize that love is not based on the physiology of erotic attraction, the rigors of sexual repression, the power of institutional transformation, or anything innately given. It is, rather, a learned response from early childhood that provides the necessary emotion-al foundation to experience romantic love. A "love crush" is nothing more than the desire to recapture the warmth and comfort of the earliest attach-ment of the child to his or her parents.

In expanding on attachment theory and giving fuller weight to the com-plexity of the experience, Jim Chisholm provides in chapter 3 of this collec-tion a biocultural explanation for the origins of romantic love. He asserts that although "the capacity for romantic love is a human universal its manifesta-tion may depend, in part, on the socioecological, political, or economic con-tingencies" that affect the level of chronic stress in early childhood. He looks less at the biology of our species and more at the life history of the individ-ual. He suggests that if the "social environment is unstable, it might be bio-logically and emotionally adaptive" to fall quickly in and out of love.

Evolutionary psychologists and anthropologists believe that romantic passion evolved to improve human reproductive strategies and solidify par-enting efforts (Buss 1988; Daly and Wilson 1978; Fisher 1992; Tennov 1984). In this view romantic passion is not derived from the psychological rigors of sexual repression or early childhood experiences but rather from a biological core, characterized by sudden, seemingly unrestrainable passion, which cre-ates an immediate, if only short-term, bond with another. Biochemical research seems to indicate that the experiences of bliss, euphoria, optimism, and exhilaration—common in the early stages of passion (sometimes called infatuation)—are caused by increased levels of phenylethylamine (PEA), an amphetamine-related compound known for its mood-lifting and energiz-ing effects (Liebowitz 1983). From this evolutionary perspective romantic love comes out of physiological forces within the hominid brain that exist independently of the socially constructed mind. Accordingly, humans have evolved the vital propensity to experience romantic passion, which is expressed as "love," enacted in courtship, and ultimately manifested as reproductive success (Perper 1985). In other words, it is a potent potential experience regardless of the presence or absence of specific cultural institu-tions or child-rearing practices. In effect, it is a human universal.

In chapter 4 Charles Lindholm offers a different explanation. For him and other existential-oriented psychologists and anthropologists, romantic love is not derived from reproductively driven sexual desire but rather springs from the existential yearning for self-transcendence. For Lindholm romantic love is one possible response to the need to experience emotional union with another. It is a transitional psychological form that is a bit like ecstasy or, rather, ecstasy is its extraordinary culmination: ecstasy, the apotheosis of love, mind, and body identified with the other. Romantic passion is kin to the creative process and accounts, in large part, for the crystallization of romantic imagination. This conception shares many features of Van Gennep's rite of passage, Turner's liminality, or Simmel's adventure (Kinget 1979).

Presently romantic passion (or romantic love or infatuation) is defined as any intense attraction involving the idealization of the other within an erotic context. The idealization carries with it the desire for intimacy and the pleasurable expectation of enduring for some unknown time into the future.

Romantic passion stands in sharp contrast to the companionship phase of love (sometimes referred to as attachment), which is characterized by the gradual and oftentimes initially unperceived change into a more peaceful (or less urgent), more comfortable (or less intense), and more fulfilling (or less ecstatic) relationship; love in this stage is built on a strong and abiding mutuality of affection, care, and respect that derives from a long-term association (Hatfield 1988). As Jan Collins and Thomas Gregor remark in chapter 5, as a result of this transformation, love is more "a matter of easy pleasure than esctasy."

Romantic Passion: The Universality of the Experience

Romantic passion is a complex multifaceted emotional phenomenon that is a byproduct of an interplay between biology, self, and society. It is this complexity that separates romantic passion from other more basic emotions (e.g., enjoyment, anger, fear, sadness, disgust, and surprise) that are readily experienced, easily recognized, and, thus, understandable around the world (see Ekman 1986; Levenson et al. 1992; Brown 1991). Romantic passion draws on, therefore, several psychological processes that range from erotic stimulation, emotional attachment, and subjective idealization. Like all complex emotions, it is "mediated by a set of distinct social institutions and cultural values that shape it in culturally specific ways" (Hinton 1993:18). In short, it has a cultural face. Before examining that face, I want to explore those elements that contribute to making it, in its most rudimentary form, on the level of private experience a cross-culturally identifiable, emotional state.

An argument for romantic passion's universality reinforced found by its very presence in societies that do not accept it or embrace it as a positive ideal. In my cross-cultural study (coauthored with Edward Fischer) of romantic love, we found it in 146 out of 166 sampled cultures. Since publication I have been able to document the presence of romantic passion in two cultures—Inuit or Copper Eskimo and Huron—previously classified as inconclusive. The revised survey brings the number of positive confirmations to 148 cultures, or 89 percent. This finding stands in direct contradiction to the popular idea that romantic love is essentially limited to, or the product of, Western culture. Moreover, it suggests that romantic love constitutes a human universal or, at the least, a near-universal.

Unlike psychologists and sociologists, anthropologists have ignored the phenomenon of romantic love. However, Helen Harris in chapter 6 wisely points out that psychologists have uncovered seven mind-centered attributes or core properties that "are common to the experience of fully being in love within almost any cultural setting." These properties include: "1) the desire for union or merger; 2) idealization of the beloved; 3) exclusivity; 4) intrusive thinking about the love object; 5) emotional dependency; 6) a reordering of motivational hierarchies or life priorities; and 7) a powerful sense of empathy and concern for the beloved." In general, the existence of romantic love can be recognized in the *perceived* specialness of another individual. It is based on the intense feelings for another, feelings of immense and complex psychological depth that need to be cultivated and renewed. It is an intimacy most readily observed, Harris writes, in "shared stories, [adventures], thoughts, and time spent together." It is heard loudly in chapter 9 when an eighty-year-old Taita man recalls his fourth wife: "She was the wife of my heart. . . . I could look at her and she at me, no words would pass, just a smile." It is found in the daring actions of an Inuit woman named Milukkuttak who, in chapter 13, refused to stay home and wait for her husband but rather went with him hunting and sealing so that they would not be separated "for a single hour." It is articulated, in chapter 14, with these words of a Moroccan youth who told his lover, "I trust you. I care for you. If I do not see you for just half a day I go crazy." It is celebrated, in chapter 6, by a Mangaian woman who, when asked why she loved her husband, replied, "He told me his life." The heights of the emotional union of romantic love are not, however, without their costs: separation, rejection, and grief. Perhaps a stronger argument for romantic love's universality can be found in the widespread cross-cultural fear of rejection and love's loss. A Mangaian man, for example, when asked how it felt to be rejected by a lover, replied, "She hurt my heart," a sentiment understood and shared by India's Society for the Study of Broken Hearts, which was established in 1992. May 3, deemed by the society as national Broken Hearts Day, is the day for the romantically disappointed and the love rejected to commiserate with one another.

What makes romantic involvement or idealization such a problematic state is its ability to flow in many ways at once. It is not uncommon for individuals to be, at least in the short run, out of sync with each other. Idealization does not have to be reciprocated. A person can be completely in love with another while that person is either uninterested or, if interested, emotionally guarded. This delay or mismatch in emotional intensity often leads to an imbalance in perception and emotional identification that can further lead to heartrending pain, dissatisfaction, and, in the extreme, obsessive behavior. It can quickly become a truly terrifying experience, a sentiment echoed by a Northeastern Brazilian who in chapter 14 remembered love being "so good and yet . . . so scary . . . because it can really hurt a person."

What may be most significant about all of the individual comments above is their lack of cultural specificity. They all sound alike, or at least sound recognizable notes. If one was not told otherwise, one could easily imagine that the speakers were American or European. In terms of the emotional experience, the remarks could have been uttered by an Inuit, a Taita, a Mangaian, a Fulbe, a polygamous Mormon, or anyone else, for that matter.

Sex, Love, and Idealization

Romantic passion, in conjunction with its cousin, lust, are two of the most powerful panhuman emotions. They are organized around different cultural and psychological criteria, which puts them, in several ways, in direct competition with one another, and this competition raises important implications for understanding their origins and manifestations in ordinary life.

Every culture highlights either sexuality or love, but has a very difficult time in blending the two together. Every culture, including the intellectuals of that culture, prefer to speak in idioms that stress the benefits of either love or sex—rarely both. This is especially true of the intellectual history of the Western world, which has repeatedly demonstrated a continuous and pronounced ambivalence toward sexuality and love.

Plato, for example, dismissed sex as something necessary for reproduction while insisting that love is coterminous with the pursuit of beauty. In essence he abstracted love both from the body and the individual beloved. This notion was further developed by the early Christians who were hostile to sexual enjoyment while glorifying the positive aspects of asexual love (agape). Later thinkers and writers were equally ambivalent. For Ovid "love is essentially a sexual behavior sport in which duplicity is used in order that a man might win his way into a woman's heart and subsequently into her boudoir"

(Murstein 1988:59). Similarly Schopenhauer, who advocated greater sexual openness, thought romantic love was "a trick" that nature played on us to ensure reproduction. Stendhal agreed, and insisted that romantic love was a delusion. The Victorian middle class, however, ignored its disgruntled intellectuals and sought to advance an idealized image of love, while viewing with ambivalent distaste the sensuality of sex.

If nineteenth-century intellectuals had difficulty synthesizing love and lust into a viable, workable, and harmonious whole, so did "utopian" experiments in family living. The Oneida society of the nineteenth century, for example, recognized lust and sexual desire as something understandably human but were convinced that the phenomenon of romantic love was nothing but sexual desire in sheep's clothing. On the other hand the Shakers deemed both romantic love and lust as undignified and irrelevant, if not threatening, to the higher aspirations of the community. In rejecting both experiences the Shakers expressed, at least, a less than dim acknowledgment of love and lust's power to undermine social order and the family. Likewise nineteenth-century Mormons looked askance at both romantic love and lust, perceiving them as disruptive forces. Yet in all three societies the persistence of romantic love and sexual entanglements among individuals confounded the rules.

In reaction to the historically growing cacophony of voices and social experiments in the West, Freud argued that the essence of cultural experience itself is the denial of lust. In effect, without sexual repression there would be no individual creativity, cultural achievement, or romantic entanglements. The implication was that in sexually unrepressive societies much of what we think of as culture would not exist. The psychologist Robert Endleman, in his analysis of the "absence" of romantic love in twelve tribal cultures, concluded that romantic passion is unknown in sexually open tribal cultures. Despite strenuous objections from many anthropologists whose work Endleman used as the basis for his conclusion, he held, like other neo-Freudians, that passionate love cannot exist in sexually expressive tribal cultures and that, therefore, there was nothing further to study.

The Endleman hypothesis closely resembles the one that informed more than two centuries of missionaries, traders, and ethnographers whose perceptions, conceptual expectations, and understanding of non-Western cultures were formed more by the presupposition of "a lusty savage" than a loving person. The story of this misunderstanding is told, in various detail, in chapters 6, 9, 10, and 12 of this collection. In practical terms, what these authors discovered was not the absence of romance but rather what Helen Harris calls the Polynesian pattern of sexual banter, which accentuates sexual imagery in ordinary speech. As with any form of speech, the use of sexual imagery has numerous connotations. At times the banter conveys good-natured joking, other times it implies real sexual desire, at other times a secret emotional attachment, and on other occasions the sexual banter disguises an ambivalence about the opposite sex. Significantly, cultures that favor the Polynesian pattern disapprove of public expressions of love and displays of emotional intimacy. These behaviors are considered to be private matters between individuals and not for public consumption. In contrast, the American pattern is organized around the notion of idealized love, which approves and glorifies public displays of affection in speech and behavior, as long as such displays are not overtly sexual. Although romantic metaphors are the preferred language of courtship, it is understood that the metaphors may range in meaning and implications from pure lust to unrequited affection. In looking back over the historical record, it is painfully obvious that ethnographers and explorers misunderstood or misperceived the numerous forms of affiliation that can exist inside and outside what Collins and Gregor call the "official" culture. This oversight is discussed in chapter 5. The two competing discourse patterns represent the individual and the official culture's inability to reconcile the two volatile emotions of lust and romantic love.

Charles Lindholm, in chapter 4, makes the critical point that a link between love and sexuality does not equate to, require, or result in pornography. Unlike lust, love cannot be bought (or for that matter, arranged, anticipated, or outlawed). If there is an attempt to buy it, love is invalid. Love is inevitably more than sexual release. Nonetheless, it is doubtful whether sexual attraction can ever be completely absent from the heart, mind, and speech. Although many cultures separate love from sexual expression, signifying distinctions in various ways, very few celebrate platonic love as its most valued ideal. More to the point, romantic passion is seldom experienced in an erotic or emotional vacuum. The recent research suggests that humankind's propensity to idealize one another, while not deriving from sexuality, is coterminous and vitally intertwined with desire (Hendrick and Hendrick 1992).

One example can be seen in eleventh- and twelfth-century aristocratic European society. Although it is routinely assumed that the code of romantic love was nonerotic in tone, implication, and experience, there is no empirical data to support this. The most that can be said, without hard data, is that courtly love, among the upper class, found cultural expression in a standardized form that purposely ignored any mention of the erotic in written communication. However, even a cautious literary reading of this code would suggest that much of the courtier and troubadour songs and poems were sublimated seductions. It can be further argued that the commonplace sublimination of erotic context bears witness to its submerged intensity (see Ackerman 1994).

The inability to satisfactorily blend and integrate the two emotions accounts for the push/pull tension between love as desire and love as enduring affection. It may also account for some of the misunderstanding and turmoil often found in male-female relationships.

Gender Differences: Culture, Biology, and Romance

Sociologists exploring the social construction of gender report that American middle-class white men are quicker to "fall in love" than women, who are consistently slower to make such an emotional commitment. Disagreeing with her colleagues over the structural explanation, Francesca Cancian holds that the differences in the timing and impact of the emotional expression does not stem from women's growing economic and social independence.[1] Rather it arises from "socialization factors that contributed to men being less responsible for working on the emotional aspects of the relationship, and therefore see[ing] love as magically and perfectly present or absent. Women, in contrast, may assume that love varies and depends on their own efforts" (Cancian 1987:77). Psychologist Dorothy Tennov (1979) maintains that there is no difference between American men's and women's experience of romantic love. Though social factors contribute to the cultural variation in the experience of romantic passion, its intensity for both genders is remarkably similar. As I indicate in chapter 10, I found that urban Chinese women are somewhat more reserved and cautious than men during the initial stages of courtship. However, once a woman becomes emotionally involved, there is no noticeable gender difference in the experience of the emotion. The argument is a difficult one.

Susan and Douglas Davis believe that cultural norms, especially regarding gender ideals, affect an individual's interest and willingness to discuss romantic involvement. Their study of Moroccan adolescent behavior found that women were more inhibited in discussing romantic yearnings and involvement. Because women are the more severely circumscribed sex in that

Muslim culture, it is simply in their best interest to adopt a pragmatic and cautious attitude toward love, sex, and marriage. Caution, restraint, and secrecy are the rule. This accounts for the infrequency of falling "head over heels" in love.

Gender differences in romantic expression also arise from biopsychological factors that shape the development of different love strategies not always recognizable or readily understood (Buss and Schmitt 1993; Hendrick and Hendrick 1992:11). Men and women are typically attracted to different qualities in a potential lover or mate, which incline men to fall in love quicker, and women to adopt a more cautious, deliberate tact. From this perspective many of the characteristic "love acts" displayed during courtship, outlined by Helen Fisher in chapter 2, are designed to enhance male and female attractiveness. For women these acts are geared toward measuring male ambition, industry, income, status, and generosity, whereas men are looking for evidence of female fertility (e.g., youth, health), sexual exclusivity, reproduction capability, and parental investment (Buss 1994; Buss and Schmitt 1993; Daly and Wilson 1978; Jankowiak, Hill, and Donovan 1992; Symons 1979).

The attitudinal differences of men and women may account, in part, for the phenomenon of instant attraction or "love at first sight." If erotic and romantic idealization for men is based on images of physical attraction, that would also account for men's ability to quickly shift between sexual fantasy and deep romantic affection. In China, for example, men often admit to "falling in love" with a good-looking woman they frequently encountered but seldom actually spoke to. In the words of one twenty-nine-year-old man, "I dreamed of someone like her last night. She was so beautiful. I knew I wanted to marry her." The word *like* may be the pivotal word, for it suggests an image, not a particular person. This phenomenon is echoed in the Brazilian proverb "Born in a glance and matures in a smile." It is heard in the remembrance of a Nigerian male of the Tiv tribe, who said of the first sight of his third wife, "When I saw her dance she took my life away and I knew I must follow her." In this way physical attraction, at least for men, might prove to be a primary catalyst for romantic idealization.

Customarily women show more interest in assessing a man's social status or in understanding his character. More so than physical attractiveness, this appears to be the more important criterion for female mate selection and the formation of romantic fantasies. Since it takes much longer to evaluate character than it does physical beauty, women may be slower to become romantically involved or make a complete commitment.

If physical appearance and social standing are valued, their very presence also increases apprehension and anxiety. The power of the love experience to distort judgment is a common cross-cultural fear. It can create imbalance, which leads men and women to think that they have been unfairly seduced or bewitched by each other. In cultures across the world countless cautionary tales warn men and women of becoming trapped in a love that is excessive. Their clearest and most vivid manifestation lies in the near universality of the femme fatale and the dangerous hero myths. The tales caution men and women to be wary and not blinded by what is most desired in the opposite sex: for men, the allure of physical beauty, for women, the power of social status. Regardless of the different dangers for men and women, the story of romantic love's painful and destructive possibilities is ancient, anchored as it is in our evolutionary wellsprings.

Love, Sex, and Marriage

It is easy to infer that choice, sex, love, and marriage are closely coterminous with one another. As various contributors to this collection make clear, however, that is not always or inevitably so. Though it is sometimes felt to be, freedom to select a mate or a lover is not a European innovation. It was long present in many tribal societies as it still is in many non-Western societies today (Westermarck 1922). Even societies that arranged marriages allowed men and women to choose mates or lovers. Once married, men in Arabic culture tended to take a second or third wife for romantic pleasure (Croutier 1989:153). As Jim Bell points out in chapter 8, Taita women prefer to be the second or third wife, rather than the first, because they would likely be married for love and thus would be treated better than other wives. It is apparent from these and other ethnographic accounts of polygamous cultures that "love marriages" are more frequent than previously reported. It has long been observed that actions are often taken that are at odds with the ideals and proscriptions of a society's "official culture," and there is no compelling reason to believe that this would not be equally the case in matters of marriage. In fact, given the high societal and individual stakes, the room to bend the rules may even be greater than in most other spheres.

Love and sex, albeit separate emotions, are inextricably intertwined and intimately connected. The critical question then must be whether they will be institutionalized inside or outside of marriage or ignored and left to the individual to reinvent anew in each generation. In each pairing it is not the singular appearance therefore of romantic love, monogamy, or individual choice but the combination of all three occurrences *inside* the institution of marriage that is historically significant.[2] What accounts for romantic love's emergence as the primary basis, as opposed to a possible consideration, for marriage?

Cultural materialists emphasize the structural impact of the transformation of the family from a unit of production to a unit of consumption, which, geographically speaking, reduced kinship ties while also providing youths with the economic and emotional resources to resist parental demands for self-sacrifice. William Goode (1959) also indicates that rapid social change separated generations in terms of cultural values, which contributed to greater adolescent freedom. In this situation love becomes the basis of inter-generational discord, as it is illustrated in chapter 6. It also becomes a discourse of defiance whereby lovers circumvent the arrangements of the senior generations and choose their own marriage partners; instances of this occurrence can be found in chapters 11, 12, 13, and 14. Once marriage was redefined as an amorous union organized around personal choice, it entered the "visible or official culture," discussed in chapter 5, which in turn patterned expectations in such a way that only "the obtuse, emotionally incapacitated, or the perversely reared are deprived of the experience of love" (Udry 1974:137). Under such circumstances love no longer had to be rediscovered anew in each generation. As cogently analyzed in chapter 5, it could become an appropriate and valued cultural experience. In the Western world romantic love gradually, and in various intensities, became the language of gentility and social distinction.

Aristocratic women, the standard-bearers for eleventh- and twelfth-century European social manners, promoted the elaboration of what had previously been a private experience into a formal ideology. Whatever meaning courtly love held for the individual, it also served to establish social boundaries between the cultural elite and the peasantry. Whereas the latter enjoyed the crudities of sexual bantering, the elite, especially its women, preferred to deemphasize the erotic in favor of romantic imagery. In this way the earthy language of eros, or what is conceptualized as the Polynesian pattern in chapter 6, was replaced by the high-flown language of romance and gentility, an idiom that is used in many strata across America today.

The ethnographers Kevin Birth and Morris Freilich in chapter 15 present a diachronic study of Trinidadian gender interaction that effectively documents the impact of disease, cultural diffusion, and social stratification on the change from the Trinidadian pattern to a recognizably American pattern. In effect, they found that romantic metaphors had replaced sexual metaphors as the preferred idiom of male-female address. Previously, the preferred idiom was organized around sexual imagery that regularly disguised or diminished underlying implications of romantic passion.[3] They suggest that it is Trinidadian women's newly obtained economic independence that enabled them to effect the change to romantic imagery, the metaphors closely related to relationships and family.[4]

In short, romantic passion may in fact be muted or hidden from easy public view, though never entirely repressed, by other cultural variables. Because researchers have rarely studied the relative frequency in which a person falls in and out of love, it is unclear if romantic love is experienced with less frequency in those cultures that deny or disapprove of the experience. The relative frequency with which members of a community experience romantic love may very well depend upon that culture's social organization and ideological orientation. What is obviously needed are many more close, fine-tuned analyses of the phenomenon of love as it is experienced and expressed in a variety of social settings, as well as ethnographic and historical contexts. Then, perhaps, in the words of Collins and Gregor, "in time we will be able to write a comparative ethnography of love [that] . . . charts human relationships whose dimensions transcend our western experience."

Overview of the Book

The collection of essays attempts to understand a fundamental, albeit seriously neglected, dimension of humankind's intimate emotional life. Because we have been so preoccupied with non-Western sexuality, heightened no doubt by its dramatic differences to our own, we denied the "natives" an essential part of their humanness—an active and profound love life.

No single theoretical perspective shapes the volume's organization. This should be no surprise, for it is to be expected when a topic is being freshly scrutinized. Although the contributors come from different academic generations and various theoretical orientations, everyone was willing to rethink and reinterpret their data, which, for some, was from a somewhat novel perspective. With the exception of the chapters in part 1, the theoretical section of the book, every chapter is based on long-term and in-depth research in a single culture. From this richly varied database the ethnographers analyze the challenges, opportunities, and dilemmas romantic passion presents to the individual, the family, and the community.

There is no gender bias in this anthropological study of love. Everyone initially ignored the topic, and both male and female anthropologists (as illustrated by the eleven male and nine female contributors to the book) working in different cultural areas have, almost simultaneously, discovered its importance for cultural analysis.

Though several contributors make evident the presence of what is called enduring love or mature love, it is, however, not the primary topic of analysis. With the exception of Collins and Gregor's chapter 6, all the contributors seek to examine romantic passion as a private experience and a form of cultural expression, thereby showing us, in some measure, what is culturally unique and what is a universal aspect of this human experience. Ethnographic, literary, and historical examples are used to document the relationship between social convention and individual desire, which often becomes entangled whenever individuals seek romantic fulfillment. However, since this approach has seldom been taken in the past, our understanding of the cross-cultural variation in the meaning and *styles* of romantic expression is lacking. By providing such richly textured accounts, the present volume hopes to correct this ethnographic oversight.

This collection is about romantic passion (sometimes referred to as romantic love, infatuation, or passionate love). The use of multiple terms is indicative of the lack of consensus present in the field over how to conceptualize and discuss romantic love. Because *romantic love* is closely identified with American culture, or, rather, monopolized to some extent by it, several contributors prefer a less culturally bounded term such as *infatuation, romantic passion,* or *passionate love.* Other contributors thought it was not important and preferred the more familiar term, *romantic love.* Regardless of terminology, each author sought to document and explore the significance of love by probing the subjective domain of an individual's emotional life within its specific cultural context.

The collection is divided into three parts. Part 1 is theoretical in its focus and provides several different perspectives for analyzing the origins, nature, and significance of romantic passion. Part 2 documents the precontact presence of romantic passion and explores its contemporary manifestation as a form of private experience and cultural expression. Part 3 examines romantic passion as a medium of cooperation and as a basis for intergenerational competition over the issue of marital choice. In effect, the reality and power of romantic love as a deeply felt and highly motivating reality is revealed.

What follows is a brief summary of each author's contribution. In chapter 2 Helen Fisher introduces an evolutionary-based hypothesis to show how feelings of attraction, attachment, and detachment evolved to coordinate and regulate the ebb and flow of affiliation, which corresponds to each species' distinctive breeding system. In chapter 3 Jim Chisholm, drawing on insights of attachment theory and evolutionary ecology, argues that love styles vary according to the degree of chronic stress present in early childhood. He further speculates that the capacity to psychologically "switch" orientations toward either a long-term or a short-term relationship can, under the right circumstances, be truly an adaptive reproductive strategy. In chapter 4 Charles Lindholm reasons that romantic love is based less in sexual biology than it is in the psychological need for self-transcendence. It is, he maintains, "most typical of the modern world [and as such is] one possible response to the human condition of contingency and self-consciousness." In chapter 5 Jan Collins and Thomas Gregor discuss the tensions between the inner world of love and the demands of the larger community. Drawing upon in-depth research conducted in American and Mehinaku culture, they hold that love is essentially a dyadic relationship organized around notions of exclusion, secrecy, and trust.

In chapter 6 Helen Harris provides convincing evidence that there is continuity of romantic love among the Mangaian that was preserved and persists into contemporary times. In doing so she effectively challenges an earlier study holding that the Mangaians were obsessed with the erotic but not love. In chapter 7 Leonard Plotnicov finds evidence that romantic love was present in Tiv society, but that not everyone experienced the emotion. In chapter 8 Helen Regis examines very closely the reasons for the Fulbe's fear, abhorrence, and tacit fascination with romantic passion. In chapter 9 Jim Bell discusses the meaning and significance of love among the Taita of Kenya. He makes the distinction between two forms of love: infatuation and romantic love. In chapter 10 I analyze romantic passion as a private experience and cultural manifestation in contemporary urban Chinese society. As a result I am convinced that it is an important and more sought-after private experience than previously reported or heretofore imagined.

The politics of love invoked as resistance or reaffirmation inside and outside the family is examined in part 3. Vickie Burbank's chapter 11 indicates that romantic passion was present among precontact Australian Aborigines. She reports that romantic passion in Mangrove, a contemporary Australian Aborigine settlement, often served as the basis for youths resisting parental authority. In a comparable case study Pamela Stern and Richard Condon's chapter 12 examines the shifts in Copper Inuit marriage and spouse exchange practices over the last sixty or more years. They demonstrate that romantic infatuation was an important, albeit unspoken, motive embedded in the Inuit Eskimo spousal exchange system. In their view one of the impacts of long-term settlement is the creation of adolescent peer groups, a new pattern of association, which enable youths to play with sexual and emotional involvement and thus delay making a spousal commitment—a pattern that is helping to undermine the stability of contemporary marriage. In chapter 13 Susan Davis and Douglas Davis also focus on adolescent identity conflict by providing a detailed study of Moroccan youths' perception of romantic love and richly textured examples of family relations and marriage. They underscore a male love dilemma as well as look closely at the reasons for Moroccan sex differences in the expression of romantic sentiment. In chapter 14 L. A. Rebhun provides an in-depth account of male-female oscillation between the desires of love and the demands of duty in Northeast Brazilian society. She found that, historically, the mother-son bond was "stronger than the husband-wife bond, and it was the location of romanticized love. Today, women who are disappointed in the weakness of their husbands' love turn to their sons for veneration and companionship that their husbands do not provide them." Kevin Birth and Morris Freilich's chapter 15 provides an overview of Trinidadian sexual love relationships across a thirty-year-period, from 1958 to 1988. Specifically, they focus on the transformation of a sexual exchange system into a romantic love exchange system. They argue that Trinidadian women's newly obtained economic power enables them to require men to court. Emilie Allen and myself in the last chapter discuss the dilemmas of men and women striving to balance romantic love and "harmonious" love, two often competing notions of love in Angel Park, one of America's oldest polygamous communities.

Finally, it is important to point out that the ethnographic cases collected here do not encapsulate the range of cultural variation that is beginning to look more and more varied than any of us could have imagined. At present, it is, however, the best that can be done. The information and analysis presented in various chapters are pathbreaking accounts. They represent the first attempt to document the significance of romantic passion in a given society. It is my hope that this book will spark renewed interest among other scholars in exploring a phenomenon that has, for the most part, been ignored or neglected. Romantic passion's vitality, uniqueness, and commonality can only be revealed through knowing it well—a task that requires renewed scholarly effort and that should be undertaken with clearer eyes.

NOTES

I am grateful to Emilie Allen, Jim Bell, Tom Gregor, Yonni Harris, Lee Munroe, Tom Paladino, Susan Pensak, and Gioia Stevens for their encouragement, advice, and assistance.

1. Sex differences in the expression of love are also shaped by cultural restraints. Like their male counterparts in Japan and urban China, American men demonstrate their love by "providing women with important resources; whereas women's style is to seek emotional closeness through verbal disclosures" (Cancian 1987:75). Because contributors did not focus on gender styles of expression, it is difficult to evaluate the significance of Cancian's American findings. Her important and noteworthy observation must wait for other scholars to research and explore.

2. Cultures differ in the way they encourage or discourage the expression of romantic passion. In some cultures romantic passion is rejected as an evil and frighteningly emotional experience. In others it is tolerated but not celebrated or asserted, and, in still others, romantic passion is praised as an important and cherished cultural ideal.

3. Trinidadians have always distinguished between the women one plays with and the women one loves. Michael Angrosino during the late 1970s found that Trinidadians were careful to affirm the permissibility of speaking openly about sex but the need to touch privately on matters of the heart. L. A. Rebhun found that Northeast Brazilians made a similar distinction. She found passionate love was always a possibility, though not a necessarily articulated fact of life, that customarily grew out of the sexual encounter. Furthermore, Oscar Lewis observed of the Puerto Ricans in the 1950s that they took a like-minded approach to matters of sex and matters of the heart.

4. Today it is deemed inappropriate, when talking to a woman, to use, even in jest, sexually explicit imagery. Not only is it considered rude and crude and, thus, the idiom of the "lower class," it is also viewed as an affront to women's image of gentility. Furthermore, emphasis on social distinction also appears to be important in shaping discourse style in urban China, Japan, and India. In every complex society issues of social distinction and social boundaries shape and mold the preferred form of public discourse. In the sixties, for example, there was an attempt to allow more explicit sexual imagery into daily speech as a matter of openness and frankness. The recent reaction to this challenge of "good taste" to the American pattern of discourse is instructive. In many ways the expansion of the definition of sexual harassment to include the issue of ambivalence (or "hostile environment") is an attempt to reinsert the positive value of asexuality back into casual conversation between men and woman.

REFERENCES

Ackerman, D. 1994. *A Natural History of Love.* New York: Random House.

Aries, P. 1962. *Centuries of Childhood: A Social History of Family Life.* New York: Knopf.

Averill, J. 1980. "A Constructivist View of Emotion." In R. Plutchik and H. Kellerman, eds., *Emotion: Theory, Research, and Experience,* pp. 305–337. New York.

Bowlby, J. 1951. *Maternal Care and Mental Health.* Geneva: World Health Organization.

Brown, D. 1991. *Human Universals.* New York: McGraw Hill.

18

Buss, D. 1988. "Love Acts: The Evolutionary Biology of Love." In R. Sternberg and M. Barnes, eds., *The Psychology of Love*, pp. 100–118. New Haven: Yale University Press.

—— 1994. *The Evolution of Desire*. New York: Basic Books.

Buss, D., and D. Schmitt. 1993. "Sexual Strategies Theory: An Evolutionary Perspective on Human Mating," *Psychological Review* 100(2):204–232.

Cancian, F. 1987. *Love in America*. Cambridge: Cambridge University Press.

Coppinger, R., and P. Rosenblatt. 1968. "Romantic Love and Subsistence Dependence of Spouses." *Southwestern Journal of Anthropology* 24:310–318.

Croutier, A. 1989. *Harem: The World Behind the Veil*. New York: Abbeville.

Daly, M., and M. Wilson. 1978. *Sex, Evolution, and Behavior*. North Scituate, Mass.: Duxbury Press.

Dion, K. L., and K. K. Dion. 1988. *Romantic Love: Individual and Cultural Perspectives*. In R. Sternberg and M. Barnes, eds., *The Psychology of Love*, pp. 264–289. New Haven: Yale University Press.

Ekman, P. 1986. "A New Pan-Cultural Facial Expression of Emotion." *Motivation and Emotion* 10:159–168.

Endleman, R. 1989. *Love and Sex in Twelve Cultures*. New York: Psychic Press.

Fisher, H. 1992. *The Anatomy of Love*. New York: Norton.

Gillis, J. R. 1988. "From Ritual to Romance: Toward an Alternative History of Love." In C. Stearns and P. Stearns, eds., *Emotion and Social Change*, pp. 87–122. New York.

Grant, V. 1976. *Falling in Love*. New York: Springer.

Goode, W. 1959. "The Theoretical Importance of Love." *American Sociological Review* 24:38–47.

Hatfield, E. 1988. "Passionate Love and Companionate Love." In R. Sternberg and M. Barnes, eds., *The Psychology of Love*, pp. 191–217. New Haven: Yale University Press.

Hendrick, S., and C. Hendrick. 1992. *Romantic Love*. Newbury Park: Sage.

Hinton, A. 1993. "Prolegomenon to a Processual Approach to the Emotions." *Ethnos* 21(4):1–22.

Hunt, M. 1959. *The Natural History of Love*. New York: Knopf.

Jankowiak, W., and E. Fischer. 1992. "A Cross-Cultural Perspective on Romantic Love." *Ethnology* 31(2):149–155.

Jankowiak, W., E. Hill, and J. Donovan. "The Effects of Sex and Sexual Orientation on Attractiveness Judgments: An Evolutionary Interpretation." *Ethnology and Sociobiology* 13:73–85.

Kinget, M. 1979. "The 'Many-Splendoured Thing' in Transition; or, 'The Agony the Ecstasy' Revisited." In M. Clark and G. Wilson, eds., *Love and Attraction*, pp. 251–255. Oxford: Pergamon.

Levenson, R., P. Ekman, K. Heider, and W. Friesen. 1992. "Emotion and Autonomic Nervous System Activity in the Minanagkabau of West Sumatra." *Journal of Personality and Social Psychology* 62(6):972–988.

Liebowitz, M. R. 1983. *The Chemistry of Love*. Boston: Little, Brown.

Lindholm, C. 1988. "Lovers and Leaders: A Comparison of Social and Psychological Models of Romance and Charisma." *Social Science Information*, 1(27):3–45.

Lowie, R. 1950. *Social Organization*. New York: Holt, Rinehardt and Winston.

MacDonald, M. 1981. *Mystical Bedlam: Madness, Anxiety, and Healing in Seventeenth-Century England*. Cambridge: Cambridge University Press.

MacFarlane, A. 1987. *The Culture of Capitalism*. Cambridge: Cambridge University Press.

Mellen, S. 1981. *The Evolution of Love*. San Francisco: Freeman.

Murstein, B. 1988. "A Taxonomy of Love." In R. Sternberg and M. Barnes, eds., *The Psychology of Love*, pp. 13–37. New Haven: Yale University Press.

Perper, T. 1985. *Sex Signals: The Biology of Love*. Philadelphia: ISI.

Pollock, L. 1983. *Forgotten Children: Parent-Child Relations from 1500 to 1800*. Cambridge: Cambridge University Press.

Rosenblatt, P. 1966. "A Cross-Cultural Study of Child Rearing and Romantic Love." *Journal of Personality and Social Psychology* 4(3):336–338.

— 1967. "Marital Residence and the Functions of Romantic Love." *Ethnology* 6:471–480.

Rougemont, D. de. 1974. *Love in the Western World*. Trans. M. Belgion. Rev. ed. New York.

Seldman, S. 1991. *Romantic Longings*. New York: Routledge,

Shaver, P., C. Hazan, and D. Bradshaw. 1989. "Love as Attachment: The Integration of Three Behavioral Systems." In R. Sternberg and M. Barnes, eds., *The Psychology of Love*. New Haven: Yale University Press.

Stearns, P., and C. Stearns. 1985. "Emotionology: Clarifying the History of Emotions and Emotions Standards." *The American Historical Review* 90(4):813–836.

Sternberg, R., and M. Barnes. 1988. *The Psychology of Love*. New Haven: Yale University Press.

Stone, L. 1988. "Passionate Attachments in the West in Historical Perspective." In W. Gaylin and E. Person, eds., *Passionate Attachments*, pp. 15–26. New York.

Symons, D. 1979. *Evolution of Human Sexuality*. New York: Oxford University Press.

Tennov, D. 1979. *Love and Limerence: The Experience of Being in Love*. New York: Stein and Day.

Westermarck, E. 1922. *The History of Human Marriage*. Vols. 1–3. New York.

Udry, R. 1974. *The Social Context of Marriage*. Philadelphia: Lippincott.

✗ PART ONE ✗

Biology, Psychology, and Cultural Factors

The Nature and Evolution of Romantic Love

HELEN FISHER

Anthropomorphizing: The charge of my critics. My counter charge: There is a sense in which, when we cease to anthropomorphize, we cease to be men, for when we cease to have human contact with animals and deny them all relation to ourselves, we . . . deny our own humanity. We repeat the old, old human trick of freezing the living world and with it ourselves.

• LOREN EISLEY, 1970

"This whirlwind, this delirium of eros," wrote poet Robert Lowell. Poems, songs, novels, operas, plays, films, sculptures, and paintings have portrayed romantic love throughout Western cultures for centuries. The love story of Isis and Osiris was recorded in Egypt over three thousand years ago (Wolkstein 1991). The Sumerian tale of Inanna and Dumuzi is among several stories, songs and poems about love dating around 2000 B.C. (Wolkstein 1991). Ovid composed poems to romantic love in the first century B.C. in ancient Rome (Melville 1990). And many other myths and legends about love come from antiquity (Bulfinch 1993). So although Americans commonly regard romantic love as an invention of the troubadours in twelfth-century France, evidence of this passion existed in Western culture long before.

Romantic love is also visible in traditional societies. In their examination of 166 cultures William Jankowiak and Edward Fischer (1992) found evidence of romantic love in 88.5 percent of them. In some people sang love songs. In others individuals eloped. Informants of some cultures recounted their personal anguish or longing. And the folklore of many societies portrayed romantic entanglements. Jankowiak and Fischer attributed the lack of evidence for romantic love in the balance of these cultures to "ethnographic oversight" or lack of access to the folklore of the culture. They concluded that romantic love, which they equate with passionate love, "constitutes a human universal, or at least a near-universal" (Jankowiak and Fischer 1992:154).

Because of the worldwide prevalence of this phenomenon, I shall propose that the fundamental components of romantic love—attraction and attachment—are primary, panhuman emotions much like fear, anger, joy, sadness, and surprise, that these feelings are based in brain physiology, as are the other primary emotions, that human romantic love stems from mammalian biochemical systems of affiliation designed to coordinate each species' specific breeding cycle, and that human cyclic attraction and attachment evolved some four million years ago in conjunction with the primary human reproductive strategy, serial pairbonding, to rear successive altricial young through their periods of infancy.

The Chemistry of Attraction

Mating is the single most important behavior pattern of any individual of any sexually reproducing species because it leads to fertilization and the perpetuation of one's DNA, and affiliative behavior plays a central role in this mating process in birds and mammals. Moreover, it is well established that there are biochemical components to several of the primary emotions. Yet until recently little work has been done on the psychopharmacology of human male/female affiliation.

In seminal work done in the 1980s, however, psychiatrist Michael Liebowitz divided human romantic love into two basic physiological stages, attraction and attachment, and he proposed that brain physiology was involved in each of these distinct affiliative behavioral complexes (Liebowitz 1983). He arrived at this conclusion while treating patients who craved a relationship. In their haste they picked unsuitable partners who soon rejected them. Their exhilaration then turned to despair, until they renewed their quest. As this cycle of failed love affairs proceeded, these individuals swung from feeling elated to feeling brokenhearted and depressed over each inappropriate romantic fling.

Liebowitz suspected that these men and women suffered from low levels of endogenous phenylethylamine, or PEA, which is chemically related to the amphetamines and is associated with feelings of elation. So he administered MAO inhibitors, antidepressant drugs that block the action of monoamine oxidase, or MAO, a class of substances that break down PEA and the monoamine neurotransmitters, norepinephrine, dopamine, and serotonin in the limbic system and associated areas of the brain. Thus, MAO inhibitors boost levels of PEA and these neurotransmitters. Within weeks of receiving MAO inhibitors, several of these lovesick patients started to live comfortably without a mate as well as choose their partners more carefully. Liebowitz hypothesized that they no longer craved the amphetaminelike feelings of exhilaration they used to get from their exciting yet disastrous love affairs.

Exhilaration, however, is only part of a larger constellation of physiological and psychological traits associated with romantic attraction. Psychologist Dorothy Tennov (1979) devised approximately two hundred statements about romantic love and asked four hundred men and women at and around the University of Bridgeport, Connecticut, to respond to her questionnaire with "true" or "false" responses. Over four hundred additional individuals answered subsequent versions of her poll. From their answers, as well as from their diaries and other personal accounts, Tennov identified a constellation of characteristics common to the condition of "being in love," a state that she calls limerence, that Liebowitz calls attraction, and that I often call infatuation.

Tennov (1979) reports that limerence begins the moment another individual takes on "special meaning"; it could be an old friend seen in a new perspective or a complete stranger. But as one informant put it, "My whole world had been transformed. It had a new center, and that center was Marilyn" (Tennov 1979:18). This phenomenon has been noted before, in literature. George Bernard Shaw once said, "Love consists of overestimating the differences between one woman and another."

Infatuation then develops in a characteristic psychological pattern, beginning with "intrusive thinking." Many of Tennov's informants claimed that as the obsession grew they spent from 85 percent to 100 percent of their waking hours in sustained mental attentiveness thinking about this single individual. And tiny details of the time they spent with their "love object" took on weight, as the "limerent" reviewed them obsessively.

The infatuated person also aggrandized trivial aspects of the adored one in a process Tennov calls "crystallization." Crystallization is distinct from idealization in that the infatuated person perceives the weaknesses of his or her love object. All of Tennov's limerent subjects could list the faults of their beloved. But they cast these flaws aside, or convinced themselves that these defects were unique and charming, and concentrated on the positive parts of their sweetheart's physical features and personality. This phenomenon, too, is well described in Western literature; as Chaucer said, "Love is blynd."

Tennov also reported a constellation of specific emotions that occurred among her "limerent" informants. Paramount was elation; hope, apprehension, uncertainty, and fear were also commonly reported. If the infatuated individual received some positive response from a "love object," he or she became ecstatic. If rebuffed, the limerent often became listless and moody instead, brooding until he or she had managed to explain away this setback and renew pursuit. And underlying the infatuated person's angst and ecstasy was fear. As a twenty-eight-year-old truck driver summed up what many informants reported, "I'd be jumpy out of my head. It was like what you might call stage fright, like going up in front of an audience. My hand would be shaking when I rang the doorbell. When I called her on the phone I felt like I could hear the pulse in my temple louder than the ringing of the phone" (Tennov 1979:49).

Tennov's informants also reported trembling, pallor, flushing, a general weakness, and overwhelming sensations of awkwardness and stammering. Shyness, fear of rejection, anticipation, and longing for reciprocity were other central sensations of infatuation. Most interesting, informants reported the feeling of helplessness, the sense that this passion was irrational, involuntary, unplanned, and uncontrollable. As a business executive in his early fifties wrote to Tennov about an office affair,

> I am advancing toward the thesis that this attraction for Emily is a kind of biological, instinct-like action that is not under voluntary or logical control. . . . It directs me. I try desperately to argue with it, to limit its influence, to channel it (into sex, for example), to deny it, to enjoy it, and yes, dammit, to make her respond! Even though I know that Emily and I have absolutely no chance of making a life together, the thought of her is an obsession. (Tennov 1979:38)

These data indicate that attraction involves a matrix of intense emotions that swing dramatically, hinged to a single other being. And this mosaic of psychological and physiological responses is only partially related to sex. Ninety-five percent of Tennov's female informants and 91 percent of her male subjects rejected the statement, "The best thing about love is sex."

Culture also plays an essential role in attraction—particularly in one's choice of love object and the timing and process of courting. As children we develop specific likes and dislikes in response to family, friends, experiences, and chance associations, so by teen age each individual carries within him or her an unconscious mental template, or "love map," a group of physical, psychological, and behavioral traits that she or he finds attractive in a mate

(Money 1986). This love map is clearly the product of one's environment.

Timing is also important, and one's environment is central to timing too. People fall in love when they are ready (Tennov 1979), as when they leave home for college, are displaced in a foreign city, or make other social, psychological, or economic changes that render them susceptible to romance. Barriers seem to enhance infatuation, as does mystery (Shepher 1971; Spiro 1958; Tennov 1979).[1] And there are all sorts of cultural rules that humans follow. In some societies, for example, individuals wed for social reasons and choose a passionate love relationship outside of marriage.

So culture plays a crucial role in who you find attractive, when you begin to court, where you woo, and how you pursue a potential partner. But parents, teachers, books, movies, songs, and other cultural phenomena do not teach you what to feel as you fall in love. Instead, like the sensations of fear, anger, and surprise, these emotional responses are generated by brain/body physiology. Liebowitz is specific about this biochemical response; he theorizes that one feels the elation of attraction when neurons in the limbic system of the brain (which governs the basic emotions) become either saturated or sensitized by PEA and/or the monoamine transmitters norepinephrine, dopamine, serotonin, triggering the feelings of attraction (Liebowitz 1983).

The Chemistry of Attachment

"Love is strongest in pursuit, friendship in possession," Emerson has written. At some point that magic wanes. Tennov measured the duration of limerence from the moment infatuation hit to the moment that a "feeling of neutrality" for one's love object began. She concluded that the most frequent interval, as well as the average, was between approximately eighteen months and three years (Tennov 1979). Sexologist John Money agrees, proposing that once you begin to see your sweetheart regularly, the passion typically lasts two to three years (Money 1980:65).

Liebowitz hypothesizes that the end of infatuation is also grounded in brain physiology; either the nerve endings become habituated to the brain's natural stimulants or levels of PEA and/or other endogenous amphetamine-like substances begin to drop. As he says, "If you want a situation where you and your long-term partner can still get very excited about each other, you will have to work on it, because in some ways you are bucking a biological tide" (Liebowitz 1983:200).

Attachment, Liebowitz proposes, is the second physiological stage of romantic love. As infatuation wanes and attachment grows, he hypothesizes that a new chemical system is taking over, the endorphins, peptide neurotransmitters that are chemically related to morphine, giving partners the feelings of safety, stability, tranquility, and peace (Liebowitz 1983). Then as partners see one another regularly, they trigger the continual production of these natural opiates, or other neurohormones that produce bonding behavior. This may explain why you physically ache when a lover dies or abandons you. Not only are you suffering from the psychological and social trauma of losing a partner, but you may also be experiencing withdrawals caused by declining levels of endogenous narcotics (Liebowitz 1983).

A host of recent data indicate that another group of neurochemicals may be associated with attachment. Oxytocin and the closely related peptide, vasopressin, play central roles in male/female bonding, group bonding, and mother/infant bonding in other mammalian species (see Pedersen et al. 1992; Winslow et al. 1993). In fact, oxytocin has been called the "satisfaction hormone" because levels rise dramatically during vaginal stimulation and male ejaculation (Jirikowski 1992) and "evoke warm positive feelings of social strength and comfort" in social interactions in several species (Panksepp 1992:243). Moreover, injection of synthetic endorphins inhibit the action of oxytocin (see Argiolas 1992) and oxytocin ameliorates morphine withdrawals (Sarnyai et al. 1985), suggesting that, in mammals, oxytocin, vasopressin, and the endorphins interact and/or operate in conjoining neuronal systems. The contributions of oxytocin and vasopressin to human romantic love are not known, but humans exhibit significant levels of these peptides, and these neurochemicals could well be additional (or alternative) psychopharmacological mechanisms for attachment in people.

A survey of world literature and mythology will probably uncover references to these two distinct physiological stages of love, attraction and attactment (Fisher in preparation). At present I have found evidence of them among the !Kung of the Kalahari Desert of southern Africa and in the Celtic love story of Tristan and Isolde. Nisa, a !Kung San woman, remarked to anthropologist Marjorie Shostak, "When two people are first together, their hearts are on fire and their passion is very great. After a while, the fire cools and that's how it stays. They continue to love each other, but it's in a different way—warm and dependable" (Shostak 1981:268). In the fatal saga of Tristan and Isolde, a young knight and a beautiful queen share an elixir known to induce romantic passion for about three years. Here is a medieval poetic reference to the chemistry of attraction.

Liebowitz does not discuss the duration of attachment. But he proposes that these two basic stages of romantic love—associated with at least two distinctly different chemical systems in the brain—evolved in the human animal for reproductive purposes. "For primitive man two aspects of relating to the opposite sex were important for survival as a species. The first was to have males and females become attracted to each other for long enough to have sex and reproduce. The second was for the males to become strongly attacted to the females so that they stayed around while the females were raising their young, and helped to gather food, find shelter, fight off marauders, and teach the kids certain skills" (Liebowitz 1983:90).

I suspect there is a third stage to romantic love associated with our human reproductive strategy: detachment. The physiology for detachment is unknown. But in trying to explain why birds abandon their nests at the end of the breeding season to join a flock and why many creatures leave the safety of their natal home after infancy, ethologist Norbert Bischof has theorized that an animal gets an "excess of security," to which it responds by withdrawing from the object of attachment (Bischof 1975a; Wickler 1976). The same phenomenon may occur in human mateships. At some point in a long relationship, the brain's receptor sites for the endorphins and/or oxytocin, vasopressin, and/or other neurochemicals may become desensitized or overloaded, and attachment wanes, setting up the body and the brain for separation.

This is not to suggest that men and women are biologically *compelled* to fall in love, attach, or detach from one another. Cultural forces play a powerful role in directing behavior, as does one's idiosyncratic perspective—what philosophers have long called "free will." But marriage is a cultural universal and divorce is common in societies around the world (Fisher 1989, 1991, 1992). Any therapist would maintain that long relationships require work. And worldwide data on the duration of marriage and timing of divorce suggest that the brain physiology for human attraction, attachment, and detachment evolved in conjunction with our primary human reproductive strategy.

Human Reproductive Strategies

Every species has a primary reproductive strategy designed to rear the young. Five of these are prevalent in birds and mammals. Two pertain to the reproductive tactics of females: monandry (forming a sexual/social/economic relationship with a single male) and polyandry (many males). Two pertain to the reproductive strategies of males: monogyny (one female) and polygyny (many females). One pertains to both males and females: polygynandry (many females, males, or horde living).

These zoological definitions do not imply that partners are necessarily sexually faithful to one another (Kleiman 1977). In fact, monogyny, monandry, polygyny, and polyandry are regularly found in association with infidelity (extrapair copulations) in nature (see Fisher 1992). Thus human marriage systems (or mateships) are only part of the human reproductive strategy; extramarital sexual activity is a secondary, opportunistic component of our "mixed" reproductive tactics. In this article only the primary human mating strategy, marriage, is examined.

Over 90 percent of American men and women in every birth cohort marry; records go back to the mid 1800s (Cherlin 1981). The *1982 Demographic Yearbook* of the United Nations lists the number of men and women who have married by age forty-nine in ninety-seven industrial and agricultural countries. Between 1972 and 1981 the proportion of married women in these ninety-seven societies ranged from 75.8 percent to 99.8 percent; the mean was 93.1 percent (Fisher 1989). The proportion of married men in these ninety-seven societies ranged from 73.9 percent to 99.7 percent; the mean was 91.8 percent (Fisher 1989). These figures have not changed significantly since (Fisher 1992). Although no worldwide tabulations have been taken on the percent of men and women who marry in horticultural and gathering/hunting cultures, the ethnographic literature confirms that marriage is a pancultural custom (Murdock 1949; Hawthorn 1970; Frayser 1985). In nonindustrial communities, bachelors and spinsters are rare (Lévi-Strauss 1985).

Moreover, most men and women are monogamous (one spouse); they wed only one individual at a time, although what is permissible to each gender varies. In 99.5 percent of cultures women are permitted to marry only one man at a time, monandry. This includes women in "monogamous" societies and women in societies that permit polygyny; in polygynous households a woman marries one man at a time even though she has co-wives. Therefore, with the exception of women who live in societies that permit polyandry, 0.5 percent (Van den Berghe 1979), women around the world pursue a marriage strategy of monandry, forming a social/economic relationship that entails sexual rights and privileges with only one man at a time.

Human males also characteristically marry one woman at a time, monogyny. In 16 percent of human cultures, monogyny is prescribed and all men who marry form a pairbond with a single female at a time (Van den Berghe, 1979). But 84 percent of the 853 human societies tabulated in Murdock's *Ethnographic Atlas* permit polygyny, and 44 percent of these cultures regard polygyny as the preferred marriage form (Van den Berghe 1979). Van den Berghe (1979) reports, however, that in most of these societies only about 10 percent of men actually practice polygyny; even where polygyny is widespread, only about 25 percent of men have several wives at once. Hence, in practice, monogyny is the predominant marriage pattern for men. Murdock concurs, saying: "An impartial observer employing the criterion of numerical preponderance, consequently would be compelled to characterize nearly every known human society as monogamous, despite the preference for and frequency of polygyny in the overwhelming majority" (Murdock 1949:27–28). Because polygyny in humans is regularly associated with rank and wealth, Daly and Wilson (1983) propose that monogamy, or pairbonding, was even more prevalent in prehorticultural, unstratified societies.

The above cross-cultural data on female and male marriage systems indicate that the formation of a pairbond with one individual at a time, monandry and monogyny, is the primary mating pattern for both sexes. Polyandry, polygyny, and extrapair liaisons are secondary, opportunistic hominid reproductive tactics. Human monogamy is not always permanent, however, and it displays several patterns of decay that are revelant to understanding the origin and nature of human romantic love.

Human Divorce Patterns

Few societies in the world prohibit divorce. The Roman Catholic Church banned divorce in the eleventh century A.D.; the ancient Incas did not permit divorce either. But with these and a few other exceptions, peoples from Amazonia to Siberia have rules about divorce, procedures for divorce, and do divorce (Fisher 1992). There are several patterns to human divorce that have purely cultural explanations (see Fisher 1992).

Divorce *rates*, for example, are correlated with economic autonomy: in those societies where spouses tend to be relatively economically independent, divorce rates are high; where spouses are dependent on one another to make a living and their resources are largely shared, divorce rates are lower (Fisher 1992). Economic independence between spouses, as well as many other cultural factors, contribute to the frequency of divorce. But four general patterns of divorce do not correlate with divorce rate; they occur in societies where divorce rates are high and in cultures where divorce is rare

(Fisher 1989, 1991, 1992). These patterns, I hypothesize, evolved during human evolution and selected for the characteristic ebb and flow of human romantic love.

The first pattern regards the duration of marriage that ends in divorce. Data taken from the *Demographic Yearbooks* of the United Nations on 62 available industrial and agricultural societies for all obtainable years between 1947 and 1989 (188 cases) indicate that divorces exhibit a skewed distribution, characterized by the occurrence of the mode during and around the fourth year, followed by a gradual, long-tailed decline in divorce counts. Divorces cluster around this four-year peak.

The second aspect of human divorce seen in these data is the age at which divorce occurs. Age at highest divorce risk was tabulated for all twenty-four available societies on selected years (80 cases) between 1966 and 1989. Divorce risk was highest among men in the age category twenty-five to twenty-nine; divorce risk for women was equally highest in age categories twenty to twenty-four and twenty-five to twenty-nine. Across the sixty-two sampled societies (189 cases), the mean percent of divorces that involved women under age 45 was 81 percent and the mean percent of divorces that involved men under age 45 was 74 percent. Thus, in the above cross-cultural samples, divorce risk was greatest at the height of one's reproductive and parenting years.

The third pattern is seen in the number of children per divorce. In the fifty-nine societies recorded between 1950 and 1989, 39 percent of all divorces occurred among couples with no dependent children, 26 percent occurred among those with one dependent child, 19 percent occurred among couples with two dependent children, 7 percent occurred among those with three children, 3 percent occurred among couples with four young, and couples with five or more dependent young rarely split (Fisher 1992). Hence divorce *counts* were highest among couples with no children or one dependent child, and they decreased with increasing numbers of dependent young.[2]

The fourth pattern of human pairbonding regards remarriage. The U.S. Census Bureau reports that 76.3 percent of American women who divorce during their twenties remarry, 56.2 percent of those who divorce in their thirties remarry, 32.4 percent of those who divorce in their forties remarry (Levitan, Belous, and Gallo 1988). Approximately 75 percent of American women and 80 percent of American men who divorce remarry (Glick 1975; Cherlin 1981; Levitan, Belous, and Gallo 1988). And one-half of all American remarriages take place within three years of a divorce (Cherlin 1981; Furstenberg and Spanier 1984).

Moreover, most remarriages occur during reproductive years. In 1979 the modal age at remarriage among American men was thirty through thirty-four; the modal age at remarriage among American women was twenty-five through twenty-nine (Fisher 1989). Cross-culturally, remarriage by divorced individuals also peaked among men and women of reproductive age. Among the ninety-eight peoples surveyed by the United Nations between 1971 and 1982, the modal age at remarriage among men was thirty through thirty-four; women who remarried following a divorce were a modal age of twenty-five through twenty-nine (Fisher 1989). The United Nations Statistical Office records the number of remarriages for specific peoples in specific years, but it does not tabulate the *percent* of divorcees who remarry. Remarriage is frequent, however, in those places for which data are available, and remarriage rates are highest for men and women of reproductive age (Fisher 1989, 1991, 1992).

These cross-cultural data indicate that human marriages have several general patterns of decay: 1) Mateships tend to disband during and around the fourth year of marriage. 2) Men and women in a variety of cultures tend to divorce while in their twenties, the height of their reproductive and parenting years. 3) Men and women most regularly abandon a partnership that has produced no children or one dependent child. 4) Most divorced individuals of reproductive age remarry. 5) The longer a mateship lasts, the older the spouses get, and/or the more children they bear, the more likely they are to stay together. There are exceptions to these patterns (see Fisher 1992). But these regularities persist in many contemporary industrial and agrarian societies as well as in several traditional cultures (Fisher 1989, 1991, 1992).

This article addresses only some of these patterns—specifically the human tendency to divorce during and around the fourth year after wedding, during the height of reproductive and parenting years, and often with a single child, followed by remarriage—because it is this constellation of mating patterns that I shall hypothesize evolved in conjunction with the human emotions for attraction, attachment, detachment, and reattachment to another.

The Evolution of Human Serial Monogamy

The evolution of human serial monogamy during reproductive years and often with one dependent child is best understood within the context of monogamy in other species. Monogamy is rare in mammals; only 3 percent pair up, and they do so under several specific circumstances (Wittenberger and Tilson 1980; Mock and Fujioka 1990). Many of these circumstances may have contributed to the evolution of monogamy in hominids (Fisher 1992). But one proposed by Kleiman is particularly relevant. She writes that monogamy is favored in evolution "whenever more than a single individual (the female) is needed to rear the young" (Kleiman 1977:51).

Canid species are good examples. The female red fox bears as many as five altricial helpless kits, and her milk is thin; she must stay in the den to feed them, and she will starve to death unless she has a mate to provision her. For the dog fox polygyny is regularly impractical because resources are spread out; he cannot acquire enough food to feed a harem. But he can provide for a single mate. So a male and female form a pairbond in mid winter, and together they raise their young during the spring and early summer months. But when the kits begin to wander parents split up to forage independently. The pairbond lasts only through the breeding season. And individuals do not always form a pairbond with the same mate in successive breeding periods (Gage 1979; Rue 1969).

Formation of a pairbond in conjunction with a breeding season is a common reproductive strategy in birds. Most avian species bear highly immature, altricial young or young that for other ecological reasons need the support of two adults. As a result, over 90 percent of some nine thousand species of birds form a pairbond to rear a brood. But Eugene Morton (pers. comm. 1985) estimates that in at least 50 percent of these species the pairbond does not last for life. Instead, it lasts only for the duration of the breeding season.

Homo sapiens share traits in common with foxes and seasonally parenting birds. The modal duration of marriage that ends in divorce, four years, conforms to the traditional period between human successive births, four years (Lancaster and Lancaster 1983; see Fisher 1992). So I propose that the human tendency to pair up and remain together for a modal duration of about four years reflects an ancestral reproductive strategy to pair up and remain together throughout the infancy of a single altricial child.

Human serial pairbonding may have evolved at any of several different times in hominid evolution (Fisher 1989). But it most likely occurred at the basal radiation of the hominid clade some four million years ago when the vicissitudes of the new woodland/grassland environment produced many other primary hominid adaptations. With the evolution of bipedalism, females were required to carry their infants in their arms instead of on their backs, increasing their "reproductive burden." It is unlikely that hominid males were able to obtain enough resources to attract or sustain a harem in a savannah environment where resources were spread out and danger constant, but, like dog foxes and male birds of many species, they could provide supplementary subsistence and protection for a single female. Hence pairbonding during the infancy of a child became critical for females and practical for males, and monogamy evolved.

The trajectory for the evolution of this reproductive strategy, serial monogamy, may have been relatively simple. Given data available on the EEA (environment of evolutionary adaptation), it is parsimonious to propose that early hominid groups traveled in communities similar to those of common chimpanzees (Foley and Lee 1989) or pygmy chimpanzees. Individual females evolved "special friendships" with particular males (Smuts 1985, 1992). And with time these "special friendships" evolved into longer partnerships designed to rear the young through infancy. Once a juvenile joined a multiage play group, however, and could be raised by other members of the band, most pairbonds broke up—enabling both partners to chose new partners and rear new young.

Despite the social disruption that detachment entails in humans (and other species), serial monogamy may have had genetic benefits in our prehistoric past. Hominids who conceived offspring by more than one partner bore more varied young, producing genetic vitality in their lineages. Moreover, males who dissolved one partnership for another had the opportunity to select a younger mate more likely to produce more viable offspring. And ancestral females who dissolved an unsatisfactory relationship had the opportunity to choose a mate who provided better protection, food, and nurturance for her, her children, and her forthcoming infants. So despite the social complexities inherent in changing partners (see Fisher 1991, 1992), those who practiced serial monogamy during reproductive years accrued genetic benefits and disproportionately survived, selecting for this reproductive strategy among ancestral hominids and leaving this legacy in contemporary worldwide patterns of divorce and remarriage.

Evolution of Romantic Love

The primary locus of selection for hominid serial monogamy must have been in the limbic system and surrounding areas of the hominid brain because neuroanatomical and neurochemical data indicate that these are the areas where the primary affiliative emotions arise in birds and mammals.

The reproductive behavior of birds and almost all mammals is markedly periodic and cyclic and is mediated by brain physiology and hormonal control, although hormonal control of reproductive behavior generally lessens as brain complexity increases. In almost all species, however, the hypothalamus and related regions of the brain play a significant role in reproductive drives (Shepherd 1988). The adjacent and connected limbic system (composed of several related regions) also contributes substantially to the regulation of the mating and breeding process by providing basic motivational responses (Shepherd 1988).

The limbic system is rudimentary in reptiles, is better developed in avian species, and is most developed in mammals (Mellen 1981). As a result emotional responses become increasingly complex in higher brained creatures. More important, although there are distinct variations in the neuronal pathways and neurochemical receptor sites in the limbic systems of different species, birds and mammals all have the neuroanatomical components necessary to experience the sensations of attraction and attachment.[3]

Birds and nonhuman mammals also share the neurochemicals associated with the sensations of attraction and attachment. Birds and nonhuman mammals have concentrations of PEA and the neurotransmitters, dopamine, norepinephrine, and serotonin, and the endorphins (Shepherd 1988), the brain chemicals associated with feelings of attraction and attachment in people (Liebowitz 1983). Humans, on the other hand, exhibit concentrations of oxytocin and vasopressin, the hormones associated with pairbonding behavior in birds and nonhuman mammals (Panksepp 1992; see Pedersen et al. 1992; Winslow et al. 1993).

Data indicate that these neurochemicals are associated with parallel emotional responses in birds and nonhuman mammals too. When Rhesus monkeys are administered MAO inhibitors to raise PEA concentrations in the brain, these primates become more social, more active, and more playful, behaviors associated with courting (Liebowitz 1983). Levels of norepinephrine rise in monogamous prairie voles during the initial excitatory stage of courting (Carter and Getz 1993). Synthetic endorphins calm infant guinea pigs that have been removed from mother (Liebowitz 1983), and, similar to humans, the endorphins play a significant role in social bonding in several other species (see Insel 1992). Levels of vasopressin rise dramatically during ejaculation in male prairie voles and stimulate male pairing behavior (Winslow et al. 1993), while rising levels of oxytocin during mating stimulate female prairie voles to pair (Insel et al. 1993). Mating also alters levels of oxytocin and vasopressin in males and females of several other mammalian species (see Pedersen et al. 1992)—including humans. Vasopressin and oxy-tocin levels rise in the plasma during sexual arousal and ejaculation among men and women (Carmichael et al. 1987; Murphy et al. 1987; Insel 1992), and copulation is often part of the bonding process for both sexes.

Equally indicative, the behavior of birds and nonhuman mammals sug-gests they may *feel* attraction and attachment. Birds distinguish between potential mates, judge which make better breeding partners, and exhibit pref-erential attraction to these individuals (Trivers 1985). Birds often exhibit attachment behaviors too. When a mated pair of zebra finch are separated, both eat more, defecate more, and lose weight, "signs of anxiety and increased emotionality" (Trivers 1985:264). Similar data for many other species suggest that the emotional sensations of attraction and attachment are at least rudi-mentary in avian species.

Attraction is clearly evident in nonhuman mammals; all distinguish between potential breeding partners and express preferential attraction to some. While courting, many mammals are energized. Moreover, chim-panzees (Goodall 1986), gorillas (Fossey 1983), baboons (Smuts 1985), ele-phants (Moss 1988), wolves (Mech 1970), and many other social mammals express their attraction with an array of pats, rubs, taps, gazes, licks, and nib-bles as well as close body contact, play gestures, and tolerance of one anoth-er. And feelings of attachment are documented for all socially living nonhu-man mammalian species. It is not difficult to observe either; anyone who owns a dog is aware of its capacity to express affection and attachment—emotional states that humans associate with "love."

Conclusion

These data support the conclusion that with the increasing behavioral flexi-bility of larger-brained creatures, genetically fixed instinctual mechanisms designed to dictate reproductive behavior gave way to the development of the limbic system and emotional responses designed to direct a more flexible (opportunistic) breeding process (see Mellen 1981). So I hypothesize that the emotions of attraction, attachment, restlessness during long relationships, and the drive to attach again (emotional states that I propose most likely arise from psychopharmacological arousal circuits located primarily in the limbic system of the brain) evolved in birds and mammals to coordinate the ebb and flow of affiliation to correspond with each species' distinctive breeding system.

Among ancestral humans these emotions evolved specifically to motivate individuals of reproductive age to become attracted and attached to one another long enough to reproduce and rear a single altrical child through the duration of its infancy, then to detach and attach to another to bear and raise another child—hence fueling the reproductive strategy of serial monogamy during reproductive years. Additionally, as a couple aged, as the length of a pairbond increased (past the critical modal duration of about four years), and/or as a couple bore successive young, these neurochemical motivational systems acted to *sustain* pairbonding behavior instead (see Fisher 1992), producing the multipart human reproductive strategy that is visible in contemporary cross-cultural data on marriage, divorce, and remarriage. Moreover, a central characteristic of the neuroanatomy and neurochemistry for attraction, attactment, and detachment that evolved among ancestral hominids was flexibility, not only to permit variation within this primary reproductive strategy (serial monogamy during reproductive years) but also to accommodate secondary opportunistic breeding strategies, including polygyny, polyandry, and extrapair copulations.

Then, with the expansion of the human cerebral cortex, our ancestors began to build upon this core of primal cyclic reproductive emotions, adding complexity of feeling as well as cultural rituals and beliefs about attraction, attachment, and detachment. And by the time Homo sapiens sapiens was wearing fox skin coats and ivory beads and drawing beasts and symbols on cave walls in southwestern France, the Pyrenees, and northern Spain some twenty thousand years ago, our forebears had developed an intricate, physiologically based constellation of emotions for loving as well as elaborate traditions to celebrate and curb what European peoples would come to call romantic love.

NOTES

1. This tendency to seek mates who are "hard to get" or somewhat mysterious may have a biological component. Among birds and nonhuman mammals individuals reared together prefer to mate with strangers; they have a natural antipathy to incest. For this and probably several other ecological reasons, either males or females regularly emigrate from their natal community at puberty to seek mates elsewhere (Bischof 1975b; De Waal 1989). A study of kibbutz marriages in Israel indicates that there is a critical time in human childhood between ages three and six when people develop a natural sexual aversion for those they see regularly (Shepher 1971).

2. The *Demographic Yearbooks* of the United Nations do not provide comparative cross-cultural data sufficient to establish divorce *risk* by number of dependent young

(see Fisher 1992). Thus these data suggest that the presence of "issue" stabilizes a marriage, but they do not prove it.

3.   Parts of the brain stem—where the endorphins and other neurotransmitters create significant activity—are undoubtedly also involved.

REFERENCES

Argiolas, A. 1992. "Oxytocin Stimulation of Penile Erection: Pharmacology, Site, and Mechanism of Action." In C. A. Pedersen, J. D. Caldwell, G. F. Jirikowski, and T. R. Insel, eds., *Oxytocin in Maternal, Sexual, and Social Behaviors. Annals of the New York Academy of Sciences* 652:194–203.

Bischof, N. 1975a. "A Systems Approach Toward the Funtional Connections of Attachment and Fear." *Child Development* 46:801–17.

— 1975b. "Comparative Ethology of Incest Avoidance." In R. Fox, ed., *Biosocial Anthropology*. London: Malaby.

Bulfinch, T. 1993. *Bulfinch's Mythology*. New York: Modern Library.

Carmichael, M. S., R. Humbert, J. Dixen, G. Palmisano, W. Greenleaf, J. M. Davidson. 1987. "Plasma Oxytocin Increases in the Human Sexual Response." *Journal of Clinical Endocrinology and Metabolism* 64:27–31.

Carter, C. S., and L. Getz. 1993. "Monogamy and the Prairie Vole." *Scientific American* (June), pp. 100–106.

Cherlin, A. 1981. *Marriage, Divorce, Remarriage*. Cambridge: Harvard University Press.

Daly, M., and M. Wilson. 1983. *Sex, Evoluton, and Behavior*. Boston: Willard Grant.

De Waal, F. 1989. *Peacemaking Among Primates*. Cambridge: Harvard University Press.

Fisher, H. 1989. "Evolution of Human Serial Pairbonding." *American Journal of Physical Anthropology* 78:331–54.

— 1991. "Monogamy, Adultery and Divorce in Cross-Species Perspective." In M. H. Robinson and L. Tiger, eds., *Man and Beast Revisited*. Washington, D.C.: Smithsonian Institution Press.

— 1992. *Anatomy of Love: The Natural History of Monogamy, Adultery, and Divorce*. New York: Norton.

— In preparation. "The Poet's Eye: Literary References to the Science of Love."

Foley, R. A., and P. C. Lee. 1989. "Finite Social Space: Evolutionary Pathways and Reconstructing Hominid Behavior." *Science* 243:901–6.

Fossey, D. 1983. *Gorillas in the Mist*. Boston: Houghton Mifflin.

Frayser, S. 1985. *Varieties of Sexual Experience: An Anthropological Perspective on Human Sexuality*. New Haven: HRAF.

Gage, R. L. 1979. *Fox Family*. New York: Weatherhill/Heibonsha.

Glick, P. C. 1975. "Some Recent Changes in American Families." Current Population Reports. Social Studies Series P-23, no. 52. Washington, D.C.: U.S. Bureau of the Census.

Goodall, J. 1986. *The Chimpanzees of Gombe: Patterns of Behavior*. Cambridge: Belknap Press of Harvard University Press.

Hawthorn, G. 1970. *The Sociology of Fertility*. London: Collier-Macmillan.

Insel, T. R. 1992. "Oxytocin—A Neuropeptide for Affiliation: Evidence from Behavioral,

Receptor Autoradiographic, and Comparative Studies." *Psychoneuroendocrinology* 17(1):3–35.

Insel, T. R., J. T. Winslow, J. R. Williams, N. Hastings, L. E. Shapiro, and C. S. Carter. 1993. "The Role of Neurohypophyseal Peptides in the Central Mediation of Complex Social Processes—Evidence from Comparative Studies." *Regulatory Peptides* 45:127–131.

Jankowiak, W., and E. Fischer. 1992. "A Cross-Cultural Perspective on Romantic Love. *Ethnology* 31(2):149–155.

Jirikowski, G. F. 1992. "Oxytocinergic Neuronal Systems During Mating, Pregnancy, Parturition, and Lactation." In C. A. Pedersen, J. D. Caldwell, G. F. Jirikowski, and T. R. Insel, eds., *Oxytocin in Maternal, Sexual, and Social Behaviors. Annals of the New York Academy of Sciences* 652:253–270.

Kleiman, D. G. 1977. "Monogamy in Mammals." *Quarterly Review of Biology* 52:39–69.

Lancaster, J. B., and C. S. Lancaster. 1983. "Parental Investment: The Hominid Adaptation." In D. J. Ortner, ed., *How Humans Adapt: A Biocultural Odyssey.* Washington, D.C.: Smithsonian Institution Press.

Lévi-Strauss, C. 1985. *The View from Afar.* New York: Basic Books.

Levitan, S. A., R. S. Belous, and F. Gallo. 1988. *What's Happening to the American Family?* Baltimore: Johns Hopkins University Press.

Liebowitz, M. 1983. *The Chemistry of Love.* Boston: Little, Brown.

Mech, L. D. 1970. *The Wolf: The Ecology and Behavior of an Endangered Species.* Garden City, N.Y.: Natural History Press.

Mellen, S. L. W. 1981. *The Evolution of Love.* San Francisco: Freeman.

Melville, A. D. 1990. *Ovid: The Love Poems.* New York: Oxford University Press.

Mock, D. W., and M. Fujioka. 1990. "Monogamy and Long-term Pairbonding in Vertebrates." *Trends in Ecology and Evolution* 5(2):39–43.

Money, J. 1980. *Love and Love Sickness: The Science of Sex, Gender Difference, and Pair-Bonding.* Baltimore: Johns Hopkins University Press.

— 1986. *Lovemaps: Clinical Concepts of Sexual/Erotic Health and Pathology, Paraphilia, and Gender Transposition in Childhood, Adolescence, and Maturity.* New York: Irvington.

Morton, E. 1985. Conversation with author. Smithsonian Institution.

Moss, C. 1988. *Elephant Memories: Thirteen Years in the Life of an Elephant Family.* New York: Wiliam Morrow.

Murdock, G. P. 1949. *Social Structure.* New York: Free Press.

Murphy, M. R., J. R. Seckl, S. Burton, S. A. Checkley, and S. L. Lightman. 1987. "Changes in Oxytocin and Vasopressin Secretion During Sexual Activity in Men." *Journal of Clinical Endocrinology and Metabolism* 65:738.

Panksepp, J. 1992. "Oxytocin Effects on Emotional Processes: Separation Distress, Social Bonding, and Relationships to Psychiatric Disorders" In C. A. Pedersen, J. D. Caldwell, G. F. Jirikowski, and T. R. Insel, eds., *Oxytocin in Maternal, Sexual, and Social Behaviors. Annals of the New York Academy of Sciences* 652:243–252.

Pedersen, C. A., J. D. Caldwell, G. F. Jirikowski, and T. R. Insel, eds. 1992. *Oxytocin in Maternal, Sexual, and Social Behaviors. Annals of the New York Academy of Sciences* 652:1–487.

Rue, L. L. 1969. *The World of the Red Fox.* Philadelphia: Lippincott.

Sarnyai, Z., G. L. Kovacs, G. Szabo, G. Telegdy, K. Jost, and T. Barth. 1985. "Influence of Oxytocin and an Analog Antagonist of Oxytocin on the Development of Acute

Morphine Tolerance in Mice." In E. S. Vizi, S. Furst, and G. Szilla, eds., *Receptors and Centrally Acting Drus,* pp. 273–276. Proceedings of the Fourth Congress of the Hungarian Pharmacological Society, Budapest.

Shepher, J. 1971. "Mate Selection Among Second Generation Kibbutz Adolescents and Adults: Incest Avoidance and Negative Imprinting." *Archives of Sexual Behavior* 1:293–307.

Shepherd, G. M. 1988. *Neurobiology.* New York: Oxford University Press.

Shostak, M. 1981. *Nisa: The Life and Words of a !Kung Woman.* New York: Random House.

Smuts, B. B. 1985. *Sex and Friendship in Baboons.* New York: Aldine de Gruyter.

— 1992. "Male-Infant Relationships in Nonhuman Primates: Parental Investment or Mating Effort?" In B. Hewlett, ed., *Father-Child Relations.* New York: Aldine de Gruter.

Spiro, M. E. 1958. *Children of the Kibbutz.* Cambridge: Harvard University Press.

Tennov, D. 1979. *Love and Limerence: The Experience of Being in Love.* New York: Stein and Day.

Trivers, R. 1985. *Social Evolution.* Menlo Park, Cal.: Benjamin/Cummings.

Van den Berghe, P. L. 1979. *Human Family Systems: An Evolutionary View.* Westport, Conn.: Greenwood.

Wickler, W. 1976. *The Ethological Analysis of Attachment.* Berlin: Verlag Paul Parey.

Winslow, J. T., N. Hastings, C. S. Carter, C. R. Harbaugh, and T. R. Insel. 1993. "A Role for Central Vasopressin in Pair Bonding in Monogamous Prairie Voles." *Nature* 365:545–548.

Wittenberger, J. F., and R. L. Tilson. 1980. "The Evolution of Monogamy: Hypothesis and Evidence." *Annual Review of Ecology and Systematics* 11:197–232.

Wolkstein, D. 1991. *The First Love Stories.* New York: Harper Perennial.

Love's Contingencies: The Developmental Socioecology of Romantic Passion

JAMES S. CHISHOLM

Introduction

Although I've never met them, I know something intimate about your parents: they had sexual intercourse, at least once. And so did their parents, and their parents' parents before them, in an unbroken chain of copulations back to the beginning of time. Reproduction, after all, is evolution's engine, and sexual reproduction is universal among higher animals. But because your parents are *human* animals, I think I know something else about them: chances are that they were "in love" around the time you were conceived—and so, probably, were their parents, and their parents' parents, back into the mists of hominid evolution. That raises the question: If sex makes evolution go around, why did love—in all its guises, with all its travails—evolve to make our sex lives go around?

For true romantics any scientific perspective on love can be no more than innocent oxymoron: How can the cold light of science illuminate the heat of youthful passion or the warm glow of mature love? But when the science is that of evolutionary ecology, many otherwise levelheaded people fear science at its most sinister: genetic determinism, narrow essentialism, and callous insensitivity to the contingencies of culture and history. I believe just the opposite, and one of my goals in this chapter is to show how recent advances in evolutionary ecology—because they recognize the contingencies as well as the functions of love—allow us to be even more human. In these worried days of spiraling sexual antagonism, teen pregnancy, broken families, and the specter of AIDS, new perspectives on love may help us simply continue being what it is we value as human.

There are about as many definitions of romantic passion as there are theories to explain it. Following Jankowiak and Fischer (1992), my image of romantic passion is that of "a sudden, unrestrained passion," or an "intense attraction that involves the idealization of the other, within an erotic context" (1992:150). Despite their diversity, however, all models of romantic passion seem to view it as promoting "bonding" or "attachment" between men and women (e.g., in psychology: Hatfield 1988; Hendrick and Hendrick 1992; Sternberg 1986; in psychobiology: Liebowitz 1983; Tennov 1979; in anthropology: Batten 1992; Fisher 1992; Russell 1993). To the extent that they even consider other kinds of love, most such models also view romantic passion as simply a passing fancy, a temporary condition that does not last but normally develops into the "deeper" and "more committed," if less intense, "companionate" love of mature men and women (e.g., Hatfield 1988). Fisher (1992) even suggests that we simply may not have the psychobiological capacity to experience passionate love for more than about four years at a time. She reasons that if our hominid ancestors had a four-year birth interval, as many suppose, then it would have been adaptive for hominid males and females to be attracted to each other for only as long as the female really needed male protection or provisioning— i.e., while she was pregnant and nursing. Thus, in Fisher's view, romantic passion per se did not increase fitness directly but was favored by selection because it provided the psychosexual "glue" that kept early hominid parents together. And because two hominid parents were better than one (if only for four years), she argues, romantic passion's ultimate adaptive function was to increase offspring survival.

A fundamental assumption of most models of love thus seems to be that romantic passion is a juvenile trait—and as such it is puerile, developmentally short-lived, and intrinsically inferior to mature love, which is "real" and (ideally) does last. It follows, for many, that romantic passion is callow, something that normal people outgrow (i.e., grow beyond). Going further, romantic passion may even be constructed as abnormal or sick, i.e., a physical disease (e.g., lovesickness), or—more dangerously—a moral disease (e.g., loose or promiscuous). In short, romantic passion has a dubious reputation—at least among middle-class love theorists. I believe, on the other hand, that this reputation comes from a too narrow view of love and its contingencies, and that in viewing romantic passion as a mere maturational step on the way to companionate love, we miss the opportunity to understand why some people, under some conditions, find it difficult to make this step. And, as always, whenever we fail to understand why people do the things they do, we run the risk of blaming them for not behaving the way we do . . . and we begin to see them as unhealthy or immoral.

What I propose, in contrast with existing models of romantic passion, is that there are individual differences within societies in the ease with which men and women can move from romantic passion to the kind of love that middle-class Westerners usually consider more committed and normal. I propose also that these individual differences in capacity to enter into this more committed kind of love are not random but are learned *facultatively* or *contingently*, according to local social and economic conditions—in such a way that what is learned (essentially a secure vs. insecure style of love, as I will argue later) may be (or once was) biologically adaptive in the environment in which it was learned. I propose, in other words, that our love styles evolved to be developmentally emergent, adaptively contingent on certain features of local socioecology, and that consequently there is no simple, "essential" style of human love. It follows, to my evolutionary way of thinking, that such ordinary constructs as average, typical, and normal are of limited use for understanding patterns of human love. Instead, we must understand the developmental and historical processes that generate all the different styles of love that we observe, regardless of their frequency or local status.

I will begin with an overview of the empirical evidence that at least in Western societies a predisposition to romantic passion seems to be part of a pattern of wary, ambivalent, and relatively precarious but also intense emotional (and consequently sexual) relations in adulthood. I will then outline the evidence that this pattern itself seems to be a predictable developmental consequence of a history of so-called insecure attachment relations. I then proceed with a brief summary of recent advances in evolutionary ecology that suggest a capacity for the facultative or contingent development of this style of adult love may be (or once was) biologically, evolutionarily adaptive in the stressful environments in which insecure attachments have probably been more common.

Attachment Theory

Attachment theory is a theory about the nature and origin of love (e.g., Bowlby 1969, 1973, 1980). Although he focused overwhelmingly on the developmental origins of love, Bowlby believed that the capacity for love existed because of its survival value. For Bowlby, love itself thus had evolutionary origins and functioned to promote mother-child proximity and thus child survival in the "environment of evolutionary adaptedness" (1969:58) (i.e., during hominid evolution).

Attachment theory holds that by the age of about seven years most children have developed what Bowlby called "internal working models"—mental images or perceptual biases—about important social relations that are derived from the quality of their interactions with their primary caretaker(s). On the basis of wide use of Mary Ainsworth's system for naturalistic observations of children's behavior in standardized situations, there is broad agreement on the existence of three major types or styles of attachment: secure, ambivalent, and avoidant (Ainsworth et al. 1978).[1] Moreover, on the basis of longitudinal studies, there is broad agreement about the major precursors of each one, as outlined below.

Secure attachment arises from the child's more-or-less consistent feelings of security—of being accepted, welcomed, and loved. These feelings motivate children to play, to explore their social and physical worlds. Such exploration inevitably increases at least the psychological distance from the child's caregiver, which causes the child to experience feelings of anxiety. This anxiety, in turn, motivates the child to return to its caregiver, to seek security in physical or symbolic closeness. A positive response to the child's approach engenders in the child feelings of security—i.e., of being loved. The circle is thus completed, and these feelings of security motivate another round of play and exploration, separation anxiety, search for security, and welcome. When this circle is repeated sufficiently often during development, children are said to be securely attached and to have positive expectations about self-with-others, which are resistant, but not closed, to change. Secure children are those who expect these feelings in their important social relations—those who feel loveable, who have positive internal working models of self and other. Longitudinal research suggests that parents of secure children are most consistently sensitive and positively responsive to their children (Ainsworth et al. 1978; Sroufe and Waters 1977).

But when attachment relations do not follow this secure course children are apt to experience feelings of anger, fear, or grief. In the language of attachment theory these children are said to be insecurely attached, with negative expectations about self-with-others, which are also resistant, but not closed, to change. The evidence suggests two primary forms of insecure attachment: in the avoidant form children seem "aloof and detached" from their caregivers; in the ambivalent form, on the other hand, children appear "clingy and dependent" and preoccupied with monitoring their caregivers' moods and guessing their intentions (Skolnick 1986:181). Longitudinal evidence suggests that caregivers of ambivalent children are relatively inconsistent and unpredictable in their sensitivity and responsiveness to their children, but not overtly rejecting, which is more common among caretakers of avoidant children. These parents, the evidence suggests, are more likely, for whatever reason, to rebuff children's bids for physical or symbolic proximity (Ainsworth et al. 1978; Isabella and Belsky 1991; Sroufe and Waters 1977).

Despite the best of intentions not to evaluate these three attachment styles, there has been a tendency to view secure attachment as more normal and thus somehow "better" than either of the insecure styles. One reason seems to be that because children with a history of secure attachment show more positive affect, less fear, and better social-emotional and cognitive development than insecure children (e.g., Matas, Arend, and Sroufe 1978; Sroufe 1983) they simply fit better Bowlby's image of what would have been adaptive during human evolution. Another reason may be that more children in unstressed middle-class samples are classified as secure (up to 66–75 percent) than in highly stressed poverty samples (as low as 35–50 percent) (Belsky and Cassidy 1994; Egeland and Sroufe 1981).

It is now apparent, however, that there is considerably more to insecure attachment than pathology, and that interpreting it as abnormal, or simply as failure to achieve the default of secure attachment, leads only to confusion (e.g., Main 1990). There seem to be two sources for this new interest in insecure attachment. First, there has been growing awareness among attachment researchers that evolution is about *reproduction* as much as survival—i.e., that survival alone without reproduction is, from an evolutionary perspective, usually no better than death. Consequently, there has also been a growing sense that attachment theory's assumptions about the survival function of attachment are too constricting, and need to be balanced by investigations of its potential reproductive function. Second, over the past decade or so, in both evolutionary ecology and attachment theory, there has been growing excitement about looking at development from a *lifespan* perspective. In evolutionary ecology this has contributed to the flowering of life history theory and the concepts of alternative reproductive and life history strategies (Roff 1992; Stearns 1992). In attachment theory this led to the development of techniques for assessing adult attachment and the consequent critical finding that adult styles of attachment—or love—may be derived from, or expressions of, attachment styles learned much earlier (as I will describe shortly).

It is in this joint evolutionary-attachment theoretical context that insecure attachment commands our attention, for there is increasing evidence that adults (at least in Western societies) with a history of insecure early attachment relations seem predisposed to adult love relationships that are simultaneously emotionally intense and apprehensive or ambivalent—i.e., those that possess the qualities of romantic passion. The argument that I will develop below is not only that early insecure attachment predisposes one to a romantic or passionate style of adult love, but that such a predisposition may constitute a developmentally contingent, adaptive, alternative reproductive strategy.

Love, Sex, and Attachment in Adults

From several ongoing prospective studies of attachment, we already have evidence that as long as a child's family environment remains fairly stable, so too does his or her attachment style, at least through early adolescence (e.g., Belsky and Cassidy 1994). However, because none of the participants in these prospective studies are yet mature, studies of the development of adult attachment are necessarily retrospective, and must rely on indirect measures of early attachment. While the problems inherent in retrospective research must be acknowledged, I believe that the results of these studies must nonetheless be taken seriously, if only because they are so intriguingly consistent with each other, with the few prospective studies that allow reasonable inferences about early attachment history—and, as I will argue shortly, with a set of robust predictions from evolutionary ecology about the adaptive function of alternative developmental patterns.

Hazan and Shaver (1987) were among the first to explore systematically the relationship between attachment history and romantic love in adulthood. Using a version of the Adult Attachment Interview (see Main, Kaplan, and Cassidy 1985), Hazan and Shaver found that men and women with secure attachment histories differed from those with insecure attachment histories in their beliefs, values, and expectations about adult love relationships. In brief, they found that secure adults—both men and women—generally described their love relationships in terms of trust, closeness, and a relative absence of jealousy and fear of intimacy. On the other hand, men and women judged to have insecure attachment histories were more likely to describe their adult love relationships in terms of fear of intimacy, emotional peaks and valleys, jealousy, obsession, and—of special interest for arguments I will make later—extreme sexual attraction (1987:515). Similarly, Brennan and Shaver (N.d.), using Simpson and Gangestad's (1991) Sociosexual Orientation Inventory, found that insecure-avoidant adults showed more so-called indiscriminant sexuality.

Hazan and Shaver's work has inspired many replications, essentially all of which report a similar pattern of secure-insecure differences in beliefs, values, and expectations about love (see Shaver and Hazan 1993 for a review). But it is also apparent that attachment history is related not only to mental representations of love but also to actual love behaviors and love relationships. Especially striking is the Hazan and Shaver (1987) finding that insecure adults had more and apparently less-committed—i.e., shorter—love relationships than secure adults. The love relationships of secure adults lasted, on average, 10.02 years whereas those of insecure adults lasted just 4.86 (insecure-ambivalent) and 5.97 years (insecure-avoidant) (in all three groups the subjects' mean age was thirty-six years). Analogous findings have been reported by Davis and Kirkpatrick (N.d.), and by Hill, Young, and Nord (N.d.), who found that on one hand insecure adults were less likely than secure adults to have ever been in a love relationship—but that, on the other hand, if they *had* ever married or cohabited they did so at a younger age than the secures, and after a shorter courtship.

Notwithstanding the need for additional research, especially prospective studies, and ignoring for now the complicating fact that there are two forms of insecure attachment (avoidant and ambivalent), I believe that there is sufficient evidence to justify the working hypothesis that insecure attachment relations during development predispose men and women toward a romantic or passionate style of adult love—one that Shaver and Hazan characterize as "preoccupation, mania, dependence, idealization, and addictive reliance on a partner" (1993:11). Assuming that future prospective research supports this hypothesis, the interesting question then would be *why should* insecure attachment relations foster the development of this sort of, on appearance, slightly "mad," passionate style of love?

The Reproductive Function of Alternative Styles of Love

One way to approach this question is by asking its opposite—that is, asking why secure attachment relations should foster the development of more levelheaded and committed (i.e., longer-lasting) adult love styles. From an evolutionary perspective the consensus is that more levelheaded and mutually committed men and women were, on average, probably more successful at rearing children. This idea—that long-term male-female bonding or attachment promotes increased or prolonged parental investment—is common to most evolutionary perspectives on the origin of the family (e.g., Lancaster and Lancaster 1987). But if the secure style of love fosters parental effort—and thus parents' reproductive success—what are we to make of the insecure or intensely passionate style of adult love, in which men and women are "crazy" about, "preoccupied" with, and "addicted" to each other—but not for very long before they move onto another such relationship? Wouldn't such fragile, short-lived male-female bonds tend to diminish parental investment (at least fathers') and thus reduce both parents' reproductive success? Is passionate love, then, only lovesickness—simply a disease, a mere psychopathology only coincidentally contingent on early insecure attachment?

Or could there be an evolutionary method to this familiar form of "madness?" There are two reasons why I think this hypothesis is worth pursuing. The first is that regardless of how the experience of romantic passion is culturally constructed and sanctioned, and whether or not it is recognized as a basis for marriage, the capacity for romantic passion seems to be a human universal (Buss 1988; Hazan and Shaver 1987; Jankowiak and Fischer 1992; Fisher 1992), and I am uneasy about dismissing as "sick" something that is so widespread. The second reason for postulating an adaptive function for romantic passion is that the evidence for the contingent development of secure vs. insecure adult love styles that I sketched above is strikingly consistent with a pair of recent models of the development of alternative reproductive strategies in humans.

Each of these models is grounded in the expectation that selection will be most likely to achieve optimal solutions to adaptive problems in the realm of evolution's engine—i.e., reproduction. This is because all organisms have had ancestors—but before these ancestors could leave descendants, each in its turn had to overcome again the problems that face all forms of life: those of survival, growth and development, and reproduction. In evolutionary ecology the work done and resources (e.g., energy, time, safety) consumed in overcoming these problems are conventionally called somatic effort (for problems of survival and growth and development) and reproductive effort (for problems of reproduction). Reproductive effort, in turn, is further subdivided into *mating effort* and *parenting effort* (e.g., Alexander and Borgia 1979; Low 1978; Williams 1966). Mating effort maximizes a parent's reproductive rate or total fertility rate (i.e., offspring *quantity*) while parenting effort maximizes the survival and ultimate reproduction of a parent's off-spring (i.e., offspring *quality*). A fundamental assumption of evolutionary ecology is that organisms that were most efficient at allocating their limited supplies of energy, time, and safety between the often conflicting demands of mating and parenting were the ones that left the most descendants. A repro-ductive strategy is thus a constellation of anatomical, physiological, psycho-logical, and developmental traits that are designed by natural selection for the optimal allocation of reproductive effort over the lifespan. Since allocat-ing reproductive effort to one function usually precludes allocating it to another, the evolution of reproductive strategies is believed to be governed by a series of trade-offs, including those between current and future repro-duction (i.e., mating and parenting effort), current reproduction and sur-vival, reproduction and growth, and number (quantity) and reproductive value (quality) of offspring (e.g., Stearns 1992).

In the first of the models mentioned above, Belsky, Steinberg, and Draper (1991) propose that the allocation of reproductive effort in adults is at least partially contingent on the developmental effects of early attachment histo-ry. They propose the existence of two evolved, conditional developmental pathways (or a continuum between two poles) thought to be adaptive in the particular socioecological contexts in which they developed. Thus, when parents in a competitive environment have sufficient social, economic, and other resources, they will be under relatively low levels of stress, and better able to foster secure attachment in their children. In turn, as we have seen from research on adult attachment, this history of secure attachment seems to constitute a learning bias toward the development of more committed adult love styles ("long-term, enduring pair bonds" according to Belsky, Steinberg, and Draper 1991:651) and so-called high parenting effort repro-ductive strategies. When parents have sufficient resources, the optimal strat-egy may be to concentrate parenting effort in a small number of "high qual-ity" offspring. Because they receive more investment, such offspring are bet-ter able to marry well and to rear highly competitive children themselves.

On the other hand, when parents in a competitive environment have insufficient social, economic, and other resources, they are likely to experi-ence higher levels of stress, which is a risk factor in the development of inse-cure attachment relations (e.g., Belsky and Cassidy 1994; Belsky, Steinberg, and Draper 1991; Egeland and Sroufe 1981). In turn, as we have also seen, such insecure attachment seems to constitute a learning bias toward the development of more romantic or passionate adult love styles ("short-term, unstable pair bonds," according to Belsky, Steinberg, and Draper 1991:651) and so-called high mating effort reproductive strategies. When parents in a competitive, stressful environment do not have the energy, time, or safety to rear competitive offspring, the optimal strategy may be to sacrifice offspring quality for a greater number of less competitive offspring.

Some additional findings from the Hill, Young, and Nord (N.d.) study will help to illustrate the relationship styles thought to be associated with these alternative reproductive strategies. Although there are few reports of gender differences in the precursors of adult attachment, Hill and her colleagues found that attachment history affected men's and women's love relationships differently: secure men had *longer* love relationships than insecure men whereas secure women entered love relationships when they were *older* and after a *longer* period of courtship than did insecure women. Because there are different constraints on male and female reproduction (e.g., Trivers 1972), this pattern of gender differences is consistent with the suggestion offered here that individual differences in early attachment may have adaptive consequences not only for survival but for later reproductive behavior.

But what is it about competitive environments that is stressful? How do they make it difficult for parents to raise competitive offspring? Elegant as the Belsky-Steinberg-Draper model is, it does not fully address the question of how a romantic, uncommitted style of adult love developmentally contingent on insecure early attachment would promote reproductive success under the stressful conditions that constituted the bias toward insecure attachment in the first place.

Following recent advances in evolutionary ecology, I have suggested that death is what makes the difference (Chisholm 1993). When mortality rates are high or unpredictable, reproductive success is more likely to be promoted by early and/or rapid fertility—i.e., high mating effort—than by the strategy of prolonged parental investment in a small number of high quality offspring. To succeed, such parenting effort strategies require that parents live long enough to bestow—and their offspring to receive—enough parental care to make a difference in the offspring's reproductive success. High mortality rates put a premium on early reproduction (to increase the chances of having at least some offspring before the parent's early death) and/or on rapid or extensive reproduction (to increase the chances that at least some offspring will survive) (Promislow and Harvey 1990; Stearns 1992).

I propose that it is under such conditions, where the adaptive premium is on early and/or rapid reproduction, that the intense emotions we associate with "romantic" passion may promote reproductive success—or have done so in the past—by increasing the likelihood or frequency of sexual intercourse, perhaps even with a variety of partners, especially if their survival, too, is problematic, or at least perceived that way. I believe, in other words, that romantic passion may constitute a psychological mechanism in the service of mating effort strategies, which are oriented toward the present—toward current or short-term reproductive success. Mature, companionate love, on the other hand, may constitute a psychological mechanism in the service of parenting effort strategies that are oriented toward the future—toward long-term reproductive success. This is where my model differs from Helen Fisher's (1992). She views romantic passion as an adaptation to keep fathers around for four years of parental investment; romantic passion for her is thus part of a parenting effort strategy. I view romantic passion instead as an adaptation to increase reproductive rate; romantic passion for me is thus part of a mating effort strategy. Mating and parenting effort cannot, of course, be mutually exclusive (e.g., Burbank and Chisholm 1992; Smuts and Gubernick 1992), but the relative balance between them—at any one time, or over an entire lifespan—may have had important fitness consequences, which might explain why our love styles today seem to develop as they do.

My evolutionary view of love holds that the capacity for romantic passion is a human universal, but that its manifestation may depend, in part, on socioecological or political economic contingencies affecting men's and women's opportunities for "secure" attachment relations—perhaps especially during early development, but probably not limited to childhood. Consistent with this argument are results from a recent behavior genetic analysis of love styles. Using a twin-family study research design, Waller and Shaver (1994) examined the heritability of particular "love styles" using Hendrick and Hendrick's (1986) Love Attitude Scale (LAS). While there remain questions about measurement and interpretation, the LAS is thought to capture dimensions of behavior or attitude that might be expected to vary with reproductive strategy (sample item: "My lover and I were attracted to each other immediately after we first met"). Subjects were 838 adult twins and 153 of their spouses from the California Twin Registry. Waller and Shaver found that, in contrast to most other attitude dimensions and personality traits, genetic factors accounted for essentially *none* of the variance in love styles. They conclude that

> shared experiences, not shared genes, account for twin similarities in love attitudes. And the correlation between spouses' love styles, which we showed cannot

be attributed to attitude convergence, indicate that love attitudes influence mate selection. . . . Hence, an orientation toward romantic love that may have been learned during childhood can eventually affect adult relationship outcomes (Waller and Shaver 1994:272).

In closing, I want to emphasize that there is no evidence that the amount of early stress one experiences neatly determines one's future love style. Not only do individual differences in temperament affect children's perception of and resiliency to stress, so too may apparently quite small changes in the stressors themselves and the means of coping available to the child (e.g., Werner and Smith 1992). Both positive and negative internal working models seem thus resistant, but not irrevocably closed, to change, and, while it may go against the statistical odds, someone with an apparently quite benign attachment history may develop a passionate style of adult love, and vice versa (e.g., Belsky, Steinberg, and Draper 1991; Belsky and Cassidy 1994; Shaver and Hazan 1993).

While it remains to be seen how love styles vary with particular socioecological and political economic contingencies, recent advances in evolutionary ecology predict that local mortality rates (or the causes or correlates thereof) may be especially important. On the other hand, it already seems clear that what has evolved is not some essential or normal reproductive strategy or style of love, but the psychological switching mechanisms that allow us to most appropriately track our developmental socioecology. However different peoples may construct it today, the propensity for passionate men and women to view each other in terms of "extreme sexual attraction" may once—under conditions of high mortality and chronic stress—have been biologically adaptive. Today, however, with our spiraling sexual antagonism, teen pregnancy, broken families, and the specter of AIDS, passionate love may be as much an effect as a cause of our distress.

NOTES

Many thanks to Victoria K. Burbank and Bill Jankowiak for their helpful comments on earlier versions of this chapter.

1. A fourth pattern (insecure-disorganized) has been proposed, but has not yet been well studied or validated in nonclinical samples. It seems, moreover, to characterize only a small number of children (Belsky and Cassidy 1994).

REFERENCES

Ainsworth, M., M. Blehar, E. Waters, and S. Wall. 1978. *Patterns of Attachment*. Hillsdale, N.J.: Lawrence Erlbaum.

Alexander, R., and G. Borgia, 1979. On the Origin and Basis of the Male-Female Phenomenon. In M. Blum and N. Blum, eds., *Sexual Selection and Reproductive Competition in Insects*. New York: Academic Press.

Batten, M. 1992. *Sexual Strategies*. New York: Putnam.

Belsky, J., L. Steinberg, and P. Draper. 1991. "Childhood Experience, Interpersonal Development, and Reproductive Strategy: An Evolutionary Theory of Socialization. *Child Development* 62:647–670.

Belsky, J., and J. Cassidy. 1994. "Attachment: Theory and Evidence." In M. Rutter and D. Hay, eds., *Development Through Life: A Handbook for Clinicians*. Oxford: Blackwell.

Bowlby, J. 1969. *Attachment and Loss*. Vol. 1. *Attachment*. New York: Basic Books.

— 1973. *Attachment and Loss*. Vol. 2. *Separation: Anxiety and Anger*. New York: Basic Books.

— 1980. *Attachment and Loss*. Vol. 3. *Loss*. New York: Basic Books.

Brennan, K., and P. Shaver. N.d. "Dimensions of Adult Attachment and the Dynamics of Romantic Relationships." *Personality and Social Psychology Bulletin*, forthcoming.

Burbank, V., and J. Chisholm. 1992. "Gender Differences in the Perception of Ideal Family Size in an Australian Aboriginal Community." In B. Hewlett, ed., *Father-Child Relations: Cultural and Biosocial Contexts*. Hawthorne, N.Y.: Aldine de Gruyter.

Buss, D. 1987. "Love Acts: The Evolutionary Biology of Love." In R. Sternberg and M. Barnes, eds., *The Psychology of Love*. New Haven: Yale University Press.

Chisholm, J. 1993. "Death, Hope, and Sex: Life History Theory and the Development of Reproductive Strategies." *Current Anthropology* 34(1):1–24.

Davis, K., and L. Kirkpatrick. N.d. "Attachment Style, Gender, and Relationship Stability: A Longitudinal Analysis." *Journal of Personality and Social Psychology*, forthcoming.

Egeland, B., and L. Sroufe. 1981. "Attachment and Early Maltreatment." *Child Development* 52:44–52.

Fisher, H. E. 1992. *The Anatomy of Love*. New York: Norton.

Hatfield, E. 1988. "Passionate Love and Companionate Love." In R. Sternberg and M. Barnes, eds., *The Psychology of Love*. New Haven: Yale University Press.

Hazan, C., and P. Shaver. 1987. "Romantic Love Conceptualized as an Attachment Process." *Journal of Personality and Social Psychology* 52:511–524.

Hendrick, C., and S. Hendrick. 1986. "A Theory and Method of Love." *Journal of Personality and Social Psychology* 50(2):392–402.

— 1992. *Romantic Love*. Newbury Park: Sage.

Hill, E., J. Young, and J. Nord. N.d. "Childhood Adversity, Attachment Security, and Adult Relationships: A Preliminary Study." *Ethnology and Sociobiology*, forthcoming.

Isabella, R., and J. Belsky, J. 1990. "Interactional Synchrony and the Origins of Infant-Mother Attachment: A Replication Study." *Child Development* 62:373–384.

Jankowiak, W., and E. Fischer. 1992. "A Cross-Cultural Perspective on Romantic Love." *Ethnology* 31(2):149–155.

Lancaster, J., and C. Lancaster. 1987. "Change in Parental-Investment and Family Formation Strategies in the Course of Human Evolution." In J. Lancaster, J. Altmann, A. Rossi, and L. Sherrod, eds., *Parenting Across the Lifespan: Biosocial Dimensions*. Hawthorne, N.Y.: Aldine de Gruyter.

Liebowitz, M. R. 1983. *The Chemistry of Love*. Boston: Little, Brown.

Low, B. 1978. "Environmental Uncertainty and the Parental Strategies of Marsupials and Placantals. *American Naturalist* 112:197–213.

Main, M. 1990. "Cross-Cultural Studies of Attachment Organization: Recent Studies, Changing Methodologies, and the Concept of Conditional Strategies. *Human Development* 33:48–61.

Main, M., N. Kaplan, and J. Cassidy. 1985. "Security in Infancy, Childhood, and Adulthood: A Move to the Level of Representation. In I. Bretherton and E. Waters, eds., *Growing Points of Attachment Theory and Research*. Monographs of the Society for Research in Child Development, no. 209.

Matas, L., R. Arend, and L. Sroufe. 1978. "Continuity of Adaptation in the Second Year: The Relationship Between Quality of Attachment and Later Competence." *Child Development* 49:547–556.

Promislow, D., and P. Harvey. 1990. "Living Fast and Dying Young: A Comparative Analysis of Life-History Variation Among Mammals." *Journal of the Zoological Society of London* 220:417–437.

Roff, D. 1992. *The Evolution of Life Histories: Theory and Analysis*. New York: Chapman and Hall.

Russell, R. 1993. *The Lemur's Legacy: The Evolution of Power, Sex, and Love*. Los Angeles: Tarcher/Putnam.

Shaver, P. R., and C. Hazan. 1993. "Adult Romantic Attachment: Theory and Evidence. In D. Perlman and W. Jones, eds., *Advances in Personal Relationships* 4:29–70. London: Jessica Kingsley.

Simpson, J., and S. Gangestad. 1991. "Individual Differences in Sociosexuality: Evidence for Convergent and Discriminant Validity." *Journal of Personality and Social Psychology* 60:870–883.

Skolnick, A. 1986. "Early Attachment and Personal Relationships Across the Life Course." In R. Lerner and D. Featherman, eds., *Life Span Development and Behavior*, vol. 7. Hillsdale, N.J.: Lawrence Erlbaum.

Smuts, B., and D. Gubernick. 1992. "Male-Infant Relationships in Nonhuman Primates: Paternal Investment or Mating Effort?" In B. Hewlett, ed., *Father-Child Relations: Cultural and Biosocial Contexts*. Hawthorne, N.Y.: Aldine de Gruyter.

Sroufe, L. 1983. "Infant-Caregiver Attachment and Patterns of Adaptation in Preschool: The Roots of Maladaptation and Competence." In M. Perlmutter, ed., *Minnesota Symposia in Child Psychology*. 16:41–83. Hillsdale, N.J.: Lawrence Erlbaum.

Sroufe, L. and E. Waters. 1977. "Attachment as an Organizational Construct." *Child Development* 48:1184–1199.

Stearns, S. 1992. *The Evolution of Life Histories*. New York: Oxford University Press.

Sternberg, R. J. 1986. "A Triangular Theory of Love." *Psychological Review* 93:119–135.

Sternberg, R. J., and M. L. Barnes, eds. 1988. *The Psychology of Love*. New Haven: Yale University Press.

Tennov, D. 1979. *Love and Limerence: The Experience of Being in Love*. New York: Stein and Day.

Trivers, R. 1972. "Parental Investment and Sexual Selection." In B. Campbell, ed., *Sexual Selection and the Descent of Man*. Hawthorne, N.Y.: Aldine de Gruyter.

Waller, N., and P. Shaver. 1994. "The Importance of Nongenetic Influences on Romantic

56   Love Styles: A Twin-Family Study." *Psychological Science* 5:268–274.

Werner, E., and R. Smith. 1992. *Overcoming the Odds: High-Risk Children from Birth to Adulthood*. Ithaca: Cornell University Press.

Williams, G., 1966. "Natural Selection, the Costs of Reproduction, and a Refinement of Lack's Principle." *American Naturalist* 100:687–690.

Love as an Experience of Transcendence

CHARLES LINDHOLM

Georges Simenon, the prolific French author who was equally active as a Don Juan, was once asked to describe the difference between sexual passion and romantic love. "Passion," Simenon said, "is a malady. It's possession, something dark. You are jealous of everything. There's no lightness, no harmony. Love, that's completely different. It is beautiful. Love is being two in one. It is being so close that when one opens his mouth to speak, the other says exactly what you meant to say. Love is a quiet understanding and a fusion" (Simenon 1984).

The erotically experienced Simenon here disengages the imperative demands of sexual desire from romantic love, which he describes as engendering a powerful and expansive sense of self-loss through merger with the beloved other. This experience of self-transcendence, I will argue in the following pages, is the essence of romantic love; it is above all a creative act of human imagination, arising as a cultural expression of deep existential longings for an escape from the prison of the self. I shall contrast this view of love with another, more prevalent view, which understands love as contingent upon sexual desire.

In making my case about the nature of falling in love,[1] I am hardly being original. Rather, the question of the nature of love has divided and puzzled

Western philosophers at least from the time of the Greeks. Irving Singer, in his exhaustive study of the philosophical and literary roots of the concept of romantic love, has outlined this debate, showing that the way love has been conceptualized throughout Western history can be divided into two opposing, but necessarily intertwined, perspectives. In the first, love is based on appraisal, and those who are beloved are thought capable of satisfying our deepest appetites. In other words, we assess the other to discover if they have the attributes we long for; if they do, we love them. Broadly defined, love is a matter of calculated self-interest.

Self-interest, however, can take on a transcendental hue. The beloved can appeal to us as an avenue to a higher level of being. There are many versions of this way of understanding love. For instance, Plato portrays love of persons as a plateau in the soul's impassioned pursuit of the ideal good. The beloved is adulated as an earthly and imperfect expression of divine harmony and beauty. But the wise man realizes that the love of persons is shallow compared to the spiritual rewards of pure reason, and progresses through enjoyment of the flawed body of the other to meditation on the abstract realm of the ideal, where beauty is absolute and eternal. Love for a person then is a means to a higher end, much like the contemplation of a work of art.[2]

A more down-to-earth stance is taken by Ovid, for whom the Platonic search for a higher love in the realm of the absolute through the body of the lover is a ludicrous subterfuge. Ovid says that what the lover wants is clear enough: sexual enjoyment. His emphasis is on the game of love, and he teaches his readers, both male and female, how the idealizing imagery of romantic passion can be used with style and grace by intelligent seducers to help them gain sexual access to those whom they desire while avoiding the attentions of others whom they find unattractive. Professions of love serve to conceal a seducer's deliberate machinations and thereby render lust more attractive.

Ovid's appetitive perspective on love has been the dominant view for scientific minds ever since Plato's notion of the spiritual progress of the soul lost its persuasiveness. But while Ovid's portrayal of sexual desire as the underlying source of love was retained, his playful attitude toward sexuality was repudiated as morally suspect by more puritanical writers such as Jonathan Swift, who wrote that love is "a ridiculous passion which hath no being but in play-books and romances" (quoted in Singer 1984:1:138).

Anthropologists, in the little they have had to say about romantic love (prior to this present collection) have tended to fall generally within the Swiftian paradigm. Most famous and representative is Ralph Linton's statement:

> The hero of the modern American movie is always a romantic lover, just as the hero of an old Arab epic is always an epileptic. A cynic may suspect that in any ordinary population the percentage of individuals with capacity for romantic love of the Hollywood type was about as large as that of persons able to throw genuine epileptic fits. However, given a little social encouragement, either one can be adequately imitated without the performer admitting even to himself that the performance is not genuine. (Linton 1936:175)

Similarly, Robert Lowie argues that in all cultures "passion, of course is taken for granted; affection, which many travellers vouch for, might be conceded; but Love? Well, the romantic sentiment occurs in simpler conditions, as with us—in fiction" (1931:95).

Romantic love, from this point of view, is nothing but a self-delusion, derived from the arts, used to persuade lovers that their sexual desires are actually ethereal and transcendent. Where Ovid saw the idealizing content of romantic love as an attractive and necessary convention, it now becomes a hypocritical lie. Jean-Paul Sartre has immortalized this modern perspective in a famous section in *Being and Nothingness* (1956), where he scathingly imagines the bad faith of a young girl absently permitting her hand to be stroked by a suitor while she simultaneously imagines herself admired solely as a creature of purity and abstract intellect.

This approach has the virtue of simplicity and coherence; falling in love is always a fraud, and men and women who claim to be in love are invariably hypocrites or, at best, seducers. But it does little justice to the actual self-reports of lovers, who clearly do not always fit into the categories of self-deceivers and sexual predators. A more sympathetic modern version of the "eros tradition" (as Singer has called it) is to be found in sociobiology, which takes a somewhat different tack toward understanding romantic love. The aim is to give more credit to the lovers' own inner experience while still retaining the materialistic view of romantic love as essentially an expression of sexuality.

The twist is that rather than debunking romantic sentiment as self-delusion, these writers understand love as a compulsive drive toward sexual contact with a specific beloved other. This compulsion is connected to evolutionary biology by utilizing contemporary theories of genetic success.

Instead of consciously manipulating one another, as enjoined by Ovid, the lovers now are themselves unconscious puppets of the deep evolutionary forces that are propelling their behaviors.

This argument was first proposed by Schopenhauer, who asserted that romantic love is a trick played by the Will in order to compel human beings to reproduce and carry on the movement of the *Geist* toward the future. Thus he writes that lovers desire a "fusion into a single being, in order then to go on living only as this being; and this longing receives its fulfillment in the child they produce" (Schopenhauer 1966:2:536); or, put more prosaically: "If Petrarch's passion had been satisfied, his song would have been silenced from that moment, just as is that of the bird, as soon as the eggs are laid" (Schopenhauer 1966:2:557).

As reworked in modern rhetoric Schopenhauer's argument is used by sociobiologists to assert that romantic love is a genetically innate mechanism serving to offset the male's natural tendency to maximize his gene pool through promiscuity. It does this by tying him to a particular female via the emotionally charged sexual contact that is understood to be the heart of romance. The enhanced pairbonding that results serves the evolutionary purpose of increasing the overall rate of survival for human children.

From this perspective falling in love is therefore a very real experience, probably a consequence of the manufacture of powerful chemicals in the brain that incite the potent feelings of merger and ecstasy lovers report; but love is not sufficient onto itself, rather it is a means to an end—perpetuation of the species. Thus sociobiology shares with the Platonic perspective a concern with teleology. But where Plato saw love as a step in the pursuit of the ideal, now the goal of romantic love is disconcertingly mundane: evolutionary success.

Some of the cultural background that informs this argument can be illustrated in a balance sheet made up by the twenty-nine-year-old Charles Darwin, who was weighing the good points and bad points of marriage. The main good point was companionship ("a nice soft wife on a sofa" . . . "better than a dog anyhow"); children were also mentioned, as Darwin expresses his fear of being a "neuter bee." The bad points were more numerous, and included the considerable financial burden a wife and children would impose on him, the inevitable constraints a family would place on his freedom of action, the "loss of time," the "anxiety and responsibility" and the fear that marriage might end as "banishment and degradation with (an) indolent, idle fool" (quoted in MacFarlane 1986:3–4).

In reading Darwin's lists, it seems clear that the disadvantages of marriage, which are many and concrete, appear to far outweigh the advantages, which are few and abstract. As Alan MacFarlane writes, speaking from a strictly rational perspective, marriage in England "was not sane behavior, for almost all the advantages of marriage could be bought in the market—from sex to housekeeping and friendship" (1986:172). But Darwin married nonetheless, persuading himself that "there is many a happy slave" (quoted in MacFarlane 1986:4). Why did he act so irrationally?

MacFarlane argues that in Western history, and especially in the history of England, romantic love has been precisely the factor that has been invoked as the source of the marriage tie. In a society where arranged marriage was never pervasive, where lineages were more or less nonexistent, and where personal autonomy prevailed, love acts as a deus ex machina, overcoming the reasonable reluctance of rational self-seeking individuals to commit themselves to marriage bonds they would otherwise avoid. Furthermore, love also focuses sexuality in the open market of potential partners, "some external force of desire is needed to help the individual to make a choice. Hence passionate 'love' overwhelms and justifies and provides compulsive authority" (MacFarlane 1987:142).

Although MacFarlane does not carry his argument through to claim a biological source for romance, it is perfectly plausible to reconcile his position with a concept of falling in love as an expression of a biological pressure that compels individuals toward erotic encounters with a specific other. The historian Laurence Stone states this point of view most candidly when he describes falling in love as "an urgent desire for sexual intercourse with a particular individual" (Stone 1988:16); a sexual encounter that, from the sociobiological standpoint, can induce the commitment and reciprocal caring necessary for maintaining a human family unit.

Following the logic of the argument further, if romantic love is simply a strong, biologically generated, hormonally induced sexual urge for a unique other, culture becomes a variable that may have an enhancing or suppressing effect on the erotic romantic impulse, and it would make sense to argue that societies valuing choice and individualism would be most conducive to romantic love, while those valuing obligation and communalism would work to control romantic desire by cultural mechanisms, such as arranged marriage, chaperoning of youth, child betrothal, and so on. On the other hand, Western culture, which favors personal autonomy and free choice, is the location where love can take its "natural," biologically induced, course, permitting romance to replace formal bonds of kinship and alliance as the motivation for marriage.[3]

To restate: from the standpoint of the contemporary sociobiological version of the eros tradition, falling in love is understood as a biological drive, probably deriving from hormonal secretions, that intensifies sexual desire and thereby leads to strong pairbonding. It is favorable to the reproduction and care of human children, and its transcendental consummation is the successful maximization of genetic potential. It can be assumed that some cultures will favor this compulsion while others will attempt to suppress it; nonetheless it will remain as a universal and ineradicable desire for mating with a particular other person—a desire interpreted as romantic love.

But there are problems with this perspective, and they have to do with the place romantic love fills in different cultural contexts. Although giving some reluctant credit to cultural processes, sociobiology generally assumes that millions of years of evolution outweigh a few millennia of culture. Therefore, human beings, like their simian ancestors, are portrayed as basically governed by instinct, though the instincts may have been distorted, channeled, and partially curbed by cultural conditioning. However, postulating a primary cause requires a demonstration of at least some discernible secondary effect; and if culture can completely rewrite, overturn, or cancel the supposed biological matrix of romantic love, sexuality, and reproduction, then the logic of the sociobiological argument is seriously challenged.

This challenge is most evident in the aspect of culture that has most to do with evolutionary biology; that is, the institution of marriage. In all human societies marriage serves as a ritualized way of formalizing and legitimizing the sexual relationship between couples. Furthermore, in almost every known culture married couples produce and raise the vast majority of children. Given this basic fact, one would expect that if romantic love is linked to reproduction, then marriage should be correlated with romantic love.

In the modern West, of course, this works well enough, since romantic love, marriage, and children indeed usually *do* go together and, as we shall see, have gone together for some centuries. However, in most human cultures this is not the case, nor was it necessarily the case everywhere in Western culture in the past. For example, in the courtly society of Louis XIV in France, marriage and love were decidedly opposed, since marriage was arranged for political advantage, not for romantic attraction. In this culture courtesans were the objects of romantic attraction, not wives. Interestingly, these courtesans, who stood outside of the political structure of the society because of their base birth, were prized not so much for their sexuality as for their charm and wit. Of course, having children was something these women avoided at all costs.[4]

Similarly, in Rome of the Imperial Age conjugal love between husband and wife was considered ridiculous and impossible, so much so that Seneca writes, "to love one's wife with an ardent passion is to commit adultery" (quoted in Grimal 1986:252). Rather, noble lineages were tied together through marriage bonds based on Roman virtues of austerity and piety; virtues that were sorely tested with the vast expansion of Roman conquests and the importation of huge numbers of slaves who could serve as concubines. In these circumstances marriage came to be regarded, as Plautus notes, as "an unavoidable calamity" (quoted in Grimal 1986:88), while love was to be found with slave prostitutes of both sexes who were outside the power struggle that pitted husband against wife.

As in France, the romantic relationship with the courtesan had nothing to do with children: reproduction was reserved for the far more mundane and pragmatic relationship of marriage. Eventually, elite evasion of the constraints of marriage in favor of romantic (but sterile) involvement with prostitutes became so prevalent that the birthrate of the nobility dropped precipitously, obliging Augustus to offer special privileges to men producing children in aristocratic marriages.

Nor is this a configuration found only in complex state societies, though many more examples from such societies could easily be cited. A similar pattern occurs in Northern Pakistan, where the patrilineal Pukhtun organized marriages to cement alliances between clans, while individual men pursued romances clandestinely. Prostitutes and adolescent boys were most often the objects of their romantic desires, and neither of these ever produced children.[5]

Furthermore, if romantic love is assumed to correlate with reproductive success, one would expect that societies most favoring the cultural expression of love would have the highest birth rate. However, the converse is the case. Cultures where marriages are between strangers and are arranged for political and economic benefit by parents have generally had far higher birthrates than the West.[6]

For instance, if we look at English and Germanic society prior to the advances of medical knowledge, we can see the birthrates there have long been low, and population growth slow, largely because of late marriage and a cautious attitude toward having children. This pattern has persisted from at least the early middle ages, and possibly much earlier. It is associated with an Anglo-Saxon cultural milieu in which personal autonomy and maximization of individual benefits outside of the extended family circle prevailed. In this context children have been (quite realistically) viewed as a cost, whose major value is as pets or as monuments to their parents. Thus Britain and Northern Europe generally have never been home to cults of fertility, nor have bachelorhood, spinsterhood, or barrenness ever been sanctioned against.[7]

All this is in obvious contrast to cultures where the extended family is the unit of production and of political power, where more children mean more labor, wealth, and physical strength invested in the extended family, and where fertility is consequently highly valued. Given these circumstances, it is difficult to see how the sociobiological paradigm could explain the fact that the Northern European constellation of low birthrate, late marriage, nuclear families, and individual autonomy *correlates* with the most highly evolved tradition of romantic love in the world!

The premise of a "deep structure" of genetic predisposition for romantic love is further undercut when we consider the relationship between romantic love and sexual desire. It is taken for granted in the eros tradition that romantic love is intertwined with sexuality and is, in fact, a consequence of the erotic impulse. Thus any disavowal of sexual desire in a romantic relationship is assumed, a priori, to be self-delusive. However, this assumption requires us to dismiss ethnographic and historical examples that point in precisely the opposite direction.

For example, consider the Southern European expressions of courtly love in the Medieval period. Here, in a transformation of the cult of the virgin Mary, the courtier explicitly denied any carnal feelings for his beloved, who was worshipped as an angel above the realm of earthly lust, not to be sullied in thought or deed. These courtiers singing of *fin amor* were often married men with active sex lives and children, and the lady herself was always a married woman, with husband and children of her own. However, romantic love was not to be found in these legitimized sexual relations, but only in adulation of the lady. To assume this chaste and idealizing ideology was simply a mask disguising sexual desire is taking for granted what one wishes to prove; rather, we should take at face value the truth of the courtier's song; that is, that the lady was, *for the poet*, beloved as a creature of sanctified innocence and virtue.[8]

Such behavior patterns and idealizations are hardly unusual, though the structure of the relationship may vary considerably. For example, the Marri

Baluch, another patrilineal Middle Eastern people much like the Pukhtun, have a highly elaborated romantic love complex. Men and women, married for political and economic purposes, long to participate in secret and highly dangerous illicit love affairs. These passionate relationships are hugely valued in Marri culture and are the subject of innumerable poems and songs.

According to the Marri, when lovers meet they exchange tokens of mutual affection and talk heart to heart, without dissimulation. In marked contrast to the elevation of the lady in courtly love, and in marked contrast as well to the reality of male domination in Marri society, Marri lovers regard one another as equals. For this reason the lovers should be chaste: sexuality, culturally understood as an expression of male power, imposes an element of oppression and subordination that the cultural ideal of mutuality and respect between lovers cannot permit.[9] How many of these relationships are indeed sexless is impossible to say, but chastity is what the Marri believe to be characteristic of the deepest forms of love between men and women; once again, to suppose that this belief is a falsehood is to do them and their culture an injustice by assuming that we know the truth behind their ideals.[10]

The separation between sexual desire and romantic love may be especially common in societies such as the Marri, where sexual intercourse is regarded as an act of violence and domination, or in Melanesia, where sexuality is associated with pollution and spiritual danger. An example of the latter is found in Manus, described by Margaret Mead, where sex is a perilous act, and marriage itself is a distasteful and shameful business. As among the Marri, Manus men and women are drawn into extramarital liaisons, but, Mead writes: "Illicit love affairs, affairs of choice, are, significantly enough, described as situations in which people need not have sex if they do not wish to, but can simply sit and talk and laugh together. . . . The wonderful thing about lovers is that your don't have to sleep with them" (Mead 1956:361, 405).

If these examples are too exotic, we need look no further than our own Victorian forbears. The familiar split between whore and virgin was a reality for the Victorians, and sexual desire was, as much as possible, divorced from middle-class marriage, since women of culture were assumed to be without demeaning sexual impulses. Men demanded virginal purity in the women they married, while wives appear, from their own accounts, to have often managed actually to live up to the ideal. Thus sexual contact between a husband and his beloved wife was regarded as an unfortunate necessity of marriage, to be engaged in as a duty; men overcome by sexual passion were expected to spend themselves in the company of prostitutes, whom they certainly did not love. This characteristic Victorian division between love and sexuality is a mode of feeling that must be taken on its own terms.

It seems, then, that the correlation between falling in love, sexual desire, and reproduction has to be reconsidered. It appears that the eros tradition in its modern guise renders biological, and therefore primary and irresistible, a peculiarly modern and Western form of relationship that does indeed unite romantic love, sexual intimacy, and reproduction—elements that may certainly have a powerful affinity, but that also may be separated, both in logic and in cultural reality. The postulated biological matrix thus does not have any provable effect.

However, there is another standard Western way of looking at love that I wish to put forward here as an alternative to the eros paradigm in all its guises. From this alternative perspective love is not motivated by the desire to reproduce, or lust, or the ideal of beauty; rather, the beloved other is adulated *in himself or herself* as the fountainhead of all that is beautiful, good, and desirable. As Francesco Alberoni puts it, when we fall in love "the possible opens before us and the pure object of eros appears, the unambivalent object, in which duty and pleasure coincide, in which all alienation is extinguished" (1983:23).

However, it is crucial to note that this adulation is offered in spite of the beloved's *actual* characteristics; in other words, falling in love is an act of imagination in which the other is invested with absolute value; the beloved can even be loved for his very faults. Singer calls this idealistic form of love the "bestowal tradition" to stress the lover's creativity in manufacturing the perfection of the beloved.[11]

From within this framework any overt or covert calculated appraisal of the other as a good provider, a useful ally, or even as an avenue to God is felt to be a sin against the very nature of romantic love, which is defined and experienced as spontaneous, total, and boundless in its devotion to the actual person of the other. Thus, to love "for a reason" is not to love at all. We love because we love, and not because of any advantage that the beloved other has to offer us.[12]

This alternative notion of unqualified love has deep intellectual and spiritual roots in the West: its heritage includes the Jewish concept of *nomos* transformed into Christian notions of God's unconditional, unreserved, and undeserved love for humanity (agape), as expressed in the sacrifice of Jesus.[13] This notion of God's boundless love of humanity made love itself a value in Western culture while simultaneously devaluing sexuality. Love was further humanized in the cult of Mary, and, as we have seen, afterward was secularized in the courtly love that bound the courtier to his lady. As Singer writes, "Henceforth the Christian could hold not only that God is Love but also that Love is God" (Singer 1984 1:340).

In this context, and over time, "the idea that love is the unmerited sanctification of the sinner degenerated into the notion that sinners become sanctified through *any* love whatsoever. God disappeared, but there remained the holiness of indiscriminate love binding one worthless person to another" (Singer 1984 1:341). Love became reciprocal and individualized, as it was secularized and institutionalized into the romantic experience that is the expected prelude to marriage in contemporary culture in the West and, increasingly, everywhere in the world.

It is this secularized form of romantic love that is rhapsodically portrayed in songs, poems, novels, and films as an ultimate value in itself: compelling, overwhelming, ecstatic, uniquely blissful—indeed, the most powerful emotional event of one's life. This is the love in which, as the young Hegel writes, "consciousness of a separate self disappears, and all distinction between the lovers is annulled" (Hegel 1948:307); it is the love apostrophized by the philosopher Roberto Unger as "the most influential mode of moral vision in our culture" (Unger 1984:29).

Is this experience of falling in love as a way of imagining and experiencing transcendence through a relationship of communion in selfless and fervent merger with an idealized other a peculiarly Western one, as Singer's philosophical approach would seem to indicate? I would say not, but it is also not universal.

Rather, falling in love can usefully be conceived as one possible response to the human existential condition of contingency and self-consciousness. As Andre Bataille writes, "We are discontinuous beings, individuals who perish in isolation in the midst of an incomprehensible adventure, but we yearn for our lost continuity" (Bataille 1962:15). In response to this unbearable but inescapable dilemma, human beings search for ways to escape the burden of loneliness while avoiding confrontation with a cold and indifferent cosmos. One of the ways this escape can be attained is in the experience of falling in love. To quote Bataille once more, "Only the beloved can in this world bring about what our human limitations deny, a total blending of two beings, a continuity between two discontinuous creatures" (Bataille 1962:20).[14] Thus, instead of resembling a biological drive, falling in love is more akin to religious revelation, but with a particular real person as the focus of devotion.

I was led to this view of romantic love because in the last few years I have been involved in cross-cultural research on charismatic movements and idealization.[15] My studies indicated that charisma, which is experienced as a compulsive and overwhelming attraction of a follower to a leader, is in almost all respects parallel to the experience of romantic love. For example, in both instances there is an intense idealization of one particular other person; in both there is a fervent subjective perception of merger with the beloved—a merger experienced as "exaltation, ecstasy and exaggeration of the ego" (Chasseguet-Smirgel 1976:356).

Furthermore, in love, as in charisma, participants feel they are capable of obliterating boundaries of convention in their quest for a state of absolute communion.[16] Both states also are characterized by a fear of loss of the idealized other—and suicidal despair if that loss occurs—and both have a strong tendency toward rationalization (charismatic groups become bureaucracies; romantic lovers become companionate couples). In both rationalization can be offset if mystery and danger are maintained by distance and obstacles that separate follower and leader, lover and beloved (the Romeo and Juliet effect).[17]

Charisma and romance also appeared to be mutually exclusive—a person involved in a charismatic group generally could not be immersed in a romantic relation, and vice versa. As Kernberg writes, following Freud, "the opposition between the couple and the group is an essential characteristic of human love life" (1977:107); an insight borne out in ethnographic data. People who leave charismatic organizations often do so because they have fallen in love; conversely, people who become devotees have often been disappointed in love. This fact also indicates that both arise from the same psychological matrix. The main differences are a result of the influence of the group dynamic in the charismatic relation, which renders it less susceptible to rationalization, while making real reciprocity between the leader and the disciples impossible.

Given these parallels, Alberoni can reasonably write that "the experience of falling in love is the simplest form of collective movement" (1983:7), and Miller can argue that there is an "equivalence between leaders and lovers that brings about the same kind of elevation, idealization and incorporation that endows the leader and lover with special status and powers" (1980:205). Falling in love and charisma thus can be plausibly conceptualized as variations on a very deep and basic human existential search—the quest for transcendence.

If we accept the proposition that charisma and love are parallel attempts to escape from contingency and solipsism, this means downplaying some of the elements that have generally been seen as diagnostic of falling in love. For instance, romantic love does not occur only among adolescents, nor does it *necessarily* imply equality between the lovers, or the transformation of love into marriage, or even powerful sexual desire.[18]

If this perspective is accepted, then further research should be oriented toward understanding what sorts of social formations and historical conditions favor various characteristic expressions of the human impulse toward self-loss in ecstatic states of union with an idealized other. We should also compare and contrast romantic love and charisma with other apparently similar experiences such as mystical and religious communion, possession trance, reverie, artistic inspiration, and so on. By taking this pathway, we can avoid reducing romantic love to an instrumentality and recognize instead that it stands on its own as a specific state of transcendence—the one most characteristic of the modern world.

NOTES

1. To begin talking about love we need first to discriminate between the ecstatic moment of falling in love and the rationalized forms that may follow from it: being in love and remaining in love. In this paper, I intend to discuss only falling in love.

2. In fact, Plato recommends sexual promiscuity as a way of ridding oneself of the delusion that any specific individual can offer perfection—perhaps the first time sexual license has been advocated as a route to spiritual enlightenment.

3. This perspective has been asserted by many theorists who do not connect their arguments with the eros tradition in its sociobiological incarnation. See, for example, Talcott Parsons (1949), Robert Solomon (1981), William Goode (1959). The argument is succinctly stated by Gideon Sjoberg: "The romantic love ideology may be seen as appropriate, even necessary, in a society where the external pressures on permanent unions through kinship are largely absent" (Sjoberg 1960:139–140)

4. See Elias (1983) for more on courtly culture.

5. See Lindholm (1982) for an ethnography of the Pukhtun.

6. Of course, the success rate of child raising is another question, and one could argue that the strong emotional investment of parents romantically involved in their own relationship might heighten the possibility of their children reaching reproductive maturity, since the loving couple will stay together, protecting and nurturing their children. However, one could also make the opposite argument, that is, that those who are romantically involved will not wish the distraction of children, and will not reproduce at the same rate as those who are married for more pragmatic reasons.

7. See MacFarlane (1986) and Goody (1983) for this argument.

8. See Boase (1977) for a comprehensive review of this literature.

9. See Pehrson (1966) for the ethnography of the Marri.

10. Middle Eastern romantic stories usually end in the death of the lovers, who never consummate their passion. Only a love remaining on the level of profound yearning has the spiritual dimension that renders it worthy of myth.

11. Singer (1987) also rightly notes, in the last volume of his work, that in fact both appraisal and bestowal are necessarily intermingled in modern romantic love—we idealize others partly for what their characteristics are. But what is important from my perspective is that it is possible to analytically distinguish the idealizing aspect of love, which allows us to see romantic attraction as parallel to other forms of idealization, and therefore to make comparisons.

12. As Singer puts it: "Love supplements the human search for value with a capacity for bestowing it gratuitously" (Singer 1984 1:14).

13. As Anders Nygren writes, "Eros *recognizes value* in its object, and loves it—Agape loves, and *creates value* in its object" (Nygren 1958:210).

14. I do not have the space here to consider Bataille's interesting argument about the crucial place of violence in romantic entanglement.

15. See Lindholm (1988, 1990).

16. In fact, most romantic attachment is located within strict boundaries of age, race, class, and even neighborhood. Nonetheless, the belief remains strong that "love conquers all." Similarly, charisma also entails a sense of extraordinary movement toward the unknown. What is symbolized in this imagery is the fundamental capacity of charisma and love to break the boundaries of the self and to produce a fusion between separate individuals.

17. See Driscoll, Davis, and Lipetz (1972) for an empirical proof.

18. This is not to say that these elements may not occur within any particular mode of romantic idealization—clearly they often do. In fact, it is quite plausible to argue, as Freud does, that sexuality is humanity's most compelling experience of the blurring of personal boundaries that is the essence of transcendence (Freud 1961). My argument is only that this association must not taken for granted.

REFERENCES

Alberoni, F. 1983. *Falling in Love*. New York: Random House.

Bataille, G. 1962. *Eroticism*. London: John Calder.

Boase, R. 1977. *The Origin and Meaning of Courtly Love*. Manchester: Manchester University Press.

Chasseguet-Smirgel, J. 1976. "Some Thoughts on the Ego Ideal." *Psychoanalytic Quarterly* 45:345–373.

Driscoll, D., K. Davis, and M. Lipetz. 1972. "Parental Interference and Romantic Love: The Romeo and Juliet Effect." *Journal of Personality and Social Psychology* 24:1–10.

Elias, N. 1983. *Court Society*. New York: Pantheon.

Freud, S. 1961. *Civilization and Its Discontents*. New York: Norton.

Goode, W. 1959. "The Theoretical Importance of Love." *American Sociological Review* 24:38–47.

Goody, J. 1983. *The Development of the Family and Marriage in Europe*. Cambridge: Cambridge University Press.

Grimal, P. 1986. *Love in Ancient Rome*. Norman: University of Oklahoma Press.

Hegel, G. 1948. *Early Theological Writings*. Chicago: University of Chicago Press.

Kernberg, O. 1977. "Boundaries and Structure in Love Relationships." *Journal of the American Psychoanalytic Association* 25:81–144.

Lindholm, C. 1982. *Generosity and Jealousy: The Swat Pukhtun of Northern Pakistan*. New York: Columbia University Press.

—— 1988. "Lovers and Leaders: A Comparison of Social and Psychological Models of Romance and Charisma." *Social Science Information* 27:3–45.

—— 1990. *Charisma*. Oxford: Basil Blackwell.

Linton, R. 1936. *The Study of Man*. New York: Appleton-Century.

Lowie, R. 1931. "Sex and Marriage." In John McDermott, ed., *The Sex Problem in Modern Society*. New York: Modern Library,

MacFarlane, A. 1986. *Marriage and Love in England: 1300—1840*. Oxford: Basil Blackwell.

—— 1987. *The Culture of Capitalism*. Oxford: Basil Blackwell.

Mead, M. 1956. *New Lives for Old: Cultural Transformation—Manus, 1920–1953*. New York: Morrow.

Miller, J. 1980. "Romantic Couples and Group Process." In K. Pope, ed., *On Love and Loving*. San Francisco: Josey Bass.

Nygren, A. 1958. *Agape and Eros*. Philadephia: Westminster.

Parsons, T. 1949. "The Social Structure of the Family." In Ruth Nanda Anshen, ed., *The Family: Its Function and Destiny*. New York: Harper.

Parsons, T., and R. Bales. 1955. *Family, Socialization, and Interaction Process*. Glencoe: Free Press.

Pehrson, R. 1966. *The Social Organization of the Marri Baluch*. Chicago: Aldine.

Sartre, J. -P. 1956. *Being and Nothingness*. New York: Philosophical Library.

Schopenhauer, A. 1966. *The World as Will and Representation*. New York: Dover.

Simenon, G. 1984. "Interview with Georges Simenon." *New York Times Magazine*. April 22.

Singer, I. 1984. *The Nature of Love*. Vol 1: *Plato to Luther*. Chicago: University of Chicago Press.

—— 1984. *The Nature of Love*. Vol 2: *Courtly and Romantic*. Chicago: University of Chicago Press.

—— 1987. *The Nature of Love*. Vol 3: *The Modern World*. Chicago: University of Chicago Press.

Sjoberg, G. 1960. *The Preindustrial City, Past and Present*. Glencoe: Free Press.

Solomon, R. 1981. *Love: Emotion, Myth and Metaphor*. Garden City: Anchor.

Stone, L. 1988. "Passionate Attachments in the West in Historical Perspective." In W. Gaylin and E. Person, eds., *Passionate Attachments*. New York: Free Press.

Unger, R. 1984. *Passion: An Essay on Personality*. New York: Free Press.

Boundaries of Love

JAN CLANTON COLLINS AND THOMAS GREGOR

Love is the most personal of relationships. It enfolds and immerses love partners in a separate world of their own construction. Yet love occurs in the larger context of families, kin, and community. Lovers must protect their world and separate it from the surrounding society. What are the tensions between the inner world of love and the demands of the encircling community? How is the loving relationship affected by where the lines are drawn? In many societies potential love partners have little choice. By tradition they are positioned in a circle of extended family households and kin. In our own culture there is a wider range of possibilities, so that love relationships may be isolated or deeply immersed in the larger community. Our society is thereby a natural laboratory for the study of the boundaries of relationships and the intersect of love and community. The purpose of this essay is to examine the nature of love in relationships that range from the most inwardly focused and deeply merged to those that blend with the surrounding community. Our data consists of information from different societies and a unique set of interviews from our own culture in which love partners recount the boundaries of their relationship.

BOUNDARIES Boundaries are lines that define and limit. Individuals have boundaries that are increasingly studied in ego psychology and in a newly emerging anthropology of the self. Our boundaries as individuals consist of tangible enclosures, such as our skin, and psychological barriers, such as the sphere of defended space that surrounds us and that others normally will not penetrate without an invitation. Things that go across personal boundaries take on deep emotional significance, whether they are physical things, such as blood and tears, or symbolic things, such as intimate and revealing words.

Like individuals, groups have boundaries that are crucial in determining their nature. Like the skin of an individual, the frontiers of a group may be physical, such as defended borders, meeting grounds, or uniforms, or they may be symbolic, such as an ethnic group's special languages and defining beliefs. As is also true of the individual, transactions across the boundaries, such as may occur in a marriage, in travel, or in trade, take on more than ordinary significance.

Standing midway between the group and the individual is the relationship. For the social scientist, relationship boundaries are perhaps the most important of all. They form molecules of social organization that join bounded egos (individuals) to one another and thereby construct groups and institutions. Like the individual or the social group, the boundaries of relationships may be physical (the household, and within the household the marital bedroom) or symbolic "tie signs," such as wedding rings or walking together while holding hands. We may say that relationships are firmly bounded when they are exclusive. They are permeable when others may participate. In the terms of Erving Goffman, those who share a well-bounded relationship are a "together," in that they form a social unit from the perspective of the rest of the society. As is also the case of both individuals and groups, transactions between firmly bonded relationship partners and the outside world take on special significance. For example, a dinner party offered by a marital couple to their friends is a presentational ritual that establishes a relationship. Its function in this capacity is clarified when there is a disruption, as could occur when a host openly flirts with a guest.

Impermeable, exclusive relationships have an additional property in common with bounded groups. Like such groups they lay claim to the individual. In common with such encompassing and intense group values as patriotism or family loyalty, exclusive dyadic relationships tend to demand full allegiance. Of such relationships in our own society love is surely the most powerful, with a first call on the individual's emotional and personal resources. The claims staked out by love are therefore often in tension with those of the group.

LOVE Romantic love is an intense, erotic relationship that involves commitment (resources and time), intimacy, and idealization of the other. The internal experience is one of merging, in which the boundaries of the ego are temporarily expanded to include the beloved. Ethel Person, the author of an insightful book on the psychology of love, puts it like this:

> If (lovers) are lucky enough to enjoy a *passionate* love, their feelings of union will be interspersed with ecstatic moments of merger. These magical moments are experienced as epiphanies. At such times, there is, if not a loss of ego boundaries, at least a permeability of ego boundaries . . . [yet] the self is preserved, the spirit exalted. (1989:127)

In English we lack a single term for this special amalgam of feelings. Passion comes close, if by it we understand the ecstasy of love.

Considering the power of the experience of love and its extravagant importance in our own culture, love is minimally studied. Until recently, the topic seemed slightly embarrassing. Just as sexual repression has inhibited research on love, so a "love repression," by which love is trivialized or ignored as a subject worthy of scientific inquiry, has barred us from fuller knowledge (see Gregor N.d.). Now, as our knowledge grows, it turns out that some of what we thought to be true is false. Until recently, we believed that the passion of love was limited to the West and a few other societies, and, within the West, perhaps only to a few periods of history. Thanks in part to the work of some of the contributors to this volume we know otherwise. In 1992 William Jankowiak and Edward Fischer, building on the work of other social scientists (see Rosenblatt 1966), examined data on love from a representative sample of 166 societies. They found clear evidence of romantic love in at least 147, or 88.5 percent, and therefore maintain that love is "a universal phenomenon," reaching across cultures and historical epochs.

Eventually we will have a comparative ethnography of love. We will be able to map its form in different cultural settings and thereby chart a human relationship whose dimensions transcend our Western experience. For the moment, however, we can use the natural variation in loving relationships in our own society, as well as the limited comparative data, to move us toward a theory of love, and perhaps, as we shall see, its history as well. Our inquiry will follow the path of increasing openness of the boundaries of love. We move from relationships that are almost hermetically sealed to those that are relatively open.[1]

The Boundaries of Love

UNBOUNDED LOVE Can there be love without boundaries? As a thought experiment we may imagine a loving relationship in which there are no limits. There are two very different ways to conjure up this vision. In one we envision the love of a pair of hermits or of those marooned on an island beyond hope of rescue. In the absence of an encircling society, the loving relationship would be unbounded: no one is excluded. We know that lovers, such as honeymooners, seek out an approximation of this environment, and, for a time, flourish within it. Would it be possible for an isolated couple to live in a permanent honeymoon of an intense, idealized, and intimate relationship? We would like to think so, but in the absence of contrasting relationships and interaction with others it seems doubtful. "Love does not consist in gazing at each other, but in looking outward in the same direction," wrote Antoine de Saint-Exupery. Enduring love seems to require engagement in something outside the relationship, whether in a shared project, or even periods of separation (Person 1989:331). Phrasing it as marriage advice, Kahlil Gibran urged, "Let there be spaces in your togetherness." Without such space, isolated love breeds habituation, habituation breeds boredom, and boredom breeds the disintegration of love (Aron and Aron 1986:94).

A degree of distance and separation between lovers may even be the essence of the experience. If the passion of love is in the yearning to merge, nothing could be as deflating of passion as total success. In partial recognition of this principle, Freud maintained that love was equivalent to goal-inhibited libido. In the absence of barriers, he believed, it would rapidly dissipate. Although Freud may have been overly cynical in equating love with libido, it is surely true that love flourishes where love partners have competing investments of resources, time, and emotion. This occurs not on desert islands, but in a society.

GROUP LOVE There is a second way to imagine love without limits. Passion can be intensely focused on a large number of love partners, all of whom are enjoyed simultaneously. No society long dedicated to this principle endures, but many have tried. Our own history of sexual communalism is a natural experiment in the extension of love to the limit. During the 1960s and '70s hundreds of communes sprang up across the United States, offering radically different sexual and residential arrangements from these familiar to most Americans. Benjamin Zablocki (1980) has studied 120 such communes, ranking them on a five-point scale in terms of their "love density." A commune in which everyone was simultaneously emotionally engaged with nearly every one else was rated as "smoldering," while others were scored as "hot," "warm," "cool," and "cold," according to the percentage of love relationships among their members. Zablocki reached a remarkable finding. The greater the love density in the commune, the higher the turnover of communal participants. The reason appeared to be that new relationships continually sprang up between both current members of the commune and those who joined it. These relationships, intertwined as they were with existing ones, rippled through the group, causing jealousies and, eventually, departures. "A close bond is possible only between two persons," warned the I Ching in 1150 B.C.: "a group of three engenders jealousy."

Even though the ideology of communal love may claim to include the entire community, the love relationship appears to be primarily dyadic.[2] Must it be so? It is certainly possible that there is an enduring commune or society, smoldering away in a region so remote that social science has not even detected its smoke. So far as we can tell, however, passionate attachments, perhaps because of their origins in the dyadic passions of the family romance, blossom in pairs. Moreover, paired love is a fragile flower, flourishing best where it is bounded.

INTENSELY BOUNDED LOVE: THE CLANDESTINE RELATIONSHIP Secrecy is the most powerful social differentiator. Those who share a secret are united by bonds of trust. When the secret is socially explosive—as is the case of sexual relationships—the boundaries are jealously guarded. The clandestine relationship is thereby a small secret society, ever vigilant and intensely conscious of itself. Following Georg Simmel, "its secret surrounds it like a boundary outside of which is nothing but . . . opposite matter." Yet, ironically, the secret may be so important that what actually occurs in the clandestine relationship is of less importance than secrecy itself. For example, one of our informants, as a young woman, fell in love with an Asian American college student. Being a Caucasian—an "outsider"—she was rejected by the boy's parents. Nonetheless, he and his beloved carried on a passionate Romeo and Julietlike affair of clandestine meetings and hidden phone calls. They risked their parents' anger for nearly a year, jealously guarding their secret. Finally, the relationship was discovered by the boy's parents. Instead of anger, however, they were struck with remorse. How could they have forbidden a relationship that was clearly so vital? Now the romance was licensed and could be conducted out in the open. The young couple were initially exhilarated, but in a week the relationship had lost its vitality and in ten days it was depleted. What had sustained it was not its internal content but the boundary of secrecy.

Clandestine relationships are extraordinarily intense for yet another reason. Like all romantic bonds, they draw some of their power from childhood. Even more than is the case in sanctioned relationships, they engage a third party (the one from whom the secret is kept) and evoke the emotional conflicts of the Oedipus complex. In the clandestine love affair described above the parallels are clear: as in the nuclear family, it is the parents who impose a sexual taboo. In adulterous relationships the triangle of lovers and their spouses may stimulate rivalries and the fear of discovery that are also reminiscent of the family romance. In such relationships, there is at least a hint of incest, with its dread and fascination. As such, hidden relationships have a potential for danger, deriving from "their instability, their hidden agendas, their connection to power considerations, and the inevitable frustrations and insecurities they engender" (Person 1989:237). Yet we should not dismiss them as necessarily pathological. Though potentially unstable, they may also endure for decades as mutually rewarding and intense relationships.[3] Within the hidden confines of the relationship, love partners neither impose on one another's independence nor temper one another's idealizations by the demands of domesticity. No one, it would seem, need quarrel about who takes out the garbage in a clandestine relationship. Finally, by virtue of its impermeable boundaries, the clandestine encounter facilitates the experience of merging.

SOCIETY OF CLANDESTINE LOVERS Law and order oppose the clandestine relationship. Like all forms of love, but even more so, it is "a loose cannon on the deck of human affairs" (Person 1989:14), ready to undermine established relationships. Yet it is alluring, especially in cultures that do not institutionalize love in more public ways, or that insist on arranged marriages, or that make divorce nearly impossible. In a few cultures the clandestine relationship is the only locus of authentic passion. This was the prevailing culture of love in the eighteenth century in some of the courts of Europe, and it lives on, in an attenuated fashion, in the institution of the casa chica in Latin America today. Such is also the case of the Mehinaku, a small society of tropical forest Indians in Brazil, as described by one of the coauthors of this chapter (Gregor 1985).

Mehinaku husbands and wives care for one another. Like ourselves, they are joined by coresidence, the division of labor, and by concern for their children. They express affection, their marriages endure, and they deeply mourn each other's death. The relationship of spouses is valued and affectionate but not romantic. However, the Mehinaku are among the world's more accomplished managers of extramarital liaisons. Each of the men maintains so-called alligator places in the forest surrounding the villagers where he can meet his girlfriends for extramarital sex. Trysts are arranged by a quick spoken word in the village or with the help of intermediaries, including children.

In a census of lovers it turned out that one young man was conducting liaisons with ten women, or most of the adult women in the tribe who were not forbidden to him on grounds of age discrepancy or the incest taboo. Most of these relationships were casual affairs in which he exchanged *yamala* (a special term for gifts given to lovers, including such items as combs, beads, cotton cords, and especially fish) and a certain amount of affection for sex. One of the affairs, however, evoked intense feeling, which was quite unlike what he felt for his spouse. His lover, he said, was "so dear to me." He added that sex with her was *kaki*, salty or spicy, and far more preferred than sex with his spouse, which he described as *mana*, a term that is applied to water and indicates tastelessness.

Clandestine relationships among the Mehinaku evoke emotion as well as sex. Their feelings are much like ours, involving commitment and a measure of passion. These relationships may endure, so that at death lovers of many years mourn each other's passing, using special, hidden symbols of grief. Yet, the prevailing culture of love among the Mehinaku is not kind to passion. Lovers who become too fond of one another may be ridiculed. In the exposed and open setting of the village, where there is little privacy and much gossip, the boundaries of clandestine relationships are hard to secure. Nor can one be sure that one's love partners will be discreet: they may kiss and tell. The exposed nature of the social setting wears away boundaries and erodes trust. Affection and commitment are sustainable, especially between spouses, but romantic love suffers.

Clandestine relationships are probably universal to all cultures, though; by their nature, they are almost certainly underreported. They have profound meaning. Men and women will take extraordinary risks to form passionate relationships. Even when such relationships are held in low esteem or are altogether denied, it appears that couples will somehow reinvent them and risk all to live them out.

Narratives of Love and Variations in Love's Boundaries

We know little of love, even in our own culture, because we are just beginning to recognize it as a legitimate object of study. But how shall we understand it? What questions shall we ask? In 1992 one of the coauthors conducted a series of interviews with love partners, with the intention of exploring the inner dimensions of love (Collins 1993). The couples were chosen for the study because of the positive character of their relationship. They had been in enduring love relationships for ten years or more; they regarded their relationship as unusually rewarding; they were perceived by others as having an unusually loving relationship; and they were seen by Collins as mature individuals who were positively emotionally and sexually engaged with one another.

Reflecting Collins's specialization as an analyst and anthropologist, the interview was a form of life history research, a cross between the technique of free association used in psychoanalysis and the ethnographic interview. Couples, in each other's presence, were asked to "tell . . . about your relationship." Although the interview gave license to the expression of marital lovingness, the informants structured the narrative. They recalled events, drew out details, intensified the emotional tone of what occurred, and reflected on its meaning. The role of the interviewer was to listen actively, to encourage and to clarify, but not to prompt or participate.

From our knowledge of the literature this appears to be the first time this technique has been used to evoke a relationship biography. The method, which is elegant in its simplicity, is new in the study of love. It requires patience and resources, since in some cases the transcribed narratives exceeded two hundred pages in length. The results are narratives of loving relationships that represent the couples' own view of their past and of who they are. The stories have been told and retold many times by our couples, to each other, to their children, and to other audiences. Subjectively, for the love partners, the narrative *is* the relationship. Further, while engaged in the narratives in the affirming setting provided by Collins, love partners emotionally experienced the events they described. They reflected on the meaning of their relationship and thereby assured one another that they had a history and a future. So deepening was the experience, and so evident was our subjects' involvement in the process, that we believe the narrative is (when spontaneously told in informal settings) a way in which love partners enact their loving relationship.

THE BOUNDARIES OF LOVE RELATIONSHIPS All of the love partners in Collins's study spontaneously described the initial boundaries of their relationships, including the obstacles they overcame, the formal ritual of marriage, and its subsequent commemoration in family celebrations. Exclusive, bounded activities, such as travel and meals and evenings together were often momentous events in the narratives. The home appears as an especially powerful symbol of marital boundaries and is a focus of intense description. Occasionally, our informants described how they actively defended the perimeters of the relationship and warded off interlopers, or resisted their spouses' excessive commitment of time and resources outside of the home. In all of the narratives boundaries appear as a significant issue and are central to understanding the inner nature of the loving relationship. We will offer two examples that represent different ends of the continuum: Jason and Ruth, whose relationship is inwardly directed, and the Clancys, whose relationship is more open to kin and community. Both relationships are loving, both are successful. Each is a different permutation on the boundaries of love.

A Bounded Relationship: Jason Wallace and Ruth Messer[4]

Jason and Ruth and their daughter Peggy are a professional family living in a suburb of Baltimore. Their partnership is the most bounded of any in the study, and probably the most intense. They are deeply intimate, they look within for sustenance and meaning, and their relationship takes up more life space than any of the others. The boundaries between their special relationship and the rest of the world are clearly marked by their use of space, time, and a special language of intimacy.

THE BEGINNING The beginning is the first boundary. Jason and Ruth and all of the couples in Collins's study vividly recall the first moments of their relationship. These moments are not simply the first time they saw one another, though this may be important. Rather the beginning is a transformation, a cleavage of time into before and after that marks love partners' view of their own histories. For Ruth the memory of the decisive moment is visually symbolic: "I remember the day, the first time we went out. I had a little balcony in front of the living room. The balcony was maybe a couple of feet off the ground, and Jason came and jumped over the balcony onto the porch."

Metaphorically, the leap over the balcony is also a step across the boundary of a relationship. Ruth sees Jason as entering both her home and her heart. Paradoxically, the boundary that marks the beginning of a relationship may be an act of parting. Early in their relationship, Jason and Ruth had to be separate for many months. The pain they felt at the moment of separation dramatized and made them conscious of the intensity of their commitment:

Jason: And then, the next day, we went to the airport, and I remember seeing you walk around behind something and then you were gone! It was very hard.

Ruth: I can still feel the pain. That was just really—but that piece of it, as far as the intensity of the pain, is something we will never forget.

INTIMACY The enfolded, intimate perspective of Jason and Ruth's marriage is expressed in memories that are emblematic of the bounded relationship. Among these are recurrent images of travel, in which they were separated from their normal social world. As was the case of other couples in Collins's study, these experiences marked narrative chronology: "When was that? Was it after Europe in '71?" A journey is a tick on the narrative clock because it is powerfully symbolic of belonging to an intense and separate partnership:

Ruth: That Christmas we went to Hendersonville, just the two of us. It was really good; it was real special, just the two of us being there, and then we gave each other those coats, remember?

Jason: And I think, in part, because during that trip we were together in ways that you aren't together, even if you spend a night in a hotel. I mean, we were two in that little box that was the camper. We got very close for six weeks, and that was wonderful. It was easy! It just felt natural and easy.

Within their narrative such trips evoked an array of detail and sensory images, suggesting the emotional importance of the experiences:

Ruth: The little memories like the girl selling the gallon jar of olives on the dirt crossroads—little things like that, and the lunches of salads every day, and those olives. We had the gallon jar of olives in the front of the car for the rest of the trip, practically, until we ate them all.

Jason and Ruth's intimate, bounded relationship is expressed in many other ways, including their house, a warm enfolding place out in the woods:

Jason: We are at the crest of a hill nearby a large farm pond. And there are trees all around. And the sense of the house is kind of being isolated and alone, and we enjoy being together, alone. We have found that we really don't want to go anywhere. We want to stay here and be here with each other. It is wonderful, but it gets embarrassing. Sometimes I feel as though we are not being social enough. But, it feels wonderful, just staying here.

BOUNDARIES AND THE EXPERIENCE OF MERGING All relationships lay claim to the individual. In our culture marriage makes the greatest claim of all. Seen from without, the identity of the individuals in a marriage disappear. A couple is a single legal, financial, and social entity, although they may not be aware of how fused they are until they attempt to separate (at which point the marital boundary may look like the bars of a prison!). From without, the loss of individuality is a matter of custom and law. Within the bounded, loving relationship the process of fusing goes much further: "The aim of love," writes Ethel Person, "is nothing less than to overcome separateness and achieve union or merger with the beloved" (1989:82). We regard the sense of merging, the overcoming of existential loneliness, as the core experience of passionate love, and surely its headiest intoxicant.

Jason and Ruth achieve merging through freely expressed emotion and tears, through touching and intense sexuality, through their common creation of a home and a child, and through their awareness of a frictionless, or, as they put it, "easy" relationship. At times their self-boundaries are so permeable that the relationship has a magical quality, in that they simultaneously dream about one another, say the same things at the same time, or have the same thoughts:

JASON: A lot of times Ruth will say something that was exactly what I was thinking. That happens frequently and, as a matter of fact, so often we can joke about it. It is amazing; never been like that with anyone else.
RUTH: That happens frequently . . . amazing. . . . Each of us senses the other, perhaps unconsciously—what the other needs.

Ruth and Jason's relationship to their three-year-old daughter, Peggy, is a particularly vivid illustration of the intense, joined quality of their marital bond. Peggy, as a third party, could be disruptive to such a relationship. In fact, as she matures, she will move beyond the marital boundary, but at present she is clearly within it. Jason observes that Peggy even looks like her parents. This is a neat trick, because her parents do not look like each other. Nonetheless, it works:

JASON: I have some pictures taken of me when I was about two years old, and she looks exactly like me, but she also looks exactly like Ruth at a somewhat later age.

Love in the Context of Community: The Clancys

One of the remarkable aspects of marriage in our society is the range of alternate possibilities it offers spouses. The boundaries they draw are, to a degree, self-selected, reflecting their own choice as much as the pattern traditional in their community. In Collins's narratives of loving relationships, that of the Clancys' stands out as especially open to a wider circle of kin and community.

Mike and Anne Clancy are in their late sixties. They have three children, all of whom live nearby with their own families. The Clancys' relationship began more than fifty years ago in courtship that was interrupted by Mike's service in World War II. On returning home he and Anne had a brief honeymoon, after which they returned to the small town of West Hawthorne, New York, where he and his family ran the town's country store. We get a hint of the context of their relationship when Mike describes their welcome: "I called West Hawthorne and said that we were coming on home, we had been gone a week. When we got back Mother and Dad had arranged a reception for us at the firehouse with the whole damn village there!" Immediately, on their return, Mike and Anne were taken in by a warm circle of kin. They moved in with Mike's parents:

ANNE: There was no place to live really.
MIKE: Mother and Dad had a room over the storeroom in the store; it was a huge room, it was heated, and had a bathroom.

Later, they moved into vacant rooms over Mike's uncle's house, but still on close terms with many relatives:

ANNE: At that time they had a connecting door that went from one side of the house to the other, and Mary and Ted had a TV at that time; we didn't have one. So we visited.
MIKE: Aunt Mary got so that she would come and have a drink with us. After two or three times Ted said, "That's all right, but make damn sure she's got dinner on the table before she joins you!"

Living on intimate terms with relatives at home, the Clancys also found themselves engaged in the town and its activities.

ANNE: Everybody was coming back from the service, there were lots and lots of parties, and we were there. . . . You were totally involved in the whole thing all the time. . . . It was every single day, there was something going on . . . the little league team . . . the clubs . . . the church.

The network of kin, friends, and acquaintances extended well beyond West Hawthorne:

MIKE: Yeah, it was fun when you travel with those people because Aunt Mary knew everybody from hell to breakfast. . . . We knew everybody. There wasn't anybody that we didn't know. It was all over, it was not just in West Hawthorne. [We] knew everybody in Arlington and . . . Dorset. We had all of our friends in Petersburg. There was always somebody around. It was a constant circus! It was!

Mike's image of a circus is intended to suggest the busyness of the town and their own social life. It is also an appropriate image of the public nature of village life. In West Hawthorne private life is also public life:

MIKE: Because we had the store, everybody knew our kids, and they knew everybody else. . . . I waited on my first customer when I was six years old, and so I was fooling around that store for fifty years. . . . It was the center of the world! Everything that went on, whether it was good or bad, it was known in that store. In two seconds it was there.

ANNE: People living in a small community, you know everybody. They knew your problems; they knew your pluses and minuses.

Even intimacies were soon public property:

MIKE: Jennifer had an affair going with Mr. Broomfield. She would leave notes for him in his mailbox and he would answer them (laughter).

The public nature of the community also extended to family responsibilities. To a degree probably unfamiliar to the city dweller, parental obligations included authority over other peoples' children:

ANNE: The village was small. I think neighbors watched out. I mean if you saw somebody going by and you saw a kid misbehaving, I don't think you would think twice about speaking to them.

The setting of the Clancys' marriage is very different from that of most urban Americans in that the Clancys were an extended, or, technically, a joint family, living in a close knit community. Together they owned, managed, and worked in a common enterprise, the family store. The boundaries of their life space were permeable: open to the flow of individuals, information and commitments of time, and emotional and financial resources.

The demands of kinship and friendship were as much a part of the Clancys' relationship as their special bond to one another. It is not surprising, therefore, that the content and tone of their relationship narrative is different from those in which the marriage is more bounded. As a consequence, while unusually successful and loving, the relationship narrative is perhaps less dramatized than others. For example, the Clancys recall the early stages of their relationship not so much in terms of passion but as a period of emerging mutual understanding: "So, we were there learning about each other and having a wonderful time." The goal was "getting along," "enjoying each other," and the result, as we see it in the narrative, was a matter of easy pleasure. Their description of their feelings gives a sense of how they perceive the relationship:

ANNE: We got along well, didn't we?
MIKE: We've had some great times together, I will tell you that. When we go to bed at night we would say "Say, wasn't that fun?"

Anne further notes that while they enjoy their mutuality, they are quite capable of considerable independence: "I think one reason our marriage has done so well, we loved each other, we like each other, we have a lot of the same interests, and you have things you do and I have things I do. So that even today it is not something that we have to be together with all day long." Both Anne and Mike see their independence and their engagement in family and community as sustaining and enriching the marital bond. When asked what it is that makes their marriage work, Mike said: "I think another thing that has been very helpful is the family. We have big families. If you don't think so, look at my telephone bill sometimes!"

Love in the Context of Community: The Kibbutz

The Clancys are only one couple, but the dimensions of their experience may have broad implications: If the boundaries of marriage are open, its emotional tone will reflect the presence of coresidents and the claims of kin and community members. It would be hard to sustain the intensity and enfoldedness of Jason and Ruth in the context of a network of friends and relatives, all of whom have their own claims to emotion and resources. Let us underscore this point by extrapolating it outward, to a society where the claims of the loving partnership are minimized and the group insists on primary emotional allegiance. Such was the case of the Israeli kibbutz, especially in the early phase of its development. What was the impact on love relationships?

In a series of landmark studies beginning in the 1950s, anthropologists and psychologists explored the utopian society of the kibbutz. For our purposes these studies are valuable as a way of examining the impact of the collective experience on love relationships. In its insistence on the primacy of the group, the kibbutz was extreme, absorbing the individual in a collectivity that was as encompassing as any other in Western culture.[5] Among the most intriguing and intimate of the studies of the kibbutz are those by Bruno Bettelheim and Melford Spiro. They document a world in which husband and wife lived apart from children who were raised communally. Marriage was deemphasized and was regarded as largely a matter of living arrangements. In at least one kibbutz in the 1920s, the prevailing ideology prompted a brief experiment in abolishing separate apartments for married couples, who had to live in barracks style with single individuals (Near 1992:89–90). At this time, as well, husbands and wives did not wear wedding rings, did not celebrate anniversaries, or even entertain as a couple. In fact, a social invitation to one was not understood to include the other. Spiro (1954) has even maintained that the nuclear family did not exist on the kibbutz. Tellingly, the phrase "our children" meant not the children of particular parents but the children of the entire kibbutz (we recall, in this context, parents' authority over all local children in West Hawthorne).

The primacy of the group on the kibbutz was linked to a pattern of bringing up children that adapted the individual to communal life. Crucially, this mode of socialization was at least partly incompatible with the passionate attachments of romantic love. Following Bettelheim, the collective socialization in children's houses, which began in infancy, diffused children's attachment to their parents. Parents lived apart and saw their children for only a short time each day. *Metapelets,* or caregivers, performed what we regard as parental functions. Children did not become deeply attached to their caretakers, who were transient: "As soon as I've learned how to hold him, and he's gotten accustomed to my way of doing things, he's moved to another metapelet (1970:111). Children did not idealize such parenting figures, who were, after all, undependable or disengaged: "A great many children . . . visit the houses where they lived before, but on these visits they don't pay any attention to the metapelets who worked with them when they lived there, so much so that the metapelets feel insulted (1970:115)." As for parents, they offered "a very pleasant but not a very important relationship" (1970:149).

The effect of collective socialization, especially in the early stage of the kibbutz movement, was to partly sever the emotional bonds between generations. Kibbutz-raised children were, in some studies, less identified with their parents and experienced less oedipal guilt and sibling rivalry than their peers raised in the traditional nuclear family (Rabin 1965). There were advantages to this mode of socialization, including the forging of peer solidarity, cooperativeness, and group harmony. The price was the partial loss of the capacity to idealize the other and experience intimacy, two of the major components of passion. What was missing, Bettelheim explains, was the child's ability to introject[6] the idealized parent within his own personality. Consequently, he could not refind the parental love object in later life within a passionate attachment. More subtly, the absence of the parental introject muted the ability to empathize and understand the other: "The Kibbutz raised youngster seems unable to project himself into the feelings or deeply personal experiences of others (Bettelheim 1970:189)."

Bettelheim does not claim that all collectively socialized children were similarly affected. Yet marriage seemed to be influenced. We would not easily find the passion of Jason and Ruth on the traditional kibbutz. Rather, the relationship was adapted to the group:

> But in the Kibbutz, husband and wife remain first and foremost part of the group. So even in the marital relationship this makes for a more outward relatedness to the Kibbutz than toward each other. There is less of the feeling (as in our best and most intimate marital relations) that "you and I belong to each other body and soul, and together we two meet the world"; and much more the feeling that "each of us belongs to the common world we share and also to each other within it." (Bettelheim 1970:274)

In such relationships, and certainly within the context of the kibbutz ideology, there could be little room for a culture of romantic love: "Although romantic love was not proscribed," we learn from a kibbutz historian, "it was felt to cut the lover off from full participation in the lives of the community, and was often subjected to criticism" (Near 1992:89).

The History of Love

THE INVISIBILITY OF LOVE The potential for loving relationships has surely existed in all societies at all times. Why then has love been all but invisible to us, so much so that reasonable scholars conclude that it hardly exists beyond our own borders:

> Something like our Western conception of love, though not entirely absent, seems to be *rare* in . . . tribal or transitional societies. And certainly it is not generally *normatively* required or expected, or considered a desideratum of the good

life. And even rarer is *"romantic love"* as reality, or as expectation or ideal. (Endleman 1989:83–84)

Endleman and other anthropologists reach this conclusion because, as a profession, anthropology focuses on official culture: the most prominent values and institutions of a people. It is clear, from Endleman's work and others, that in many societies this culture is not kind to love. It includes arranged marriages that meet economic rather than emotional needs, communal households that diffuse emotional attachments, the near absence of restrictions on extramarital sexuality, men's cults with their attendant patterns of gang rape and the subordination of women, ritualized (and often forced) homosexuality, magical beliefs about the relationship of sexuality and disease, female genital operations, and the explicit denigration of romantic love and becoming "too involved" with a woman. That love exists amidst this massive repression is testimony to its power and its basis in fundamental human needs. An achievement of this collection of essays has been to look past official culture to the actual behavior and motivation of individuals.

VISIBLE LOVE Love has been underreported and underrepresented in many of our accounts of non-Western peoples. But it is equally true that there are major differences between love-facilitating societies, where love is culturally salient and likely to be actually experienced, and many of the other societies of the world. We can put the matter more emphatically: an emphasis on love is a sea change in the evolution of the human emotional habitat. In all cultures, at all times, the experience of love was a possibility, but it was one that had to be reinvented each generation, by each love partner. Love-facilitating cultures institutionalize love. In our own culture, for example, we find everywhere around us scripted love stories we can make our own. They slip easily from popular culture to personal expectation, from expectation to experience, from experience to reflection, and, ultimately, from reflection to the narratives of love in Collins's study.

Why has it happened? Why is love visible in some cultures but not in others? We have partial answers. Love repression wanes when there is an institutional basis to the dyadic commitments that are necessary for love. William Goode writes of the facilitating conditions for love:

First, the family unit is relatively independent of the larger kinship group so husband and wife are free to love each other without serious competition from kin. . . . Second, the parent-child tie is strong, and falling in love permits the young person to free himself from this attachment in order to enter the independent status of spouse. Third . . . (there is) considerable freedom to adolescents, thus increasing the likelihood that they will fall in love. (1982:54)

Of these explanations the focus on kinship and the relatively isolated family structure strike us as fundamental. The way families are linked to one another is a reasonable basis for identifying broad categories of kinship systems corresponding to cultures that institutionalize love and those that do not. A useful typology has been suggested by Francis Hsu (1972), who proposed that each kinship system is based on an essential and emotionally important dyadic link. For example, the key kinship relationship can link fathers and sons in lineages and clans that would endure over generations. Alternatively, the crucial link may be between husband and wife, a family form that is the primary unit in contemporary Western and other industrialized cultures. A major characteristic of such systems is their exclusiveness, or, in our terms, their boundedness:

> It is exclusive of other individuals because each husband-wife dyad is not only complete by itself but is intolerant of intrusion by a third party. It must, therefore, insist on monogamy as an absolute *ideal*. . . . In contrast to [other] societies, the husband-wife union is the only relationship which is expressly and elaborately sanctioned, guaranteed and safeguarded by the church as well as by the law. (Hsu 1972:525)

Hsu was mainly concerned with how the isolated marital dyad of Western systems generates characteristic ideologies and institutions of individualism and self-reliance. Nonetheless, he notes that "this is the only type of kinship system in which all sorts of public display of erotic expressions between lovers and between spouses is encouraged, pictorialized, glorified . . . played up so that they can almost stop traffic in the busiest thoroughfare" (1972:526).

Hsu's model of kinship parallels our perspective on loving relationships. For us the key variable is the degree to which potential love partners are insulated from the claims of the group or exposed to it. Systems of Hsu's first type, those that link different generations, open husband and wife to the competing demands of clan, lineage, extended family, and resulting arrays of in-laws. In this setting, Hsu writes with reference to traditional China, "Romantic love as an ideal is absent and public expressions of intimacy . . .

are taboo. A son can be required by his parents to divorce his wife if she fails to please them, just as he is duty-bound to take a concubine if his wife fails to provide a son" (1972:518). A saying holds that "you have only one family, but you can always get another wife." Reflecting the same disorganizing power of love for a lineage, the Arabic term for a beautiful woman, *fitna*, also means "chaos." The group-threatening characteristics of the love relationship are also a hazard to generational systems like that of the kibbutz or other experiments in collectivization. Here, too, spouses are exposed to the competing demands of the peer group, and the unbounded marital relationship is relatively defenseless.

In general, as Hsu maintains, societies with relatively permeable martial relationships are those of traditional cultures, while the bounded dyad is more characteristic of industrialized societies. Love, as a cultural ideal, is less frequent in the former, while in the latter it reaches the proportions of a major industry. In the absence of competing allegiances to kin and community, it flourishes as a goal, as a focus of popular culture, and, for many, as actual experience. But even in contemporary Western societies, love continues to reflect the boundaries that love partners draw around the perimeters of their relationship. The range of possibilities is substantial, from airtight clandestine relationships, through enfolded families represented by Jason and Ruth, to the relatively open love relationship of the Clancys. All are different resolutions to the paradox of romantic love, by which lovers seek a world in one another, yet must remain connected to their society.

But it is well to post a note of caution about the florescence of love in modern cultures. The state, as well as the family, the clan, and the peer group, may lay claim to the individual. In the totalitarian regime the loving partnership is a source of potential resistance, a form of relationship not subject to the discipline of the state. The Soviet state recognized this in its early years and set out to deliberately destroy marriage. Church weddings ceased to have legal effect, marriage was denigrated, and husband and wife could be assigned to work in different towns by an obligatory labor law. Couples who objected were advised (in a way that echoes the Chinese maxim quoted above) that they could probably find a new spouse in their place of work (Timasheff 1968). The impact on the family was catastrophic and the experiment was short-lived. But even afterward, as has also been the case of other despotic societies,[7] the Soviet regime remained harshly puritanical and suspicious of loving relationships.[8]

Because of its intensity, love has the capacity to disrupt social norms. In societies that worship high gods, love is a celebration of individuality and relationship, "a church and religion of two." Romantic love may thereby conflict with the restraints of convention and the structure of ordered society (Person 1989:14–15). The moral lesson is that love is intrinsically related to personal freedom and respect for the individual.[9] It is powerful enough, as the contributors to this volume show, to survive in virtually all environments, no matter how repressive (see, for example, Gregor 1988). But it flourishes only if we allow love partners to make choices that reflect their feelings, if we permit them to form intense loyalties that may conform to or confront the encircling society, and if we accept and protect the diverse expressions of lovingness that naturally emerge in the setting of a complex culture.

NOTES

1. Williams and Barnes (1988), following a perspective different from that developed here, usefully examine the boundaries of love in terms of the relative success of different forms of relationships.

2. "Open marriages," in which sexual relationships coexist with a commitment to a single partner, also appear difficult to sustain (Hatfield and Walster 1978).

3. Person (1989:341) maintains that "some of the most transforming and positive love affairs are in fact adulterous." See also Person's more extended discussion of the points that follow.

4. Names and all identifying information has been changed to protect the privacy of Collins's subjects. They, however, have chosen their own pseudonyms for publication.

5. The discussion that follows describes the kibbutz movement as it was during its most intensely collective phase. In recent years marital relationships among the members of the movement have become more similar to the surrounding society (see Spiro 1975).

6. Introjection is the capacity to build an image of the caretaking figure into oneself, so that security and the experience of love are no longer dependent on the physical presence of that individual.

7. Interestingly, the control of sexuality by the totalitarian state is also recognized in the two most prominent fictional renderings of despotism, Orwell's *1984* and Aldous Huxley's *Brave New World*.

8. Alexander Zalkind, a Party sexologist, urged that "sexual selection should proceed according to the line of a class revolutionary-proletarian consciousness. The elements of flirt, courtship, coquetry should not be introduced into love relationships." The 1940 edition of the *Great Soviet Encyclopedia* stated that the goal of sex education was to divert the sex drive into "the sphere of labor and cultural interests" (quotes from Kon 1993).

9. One writer, in what is surely an overstatement, puts it like this: "Only in a society

with an enormously powerful ideology of the individual, in which the 'alienation' of the individual from the larger society is not only tolerated but even encouraged and celebrated, can the phenomenon of romantic love even be conceivable" (Solomon 1981:136).

REFERENCES

Aron, A., and E. N. Aron 1986. *Love and the Expansion of Self.* New York: Hemisphere.

Bettelheim, B. 1970. *Children of the Dream.* New York: Avon.

Collins, J. C. 1993. "Narratives of Positive Gender Relationships." Ph.D. diss. Ann Arbor: University Microfilms.

Endleman, R. 1989. *Love and Sex in Twelve Cultures.* New York: Psyche.

Goode, W. J. 1982. *The Family.* Englewood Cliffs, N.J.: Prentice-Hall.

Gregor, T. A. 1985. *Anxious Pleasures.* Chicago: University of Chicago Press.

— 1988. " 'Pahikyawalu: She Who Is Covered with Feces': The Dialectics of Gender Among the Mehinaku of Brazil." In R. Randolph, D. M. Schneider, and M. N. Diaz, eds., *Dialectics and Gender: Anthropological Approaches,* pp. 80–90. Boulder: Westview.

— N.d. "Sexuality and the Experience of Love." In P. Abramson, ed., *Sexual Nature and Sexual Culture.* Chicago: University of Chicago Press, forthcoming.

Hatfield, E., and G. W. Walster. 1978. "A New Look at Love." *Addison Wesley Reading Module.* Reading, Mass.: Addison Wesley.

Hsu, F. L. K. 1972. "Kinship and Ways of Life: An Exploration." In F. L. K. Hsu, ed., *Psychological Anthropology,* pp. 509–572. Cambridge: Schenkman.

Jankowiak, W., and E. Fischer. 1992. "A Cross-Cultural Perspective on Romantic Love." *Ethnology* 31(2):149–155.

Kon, I. 1993. " 'We Have No Sex!' Rediscovery of Sexual Pleasure in Russia." Paper for Symposium 116, Theorizing Sexuality: Evolution, Culture, Development. New York: Wenner Gren Foundation.

Person, E. S. 1989. *Dreams of Love and Fateful Encounters: The Power of Romantic Passion.* New York: Penguin.

Rabin, A. I. 1965. *Growing Up in the Kibbutz.* New York: Springer.

Rosenblatt, P. 1966. "A Cross-Cultural Study of Child Rearing and Romantic Love." *Journal of Personality and Social Psychology* 4:336–338.

Solomon, R. C. 1981. *Love, Emotion, Myth, and Metaphor.* Garden City, N.Y.: Anchor.

Spiro, M. 1954. "Is the Family Universal?" *American Anthropologist* 56:839–846.

— 1975. *Gender and Culture: Kibbutz Women Revisited.* Durham: Duke University Press.

Timasheff, N. 1968. "The Great Retreat." In N. W. Bell and Ezra F. Vogel, eds., *A Modern Introduction to the Family.* New York: Free Press.

Williams, W. M., and M. L. Barnes. 1988. "Love Within Life." In R. J. Sternberg and M. L. Barnes, eds., *The Psychology of Love.* New Haven: Yale University Press.

Zablocki, B. 1980. *Alienation and Charisma: A Study of Contemporary American Communes.* New York: Free Press.

✶ PART TWO ✶

Romantic Love as a Private Experience

Rethinking Polynesian Heterosexual Relationships: A Case Study on Mangaia, Cook Islands

HELEN HARRIS

From the time of French and British exploration of the South Seas, Europeans constructed identities for Polynesians that revealed more about their own attitudes than Maori reality. Eugene Burdick (1961:285) is speaking of Westerners in general when he observes that "in some subtle haunting way a vision of Polynesia creeps into the knowledge of all Americans, a vision flawless and jewelled. In Polynesia the defects of America are magically eliminated. The place is warm and sunny. It glows." For the ordinary traveler accustomed to living within the constraints of a repressive moral system, Polynesia held out the promise of sexual liberation and guiltless pleasure. For Western philosophers it served as the confirmation of *l'homme naturel* and the Rousseauean ideal state of nature. For Calvinist missionaries it was a world of profligates awaiting the message of Christian salvation. And for anthropologists it has stood as a compelling example of the exotic "other."

Common and central to each of these perceptions of Polynesia is an obsession with sexual attitudes and behavior. The premarital sexual license that delighted the first explorers and seamen has dominated and defined Western notions of island life and pervaded all subsequent accounts, at once creating and drawing upon a myth of the South Seas. One of the more detailed and influential portraits of Polynesians as fundamentally sexual beings is anthropologist Donald Marshall's study of "Sexual Behavior on Mangaia" (1971a). Conducting field research in the Cook Islands during the 1950s, Marshall found that "copulation is a principal concern of the Mangaian of either sex," and he supplied orgasm frequency data that seem to substantiate this assertion. His data indicate that eighteen-year-old males experience an average of three orgasms every night of the week; twenty-eight-year-old males have an average of two orgasms per night five to six nights a week; forty-eight year olds slow down to an average of one orgasm per night two or three times a week (1971a:123). The effect of this report has been to confer almost legendary status on Mangaians, distinguishing them as the most sexually motivated people in the world.

While emphasizing sexuality, Marshall downplays affection in Mangaian male-female relationships, and, in so doing, joins an academic tradition that generally minimizes emotion in accounts of Polynesian life. The most consequential proponent of this approach was Margaret Mead, whose popular *Coming of Age in Samoa* (1961 [1928]) shaped perceptions of all Polynesians with its claim that Samoans lack a capacity for strong emotion, specialized feeling (such as romantic love), and caring personal interactions. Mead contends that Samoan heterosexual relationships are casual, frequent, often overlapping, always sexual, and devoid of affectional ties. Sex is an end rather than a means, "something which is valued in itself but deprecated inasmuch as it tends to bind one individual to another" (Mead 1961:222 [1928]).

"Sexual Behavior on Mangaia" (Marshall 1971a) belongs to this tradition formalized by Mead but initiated by explorers, advanced by missionaries and travelers, and reiterated by a lineage of ethnographers who characterized Polynesians as emotionally stunted yet exuberantly sexual people whose uninhibited libidos set them apart from the rest of humanity (see Danielsson 1986; Marshall 1961, 1962; Russell 1961; Suggs 1962). The works of Gerber (1975) and Freeman (1983) on Samoa and Levy (1973) on Tahiti, among others, have helped to correct this distortion by starting to fill in the emotional blanks in Pacific research. But as Brain (1976:229) asserts, despite the countless books written about "the most-discussed lovers of all times" there is still relatively little known about Polynesian intimate emotional life. Whether enthralled or scandalized by a sexual freedom never available to them, Europeans have been so preoccupied with sexuality that they have denied Polynesians an essential part of their humanness—an active and profound love life.

Marshall's chapter on Mangaian sexuality contains several confusing, if not contradictory, statements about heterosexual interactions. At one point he comments that "personal affection may or may not result from acts of intimacy" (Marshall 1971a:119), leaving the impression that personal affection among youthful couples is possible in some circumstances, yet he later says that Mangaians were "puzzled" by the components of affection and companionship attributed to the European version of love (Marshall 1971a:151). And although he acknowledges that a few suicides have occurred when parents forbade young people to marry lovers of their own choosing, he inexplicably attributes these deaths to sexual jealousy. Marshall also notes that bilingual Mangaians use the English expression "I love you," but only to mean "I want to copulate with you," and then reports that according to informants affection and intimacy arise only late in a relationship: "When the Maori gets old, that's the time to 'get close' to his wife; but this is when they are over fifty years of age" (1971a:157). He adds that some Mangaian couples never acquire "a good feeling" for each other, being bound together only by sexual jealousy.

Although the role of affection is obscured by these conflicting statements, other comments unequivocally establish sexuality as the basis on which young people (*mapu*) build their relationships. Marshall contends that "there is no contact between the sexes, no rendezvous, no equivalent of our 'necking' that does not culminate directly and immediately in copulation" (1971a:117) and that "copulation is the only imaginable outcome of heterosexual contact" (1971b:44). The general impression conveyed by Marshall's account of Mangaian intimacy, despite the confusion of contradictions, and by his assertion that Mangaian sexual interest is not a *morbid* preoccupation (1971b:43) is that the islanders are sexually obsessed and seemingly innocent of the experience of romantic love that often characterizes the initial phase of male-female relationships in the West. The strength of that impression is demonstrated, for example, by Robert Endleman's (1989) recent summary of Marshall's data:

> Sexual activities [on Mangaia] appproach being a national pleasure, in which both males and females participate enthusiastically. . . . There is no indication whatever of anything at all like romantic love involved, only sexual attraction. All the Mangaians place great value on erotic technique, none on any affection or caring between sexual partners, preceding sexual encounter. (57)

In the wake of Marshall's research Mangaian intimacy is reduced to no more than a series of one-night stands.

Love in the Social Sciences

The case of a Polynesian society whose members purportedly negotiate their intimate relationships solely on the basis of sexual attraction and performance, knowing nothing of falling in love, concerns not just Pacific specialists but also those social scientists participating in the ongoing debate over the nature of romantic or passionate love. A central question in this debate involves the prevalence or distribution of romantic attraction across cultures. Goode (1959:40) notes that "the implicit understanding [among anthropologists] . . . is that love as a pattern is found only in the United States" or at least in societies whose ideological systems derive from the Western European cultural tradition. Indeed, many other social scientists concur that romantic love is a relatively recent and localized cultural invention whose origins lie in the doctrine of courtly love that arose in southern France around the twelfth century (see Averill 1985; Branden 1981; Coppinger and Rosenblatt 1968; Rougement 1940; Merrill 1949) or at least in the complex social milieu of developed civilizations (see Durant 1954; also Stone 1988). On the other side of the debate are poets, philosophers, and some social scientists who propose that romantic love is a human universal or a universal human potential manifested minimally in all societies as occasional "violent emotional attachments between persons of opposite sex" (Linton 1936:175).

While this debate has long been part of more general discussions of human emotions, it has recently resurfaced with vigor as a result of two developments in the social sciences: first, the accumulation of twenty-five years of extensive psychological research on romantic love (e.g., Berscheid and Walster 1978; Brehm 1985; Cook and Wilson 1977; Dion and Dion 1973; Hatfield and Sprecher 1986; Hatfield and Walster 1978; Hendrick and Hendrick 1986; Knox 1970; Knox and Sporakowski 1968; Lasswell and Lasswell 1976; Lee 1973; Rubin 1973; Sternberg and Grajek 1984), and, second, the emergence of the subdiscipline of evolutionary psychology (see Barkow 1973, 1991; Buss 1989, 1991; Cosmides 1989; Cosmides and Tooby 1987; Cosmides, Tooby, and Barkow 1992; Daly and Wilson 1988; Symons 1979, 1989). These two innovations invest the island of Mangaia with significance beyond the interest it might hold for aficionados of exotica or erotica. As a result of Marshall's ethnographic report, Mangaia emerges as an intriguing and important test case for anyone pondering the cross-cultural status of romantic love and the possible implication of evolutionary processes in its existence.

Anthropologists have only recently initiated systematic or coherent investigations of the emotional content of heterosexual relationships (see Abu-Lughod 1986; Gregor 1985; Haeri 1989; and Jankowiak 1993); consequently, the preponderance of data on love available in the ethnographic record is scattered, incidental, uneven in quality and content, and compromised by the lack of a commonly held definition of romantic love and by the tendency to link love with marriage. In fact, only a few societies recognize or sanction mutual romantic attraction as a requisite or even appropriate basis for long-term unions (Goode 1959). In most societies, and in most historical periods, marriage is a social institution based on an array of familial considerations rather than on the personal emotions that often unite couples in contemporary America. While arranged or loveless matches may be the cultural ideal, this fact reveals relatively little about the involvement of passionate love in illicit relationships, such as elopements and extramarital affairs (see Jankowiak and Fischer 1992), yet anthropologists typically have regarded the presence of arranged marriages as evidence for the absence of love.

Until the late 1960s not only anthropologists but social scientists in general eschewed the study of love primarily because they considered it to be a vague, subjective feeling defying quantification and scientific analysis (Berscheid 1988; Gaylin and Person 1988; Rubin 1988; Safilios-Rothschild 1977). However, Zick Rubin's groundbreaking study "Measurement of Romantic Love" (1970) established love as a legitimate topic of scholarly interest and scientific inquiry and inaugurated a period of active research. Most of the subsequent data have been generated by psychologists, who have attempted to identify the distinctive features of different types of love and to measure love from various perspectives.

One of the most significant contributions is Dorothy Tennov's *Love and Limerence: The Experience of Being in Love* (1979), a systematic analysis of over five hundred cases of romantic love in the United States from which Tennov abstracted a pattern of emotions, cognitions, and behaviors that she labeled "limerence." As a neologism roughly equivalent to infatuation, falling in love, or romantic love (which are employed as loosely synonymous throughout emotion literature), limerence is said to possess the following set of identifiable and transpersonally stable components:

1. Intrusive thinking about the limerent object (LO)
2. Acute longing for reciprocation and for complete merger or union
3. Dependency of mood on the LO's actions or perceived actions
4. Inability to react limerently to more than one person at a time
5. Some fleeting and transient relief from unrequited limerent passion through

vivid imagination of action by the LO that means reciprocation

6. Fear of rejection and sometimes incapacitating but always unsettling shyness in the LO's presence, especially in the beginning and whenever uncertainty strikes

7. Intensification through adversity

8. Acute sensitivity to any behavior that might be interpreted favorably and the extraordinary ability to see hidden passion in the seeming neutrality of the LO

9. An aching of the "heart" when uncertainty is strong

10. A general intensity of feeling that leaves other concerns in the background

11. Buoyancy when reciprocation seems certain

12. A remarkable ability to emphasize what is truly admirable in the LO and to avoid dwelling on the negative, even to render the negative into a positive quality

13. Sexual attraction to the LO as a potential sex partner

The significance of Tennov's work lies first in the identification and documentation of a complex pattern of thought, emotion, and action (with emphasis on thought and emotion) that occurs in a similar form among extraordinarily dissimilar people (Tennov 1979:173) and that offers, at last, a precise, empirically derived definition of romantic love. Second, her description of limerence as a set of almost exclusively cognitive and emotional features, in spite of references to behavior and action, points to the fact that the stable components of the pattern are found reliably at the psychological rather than the behavioral level, since overt behavior is much more susceptible to situational or cultural distortion and suppression than are mental processes. This mind-based perspective is an essential precondition to her third contribution: the wedding of an impressive body of empirical findings to a theoretical perspective that has the potential to bring coherence and meaning to many of the disparate research findings from the past two decades.

The emergence of a stable pattern of thought, emotion, and behavior implied, in Tennov's mind, a kind of human instinct, prompting her to interpret limerence as one of the psychological features that constitutes what is popularly known as "human nature" (Tennov 1979:173, 242):

> Granting that we do not operate through full-blown instincts in the old-fashioned sense of a complex pattern fully prewired, it is still hard to believe that we do not at least have built-in reactions in our basic natures that make the learning of significant strategies for biological survival (evolutionary development) easier than if culture operated on the proverbial blank slate. Furthermore, if any of our

behaviors are under direct influence of the genes, surely those related to reproduction are most likely candidates. . . . Similarity of experience among diverse
persons as well as involuntariness suggests that limerence is well rooted—whatever our cultures and lifestyles—in the very nature of our humanness.

Tennov's assertion that her data on romantic love imply a kind of human
instinct prepares the way for the application of principles derived from evolutionary psychology and the evaluation of love as a possible human psychological adaptation.

Evolutionary psychologists assume that human beings, like all other life
forms, are products of natural selection (Tooby 1985) and that an understanding of human behavior will result only from an examination of the mul-
titude of special-purpose psychological mechanisms that have been shaped
by evolutionary processes to produce or motivate action (Cosmides and
Tooby 1987). The mechanisms composing the human mind exist because
they solved specific adaptive problems or served particular functions in the
Pleistocene environment in which they evolved (Cosmides, Tooby, and
Barkow 1992). The implication of the research of Tennov and other evo-
lution-minded psychologists, such as Hatfield (1988), Shaver, Hazan, and
Bradshaw (1988), and Buss (1988), and anthropologists, such as Mellen
(1981) and Fisher (1982; 1989), is that because of the stability and complexity of its set of features and its intimate connection to reproduction romantic
love should be viewed and tested as a likely psychological adaptation.
Common to all interpretations of romantic love that invoke some type of
biological or genetic explanation is the expectation that the components of
the pattern will be not only transpersonally but cross-culturally stable, manifested at least occasionally in all societies and in all historical periods.
Logically, the ideal approach to testing such an expectation of universality is
cross-cultural comparison. In spite of anthropologists' previous resistance to
conducting research on romantic love, it is now clear that without focused
and thoughtful ethnographic projects that test the hypotheses generated by
both traditional and evolutionary psychologists, the questions about the
nature of romantic love will remain unanswered.

Noted earlier, one of Tennov's contributions has been to propose a mind-
centered set of components that she calls limerence. This empirically based
description of romantic love possessed the potential to solve the definitional
problem that plagued previous research efforts, especially cross-cultural
studies, but while promising, her model proved excessively rigid and exclu-
sionary. Tennov equates falling in love with the *full* complement of compo-

nents, defining limerence as an absolute state of being with no degrees of intensity or flexibility of content. Other love researchers (Hatfield and Sprecher 1986; Liebowitz 1983; Money 1980; Peele 1988; Shaver, Hazan, and Bradshaw 1988; Sperling 1985; Sternberg 1988) point to Tennov's use of such qualifiers as "acute," "incapacitating," and "extraordinary" as well as to certain of the features and interpret limerence as an extreme or obsessive form of love. Evaluated against the collective research of the past quarter century, limerence appears more accurately to represent a subvariety of romantic love that is located at the extreme end of an emotional continuum.

If the term *limerence* now appears to express an extreme or anxious love experience, what are the properties of a more generalized form of passionate love? In their recent evaluation and summary of love research, Hendrick and Hendrick (1992) are unable to offer a formal definition of the very topic about which they are writing, proposing instead "to let the context of the entire book engage in the defining process" (1992:6). This approach may be convenient for their purposes, but a book-length, impressionistic definition of love lacks the precision, coherence, and consensus necessary for a working description that can serve as a basis for ethnographic research. Without some general agreement on the emotions and thoughts involved in romantic love, the cross-cultural evaluation essential to addressing the issue of its status as a human universal and, ultimately, as a psychological adaptation remains impossible.

In an attempt to extract some definitional consensus from the love research of the previous twenty-five years, I compared a number of discussions of romantic love, including Tennov's, and compiled a list of seven mind-centered attributes that were the most frequently noted and convincingly supported in the psychological literature (see Averill 1985; Brehm 1988; Buss 1988; Davis 1985; Hatfield 1988; Knox 1970; Levinger 1988; Lindholm 1988; Money 1980; Murstein 1988; Orlinsky 1977; Shaver, Hazan, and Bradshaw 1988; Sternberg 1988; Tennov 1979).

1. desire for union or merger, both physical and emotional—initially sexual attraction or sexual involvement that broadens into a desire for physical and psychological intimacy, which requires reciprocation of feelings and maintenance of physical proximity
2. idealization of the beloved (called crystallization by Tennov)—a tendency to emphasize a love object's positive qualities and minimize, ignore, or rationalize the negative ones. It may also involve varying degrees of constructed images of the beloved, at the beginning of the relationship when knowledge is

limited, and a couple "fill in the blanks" with imagined or projected attributes

3. exclusivity—a focus of emotion and desire on one particular person and a desire for this exclusive focus to be returned. Fundamental to exclusivity is the often unstated presupposition that love is directed toward one individual whose real or idealized qualities distinguish him or her from all other people

4. intrusive thinking about the love object (or fascination)—a cognitive preoccupation with the love object

5. emotional dependency—in general, an emotional state dependent on reciprocation and especially on the maintenance of physical and emotional access to the beloved; "happiness is coming closer to the beloved; unhappiness is falling away from the beloved" (Brehm 1988:255)

6. a reordering of motivational hierarchies or life priorities—central importance accorded maintenance of the relationship (i.e., physical and emotional proximity) at the expense of other concerns, interests, responsibilities, and activities in life

7. a powerful sense of empathy and concern for the beloved—an equivalent to what is called "caring" about someone or wanting to satisfy someone's needs. It does not involve altruism in the real sense but rather self-interest and personal need. As Steck, Levitan, McLane, and Kelley (1982) find in their study of caring versus need, people conceive of love as caring but operationalize it in terms of need. In light of how easily love turns to hate and revenge motivates jilted lovers, concern for the beloved must be viewed in terms of its ability to maintain access to the beloved and pave the way for reciprocal feelings

Equipped with a working definition of a syndrome of traits that encompasses a broader array of intimate experiences than limerence, I designed a field project to investigate Marshall's contention that romantic love is absent on Mangaia.

Mangaia, Cook Islands

As the southernmost island of the fifteen-island Cook Archipelago, located in the Central Pacific, Mangaia is a mere twenty-five square miles in area with a population in 1986 of 1,235 people living in three villages situated on different sides of the island. During three separate trips to Mangaia I conducted a total of ten months of field research there, maintaining a household and participating in the daily life of Oneroa, the largest of the three settlements. In addition to engaging in participant-observation, which yielded general cultural information but little insight into heterosexual relationships, because of the strict public gender segregation practiced on the island, I relied heavily on collecting life histories and biographies from sixty individuals ranging in age from eighteen to eighty and descriptions of almost ninety intimate heterosexual relationships. In the collection of these life histories, I allowed informants to tell their stories in their own way, with minimal direction or prompting, although at some points in the interview I asked questions to draw out and deepen the discussion. Because of that ambiguous status often accorded Western women in gender-segregated third world societies, I enjoyed increased freedom of movement between the sexes and was able to interview both men and women, and even to engage several male elders, some of whom had worked with Marshall as primary informants. These and other sources helped to contextualize the personal biographies and enabled me to reconstruct the social milieu of the 1950s, the period on which Marshall based his conclusions.

Precontact Mangaia

The debate over the universality of romantic love can be distilled into a central contention that love is an invention of Western European culture, having been transmitted to other parts of the world by exploration and colonization. With this issue in mind as well as with the aim of preparing for fieldwork, I researched precontact courtship and marriage on Mangaia and found a scant eight pages devoted to these topics in Te Rangi Hiroa's *Mangaian Society* (1934:88–96), a reconstruction of precontact island life and history. In these pages Hiroa confirms a pattern of premarital sexual experimentation (common throughout Polynesia), terminating in the contraction of some type of more enduring heterosexual relationship in which the partners were expected to renounce other sexual entanglements. Although trial and informal marriages were acceptable among commoners, Hiroa is unclear regarding the extent to which formal, parentally arranged unions, which prevailed among the upper class, characterized marriages of lower-ranking couples. He does leave the impression, however, that all long-term relationships were subject to parental arrangement. At no point in his ethnography does Hiroa discuss Mangaian emotional life or provide information about the affective content of heterosexual bonding.

The few available clues about the emotions attending precontact male-female relationships come from a corpus of oral literature preserved by missionary William Wyatt Gill, assigned to Mangaia between 1852 and 1872. Although most of the myths and songs recorded by Gill feature themes of intertribal warfare and interpersonal strife (serving no doubt to exaggerate the "darkness" from which Mangaian souls were being rescued), there are a few works that also display love themes and provide a glimpse of pre-European intimate life. The first example, a myth entitled "A Bachelor God in Search of a Wife" (Gill 1977:107–114), describes the rivalry for the love of a woman between the well-known god Tane and a local chief named Ako. The myth supplies evidence of intense romantic attachment (on Ako's part), a description of Ako's courtship, and a reference to love at first sight (on Tane's part). The other evidence comes from several *pee*, or historical songs, that recount the vicissitudes of love affairs, albeit against the ever present backdrop of violence. The first *pee*, forming a part of a chapter called "Unforgiving and Unfortunate Lovers" (Gill 1984:168–172), tells the story of a warrior named Vete who "fell violently in love with a pretty girl called Tanuau" and then turned on the young woman when she rejected him. Most of the tale dwells on the details of Vete's revenge, including a murder plot, grave robbing, and cannibalism, all of which demonstrate the strength of emotion of which Mangaian lovers are capable. With a Romeo and Juliet theme, the second *pee* involves a famous warrior, Oimara, and his lover from an opposing clan. Despite the defeat of Oimara's tribe by his lover's, the couple continued to see each other, with his lover secretly supplying him with food as he hid near her village. When the lovers were discovered, Oimara was killed, and his beloved was left to mourn his untimely end with many and loud lamentations. In the 1950s a song composed by a Mangaian man to commemorate the couple's love and Oimara's death became popular throughout the Cooks. The final *pee*, composed in the late 1600s, described another intimate relationship that developed while warriors were in hiding after a military defeat. The song tells the story of the leader of the exiles, Inangaro, a handsome and talented poet, who feigned love for a maiden of the opposing tribe in order to acquire provisioning but then fell truly in love with another woman, Kurauri, who was bringing food to his younger brother. The younger brother deferred to his elder sibling, and a love affair developed between Inangaro and Kurauri. The inevitably tragic end came when Inangaro's first lover discovered his infidelity and betrayed him to her clan. A poem reputedly composed by Inangaro for Kurauri and recited by her as he was put to death was passed down through generations of Mangaians and eventually recorded by Gill (1984:88–98).

Taken together, these samples of oral literature demonstrate that individuals in ancient Mangaia did form attachments with recognizable components. These relationships exhibited proximity seeking (lovers' striving to be together at great risk), rearranged life priorities (the willingness to risk death to continue a forbidden relationship), emotional dependency (the anger or sadness resulting from loss of love by rejection or death), exclusivity (the jilted woman's anger when she discovered her rival), and a sense of empathy and concern (the willingness of women to provision fugitive lovers). It is important to note that these stories also show that empathy and concern exist within a reciprocal relationship but cease when love is betrayed or rejected. Both Vete and Inangaro's first lover turned on the beloved when access was denied to them, with both seeking violent revenge. As is typical of folk tales of love, the idealization of the lovers is supplied by the narrative itself, which extols the physical attributes of the protagonists. An example is found in the story of Inangaro, who is described in several places as a handsome man with considerable poetic talent. Gill generally refrains from direct references to sexual expression, making confirmation of that feature difficult; however, Hiroa's ethnography clearly subtantiates premarital sexual license. Thus, the seven components of the romantic love syndrome are confirmed by Hiroa's ethnography and by the few pieces of precontact oral literature preserved by Gill.

LANGUAGE OF LOVE: *"Maoris have heaps of words for falling in love, but the Europeans have only one."* Marshall (1971a) documents a substantial Mangaian sexual vocabulary as evidence of the islanders' concern with sex, but he fails to mention a variety of terms that allow Mangaians to articulate heterosexual love. The only reference made to terms of endearment is a parenthetical explanation of the Maori word *tika*, which he contends "is the term for proper affection between husband and wife" (Marshall 1971a:159), although its literal translation is "to be straight, correct, to the mark" (see also Savage 1980). During my research on emotion language I learned, however, that *tika* expresses only sexual fidelity and not emotion. Informants were unanimous and resolute in their contention that the proper gloss for strong affection between men and women is *inangaro* and its derivatives. (Note that *inangaro* is used as a proper noun, a common noun, and a verb.) As the opening informant statement indicates, Mangaians actually possess a rich lexicon of love.

Inangaro is a multipurpose word translating broadly as "wanting, needing, liking, or loving." Although, as one informant noted, "*inangaro* is a big word having many meanings," when referring to a male-female relationship, it expresses "the real love from within . . . the feeling inside you, from your heart, for someone. It is the thing that makes people want to get married." Perhaps because of its multiple meanings and because, as women asserted, the word is often used by men trying to seduce them with insincere sweet talk, *inangaro* is usually qualified or intensified by the adverb *tikai*, meaning "very or really." The standard way to say "I love you" in Mangaian becomes *Te inangaro tikai nei au iaau.* However, since even this expression has been corrupted by the *puaka kuri* (pig dogs), as Polynesian playboys are called, most informants insisted that to convey properly the experience of falling or being deeply in love, a speaker must choose from a trilogy of derivatives: *inangaro kino*, *matemate te inangaro*, and *pau te inangaro*, all of which convey a measure of certainty and sincerity about the depth of emotions.

In the first expression, *kino*, literally meaning bad or evil, is used as a powerful intensifier, much in the way that English speakers employ *terribly* as a positive intensifier in the expression "I am terribly in love." According to one informant, *inangaro kino* is

> the strongest feeling you can have about another person; it means you really love someone and you'll be wanting to find out what the other person's feeling is for you. It is trying to see if the feelings are the same; maybe you're the only one loving, and he or she is not [loving you]. You really want to fulfill it. If the man agrees to be your [lifetime] partner, then you know the love is fulfilled.

Matemate te inangaro, literally meaning "dying of love," was evaluated by other sources as the strongest feeling of affection because in their minds dying for something is the most powerful evidence of a deep emotion: "You don't want anything else; you die for love, but you don't mind if you die; you don't feel ashamed about loving that person to death. If you really love someone, nothing will stop you."

Pau te inangaro, translating as "empty of love," conveys the message that "all your feelings are gone to your lover; none is left inside you; you have nothing more to think of but him or her; all your heart is gone. You don't think anymore; you don't want anyone else anymore." In addition to intrusive thinking, *pau te inangaro*'s most striking feature is its emphasis on exclusivity. Conveying a sense of having given all of one's love to a particular person, it represents a linguistic acknowledgment of the inability of individuals truly in love to be involved in another equally intense and intimate heterosexual relationship.

As I collected data on the vocabulary of love, I began to discern in informant comments a familiar pattern. For example, in the preceding definitions of *inangaro* there are statements about reciprocity and intimacy, reordering of priorities, exclusivity, sexual interaction, and intrusive thinking that signal a correspondence between romantic love and *inangaro* and contradict Marshall's claim that love is absent on Mangaia. The precontact literature had already alerted me to the possibility that Marshall had erred, but once on the island I quickly confirmed that Mangaian male-female relationships were in the 1950s and are today often marked by both emotional and physical involvements whose attributes are consistent with the descriptions of romantic love in recent American psychological literature.

Early in my fieldwork I also had the opportunity to observe a Mangaian reaction to Marshall's depiction of local sexual behavior. About a month after I arrived on the island for my first extended visit, the *Cook Islands News* published an excerpt from a story appearing in a popular Australian magazine. According to the Australian article, Mangaians are "the most highly sexed people in the world, getting it off an average of about three times a night at age 18, dropping off to a still impressive twice a night by the time they hit 30." Neither the *Cook Island News* nor the Mangaians themselves knew the actual source of these data, as attribution was omitted in the Australian article, but it is clear that these impressive figures were derived from Marshall's orgasm frequency chart. The newspaper's response was to label the characterization of Mangaians as "ridiculous trash and a load of twaddle" and to decry the typical treatment of Cook Islanders in the foreign press.

Mangaians with whom I spoke about the news article disputed its accuracy and resented the implication that they were obsessed with sex. They declared that the original source, whoever he or she was, must have been the victim of Mangaian braggadocio, and they scoffed at the frequency figures, saying that "after all, Mangaians are only human." One man contended that the principal concern of Mangaians is not sex but rather sleep and food, while another joked that if the article were correct, Mangaians would be too tired to get out of bed in the morning. Several men were not so restrained, calling the claims "bullshit," while some of the female informants who reviewed the story laughed and wondered aloud if the source of the figures had ever talked to women.

During my second field period I verified that Marshall had indeed been the victim of some good-natured recreational lying. According to a story that is now part of local folk history, Marshall had questioned a drinking group whose members bragged to him about their sexual accomplishments, never thinking that their wishful fantasies would be uncritically included in a scholarly work defining the island as a carnal paradise. Although some Mangaians knew that a document about their sex lives existed, no one had ever actually seen it.

Inangaro and Romantic Love Compared

Contradicting Marshall's negative report for romantic love but supporting my own preliminary literary and linguistic findings, Mangaians readily acknowledged that love is one of several historical motivations for choosing a lifetime partner and entering into a permanent union. In the first half of this century a match arranged by parents to improve the family's landholdings, political clout, or social standing was the expressed cultural ideal although not the most common form of marriage. While matches of personal choice easily outnumbered arranged marriages, all permanent unions or "serious relationships" were nevertheless subject to parental approval, which was usually granted on the same bases as marriages were arranged. Anecdotes abound of intrafamily conflict over mate choice and parental interference. Because romantic love lies at the heart of a significant portion of intergenerational discord, love is not a cultivated or even anticipated psychological experience; it is conceived as an emotional state that arises involuntarily, sometimes intensely—and often unfortunately—as it overturns the plans of parents and disturbs the web of relationships that binds individuals to their family and community.

In spite of its low institutionalization, the frequency with which romantic love occurred and continues to occur on Mangaia provided ample data for evaluating the presence of the seven components of love identified by psychological researchers. In this section I will examine the features of the romantic love syndrome from a Mangaian perspective and verify that they are present and recognizable. During this review I will approach the seven features of romantic love not as discrete and independent components but rather as integrated and interactive elements, often relying on each other for meaning. Additionally, I will briefly discuss the particular cultural signature that distinguishes the Mangaian version of romantic love from the basic pattern identified by American researchers.

SEXUAL AND EMOTIONAL INTIMACY: *"it's both feelings and sex. It's when both things come together; that is falling in love."—A Mangaian man in his sixties* Berscheid (1988:361) asserts "that the role of sexual desire and experience has been neglected in contemporary discussions of romantic love" and commends Freud for his perceptive positioning of sexual desire at the center of his analysis of love. For Mangaians sexual expression, or its possibility, is an undisputed component of an intimate heterosexual relationship, before as well as after marriage. A Mangaian woman in her fifties remarked, for example, "when girls and boys like each other, they usually sleep together. They want to enjoy themselves." What is distinctive about Mangaia and many other Pacific societies is the stubborn retention of a thoroughly Polynesian attitude toward the pursuit of sexual pleasure in the face of vigorous and sustained missionary efforts to inculcate precisely the opposite disposition. While Mangaians are a pious Christian community, they retain the belief of their ancestors that sex is a good and natural part of life and that premarital sex, if practiced discreetly (that is, away from the watchful eyes of controlling parents and moralizing ministers) is an appropriate, if not requisite, part of the *mapu* or postadolescent, premarital period. Despite a cult of virginity for high-ranking young females in precontact times and the aforementioned post-contact pressure for premarital celibacy from the London Missionary Society, Mangaians have generally engaged in more premarital sex than did Americans, for example, before the sexual revolution of the 1960s. (The mid-century cultural upheaval in the United States brought Polynesian and American patterns of intimacy into closer conformance, liberating American youth from the constraints of Victorian sexual mores and affording them freedoms similar to those routinely enjoyed by their Polynesian counterparts.)

Although a virgin bride or groom was a cultural rarity in the fifties on Mangaia, male-female relationships were not as inexorably, instantaneously, or exclusively sexual as Marshall suggests when he writes that there was "no contact between the sexes, no rendezvous, no equivalent of 'our' necking that does not culminate directly and immediately in copulation. Coitus is the only imaginable end for any kind of sexual contact among Mangaians" (Marshall 1971a:117). For Mangaians the courtship process was and remains a time not just for experimenting with physical intimacy, which, as I have noted, eventually occurs for most couples, but for establishing a close emotional relationship as well. According to numerous informants courting couples spend substantial time together, both making love and sharing stories about their lives. "When a boy and a girl feel *inangaro*, they want to see each other all the time." Mangaians are normally taciturn, reserved, and cautious toward one another as well as outsiders, but within the context of *inangaro*, they abandon these psychological protections and share their time, thoughts, and secrets. A man in his late forties recalled, for example, that when he and his wife were courting, "we talked a lot and we shared things about ourselves. We talked about all of our parents and a lot about kids. We both liked kids and talked about having children." When asked why he decided to marry, a younger man replied that he had both sexual and emotional needs to satisfy: "When you are a single person you need someone to talk to and to be with." Finally, an elderly man offered these summary remarks:

> *Inangaro* is a very important thing—that's the main thing for the wife and for yourself. Sleeping with her and talking with her was what I did with my wife. We felt together—close. When you look at some ladies, you know they are bright and good and beautiful, but someone else keeps coming into your mind. It's the feeling you get when you're close with someone; there is a deep feeling.

Contrary to Marshall's contentions, courtships can remain chaste for weeks or months, and emotional intimacy may precede sexual involvement. When I asked a woman why she decided to have intercourse with her lover, she replied, "He already told me his life." That is, they had developed a certain level of emotional intimacy. Indeed, the principal governor on the speed with which a couple approach sexual intimacy is usually the woman's wariness of the man's intentions. One elderly man said simply that "it is the Polynesian way for women to be cautious about men; therefore, the men must continue to return and talk about their lives to reassure women."

Fundamental to experiencing intimacy is reciprocation of interest, desire, and emotion. Intimacy cannot be accomplished without a willingness of both parties to permit physical and emotional access. Several informants revealed that a significant portion of the conversation occurring during courtship centers on the relationship itself and how each person feels, allowing the lovers, but especially the woman, to assess the depth and sincerity of emotion between them. As one middle-aged woman put it, "when you feel *inangaro kino*, you will want to see if the other person is feeling like you." She labeled this desire for reciprocity as seeking fulfillment.

EMOTIONAL DEPENDENCY: "INANGARO *can make you sad and happy; when you are in love and one of you leaves, you feel sad; but as long as you are together, you are happy.*"—*A Mangaian woman in her fifties* As noted earlier, the various features of romantic love are integrated and interactive elements, some of which are made meaningful only by the presence of others. Emotional dependency, for example, requires content derived from other components, but most especially from the desire for physical and emotional closeness. Mangaians recognize that certain predictable emotional states arise in response to the status of a love relationship; love brings both happiness and sadness. Separation or threat of separation from the beloved, caused by nonreciprocation of affection, geographic distance, or parental interference was unanimously identified by informants as the key determinant of emotional distress:

> Once a boy and a girl are in love with each other and one goes away to another island, they become sad. Just to see her face—only to see her face—makes him feel better. He doesn't even have to have sex with her—just to see her face. The one who stays on the home island will be sadder because everything reminds that person of the one who went away. He will be sad until he finds another girl. The man can go and join a group to make him happy drinking, but the man who isn't drunk will keep being sad and will still wait for the girl to return.

I noted earlier that Mangaian marriage is a social institution used by parents to improve family landholdings, social status, or political power. Because of this broader signficiance, long-term relationships require parental approval, but parents often refuse to give consent to a proposed marriage, holding out for a more favorable match. One parent remarked, for example, that "if we leave the decision of a lifetime partner up to our children, they'll just choose someone because of looks." In the 1950s parental disapproval of a liaison and the subsequent forced separation of the couple were powerful and frequent sources of emotional distress for lovers.

Because of strict public gender segregation, courtships are secret affairs, usually initiated by the male and conducted in the bush or on the beach under the cover of night. Even in this constrained social environment, thirty to forty years ago as well as today, *mapu* find opportunities at school, church, community dances, and other social gatherings "to meet one another and fall in love," as one informant noted. Typically the young man discreetly approaches the girl and lets her know that he has noticed her. He then begins a courtship of secret nocturnal visits to her family's home. Responding to a prearranged signal, the girl slips out of the house and joins the boy for a late-night stroll or lovemaking session.

Concerned parents do not usually wait until a liaison becomes serious to intrude into their children's affairs; as soon as a clandestine relationship is discovered, they may demand an immediate cessation. For example, Tangi's parents discovered her trying to leave the house at night to meet Moeroa at their trysting spot. Disturbed by his reputation as a *puaka kuri* and fearful that he would abandon their daughter if she were to become pregnant, they forbade Tangi to see him again. Initially, Tangi and Moeroa obeyed her parents' wishes and stopped meeting. Tangi recalled that this was "a terrible time" when she felt empty inside and could not conduct her life properly. Equally distraught, Moeroa decided to move to Rarotonga, the capital of the Cooks, to look for a job and to start a new life. But neither was able to get the other out of mind. Eventually concluding that they could not bear to live apart, Moeroa returned to Mangaia and the couple embarked on a three-year, ultimately successful, campaign to gain parental approval. They were finally married in a church ceremony and now have several grandchildren.

In a similar case, Metu and Moana were discovered by Moana's parents and forbidden to continue the relationship. Metu recalled that during the ensuing weeks of forced separation he felt "sad with tears," unable to console himself even with the company of another woman. Finally the couple secretly began seeing each other again, and Metu said that he then "felt like jumping in the sky!" When I questioned Moana about her feelings during the separation, she talked of being *atingakau*, or brokenhearted: "I was lonely and really sad and I cried. I stopped eating and didn't sleep well; I couldn't keep my mind on my work." At the point that the couple recommenced their relationship, Moana's sadness dissolved and she was happy whenever she and Metu were together. After some years of conflict with both sets of parents, Metu and Moana are now living together, trying to save money for a formal wedding.

An intense response to separation from a beloved is glossed by the term *atingakau*, or a broken heart. *Atingakau* is perceived as a potentially fatal physical condition to which true love (*inangaro kino*, etc.) exposes an individual. Its most common manifestations or symptoms are loss of appetite and inability to sleep, social isolation, and, in men, heavy drinking. The actual cause of death in the fatal cases of *atingakau* remains obscure both to me and to the Mangaians I interviewed, although several suggested that suicide by starvation was a possible explanation.

While most of the fatal cases of *atingakau* brought on by family interference occurred before the 1960s, when a slow liberalization of attitudes and parental restrictions began, there are numerous cases of parents continuing to intrude in their children's mate selection by attempting to break up relationships of which they do not approve. These parental intrusions inevitably produce emotional distress in the affected lovers and often lead to family schisms, which I will discuss in a subsequent section.

Like lovers elsewhere, alienation or loss of affection also causes heartache (*Ua ongo toku ngakau*). A woman now in her late forties remembered the ending of her only love affair as particularly painful: "My boyfriend went with others. He made me hurt. He didn't care; he would go to dances and then I'd hear that he'd been with other girls. Love can make you happy but it can also make you sad."

Women feel especially vulnerable to the threat of suffering heartache, believing that males will seduce and then abandon them to go to someone new. While I recorded ample evidence to justify this caution, I also learned that women are able to inflict pain on men as well. Tamariki, now in his mid-thirties, revealed that he had contemplated suicide when his girlfriend left him for another man. As many heartbroken men do, he left the island and lived abroad until he could recover from the loss.

INTRUSIVE THINKING: *"Your mind goes wandering."—A Mangaian woman in her forties* When I asked Tangi to describe her feelings after meeting Moeroa, she reported a strong tendency to think about him repeatedly. Additionally, during their forced separation both reported being preoccupied with the other, a condition that led them ultimately to reject the demands of Tangi's parents. Intrusive thinking or cognitive preoccupation was mentioned frequently by Mangaians when they talked of their love relationships, especially in the early stages. One woman in her late fifties described her reaction to a declaration of love by a suitor:

> We had talked all night and he said that he loved me. He said he had fallen in love with me. We talked and talked, and finally it was morning and I said, "You'd better go now, because my father will see you." He answered that he would come back on another night. All that next day I stayed on my bed and did no work. I was just thinking "Oh, when is my boyfriend going to come back?" Just thinking about him like that. Just waiting and thinking of him—my mind lost. And I waited. And then he came back. We talked together again, and I told him what happened to me that day. He said the same; he was hurting for me. He said he had the same feeling on that day. . . . And I said, "I am thinking of you, too." And I told him I loved him. *Te inangaro tikai nei au iaau.*

This woman's description points up the functional connection between intrusive thinking and maintaining access to the beloved. Cognitive preoccupation compels the individual to seek proximity by creating longing during separation that in turn hastens the reunion of the couple. It also demonstrates that the intrusion of thoughts about the beloved interferes with other thoughts and with the normal conduct of daily life.

The same intrusive thinking occurs during a forced separation. Tamariki, introduced in the previous section as the young man who contemplated suicide, described how thoughts of his former girlfriend continued to haunt him. Each time that he went to his plantation to work, he saw the places they had been; he remembered the good times and the bad times:

> All places reminded me of her; I didn't eat much or sleep. And one day at the plantation I walked right up to the edge of the *makatea* (cliff face of the raised coral reef) and thought about jumping to commit suicide, because the plantation reminded me of her. She hurt my heart. I wasn't jealous (*vareae*), I was hurt (*maromaroa*). I didn't jump from the *makatea*, but I almost did.

Another man in his mid-forties spoke of a time when he was working on another island and fell in love with a local girl whose parents would not give their permission for her to move to Mangaia with him. He recalled that when he left the island after three months of residency he really missed her and he felt great sadness: "I could not get her out of my mind."

EXCLUSIVITY: *"I didn't want any other men, and I wanted him to look only at me, not at other girls."*—*A Mangaian woman in her forties* One of the characteristic assertions of many Polynesian specialists of the Mead tradition is that there is such mental uniformity among Maoris that one person is as good as another, and, therefore, no one is special or "right." This stereotype of unromantic Polynesians is summarized by Danielsson (1986:67):

> According to our romantic idea of love everyone should endeavor to find the "right" partner, who is assumed to be one person and one person only. Such a point of view was quite unknown to Polynesians: on the contrary a man or a woman was extremely surprised if now and again it happened that a person of the opposite sex was *not* suitable as a partner in love or marriage. The difference is easy to understand if we remember how similar and standardized people were in the small Polynesian racial groups.

Underlying all discussions of romantic love in Western psychological literature, on the other hand, is a belief in the uniqueness of individuals and the noninterchangeability of lovers.

Returning to Tangi and Moeroa's case we find both direct and indirect evidence contradicting Danielsson's portrayal of Polynesian heterosexual behavior and supporting a model that includes recognition of individual distinctiveness. Implicit in their story, as well as in all Mangaian anecdotes involving personal preference, parental opposition, and persistent attachment, is an awareness of individual differences and the effect that these differences have on attraction. If people were truly interchangeable there would be no resistance to arranged marriages, no stubborn attachment to a particular man or woman, no family upheaval, and no incidences of intense attraction—all common themes in tales of Mangaian relationships. In reality, strong attachments arise between certain individuals and not between others, and lovers are often willing to face dire opposition from their families to preserve their romantic liaisons.

In Tangi and Moeroa's case there is also explicit evidence of exclusivity, or the narrowing of the focus of attraction and affection to one person. Moeroa had a well-deserved reputation as a ladykiller, yet after he met Tangi, he became a devoted and faithful "one-woman" man. At the same time, Tangi, an attractive young woman, was being pursued by a number of *mapu* when she met and fell in love with Moeroa. She recalled, "I wasn't interested in any of [those men]; I felt as if they were nothing. My strong feeling for Moeroa made it easy to resist them."

Because of a pronounced double standard and the tendency of young men to seek sexual opportunities whenever possible, ever cautious women look for a sign of "real love" (*inangaro kino*, etc.) and find it most often in the willingness of the man to forsake all other liaisons. In interview after interview, women stated that when their man demonstrated a singular interest in them they became convinced of the sincerity and depth of his feelings. As one middle-aged informant noted, a woman looks for a man who "isn't going around with other women" and who wants to marry her. Marriage is perceived as the ultimate expression of exclusivity.

Several of the informants who acknowledged the exclusive nature of romantic attachment felt, however, that it was an unwelcomed burden in some circumstances. When Tuaine discovered that her boyfriend was seeing other girls, she tried to take a relative's advice and find another man: "I went to dances, but I didn't like any of the boys there . . . I didn't want anyone else, even though I was very angry with my boyfriend at the time." A male informant, Tere, tried the same strategy when he found himself in love with a woman who was still involved with a previous lover. He related that he became *vareae* (jealous) and *ririri* (angry) over his lover's lingering liaison and decided to "go around with other girls" to teach her a lesson. By his own appraisal, it was "a crazy time" culminating in the impregnation of both his girlfriend and another woman he was "just seeing." Tere confessed that when he learned of the two pregnancies he did nothing about the other woman, wanting only to return to his girlfriend and rebuild their relationship. In the end, Tere and his girlfriend worked out their problems, were married, and produced two children.

IDEALIZATION: *"At first I thought he was wonderful."—A Mangaian woman in her forties* As I noted in the previous section, exclusivity requires a perceived specialness about another individual, but not all of that perception derives from real attributes of the beloved. Murstein (1988:29) observes: "In the absence of much real knowledge of the other, each member of the couple may project fantasized real qualities onto the other. The qualities of the other are apt to be exaggerated, and much attention is paid to the beloved." On Mangaia, where the two sexes are publicly segregated and males usually initiate the secret courtships that characterize premarital heterosexual interactions, men often reported falling in love by simply observing a woman and perhaps speaking to her on a few occasions. The following description of a declaration of love illustrates this element of early idealization:

> Maara came to talk to me. He had been waiting, waiting for me to return from Rarotonga. He didn't forget the time we were in school together. He said to me, "You know what? I've been looking at you. I've seen you going around." Then he said that he loved me. He said he had fallen in love with me. Yes, seeing me all around, day and night, waiting for me. I asked him, "Why me?" He said he had seen how I was at school; how we laughed, how I shared with people. I'm just the one he's looking at. He said his heart was hurting for me.

The woman relating this anecdote believed that her boyfriend was attracted by her pleasing nature, but most men admitted to being heavily and initially influenced by physical beauty alone. When captivated by an attractive face, flowing hair, and full hips, men typically fill in the blanks about the woman's other attributes, assuming that these will be as alluring as her appearance. For example, Maki, a man in his sixties, fell in love with his wife Tama before he really knew her. As an adolescent still in school, Maki was struck by Tama's beauty, and even as he enjoyed his share of sexual adventures with other girls, his thoughts and desire continued to return to Tama. He finally approached her and, after some earnest wooing, convinced her to become his lover. When their liaison eventually led to plans to marry and Maki informed his father of their intentions, his father reponded negatively, reminding him that Tama had been a spoiled child (*tamaine kata*) and would be an unsuitable wife. Here again idealization influenced Maki's decision making, and he chose to ignore his father's cautionary advice. Maki and Tama were married in the mission house without the consent or attendance of Maki's father. After forty sometimes difficult years of union, Maki now believes that his failure, unwillingness, or inability to heed his father's warning set him up for a less than happy marital life. He agreed with another informant who commented that "a young heart is not careful."

Mangaian women are cautious and less likely to engage in the kind of "minimal-data" idealization characteristic of men, although love at first sight clearly involves this type of idealization. Woman demonstrate a type of idealization that typically arises after initiation of active courtship and is more properly defined as emotionally ignoring or minimizing the other person's faults. Also, when women recalled their courtships and the men in their lives, they described the men in glowing terms, fixing on perceived talents or skills or personality attributes: he was a very good fisherman; he was the best planter; he was a fine musician; he was kinder than the other men. Many women claimed that although a particular man had a reputation as a philanderer, they suspended their distrust and evaluated their suitor in a more positive light than reputation would seem to have warranted. For example, when her parents objected to her relationship with Moeroa, Tangi disregarded their counsel and his reputation as a womanizer, being convinced that he had changed when he met her. (She was right, as it turned out.) Similarly, the wife of a prominent subchief was aware that the man who would become her husband had several children by different women, none of whom he was willing to claim. Just after they became lovers she chose to ignore his past: "He told me that I was the one he was choosing. He had had many girls, but I didn't care about that. I loved him and I believed him."

REORDERING OF MOTIVATIONAL HIERARCHIES: *"Because I had that feeling inside, I couldn't do what my parents wanted; I had to go after my boyfriend."*— *A Mangaian woman in her fifties* The inhospitable social milieu in which courtships are enacted and the frequency with which parents interfere in their children's intimate relationships often force lovers to make hard choices that highlight the fact that a new set of priorities is guiding action. Socialized to honor and obey their parents, children who are at odds with their families over the issue of mate selection may find themselves in a position of having to decide if they can continue to put their parents and relatives first. More frequently than not, the young man or woman will opt in favor of maintaining the love relationship, risking and often losing important family connections and support. A couple in their eighties recalled with regret that parental opposition to their plans to marry forced them to elope to Rarotonga, where they remained painfully estranged from the objecting family for five years. Another elderly couple related how they had eloped to the interior of the island and stayed hidden there until opposing parents consented to their marriage and allowed them back into the family. These daring actions evidence a significant shift in the priorities that inform decision making for normally respectful and docile *mapu*.

An even more dramatic and poignant example of reordering of priorities came from a woman now in her late fifties. In her youth Tiare had had three children by her first boyfriend, who eventually left her for another woman. Tiare recovered from the heartbreak of losing her man by focusing all of her love and attention on her children, whom she was rearing with the help of her father. It was some years after the collapse of her first relationship that she met Turi and fell in love again; but Tiare's father did not approve of Turi and refused to consent to a marriage. Here is how she described the resulting change in her priorities:

> The feeling that I had for my children was now going to my boyfriend. I loved my children very, very much; but at that time I loved my boyfriend more. Sometimes I would leave my children, especially at night, and go to my boyfriend. For my boyfriend only.... Finally, I left the island with my boyfriend; I left my children behind with my father. When I left I was just thinking of my children and I cried. But on the boat, while I was sleeping, I just forget everything. I'm clean. I didn't remember anything. All those things that had been causing me troubles were washed away by the sleep.... I was happy. I forgot everything; there was nothing troubling my mind. What a man; what a woman. Not thinking about the home, the parents, or my children.

Whenever informants mentioned parental opposition to mate choices, they typically described significant emotional distress and long-term, intrafamily upheaval that jeopardized their standing in the all-important family and lineage. But even more compelling than stories of family strife are the reports of fatal cases of *atingakau*. As I have previously mentioned, forced separation and *atingakau* sometimes ended in suicide, especially in the first half of the century. Placing love above life itself represents the ultimate reordering of motivational hierarchies.

CARING OR CONCERN FOR THE OTHER: *"What is being in love? It is caring about someone, taking care of someone, showing care."—A Mangaian man in his forties* During a previous survey of ethnographic and literary sources to confirm features of the romantic love syndrome cross-culturally, I located few references reflecting a concern for the welfare of the beloved. I surmised either that the demonstration of concern is simply not the stuff of which lyric poems or legends are made or that, in fact, the feature is more characteristic of Euro-American love. I was therefore surprised to encounter a number of Mangaians who recognized and cogently expressed the solicitous concern and caring that are mentioned in American research and are defined in a way that differentiates them from those obligations that fall to men and women because of their respective roles in the cooperative household unit.

As I sat one morning watching a woman prepare a meal for her family, we began talking about her own courtship, and I asked her how a person knows when she is in love. Taken aback momentarily, she stopped her cooking, wrinkled her face in concentration, and then replied, "I guess you're in love or you're 'serious' when you worry about your man when he is out fishing." (Fishing beyond the reef from an outrigger is perilous work.) The story of Taeake's love affair illustrates this concern. Taeake is a woman in her mid-forties who had been deeply in love with a married man. When I spoke to her about her relationship with her lover, she complained about the treatment he received from his wife: "If I was the woman living with him, I would have done anything to make him happy. Anything for him. I kept thinking that he needed someone who suited him better. He needed something nice to eat, something cool to drink, but he wasn't getting that kind of treatment." Taeake's desire to contribute to her beloved's happiness, I am convinced, was deep and sincere, yet it did have its limits. When her lover refused to leave his wife, she reluctantly withdrew from the relationship, despite his pleas to continue the affair. Taeake's concern for her lover's happiness was ultimately superseded by her own increasing need for intimacy and by her growing dissatisfaction. When her needs were unmet she opted to discontinue the relationship, inflicting significant emotional pain on the man whose welfare had previously been such a central concern to her .

It was with Taeake's story that I came to realize that the element of caring and concern in romantic love is also informed by the other components, again most notably by the desire for union and intimacy. Caring is not simply an abstract concern for the welfare of the beloved but rather a concern connected to the desire to prevent separation and loss of access. Caring is ultimately defined by how it contributes to maintaining access, increasing intimacy, and fostering reciprocation. Underlying a deeply felt anxiety over the welfare and happiness of a lover is an understanding that the safety and happiness of the beloved are fundamental to maintaining proximity.

Other Features

The goal of cross-cultural research on romantic love is to identify a basic pattern that is universal, or nearly so. The seven components synthesized from the work of a number of American researchers and used as the basis for my field research have been confirmed for Mangaia. But several additional features were mentioned often enough by informants to require acknowledgment and inclusion in the description of romantic love as it occurs on the island.

First, Mangaians conceive of *inangaro* as an *involuntary* emotional state or feeling emanating from the *ngakau,* or heart (literally, the bowels). A woman now in her fifties stressed that *inangaro* is "not a choice, but suddenly it is a feeling" that overtakes a person. Involuntariness possesses a negative as well as a positive side. Sometimes informants talked about relationships that should have been but were not because "that feeling" just was not there. For example, Ani was energetically courted by a "good and loving" man who wanted to marry her but for whom she did not feel *inangaro*. Instead, she fell in love with a man who turned out to be unfaithful to her after they were married, causing her considerable unhappiness. As she reflected on her life, Ani regretted not being able to love her first suitor, who, in hindsight, would have been a better spouse.

Second, as I mentioned earlier, Mangaians acknowledge unapologetically that physical beauty is a powerful initiator of relationships between men and women. Polynesians in general have a profound appreciation for the aesthetics of the human body and have no difficulty admitting that it is the essential beginning of passionate love. Although on Mangaia parents attempt to redirect their children's focus to more practical criteria for mate selection, such as land, power, or personal qualities like industriousness, *mapu* continue to be swept away by physical allure. Indeed, even elderly informants remembered wistfully the beauty of a particular lover of long ago.

Involuntariness of onset and the decisive role that physical beauty plays in initiating relationships set the stage for a third feature, the occurrence of love at first sight. A number of informants described experiences of intense and sudden attraction to a person they had just met, and, although there is no local lexical representation for this phenomenon, it is clear that the English term *love at first sight* appropriately captures what informants were describing. Now a grandmother, Rimaputa recalled the first time she met the man who would be her husband:

> I was in the shop buying some food and I turned and saw him. I got a feeling inside me that I had never felt before with anyone. I had already had a boyfriend and a baby and other boys had come around too. But when I saw this man, I wished that he would be my husband, and this feeling was a surprise because I had never seen him before. Although I had that feeling, I didn't expect that the feeling would come true.

In fact, that feeling did come true, for as Rimaputa's husband confided later, he also experienced an instant attraction to her on that day in the shop. And as both of them reflected on what had occurred between them, they concluded that this feeling was "nature's work," that is, nature's or God's way of bringing and keeping them together.

Although Tennov (1979) does not include these features in her list of primary limerent components, she does acknowledge two of them at other points in her text. She admits that "looks count" and that "we fall for beauty" (253) in America, despite our belief that it is a superficial and insubstantial basis for a relationship, and she refers to involuntariness of onset (173; 183), which carries a similarly negative connotation in this culture because it violates our view of ourselves as "free, rational, and therefore, responsible creatures" (173). Ironically, Tennov does not pursue the topic of love at first sight, which seems simply to be lexicalization of an intense physical attraction that develops into a continuing relationship. While Americans in general seem to be ambivalent about love-at-first-sight experiences, believing that a "serious" relationship cannot be initiated exclusively on physical attraction, but recognizing that cases exist, Mangaians who spoke of an intense and immediate initial reaction to a member of the opposite sex were unconcerned. I suspect that as more cross-cultural study is conducted we will find in those cultures not influenced by an ideological discomfort and suspicion of the body a greater willingness to admit the power of physical attraction and incidences of love at first sight.

Conclusion

The psychological literature of the past quarter century has provided anthropologists (and other social scientists) with an initial symptomatology or list of emotional, cognitive, and behavioral characteristics of romantic love that can be used as a basis for cross-cultural evaluation of the possible universality of the phenomenon. As scholarly interest in romantic love increases, and

I believe it will, a variety of ethnographic initiatives will surely give us the ability to refine our understanding of love and to redefine or confirm its core properties-that is, those elements that are common to the experience of falling or being in love within almost any cultural setting. We will be able to determine whether romantic love is universally involuntary, whether its initiation is everywhere strongly influenced by physical beauty, and whether in all cultures intense and immediate attractions, or episodes of love at first sight, occasionally occur and sometimes lead to enduring unions. My own survey of cross-cultural literature suggests that there is support for their inclusion in the universal model, but the construction of that model lies in the future as we acquire data and sort the features that are universal from those that are culture specific.

When compared with the American pattern of romantic love, Mangaian heterosexual bonding differs in emphasis more than content. With all seven basic components verified, and some not too unusual additional features identifed, we discover that the significant differences between American and Mangaian love lie in the relative weighting of features. Highly dissimilar sexual attitudes have created two distinct patterns of heterosexual interaction. The Polynesian pattern emphasizes sexual expression to the point that researchers like Marshall actually overlook the other features of heterosexual relationships while the American pattern minimizes sex to such an extent that our own social scientists fail to consider it when discussing romantic love. I predict that the issue of emphasis will prove to be central to the understanding of many of the perceived differences in cross-cultural heterosexual interactions. The same elements will continue to be verified but the cultural valuation assigned to each will create an illusion of greater differences than actually exist. Much like a stamped embroidery pattern on which the individual embroiderer creates a distinctive work with choices of color, thread, and stitching, the core properties of the romantic love syndrome are embellished, distorted, or even obscured by cultural elaborations to produce a myriad of variations on a theme. Our ability to perceive clearly the basic pattern and to identify distinctive cultural signatures will come only with a robust cross-cultural research program.

REFERENCES

Abu-Lughod, L. 1986. *Veiled Sentiments.* Berkeley: University of California Press.
Averill, J. 1985. "The Social Construction of Emotion: With Special Reference to Love." In

K. Gergen and K. Davis, eds., *The Social Construction of the Person*, pp. 91–109. New York: Springer-Verlag.

Barkow, J. 1973. "Darwinian Psychology Anthropology: A Biosocial Approach. Current." *Anthropology* 69:506–510.

— 1991. *Darwin, Sex, and Status: Biological Approaches to Mind and Culture.* Toronto: University of Toronto Press.

Berscheid, E. 1988. "Some Comments on Love's Anatomy." In R. Sternberg and M. Barnes, eds., *The Psychology of Love*, pp. 359–374. New Haven: Yale University Press.

Berscheid, E., and E. Walster. 1978. *Interpersonal Attraction.* Reading, Mass.: Addison-Wesley.

Brain, R. 1976. *Friends and Lovers.* New York: Basic Books.

Branden, N. 1981. *The Psychology of Romantic Love.* New York: Bantam.

Brehm, S. 1985. *Intimate Relationships.* New York: Random House.

—1988. "Passionate Love." In R. Sternberg and M. Barnes, eds., *The Psychology of Love*, pp. 232–263. New Haven: Yale University Press.

Burdick, E. 1961. *The Blue of Capricorn.* Cambridge, Mass.: Riverside Press.

Buss, D. 1988. "Love Acts: The Evolutionary Biology of Love." In R. Sternberg and M. Barnes, eds., *The Psychology of Love*, pp. 100–118. New Haven: Yale University Press.

— 1989. "Sex Differences in Human Mate Preference: Evolutionary Hypotheses Tested in Thirty-Seven Cultures." *Behavioral and Brain Sciences* 12:1–49.

— 1991. "Evolutionary Personality Psychology." *Annual Review of Psychology* 42:459–491.

Cook, M., and G. Wilson, eds. 1977. *Love and Attraction: An International Conference.* Oxford: Pergamon.

Coppinger, R., and P. C. Rosenblatt. 1968. "Romantic Love and Subsistency Dependence of Spouses." *Southwestern Journal of Anthropology* 24:310–319.

Cosmides, L. 1989. "The Logic of Social Exchange: Has Natural Selection Shaped How Humans Reason?" *Cognition* 31:187–276.

Cosmides, L., and J. Tooby. 1987. "From Evolution to Behavior: Evolutionary Psychology as the Missing Link." In J. Dupre, ed., *The Latest and the Best: Essays on Evolution and Optimality*, pp. 277–306. Cambridge: MIT Press.

Cosmides, L., J. Tooby, and J. Barkow. 1992. "Introduction: Evolutionary Psychology and Conceptual Integration." In L. Cosmides, J. Tooby, and J. Barkow, eds., *The Adapted Mind*, pp. 3–15. Oxford: Oxford University Press.

Daly, M., and M. Wilson. 1988. *Homicide.* Hawthorne, N.Y.: Aldine de Gruyter.

Danielsson, B. 1952. *Raroia.* Chicago: Rand McNally.

— 1986. *Love in the South Seas.* Honolulu: Mutual.

Davis, K. 1985. "Near and Dear: Friendship and Love Compared." *Psychology Today* 19:22–28+.

Dion, K., and K. Dion. 1973. "Correlates of Romantic Love." *Journal of Personality* 43:39–57.

Durant, W. 1954. *Our Oriental Heritage.* New York: Simon and Schuster.

Endleman, R. 1989. *Love and Sex in Twelve Cultures.* New York: Psyche.

Fisher, H. 1982. "Of Human Bonding." *Sciences* 22:18–21.

— 1989. "Evolution of Human Serial Pairbonding." *American Journal of Phyical Anthropology* 78:331–354.

Freeman, D. 1983. *Margaret Mead and Samoa: The Making and Unmaking of an Anthropological Myth.* Cambridge: Harvard University Press.

Gaylin, W., and E. Person. 1988. "Introduction: Thinking About Love." In W. Gaylin and E. Person, eds., *Passionate Attachments*, pp. ix–xii. New York: Free Press.

Gerber, E. 1975. *The Cultural Patterning of Emotions in Samoa.* San Diego: Unversity of California.

Gill, W. W. 1977. *Myths and Songs from the South Pacific.* New York: Arno.

— 1984. *From Darkness to Light in Polynesia.* Apia, Western Samoa: University of the South Pacific.

Goode, W. 1959. "The Theoretical Importance of Love." *American Sociological Review* 24:38–47.

Gregor, T. 1985. *Anxious Pleasures: The Sexual Lives of an Amazonian People.* Chicago: University of Chicago Press.

Haeri, S. 1989. *Law of Desire: Temporary Marriage in Shi'i Iran.* Syracuse: Syracuse University Press.

Hatfield, E. 1988. "Passionate and Companionate Love." In R. Sternberg and M. Barnes, eds., *The Psychology of Love,* pp. 191–217. New Haven: Yale University Press.

Hatfield, E., and S. Sprecher. 1986. "Measuring Passionate Love in Intimate Relationships." *Journal of Adolescence* 9:383–410.

Hatfield, E., and G. W. Walster. 1978. *A New Look at Love.* Reading, Mass.: Addison-Wesley.

Hatfield, E., and R. L. Rapson. 1987. "Passionate Love: New Directions in Research." In W. Jones and D. Perlman, eds., *Advances in Personal Relationships,* pp. 109–139. Greenwich, Conn.: JAI.

Hendrick, S., and C. Hendrick. 1986. "A Theory and Method of Love." *Journal of Personality and Social Psychology* 50:151–157.

— 1992. *Romantic Love.* Newbury Park, Cal.: Sage.

Hiroa, T. R. 1934. *Mangaian Society.* Honolulu: Bernice P. Museum.

Jankowiak, W. 1993. *Sex, Death, and Hierarchy in a Chinese City.* New York: Columbia University Press.

Jankowiak, W ., and E. Fischer. 1992. "A Cross-Cultural Perspective on Romantic Love." *Ethnology* 31(2):149–155.

Knox, D. 1970. "Conceptions of Love at Three Developmental Levels." *Family Coordinator* 19:151–157.

Knox, D., and M. Sporakowski. 1968. "Attitudes of College Students Toward Love." *Journal of Marriage and the Family* 30:638–642.

Lasswell, T., and M. Lasswell. 1976 . "I Love You But I'm Not in Love with You." *Journal of Marriage and Family Counseling* 2:211–224.

Lee, J. 1973. *Colors of Love.* Toronto: New Press.

Levinger, G. 1988. "Can We Picture 'Love?' " In R. Sternberg and M. Barnes, eds., *The Psychology of Love,* pp. 139–158. New Haven: Yale University Press.

Levy, R. 1973. *Tahitians: Mind and Experience in the Society Islands.* Chicago: University of Chicago Press.

Liebowitz, M. 1983. *The Chemistry of Love.* Boston: Little, Brown.

Lindholm, C. 1988. "Lovers and Leaders: A Comparison of Social Psychological Models of Romance and Charisma." *Social Science Information.* London: Sage.

126 Linton, R. 1936. *The Study of Man.* New York: Appleton-Century.

Marshall, D. 1961. *Ra'Ivavae.* New York: Doubleday.

— 1962. *Island of Passion.* London: George Allen and Unwin.

— 1971a. "Sexual Behavior on Mangaia." In D. Marshall and R. Suggs, eds., *Human Sexual Behavior*, pp. 103–162. New York: Basic Books.

— 1971b. "Too Much in Mangaia." *Psychology Today* 4:43–44+.

Mead, M. 1961 [1928]. *Coming of Age in Samoa.* New York: Morrow Quill.

Mellen, S. 1981. *The Evolution of Love.* Oxford: W. H. Freeman.

Merrill, F. 1949. *Courtship and Marriage: A Study in Social Relationships.* New York: William Sloane.

Money, J. 1980. *Love and Love Sickness.* Baltimore: Johns Hopkins University Press.

Murstein, B. 1974. *Love, Sex, and Marriage Through the Ages.* New York: Springer.

— 1988. "A Taxonomy of Love." In R. Sternberg and M. Barnes, eds., *The Psychology of Love*, pp. 13–37. New Haven: Yale University Press.

Orlinsky, D. 1977. "Structural Features of the Romantic Love Relationship." In M. Cook and G. Wilson, eds., *Love and Attraction*, pp. 209–211. Oxford: Pergamon.

Peele, S. 1988. "Fools for Love." In R. Sternberg and M. Barnes, eds., *The Psychology of Love*, pp. 159–188. New Haven: Yale University Press.

Person, E. 1988. *Dreams of Love and Fateful Encounters.* New York: Norton.

Rougement, D. de. 1940. *Love in the Western World.* New York: Harcourt.

Rubin, Z. 1970. "Measurement of Romantic Love." *Journal of Personality and Social Psychiatry* 16:265–273.

— 1973. *Liking and Loving: An Invitation to Social Psychology.* New York: Holt, Rinehart, and Winston.

— 1988. "Preface." In R. Sternberg and M. Barnes, eds., *The Psychology of Love*, pp. vii–xii. New Haven: Yale University Press.

Russell, A. 1961. *Aristocrats of the South Seas.* New York: Roy.

Safilios-Rothschild, C. 1977. *Love, Sex, and Sex Roles.* Englewood Cliffs, N.J.: Prentice-Hall.

Savage, S. 1980. *Dictionary of the Maori Language of Rarotonga.* Suva, Fiji: University of the South Pacific.

Shaver, P., C. Hazan, and D. Bradshaw. 1988. "Love as Attachment." In R. Sternberg and M. Barnes, eds., *The Psychology of Love*, pp. 68–99. New Haven: Yale University Press.

Sperling, M. 1985. "Discriminant Measures for Desparate Love." *Journal of Personality Assessment* 49:324–328.

Steck, L., D. Levitan, D. McLane, and H. Kelley. 1982. "Care, Need, and Conceptions of Love." *Journal of Personality and Social Psychology* 43:481–491.

Sternberg, R. 1988. "Triangulating Love." In R. Sternberg and M. Barnes, eds., *The Psychology of Love*, pp. 119–138. New Haven: Yale University Press.

Sternberg, R., and S. Grajek. 1984. "The Nature of Love." *Journal of Personality and Social Psychology* 47:312–329.

Stone, L. 1988. "Passionate Attachments in the West in Historical Perspective." In W. Gaylin and E. Person, eds., *Passionate Attachments*, pp. 15–26. New York: Free Press.

Suggs, R. 1962. *The Hidden Worlds of Polynesia.* New York: Harcourt, Brace, and World.

Symons, D. 1979. *The Evolution of Human Sexuality.* New York: Oxford University Press.

— 1989. "A Critique of Darwinian Anthropology." *Ethology and Sociobiology* 10:131–144.

Tennov, D. 1979. *Love and Limerence: The Experience of Being in Love*. New York: Stein and Day.

Tooby, J. 1985. "The Emergence of Evolutionary Psychology." In D. Pines, ed., *Emerging Synthesis in Science*, pp. 1–6. Sante Fe: Santa Fe Institute.

Love, Lust and Found in Nigeria

LEONARD PLOTNICOV

This chapter, like many others included in this volume, aims to help dispel the misconception that the experience of romantic love is an oddity among human societies, a peculiarity of modern times or Western civilization. To provide data that the Western and modern worlds have not cornered the market on Cupid's services, I offer illustrative cases from Nigeria, where its presence under traditional conditions is unexpected. These ethnographic examples are anecdotal, to be sure, but evidence of romantic love is restricted to such materials. I will also try to demonstrate that for the most part these cases cannot be attributed to the influence of Western notions of romantic love or other exogenous influences.

Psychologists apparently have been aware for some time that romantic love may be quite common to humanity,[1] so I feel some discomfort if this essay cannot go beyond the exercise of being iconoclastic. However useful myth dispelling might be, something more is required. Ideally, misconceptions not only should be replaced with more accurate information but also with better explanations that provide the basis for raising new questions. This chapter aims to meet such objectives.

The case material presented here required addressing some implicit questions that include 1) How does one determine the presence of romantic love with some assurance that it is the genuine article? 2) If one is certain of romantic love's existence in a non-Western setting, and if one's data are to be used as evidence in refuting the notion that love is absent or rare in non-Western traditions, how can one be sure that the examples are endogenous and not due to diffusion from the West? 3) Is romantic love biologically predetermined or a culturally induced condition?

The last question is a version of the nature/nurture dichotomy and should not be expressed in either/or terms. It may be rephrased in different ways: What is the relationship between the experience of romantic love and the cultural environment that either nourishes or inhibits its expression? Are people biologically predisposed to experience romantic love but require a cultural elaboration of the condition in order to do so? Is romantic love possible in a cultural context lacking a concept for it? Where romantic love is an expected condition of adulthood, what do we make of those who lack the experience?

But Is It Romantic Love?

Ethnographers and teenagers are not alone in wondering when and whether they are in the presence of the genuine article. How can one tell? Unlike a rose that looks and smells as sweetly anywhere, love is an attitude, an emotion that does not speak for itself but requires inference and interpretation. What signifies its presence? Can it be detected objectively or must self-reporting determine certainty? If self-reporting is necessary, as with an ecstatic religious experience (assuming the report is trustworthy), how is this possible if the cultural context ignores the phenomenon? Further, romantic love is hardly a sharp and clear subjective state even where it is an expected, normal condition: one often is unsure of one's own feelings. It has a strong erotic component, to be sure, so how can one differentiate it from similar emotional states like infatuation or lust? How can we be certain when someone has fallen in love in a non-Western society, when the distinctions made in European languages between different aspects of amorous affect may be culture bound and, in any case, offer few clear guideposts?[2]

These caveats noted, and in order to provide some direction to frame the discussion, I use here as a definitive criterion of romantic love the ardent, fervent, and passionate desire for another without whom the lover experiences the feeling of being acutely incomplete, as if a vital part of her or him was lacking. In the illustrative cases of romantic love from Nigeria presented here, the determination of the presence of love depends almost always on my judgment, rarely on an informant's admission.

The examples of romantic love are recalled from research on personal adjustments to modern urban life in Nigeria, conducted between 1960 and 1962 in Jos, a city at that time with a heterogeneous population of over sixty thousand. Through intensive work with adult male informants recording their biographies and routine activities, intimate personal data were obtained.[3] Important for consideration here is that my topical schedule did not include questions on romantic love; I do not recall whether the thought to do so crossed my mind. Thus examples of romantic love elicited from my informants were not prompted by me or my questions but were independently offered in the course of discussing other issues.

But Is It Indigenous?

For this essay I returned to my field notes with an initial view of seeing what I might glean, having felt encouraged to do so because memory convinced me that I had two or three firm cases. I was also convinced that the possibility of having learned about romantic love through Western cultural diffusion was exceedingly remote for many of my informants, but the cases presented below include sufficient contextual information to permit independent judgment.

According to cross-cultural research on the subject (Jankowiak 1992; Rosenblatt 1967), Africa shows the lowest incidence of reports of romantic love under traditional conditions and, conversely, the highest incidence of reports of its absence. This suggests that when examples of romantic love are identified in present-day African cities they reflect Western cultural penetration. We should also expect Western acculturation to be most prevalent in modern-oriented men—who generally are younger, work at trades or occupations introduced from Europe, prefer living in cities to life in rural areas, and are fond of Western material and cultural products—while absent or negligible among traditionalists, because the latter (excepting Muslims literate in Arabic) have had little or no schooling. If one expects Western notions of romantic love to be manifest in modern-oriented men and absent or negligible among traditionalists, one will be disappointed. My data show no such correlation. Cupid's arrows appear to strike at random.

Romantic love was of little interest as a topic of conversation when I did my research. The expression of lust, however, was an important part of men's culture among most male urbanites between the ages of fifteen and fifty, in the sense that it was talked about, and the physical endowments of women provided a genre for joking. Philandering was expected of men:

some were devoted to it with the passion of pursuing a favorite sport, while others showed little or no interest. Lust also was recognized as related to romantic love by contrasting womanizing and a serious relationship. Joking among friends and acquaintances was expected with the former, but one had to be circumspect about the latter.

I begin with a brief consideration of lust, followed by examples of courtship: first where romantic love is absent, followed with cases of its presence. Not surprisingly to those familiar with African societies, we shall see that men who experienced romantic love frequently married in its absence.

Lusting

While almost all my informants had girlfriends before being or while they were married, only wealthy men could afford philandering as a regular pastime. Men tried to conceal their womanizing from their wives. Most wives seemed aware of these indulgences when they occurred, many had grounds for suspicion, and few hesitated expressing their disapproval. Over rounds of bottled beer in the local bars, men circulated stories of philandering, and occasionally told how some wives made trouble when they learned the identity of a girlfriend.

One story was about a local wealthy man, a polygynist, whose wives had warned him several times against pursuing his addiction to chasing women. When he ignored a final warning, they obtained a native "medicine" they put in his food. This allegedly caused him a permanent erection, for which an antidote was withheld until his promises at reform were accepted.

Three Men Cupid Missed

My principal Yoruba informant was a staunch traditionalist and respected elder. As a young man, Olu was more concerned with furthering his trading than marrying, but did marry at his parents' insistence. They chose his wife from a "family without blemish." Olu said, "Until my wife stepped into my father's house, we had never exchanged words. That was the custom of our time. . . . Whatever our parents decided we had to do. The only thing a son could say was, 'Father, pray for us to have a successful marriage.' " A few years after his first marriage, another girl's parents proposed to his that Olu marry their daughter because he was a model husband. Olu did not know her, and was reluctant to have a second wife until he was confident of financial stability, but married again at his father's urging. Both marriages were highly successful by traditional measures, that is, both women had many children, and the co-wives got along well with their husband and with each other.

Olu married a third time when his wives, who did not practice birth control, no longer wished to bear children. He then still enjoyed and wanted sex, but thought his dignity would be jeaopardized if he took a mistress or went to prostitutes. He divorced this wife within several years when her jealousy of the other wives proved disruptive. Not even with the third marriage did Olu give any indication of a romantic interest, even though he alone was responsible for initiating it.

Musa Ibrahim, born about 1902, was unusual for a Hausa man (virtually all of whom are Muslim) because he was raised as a Christian and converted to Islam in middle age. For someone of his generation he also was unusually well educated. He had been the headmaster of a teachers training college and had held other important administrative positions in education. Musa's lengthy account to me of how he followed Hausa custom in obtaining his first wife gave no indication of love's involvement. His only evaluative statement about her was, "She was a good wife to me. There were no misunderstandings between us." Musa's reserved, detached attitude characterizes his subsequent marriage. Shortly after his first wife's death in 1950, while on tour inspecting rural schools, a friend introduced him to a divorced woman, saying she was his ward and that he was holding her for Musa to marry. Musa recalled remonstrating with this friend.

> "How can you [do this] without first consulting to find out whether they [the principals] are interested in each other?" His only reply was, "Don't you like her?" "I don't say that, but how do you know that she likes me?" Then he said, "Everything has been arranged, it only remains for you to agree." Then I asked him to call her so that I could see her and study her before giving my verdict. They returned together in about five minutes, and we sat for about ten minutes, [after which] I gave her ten shillings [as a gift].

Musa did not pursue the matter. Some seven months later his friend wrote to ask about Musa's intentions. Musa's response was for marriage arrangements to proceed, but that the woman first be converted to Islam. They were married in absentia and he did not see her until she entered his house as wife, one year and three months after their initial meeting. They had one child and divorced after seven years of marriage.

A year and a few months after this divorce, Musa married for a third time under circumstances similar to his second marriage. This wife proved far less satisfactory than the others, so Musa sent her home in anticipation of a divorce, and was considering the possibility of marrying yet again, perhaps even to his second wife, who he said was generally good. He had several prospects but pursued none, calculating that he might marry one or two if and when his financial circumstances improved. Nothing in Musa's account hints of love in these relationships.

Isaac, an Ijaw man born in 1918, was a civil engineer and contractor who enjoyed displaying his facility to quote in Latin and claimed to read voraciously in science, metaphysics, and the occult. His parents began urging him to marry when he was about twenty-four or twenty-five, and suggested several girls, all of whom he rejected. He then had a dream in which omens directed him to the family of the woman he came to marry. When they too said that they had been experiencing strange things, he was convinced that supernatural forces guided him to her, and proposed marriage. Isaac claimed that he had no prior knowledge of his fiancée's existence.

When asked to talk about his wife, Isaac's respose was to list her many virtues that suited his ambitions to succeed as a leader in traditional institutions and also be accepted among the modern elite. Nothing he said indicated that he felt any affection for her at any time. They separated after some twenty-five years of marriage and remained living apart.

Olu, Musa, and Isaac seem never to have experienced romantic love. Of the three, Olu is clearly a staunch traditionalist (albeit a good Christian) who had no formal education, spoke no English, and always dressed in traditional style. Musa and Isaac had an extensive Western education, and both men were justifiably proud of their command of the Queen's English. They differed in dress: Musa preferring traditional styles and Isaac almost always wearing Western attire. Although I call the latter two men modern oriented, one can appreciate how terms like modern and traditional apply imperfectly.

Well-Aimed Arrows

Gande in 1961 was probably older than his claimed age of fifty-five. The most culturally conservative of all informants, he had no formal education, and as a boy saw the first Europeans arrive in Tivland. He had married five times. Two wives were dead, one he divorced. He married the first time when, in his mid-twenties, he worked as a carrier for the district officer touring Tiv villages. Gande saw a girl he was attracted to, observed her behavior in the market, then asked someone to introduce them. The next morning he asked her father for permission to marry, which was given, and Gande's father covered the bridewealth, which was thirty iron bars. This woman died when Gande was in the army, in the late 1920s or early 1930s. Discharged after contracting tuberculosis, he met a girl he liked and wanted to marry. Her father, however, insisted on a sister exchange, so the couple ran away to force a marriage. My notes offer no hint about romantic love in these two cases.

Gande's remarks about women, courtship, and marriage were predictably conservative. He mentioned how he had observed his first wife's behavior for several days before deciding to ask her father's consent to marry and, like Musa and Isaac, easily could tick off a list of conditions expected of a good wife. Once he even volunteered that beauty is of no concern when considering marriage. So his account of how he met and fell in love with his third wife astonished and moved me. I asked him why he wanted another wife, as he was then married. He answered,

> Onabu was very beautiful. When I saw her, she took away my life. Most of our people are dancers. When they were dancing [in the market] I went there. When I saw how she danced, I was very pleased to look at her. When I saw all this I tried to marry her. I asked her if she had a husband and she said she had none. I told her I wanted to marry her. She said she had nothing to say about that, and directed me to her parents.

Onabu became ill during their second year of marriage, when she was eight months pregnant. Native medicines proved useless and she died en route to a hospital. The baby could not be saved. Gande's subsequent marriages were not at all similar, being prosaic affairs.

Daniel Njoku, a licensed lorry driver (despite being illiterate), estimated his age at fifty or fifty-two when we met, and his facial scars identified him as a Western Igbo. He spoke several Nigerian languages well because of his extensive travels in the country. Despite having lived in cities, Daniel had never seen a motion picture and had no desire to. His work required him to live away from his hometown, from which his first wife was chosen for him by a classificatory sister. Daniel's first wife proved barren, and after fifteen years of marriage he married again. The second wife also having no issue after five years of marriage, he married a third time, this woman also having been chosen for him by a sister.

Although Daniel said he had gotten on well with all his wives, he confessed that the second was his favorite, describing her as very beautiful, "slender and fine." He said that the first time he saw her he fell in love with her beauty. This was on a visit to his relatives at home. He had arrived late at night, and he noticed her among those helping to unload his lorry. She had

moved into the compound as a teenager after her mother died to stay with a
female relative who had married into Daniel's family.

> I see her then and ask where the father of this girl. I say I like for marry. They say
> many people want for marry her but she refuse them all. Make I talk to her, see if
> she agree. I ask the girl. I say, "I like you. You like me?" She laugh, she go for
> house. Next day, I call. I tell her not to play because I come for marry some girl.
> So I push my sister for go to her, come tell me if girl thinks I play [joke]. She say
> if he mean it, she mean it, too. Then I talk to father's sister [who had married into
> the family] and she laugh, think I play. Then she ask girl, and girl say yes. The
> father's brother call girl and ask her and she say yes. So he glad because she refuse
> so many before.

Pam Choji held a high post in the Provincial Native Administration and
estimated his age in 1961 at about thirty. He and his friends, with whom he
spent evenings drinking beer, were both traditional and modern elite. Pam
was raised under traditional Birom conditions and, although a Christian, had
two wives, both Birom and both culturally conservative. Two years after
marrying the first, he married the second, basing his decision on traditional
values, that is, she was "a well-mannered woman [and] I was convinced she
would be a good housekeeper."

Pam met his first wife when, at around age fifteen, he and his schoolmates
were on holiday and visited her school. She must have impressed him, for
when he later was assigned to her school as an assistant teacher and she was
a pupil in his class, he remembered her. He related that he liked her looks and
behavior, so asked friends who were her classmates to intervene.

> I told them that I loved her. They spoke to her and she told them that she loved
> me too. Then I asked my friends to invite her to my house so I could speak with
> her privately and find out if she really loves me. She came to my house with some
> friends and she was very shy. She couldn't speak to me directly. We had to use her
> friend as a go-between. . . . It was only as an afterthought that I considered her
> family background.

Like Pam Choji, David Kagoro was from one of the many central
Nigerian ethnic groups. A certified electrician, he worked for a government
agency at relatively good wages. He was twenty-three years old in 1961 and
had married eight years earlier, when he was still at school, being forced to
do so by his father, a Baptist pastor. David initially explained that he had
refused to marry ten girls prior to that one by protesting he was too young.

Later he said that his father wanted him to marry a Kagoro woman because his older brothers had taken wives from another ethnic group and he insisted on the marriage to quash David's romance with a Kafanchan girl.

This girl and he had been neighbors and playmates as children. When David was about fourteen, he said he jokingly asked her to be his sweetheart. She responded that she wanted to marry him, and they agreed to marry when adult. Time only strengthened their determination, and David looked forward to her graduation from nursing school so they could marry. His wife and the girl's parents were agreeable to this, and he hoped his father would be as well.

The four men just depicted, to whom I attribute having fallen in love, are not easily classified with regard to the modern/traditionalist spectrum. Regardless of how one might code them, they were not chosen for illustration because they appear conservative, but only because they offer the clearest evidence I have of romantic love experienced by my informants.

Companionate Love

The circumstances of research permitted my observing a few instances of lusting and infatuation but almost nothing of other behaviors or emotions Westerners associate with aspects of love. Traditional African social occasions are marked by gender segregation; public events do not provide opportunities to observe the expression of companionate love. Married couples, for example, even modern-oriented couples, never displayed affection in public. In one sense lust, infatuation, and conjugal (or companionate) love represent positions on the same continuum. That is to say, these feelings are marked by different intensities of eroticism (cf. Berscheid 1988:373) and attitudes about the permanence of the relationship. Whether or not this is so, the present essay would be incomplete without some consideration of companionate love, which Hatfield (1988:191) defines as "the affection we feel for those with whom our lives are deeply entwined," and to which she adds the attributes of friendship, understanding, and concern.

By Hatfield's definition, my informants clearly articulated experiencing companionate love for parents, siblings, offspring, and spouses. The Tiv man, Gande, was particularly close to his mother. She died when he was about twenty-five, after which he said his sorrow would not allow him to remain at home. Olu, the Yoruba traditionalist, was deeply attached to his older sister and father. When the latter died "I went home for the funeral and relatives and friends gathered round me. . . . Although I showed smiles to everyone, deep in my heart I was the gloomiest man on earth because we were great friends." That he once told me he loved his sister more than he did his own children should not be taken literally but as an indication of how his intense affection for her.

I have ample evidence that Olu cared strongly about his children's welfare and happiness—all twenty-three of them—and acted appropriately in their interest, but his concern with proper appearance governed his behavior toward them. Aware of the aloof impression he gave, he said, "We don't show our love to our children in public; we love them privately and we love them very much, but the world won't know about it."

Many aspects of traditional African social organization and culture suggest an environment of conditions that discourage the nurturance of companionate love. These include arranged marriages, gender segregation for work, recreation, and companionship (especially in Muslim areas), high rates of marriage and divorce with some peoples, and male attitudes about women. Husbands regard it as their right to use corporeal sanctions with errant wives, for example, and some said they had to treat them like children.

Men like Isaac, Musa, and Gande talked about women and wives in a detached manner, more like objects than as social persons with whom one is intimately related. Gande's attitude toward women was not uncommon, saying God created them to serve men and bear their children. He claimed that each time he married (five in all) he lectured his bride on expectations and laid down the rules. Among other things, a good wife should be respectful and obedient to her husband (never talk back), seek his permission to go anywhere, work vigorously and cheerfully, and prepare food for visitors immediately upon their arrival. With such indications of male chauvinism and Gande's cultural conservatism in particular, I was quite unprepared for his display of emotion and affection to the wife he left at home.

Gande had spent most of his adult life employed and living away from his home area. Old now, he yearned to return home to retire. His second wife, whom he married thirty-three years previously, and an unmarried son were there. He had not been home and had not seen her in over ten years. In December 1961, having to travel to southeastern Nigeria, I offered to take him home for a visit and he accepted.

He had spoken little about this wife during interviews, perhaps because she caused him no trouble, and was silent for most of the several hundred miles' ride from Jos. To reach his homestead required leaving the main road and taking a dirt track for four or five miles, then walking for almost another mile. I am not certain that his wife was expecting him, but assume so. When we arrived at his compound, he and she embraced and hugged one another for several minutes. Both were crying, tears streaming down their cheeks. When Gande left her to greet others, she continued weeping. Every once in a while Gande returned to her, put his arm around her shoulder, and spoke softly to her. This continued until I left to resume traveling. Were it not for such rare, fortuitous observations, I would have no evidence of the presence of companionate love among culturally conservative Nigerian spouses.

Conclusion

This essay began with three interrelated questions regarding romantic love: how to recognize its genuine presence in others, whether it is a culture specific phenomenon, and whether its presence anywhere is the natural expression of an innate disposition for the experience, which different cultural contexts may encourage or inhibit.

Irrefutable evidence of romantic love is virtually impossible to obtain even under optimal conditions—i.e., where it is an expected part of normal life, where it is culturally elaborated and given a rich vocabulary—because it depends on subjective evaluation and self-reporting or imprecise objective criteria. In addition, all emotions in their descriptions and behavioral expressions are culturally conditioned, which raises the problem of their translation from one culture to another,[4] i.e., we cannot be sure we are feeling and talking about the same thing. And as we have not the means of detecting in the brain's limbic system or in blood chemistry the distinctions between different kinds of love and erotic attachment, I have based my judgment of love's presence on such evidence as my Tiv informant describing his feeling about the woman who became his third wife: "When I [first] saw her she took away my life." It appears he fell in love then, and it appears from the reunion scene I witnessed that he and his second wife experienced companionate love for one another.

The problem with verifying romantic love's presence anywhere lies not with population sample size but with the quality of data and the criteria of judgment. The evidence that my informants experienced romantic love is convincing, although we are less sure about the involvement of Western cultural influences. Anyway, the Western/modern-oriented men had no advantage in this over the cultural conservatives.

These data provide little guidance for answering the question of whether the potential for romantic love is universal and, if so, in what ways. Where the concept is absent, persons may still have that special, intense feeling without being able to verbalize it with appropriate clichés. If there is a panhuman predisposition for it, there still is no assurance that even within a culturally encouraging environment the experience will come as a birthright. Some people will not achieve the state while others will have little trouble doing so. Some will be convinced of their success, some probably fake the experience, others remain uncertain, and some may wonder why they are singled out for disappointment. Perhaps the experience is like religious ecstasy and possession trance, and, as with the American Plains Indian personal spirit quest, some just never get it.

NOTES

1. Hatfield and Rapson's (1987:135) review of the literature suggests to them that passionate (romantic) love is "universal," and not one of the "inventions of the twentieth century," probably because the "predisposition . . . [is] 'prewired' into primates." The genetic basis, however, does not deny "the power of cultural, demographic, economic, social, and historical factors in . . . shaping the manifold ways in which that emotion is expressed, repressed, and suppressed."

2. There appears to be little agreement among psychologists on what romantic love is. Hatfield (1988) offers several definitions and Berscheid (1988:373) confesses not really knowing what it is, since it consists of a great assortment of things, adding, however, that sexual desire is an overwhelming component. Similarly, Rubin (1988:viii) suggests that the meaning of the concept varies subjectively with people, and asks rhetorically whether it is "an attitude, an emotion, a set of behaviors . . . an individual orientation or a dyadic bond?"

3. Fuller treatment of these men appears in Plotnicov (1967).

4. See Shweder (1993) for a discussion on the difficulties of translating intercultural concepts of basic emotions into English equivalent terms.

REFERENCES

Berscheid, E. 1988. "Some Comments on Love's Anatomy: Or, Whatever Happened to Old-Fashioned Lust?" In R. J. Sternberg and M. Barnes, eds., *The Psychology of Love*, pp. 359–374. New Haven: Yale University Press.

Hatfield, E. 1988. "Passionate and Companionate Love." In R. J. Sternberg and M. Barnes, eds., *The Psychology of Love*, pp. 191–217. New Haven: Yale University Press.

Hatfield, E., and R. L. Rapson. 1987. "Passionate Love: New Directions in Research." *Advances in Personal Relationships* 1:109–139.

150   Jankowiak, W., and E. Fischer. 1992. "A Cross-Cultural Perspective on Romantic Love."
       Ethnology 31(2):149–155.

Plotnicov, L. 1967. *Strangers to the City: Urban Man in Jos, Nigeria.* Pittsburgh: University of
       Pittsburgh Press.

Rosenblatt, P. 1967. "Marital Residence and the Functions of Romantic Love." *Ethnology*
       6:471–480.

Rubin, Z. 1988. "Preface." In R. J. Sternberg and M. Barnes, eds., *The Psychology of Love,*
       pp. vii–xii. New Haven: Yale University Press.

Shweder, R. 1993. "The Cultural Psychology of the Emotions." In M. Lewis and J. M.
       Haviland, eds., *The Handbook of Emotions,* pp. 417–431. New York: Guilford Press.

The Madness of Excess: Love Among the Fulbe of North Cameroun

HELEN A. REGIS

"Her charms are too much for him. He has lost his head completely!"

"Siiri maako 'buri mo sembe. Hakkilo maako kam majji pat!"

Love as a Disease[1]

As each chapter in this book illustrates, the capacity to love passionately is a widespread phenomenon. It is crucial to remind the reader, however, that the expression of love is not universally the same.[2] The Fulbe lover is constantly on guard, lest he or she reveal authentic feelings in an inappropriate context and expose him or herself to public opprobrium. On the other hand, through friendly discussions American lovers enjoy announcing and savoring their emotional involvements. For most Americans love is one of the culture's highest ideals.

In this chapter I will explore how Fulbe think about and express respectability and emotionality. In particular, I will examine their conception and articulation of passionate love. Although Fulbe do experience the emotional states we refer to as love, the culture does not recognize it as an ideal. It has no legitimate place in the social life of the community. The Fulbe therefore have a tremendous incentive *not* to fall in love (i.e., to keep a level head on their shoulders), yet time and time again they fail.

The research on which this chapter is based was conducted in a community of sedentary Fulbe in the Extreme North Province of Cameroun. They cultivate millet for domestic consumption and onions and cotton for cash. Unlike the nomadic and seminomadic groups, sedentary Fulbe hold the seclusion of married women as an ideal. The gendered segregation of social space is much more elaborated, with high mud walls effectively excluding the casual gaze from the enclosed family compound. Koranic education is nearly universal as most parents keep their children home from the government-run secular schools. Fasting, the five daily prayers, and almsgiving are taken very seriously, and the few who are able to make the pilgrimage to Mecca are held in the highest esteem. Although they share a common language with the pastoral Wo'daabe of Niger (Beckwith 1989; Dupire 1962) and the semisedentary Fulani of Burkina Faso (Riesman 1977), the settled Fulbe are much less involved in cattle and more identified with commerce and Islamic discourse.

The Fulbe construction of normalcy and deviance is anchored in their rules for when, where, and how to express emotions.[3] The ability to control emotions lies at the heart of the Fulbe construction of personhood. In order to understand love and romantic expression among the Fulbe, we must first briefly examine the importance of restraint and self-control in their lives.

The disclosure of reticence: The display of personhood and the concealment of emotionality

The Fulbe take pride in their poised reserve. Their very identity as free people—in a land where slavery is to this day a social fact—hinges on their success in mastering their emotions (Riesman 1977; 1992). A man who cannot control his emotions is not master of himself. If he is not his own master, he is a slave.[4]

Very early, Fulbe children are taught not to express pain. They learn from their mothers not to share the pain of injury or sickness with others. When asked how they are doing by concerned friends and neighbors, they respond dutifully, "Much better now (*daama*), thanks be to Allah." Riesman asserts that the demonstration "that one is in control of normal human emotions and above human needs is constantly taking place in [Fulani] formal behavior" between members of the same community (Riesman 1975:63).[5] In response to the pain of sickness and the pain of a cure, as well as in competitive games, Fulbe adults and children make a virtue out of the suppression and even the complete denial of pain.[6] Men often play a game of verbal taunting in which the one who becomes angry loses. Under customary law as well as in popular opinion, a person who commits a crime in the heat of passion is judged particularly severely. Loss of temper, rather than being viewed as "mitigat-

ing circumstances," further discredits the accused, who is viewed as mental-
ly unstable.[7] When grief over the death of a child exceeds culturally prescribed norms, the distraught parent is scolded by relatives and kin. The will
of Allah must be accepted. Excessive parental love, like anger, grief, and
pain, cannot be publicly acknowledged.[8] Excessive happinesss, expressed
through laughter or abandoned dancing, is frowned upon because it is said to
involve a denial of death. Grief and anger, like pain, are part of human existence everywhere. But the Fulbe strive to conceal their experience of emotions, however intense. As children become adults, they seek to control and
internalize their emotional experience.

Shame (*semteende*) is different from all the emotions in that it is the only
emotion that is expected to influence public behavior.[9] The anticipation of
shame and the fear of being called shameless is perhaps the principal deterrent to the public display of romantic love. Although *semteende* is a multivo-
cal concept in Fulbe culture, and a full discussion of it cannot be undertaken
here, its core meaning springs from deference and respect for the social group.

The Fulbe discourse about their relation to the community in the language of posture, gesture, and ceremonial greeting continually reiterates the
healthy individual's availability to fellow villagers[10] and his or her respect for
the power of others. Availability to others, commensality, respect/deference
for elders are all expressed in Fulbe practices of eating, greeting, patterns of
visiting and sitting together, and body language generally. The individual
affirms both the egalitarian and hierarchical principles of the social order in
his or her everyday bodily discourse.[11] Both of these principles are threatened by an individual's total passionate involvement in a dyadic romance.[12]
By its very nature romance competes with and contradicts the complex and
multifaceted relations of the individual to the community. It is apart from
and more powerful than the social group that first claimed the individual in
his or her naming ceremony, seven days after birth.[13] The hostility of the
community to the dyadic bond is consistent with cultural principles about the
nature of human relationships that are constantly performed in the everyday
acts of the community. Because falling in love strengthens the egos of the
lovers, at least for a time, it separates that amorous dyad from the power of
the community. This is one reason why the family and others publicly react
against those who fall in love. The Fulbe would agree with classical Freudian
theory that there is a fundamentally antagonistic relationship between passionate emotions and societal obligations.

Love: The Defiant Emotion

During field research in a Fulbe village over a period of eighteen months, I often heard public criticism of people who were in love. Some of this criticism concerned people who acted inappropriately. For example, a man should not loiter around a woman's compound during the day but should be out in public socializing with other men. Other criticism concerned people who did not follow the advice of family and friends; they refused to take a second wife or remarry after a divorce. For example, Hamman Ga'bdo refused to take a second wife even though his current spouse, Dija, was childless. He was repeatedly the subject of this tirade: "Her charms are too much for him. He has lost his head completely!" (Siiri maako 'buri mo sembe. Hakkilo maako kam majji pat!). Excessive love also makes it difficult for a man to treat his wives equally. The village chief Yaya Atiiku was known to give preferential treatment to his wife Ubbore over the younger Fa'dimatu. His own brother noted this imbalance: "He loves her too much!" (O yi'di mo jammum!). His affection for Ubbore prevented him from treating his two wives equally, as required by Islamic law. Fa'dimatu's resentment of her less considerate treatment was thus legitimated by religious authority. When the chief repudiated her in a fit of anger one night, her family refused to negotiate for a reunion. "He has mistreated her enough," her father said.

In everyday conversations among neighbors, women routinely and vehemently deny emotional attachment to a husband. Perhaps correctly, they seem to sense that their freedom of action depends on a practical stance toward marriage. If they get what they want in terms of good treatment and material support, following this logic, they will stay. Otherwise, they will leave. It is the believable threat that they will leave a husband who is neglecting or mistreating them that can act as an effective deterrent to male abuse.[14] In spite of these customary denials of feeling, when Fa'dimatu was teased by a group of women at the well one night, she did not deny her love for her husband the chief. She merely gave a pained smile, which served as an affirmation. She loved him, but she did not disobey her father to return to this man. She accepted his view that the relationship would never work out well.[15]

However, there were couples in the village who seemed to be in love but did not act inappropriately and were not the object of critical gossip. Another ethnographer, Paul Riesman, who worked with Fulbe of Burkina Faso, also writes that he believes couples he knew were in love (Riesman 1971:608). The problem is that if these couples were not being criticized and they were not talking about their emotions, how is it possible to know that they were in love? I received a number of nonverbal cues when I was alone with them: a man lingering near his wife, an affectionate look, a couple's shyness in each other's presence. These couples, I believe, were careful not to show their feelings in public and not to allow their feelings to influence their public behavior.

Other couples, who were less successful in hiding their feelings or who were more in the public eye, came to be labeled by fellow villagers as sick, socially impaired individuals whose symptoms were caused by loving their partner too much. A man who is in love with his wife will tend to stay home during the day or in the evenings, when he is expected to meet his friends on the *buwol*, or main street. This violates the norm that men must be available to their fellow villagers. For example, Abdu was known to be in love with his wife. His conspicuous absence when other men were gathering near his house led to derisive statements that he was a man under the power of a spell. (Implicit in these allegations is the assumption that the spell was being cast by his wife. In other words, he was under the power of his wife.) Such a man is thought to be reluctant to remarry, slow to discipline his wife, and slow to divorce her in case of a serious breach of conduct. If he has more than one wife, he will be unable to treat them equally. He will be vulnerable to teasing from his peers and more likely to become angry at the (too truthful) taunts that he has lost his head over a woman. He will lose the respect of his peers and the consideration of his elders. Like Mahmudu, rebuked for hitting his wife in her father's house, he will be the subject of villagewide gossip should any incident occur that further corroborates the imbalance of his mental state.

A woman who is in love will be inordinately jealous of her co-wife, will ignore the advice of parents on whom to marry, and will be absentminded and lackadaisical in her work. She will marry a poor man and spurn a rich one, like Ditti Hurrey, who left a powerful chief of the region to marry a struggling market vendor. She was teased for this impractical marriage. A woman in love, if she is married to someone else, will be tempted to be unfaithful to her husband, which, in the social space of the village, can be a difficult and risky venture.

The dangers of loving the wrong person and of loving without restraint are illustrated with grotesque and fearful humor in Fulbe stories. A collection of Fulbe tales from Maroua (Eguchi 1978), the provincial capital of the Extreme North of Cameroun, contains the story of a man and a woman, strangers, who meet on the road and fall in love. He discovers by spying on her that she is in fact a *waylooru* (person who can turn into a hyena and eat people) and thus a cannibal. In fact all of her people are *waylooji*. After a long struggle in which he is pursued by her relatives (who have been transformed into hyenas), he is able through the use of magical powers to marry her. When he brings her home his relatives and friends find her strange and question his emotional involvement with her.

This story is a cautionary tale about the hazards of falling in love with a stranger. Indeed, it would be difficult to construct a more frightening scenario. Her kin, as hyenas, literally tried to eat him alive. The message is clear: Obey your parents and marry "one of your own," preferably a cousin.

Love is no exception: A comparative perspective on love-madness

In examining the cross-cultural expression of love, it is relevant here to see that the Fulbe are not alone to characterize love in negative terms. In fact, a number of other Islamic peoples share Fulbe misgivings about romance. The Fulbe posture toward the expression of love resembles medieval Islamic medical thought on passionate love, or *'ishq*: "It exceeds the limit of mere inclination and [normal] love and, by possessing the reason, causes its victim to act unwisely. It is blameworthy and ought to be avoided by the prudent" (Dols 1992:319). Medical textbooks used passionate love to illustrate the relationship between psychic and bodily ailments. Unwise behavior is exemplified in ill-advised efforts to make one's ardent love public. Such indiscretion leads to the lover's being labeled "mad." "Ar-Rhazi's remedy for lovesickness was to wean oneself away from seeing the beloved, remembering that ultimately death separates all lovers" (Dols 1992:317). The contemporary Fulbe agree: to engage fully in a feeling—be it grief, pain, anger, happiness or love—is tantamount to possession. It is a loss of reason or sense—madness.

Love, passion, and madness are so intertwined in Islamic thought that they shape the character development of folk tales. The story of Qays and Lila and their ill-fated love became a classic in Islamic literature, like Romeo and Juliet in Europe. Both stories tell of star-crossed lovers, but the Islamic tale paints Qays as a "majnun," a madman (Dols 1992:332). The theme of madness that arises as a consequence of ardent love is a pan-Islamic theme.[16]

The Muslim Tuareg of Niger share similar notions of love-madness whose similarities to Fulbe thinking are worth noting. Rasmussen reports that the "Tuareg cultural values . . . discourage revealing personal sentiments directly, in particular love preference." The emphasis on reserve is particularly strong for women. It is therefore not surprising that they are the principal suffers of *tamaẓai*. It is "an illness of the heart and soul" that is often attributed to possession by a spirit due to a "hidden love" or not acting on desires (Rasmussen 1992:339). A person suffering from *tamaẓai* feels harassed by people and withdrawn from them. Among the Tuareg the cure involves exorcism of the spirit (Rasmussen 1992:337). Ironically, the curing rituals, which are held in the evenings, are customarily occasions for flirtation and courtship.[17] "Love is often outside of marriage; it is called *tara tan iblis*, love of Iblis (the devil). The devil, present at nightly festivals and during courtship conversation, is believed to incite illicit love" (Rasmussen 1992: 357). Fulbe cures also center on exorcism, yet they are not social events but private sessions between the religious practitioner and the afflicted.

The Tuareg view on passionate love as inappropriate and excessive mirrors Fulbe thinking. For the Tuareg, emotional imbalance is thought to create a *vulnerability* to spirit possession, whereas the Fulbe see possession as the *cause* of emotional imbalance. In both cultures the imbalance is linked to an individual's vulnerability to external influence in the form of spirits.[18] Although the parallel influence of Islam could be invoked to explain the similarities in Fulbe and Tuareg thinking, it cannot explain resemblances with a non-Muslim group in southeastern Nigeria.

Elechi Amadi's treatment of the relationship between the newly widowed Ihuoma and the bachelor Ekwe in a village he calls Omokachi (Amadi 1966) displays the familiar construction of excessive love as madness.

> Whatever she felt was safely locked up in her mind. Not even her mother could probe into its depths and wrench its secrets. She had admitted to herself that she liked Ekwe very much. But what woman does not like some man? Her liking for Ekwe was not frantic nor was it sudden. It had grown gradually over a long period. Since it did not take her by storm she was able to keep it firmly under control.
>
> . . . Omokachi village life was noted for its tradition, propriety, and decorum. *Excessive or fanatical feelings over anything were frowned upon and even described as crazy.* Anyone who could not control his feelings was regarded as being unduly influenced by his agwu [personal spirit]. (Amadi 1966:127, emphasis mine)

This passage in Amadi's novel *The Concubine* seems to capture that society's view on love and emotions in general. They are to be accepted in moderation, but excessive emotion is madness, which can either be caused by a disproportionately strong personal will or by a love potion.

Fulbe and Tuareg attribute passionate love to an external force that pos-

148   sesses and controls the conscience; Amadi's villagers blame an overly strong personal spirit (or *agwu*). Both etiologies suggest that people in love are influenced by a force beyond their conscious control, though this force is alternately conceived as external or internal. Rasmussen emphasizes the element of exaggeration (rather than deviance) inherent in the syndrome. This makes it possible to see the similarities between cultural constraints on the expression of grief, pain, anger, affection for children, and romantic love. While these are normal feelings in moderation, when indulged in excessively they are seen to cause an imbalance in people that prevents them from participating in the ordinary life of a face-to-face community.

In sum, any emotion, when taken up obsessively, makes a person unavailable to peers, less than fully respectful of elders, contemptuous of convention, and forgetful of death (and of god). For the Fulbe, "if there is death, there is no pleasure." That is, there is no tyranny of emotion, no passion that is allowed to possess the personality. In this way love is no exception.

NOTES

The research on which this chapter is based took place between January of 1990 and June of 1991. Funding for my field work came from USAID and the Tulane University School of Public Health and Tropical Medicine in cooperation with the Ministry of Public Health of Cameroun and the Institute for the Study of Medicine and Medicinal Plants. I am grateful to Barry S. Hewlett for his guidance during this period. I would also like to thank Lawane Yaya Atikou and his family, who welcomed me into their lives, and Halidou Limane for everything. All Fulbe names have been changed. Bill Jankowiak's enthusiasm, encouragement, and criticism made this chapter possible.

1.   Although I tend to think of the sickness *soynde hakkilo* (loss of sense) as a metaphor for emotional states, the Fulbe would deny that it is a metaphor. The emic view is that a sickness exists. It is caused by caring too much. The disease is expressed in inappropriate behaviors.

2.   Lock and Scheper-Hughes (1990) have argued against a persistent cartesian dichotomy in discussions of the body as materially constituted in isolation from a culturally constituted mind. Merleau-Ponty and other processual philosophers have worked toward a unified view of the person in "lived experience" which speaks of the embodied mind and the intelligent body. I would argue further that there is no experience of the body which is not already culturally interpreted. Thus, when I say that love is not experienced in the same way everywhere, I mean that love is not a discrete physiological process which can be identified in isolation from cultural interpretation (though such biological processes may make love possible).

3. Foucault (1988) has shown how the definition of some people and behavior as deviant is crucial to solidifying societal notions of normalcy. The relation between emotional expression and personhood is developed in Trosset (1993).

4. Riesman has developped this theme at length in *Freedom in Fulani Social Life* (1977) and *First Find Yourself a Good Mother* (1992). Slaves grew up in a Fulbe environment and spoke Fulfulde, but remained outsiders to the only culture they knew. An account of how some people became Fulbe slaves is in Baldus (1977).

5. This section owes much to Riesman's (1975) thinking on the meaning of Fulbe greetings.

6. Women often displayed an impressive ability to pick up hot things (coals, cooking pots) with their hands, but I never saw them play a testing game with heat. Their silence about the pain of childbirth is noteworthy.

7. Constraints on the public expression of grief sometimes conflict with individuals' feelings, leading to the labeling of a woman I knew as "imbalanced" when her feelings exceeded the culturally prescribed norms.

8. Excessive parental love is blamed for childhood illnesses with a broad range of symptoms. For example, *garsa*, which is manifested in any kind of lopsidedness in the body, is caused by the mother's affectionate gaze at her infant.

9. Abu-Lughod has written extensively about the Awlad 'Ali concept of *hasham* and the complex linkages between modesty, ethics and power exemplified by it (1986;1990b). Many of the things she says about *hasham* could also be said about *semteende*. I have been repeatedly surprised at the striking resemblances between Bedouin and Fulbe discourse, although to what extent these similarities are due to a shared missionization and to what extent they are due to a shared ethnographic tradition is difficult to determine.

10. I was amazed several times when my hosts would anticipate my thirst and offer me water during a meal when I didn't ask for it. I gradually realized that my eyes were betraying my thirst because I was looking at the water, thinking of asking for it, but not wanting to interrupt the conversation. My host had noticed the direction of my gaze and handed me the water. This suggests a tremendous sensitivity to guests as well as an interest in showing awareness of their needs (as well as showing a keen awareness of the relationship between looking and wanting).

11. Schmitt (1989) and Vigarello (1989) show how ethics have been conveyed through gesture and posture in Europe.

12. Nelli (1989), writing about the practice of the *Asag*, or test of love, in medieval Provence, indicates that romantic involvements outside of marriage, in which the "lady" was in complete control, were defined in opposition to marital relations, which were very much controlled by the husband (Nelli 1989:229).
    Abu-Lughod has indicated that heterosexual or romantic love is talked about as a threat "to the solidarity of the paternal kin group." The Awlad 'Ali view sexual bonds and the bonds of agnation as competing (1990b:34). Love poetry is a "discourse of defiance" and "a discourse of autonomy and freedom" (Abu-Lughod 1990b:36).

13. Fulbe naming ceremonies, like Catholic baptisms, function to integrate a new person into the social group. In the Fulbe ceremony relatives (especially patrilineal relatives) of the child and members of the community come to witness the naming. Women bring small gifts to the mother's house while men gather with the father in front of

the family compound. The father's sister carries the baby out of the mother's house for the first time.

14. Of course, the credibility of the threat also depends on the proximity of a woman's relatives and/or her own savings, which she might use to pay for transport or to support herself in a transitional period.

15. She is now married to a merchant in Maroua.

16. Smadar Lavie (1990) notes a similar imperative among the Mzeina of South Sinai to be discrete about feelings of love, lest one become marked as a crazy person.

17. Bovin (1975:466) documents the practice of possession among pastoral Fulbe of Niger (Wo'daabe). The possessed person is described as "crazy" and "not quiet/sane." Interestingly, these rituals also lead to love trysts in the bush after the performance.

18. The Fulbe also believe that emotional imbalance can be caused by spells.

REFERENCES

Abu-Lughod, L. 1986. *Veiled Sentiments*. Berkeley: University of California Press.

— 1990a. "Shifting Politics in Bedouin Love Poetry." In C. Lutz and L. Abu-Lughod, eds., *Language and the Politics of Emotion*. New York: Cambridge University Press.

— 1990b. "Introduction: Emotion, Discourse, and the Politics of Everyday Life." In C. Lutz and L. Abu-Lughod, eds., *Language and the Politics of Emotion*. New York: Cambridge University Press.

Amadi, E. 1966. *The Concubine*. London: Heinemann.

Baldus, B. 1977. "Responses to Dependence in a Servile Group: The Machube of Northern Benin." In S. Miers and I. Kopytoff, eds., *Slavery in Africa*. Madison: University of Wisconsin Press.

Beckwith, C. 1989. "Geerewol: The Art of Seduction." In *Fragments for a History of the Human Body*. ed. M. Feher. New York: Zone.

Bovin, M. 1975. "Ethnic Performance in Rural Niger: An Aspect of Ethnic Boundary Maintenance." *Folk* 16–17:459–474.

Dols, M. 1992. *Majnun: The Madman in Medieval Islamic Society*. Oxford: Clarendon Press.

Dupire, M. 1962. *Peuls Nomades*. Paris: Institut d'Ethnologie.

Eguchi, P. 1978. *Fulfulde Tales of North Cameroon*. Tokyo: Institute for the Study of Languages and Cultres of Asia and Africa.

Feher, M. 1989. *Fragments for a History of the Human Body*. New York: Zone.

Foucault, M. 1988. *Madness and Civilization: A History of Insanity in the Age of Reason*. New York: Vintage/Random House.

Hopen, C. E. 1958. *The Pastoral Fulbe Family in Gwandu*. London: Oxford University Press.

Lavie, S. 1990. *The Poetics of Military Occupation*. Berkeley: University of California Press.

Le Goff, J. 1989. "Head or Heart? The Political Uses of Body Metaphors in the Middle Ages." In M. Feher, ed., *Fragments for a History of the Human Body. Part Three*. New York: Zone.

Lock, M., and N. Scheper-Hughes. 1990. "Rituals and Routines of Discipline and Dissent." In T. M. Johnson and C. E. Sargent, eds., *Medical Anthropology: Contemporary Theory and Method*. New York: Praeger.

Nelli, R. 1989. "Love's Rewards." In M. Feher, ed., *Fragments for a History of the Human Body*. New York: Zone.

Rasmussen, S. 1992. "Reflections on *Tamaẓai*: A Tuareg Idiom of Suffering." *Culture, Medicine, and Psychiatry* 16:337–365.

Riesman, P. 1971. "Defying Official Morality: The Example of Man's Quest for Woman Among the Fulani." *Cahiers d'Etudes Africaines* 44:602–03.

— 1973. "Love Fulani Style." *Society* (Jan/Feb), pp. 27–35.

— 1975. "The Art of Life in a West African Community: Formality and Spontaneity in Fulani Interpersonal Relationships." *Journal of African Studies* 2:39–63.

— 1977. *Freedom in Fulani Social Life: An Introspective Ethnography*. Chicago: University of Chicago Press.

— 1992. *First Find Yourself a Good Mother: The Construction of Self in Two African Communities*. New Brunswick, N.J.: Rutgers University Press.

Schmitt, J. -C. 1989. "The Ethics of Gesture." In M. Feher, ed., *Fragments for a History of the Human Body*. New York: Zone.

Scheper-Hughes, N. 1992. *Death Without Weeping: The Violence of Everyday Life in Braẓil*. Berkeley: University of California Press.

Trosset, C. 1993. *Welshness Performed: Welsh Concepts of Person and Society*. Tuscon: University of Arizona Press.

Vigarello, G. 1989. "The Upward Training of the Body from the Age of Chivalry to Courtly Civility." In M. Feher, ed., *Fragments for a History of the Human Body*. New York: Zone.

Notions of Love and Romance Among the Taita of Kenya

JIM BELL

Throughout the nineteenth and twentieth centuries a prevailing European image of Africa held that the native was nonhuman and thus driven entirely by animalistic desires for sexual satisfaction. This image, which Katherine George (1958) calls "antagonistic fantasy," found its strongest voice in the works of some Western missionaries (Hulstaert 1938; Johnston 1911; Lugard 1904; MacDonald 1916; Noble 1899; and others). Their early accounts of daily African life are filled with tales of lust and other forms of "sexual debauchery." They are silent, however, about the presence of passionate love. For most it was a moot point: the African was not capable of experiencing passionate love, so there was nothing to discuss.

The proper business of missionaries was to save souls, which meant that they had to instruct the Africans on how to live according to the Christian ideals of family and virtue. They seldom were successful in this endeavor. Donald Fraser's (1928) account of Africans' inability to achieve the Western ideal of good family is highly representative. He writes:

> In spite of all that we have said of the magical sanctions which preserve a comparatively high fidelity between husband and wife in primitive African society, the standards of social purity are shockingly low. The cases that demand most of

the attention of the native and magisterial courts are breaches of the seventh commandment [adultery is forbidden] (1928:107).

Another missionary, Ellen Parsons (1906), working among the Taveta (a close neighbor of the Taita), also noted similar behavior. She writes:

> One great hindrance stood in the way—sensuality. The awfulness of the bondage to the flesh in which the people are enthralled only incites their teachers the more to point them to Christ the Liberator, for He is able to so renew their minds that even they can learn to say, "In thy presence is fullness of joy; at thy right hand are pleasures for evermore." (1906:173)

The Christian obsession with "proper" family structure and sexual behavior prevented a clear understanding of romance among Africans. In many ways this misunderstanding, first expressed in the early missionary accounts, continues as a predominant Euro-American image of Africa (Jablow and Hammond 1977:16).

In this essay I examine the ideal of lust, love and romance, as they are remembered, lived, and performed among the Taita (sometimes also refer to as the Wataita, or Wadawida) of Kenya, East Africa. I argue that the notion of marriage for love (or passionate love) may not be new to Taita culture and might not depend on European contact. Rather, passionate love or romantic love existed before the arrival of what Ali Mazrui (1986) calls "European Christianity" and, as such, has been an integral part of African culture.

Missionaries and the Development of Passionate Love

For most missionaries the primary evil in African society was the widespread custom of females and males becoming deeply involved with one another (for whatever reason and on whatever terms) *outside* the institution of *monogamous* marriage—with an equal emphasis on both words: *outside* and *monogamous.* This emphasis on standard marriage and monogamy serves to blur the notion of romantic love.

The religious preoccupation with monogamous marriage helped to prevent recognition of an important human phenomenon. Because the missionaries favored monogamous marriage over polygynous marriage, they actively sought to persuade all converts of the cultural and religious superiority of monogamy through the introduction of symbols and rituals that glorified monogamous marriage. In this way early missionaries (cf. Clark 1890, Lovett 1899, Parsons 1906, Thomas 1885, and others) who toiled in the

African bush strove to introduce a number of Western-inspired cultural features, including certain forms of romantic expression, into contemporary
African marriage and daily life. The words "love, honor, and obey" in the
marriage rite is one such introduction. Promotion of monogamous marriage
was initiated with the moral imperative to "cleave to one wife or husband."
Further evidence of the missionaries' misunderstanding of the variety of
expressions that love can take, both inside and outside of marriage, can be
found in their depictions of polygynous marriage among the Kikuyu. The
missionaries believed this practice was based on the principle that women
were chattel. Jomo Kenyatta, a Kikuyu who was also Oxford-educated,
insists, however, that the "*Gikuyu* [or Kikuyu] have always been free to
choose a mate without any interference on the part of the parents on either
side" (Kenyatta 1959:165). He further insists that in traditional Kikuyu society "love" was a strong motive in mate selection. Kenyatta also notes that
when a "boy falls in love with a girl he cannot tell her directly that he loves
her or display his devotion to her in public, as this would be regarded by
Gikuyu as impolite and uncultured" (1959:165). The early missionaries were
ignorant of such customs of public decorum and politeness.

I found among the Taita a similar attitude toward choice and public decorum. For example, younger Taita women prefer becoming involved with
what they call a "chosen lover," usually a member of their age group. Many
of these involvements arise out of a sense of deep affection, physical attraction, romantic love, or a mixture of all three. In the last case, some of these
relationships last a lifetime. Given the missionaries' obsession with reporting
on the "native's" sexual behavior, this type of love arrangement was, perhaps,
predictably, condemned in some accounts and curiously ignored in others.

For the Taita two cultural features are important: 1) European missionaries tried to change the indigenous ideals of marriage and love affairs.
Marriage practices have changed; polygyny, however, remains a popular
institution. 2) Romantic love appears to have always been part of Taita history. Consequently, love affairs (and not just sexual liaisons) are a regular
fact of daily Taita life. As one old and thoughtful grandmother informed me,
"Lovers will continue to walk the hills of Dawida (the mountain range in
which she lives)."

Lust, Love, and Beauty in the Taita Hills

The Taita are highland farmers who have inhabited a mountainous area in
southern Kenya for four or five hundred years. During this period the Taita

have engaged in wars with the nomadic Maasai and the slave-trading Arab and Swahili peoples from the coast. In addition, the culture has, for at least 140 years, sought to assimilate and accommodate European missionary efforts to alter their view of the world. These efforts have led to the adoption of certain Western linguistic expressions like *love* and *lust*. Nevertheless, Taita informants assert that prior to European contact *ashiki* (lust) and *pendo* (love) were terms already in existence. It would stand to reason therefore that just as these experiences were found in European cultures before the French coined the word *romance* in the twelfth century, the emotions underlying them would have existed before the linguistic invention of the term itself. Although the Taita have adopted many aspects of Christian cosmology, which frame and filter their descriptions and accounts of lust, love, and romance, their adoptions only constitute a gloss over indigenous human sentiments. In short, the terminology reflects feelings of private experience that have always been present, if not warmly celebrated, in Taita culture.

An examination of East African folklore finds that there are only a few precontact tales of romance. Because folklorists initially showed some interest in narratives of subsistence and warfare tales, they did not collect very many love tales. The small number of love stories collected does not therefore mean that the sentiment was foreign to the Taita. It only suggests that the phenomenon was ignored by earlier students of Africa and, in particular, students of the Taita. When the folklore of the entire region is analyzed, I suspect that future folklorists will find the Taita to be correct in their contention that the lack of East African love stories is due to the failure of previous anthropologists to identify the presence of romantic love, and is, thus, more a product of ethnographic oversight than the lack of indigenous desire or interest.

The Ideal Mate: Beauty as a Factor in Love and Marriage

Observers of polygynous family life often ignore the fact that within the nuclear family each co-wife and her offspring form their own social unit. For centuries the Taita have practiced arranged marriages, which advance the interests of the larger family group. The criteria for these marriages seldom focus on an individual's physical beauty. Rather, the senior generation looks for evidence of health and an accommodating personality. Individual desire is deemed irrelevant. It is understood by everyone that the welfare of the family, and not the individual, is the primary objective of arranged marriages. Nevertheless, Taita males have definite ideas of female beauty, and beauty plays no small part in the selection of a mate. Although there are differences in opinion, there is a general consensus over what constitutes a beautiful woman. Many young men describe their ideal mate as possessing the following attributes:

A full face, with "bright eyes and a pretty nose that flares broad on the face." She should "have a full mouth and thick lips, with a large smile, white teeth, and fresh breath." Her neck should "possess smoothness and be thick near the shoulders." Together these features "make for a pleasant woman to look upon." In addition, a beautiful woman has soft skin and "delicate eyes and sharp cheeks (high cheek-bones)." The last feature is a sign of "a woman who will love you for life." Finally, her ears should be small and close to the head. The young males were all certain that these particular features of beauty are self-evident and, thus, universal.

Women's hair, never heretofore a specially expressed element of beauty among the Taita, today has a place in the attributes of beauty looked for by young men. Some young men expressed preference for the traditional close-cropped head, where the shape of the head is clearly seen and the hair is clean and shiny. Others preferred long hair, plated in some style resembling the European styles commonly seen in magazines. Either way, the face and neck must be accentuated.

The eyes, as mentioned, should be "delicate" and reflect what many young men claim is "the heart of the girl's mind." The darker the eyes, the better. Since the Taita are a combination of several different East African ethnic groups, some have light brown eye coloring while others exhibit the almost olive-shaped black eyes found among coastal peoples. It is the dark-eyed women that young men find so attractive. A young man in his early twenties told me, "Such eyes of a woman speak of love in late evening, just prior to the setting of the sun."

The ideal body shape of a beautiful female is hefty overall, with large breasts (for feeding children), thick legs, and small ankles. She should walk "as if floating in the air" and "she should smell of fresh flowers always." Her buttocks "should be round and firm, moving to the sway of her hips in such a manner as to appear to be in a dance as she walks." Finally, all agreed that the women must have a pleasing personality. Such a personality is a sign of great beauty.[1]

A Female View of Males as Love Objects

Taita females, also have an image of the "ideal" man. Young women (fifteen to twenty years old) spoke of the men they *would like* to marry, although most admitted it would be unlikely they would have such a husband. The ideal man for a few Taita women is someone who is honest and kind. Others thought the ideal man should be "tall and handsome." Everyone interviewed stressed that a husband should be intelligent and a good farmer/provider. Clearly, a male's physical attractiveness is not as important as how he interacts with his wife and how he treats her. Some of the informants, however, believed that a man could enhance his manliness if he bathed everyday (an activity Taita women do daily). A man should have "a strong look to his face, with no hair on it." Facial hair connotes a dirty person. Or as several informants put it, "white men have hair on their face and they are dirty for that reason."

The ideal man's eyes "should shine with life like the morning sun on the grasses." His mouth "should smile often to reveal his kind nature." One young woman told me, "Some men believe they must speak in a loud voice, but a man should speak in a low tone so others will respect him." His head "should have a close cut with the hair. It should be kept clean and carefully managed." Men should possess "a thick neck so as to carry his head in a proud manner."

Most women were not as forthcoming about the ideal male body (perhaps because I was male and a foreigner). Nevertheless, a few women of various ages did agree that a male must not have small genitals or a penis that is too large. In addition, "his arms and legs should show musculature, and he should be the dark color of the sky before sunrise (a copper brown or a reddish brown), with dark eyes."

In the main, both males and females hold different ideals of beauty and personality that influence the choice of lovers they select, or would select, if completely free to do so. Males emphasize physical attributes, whereas females, as in our society, focus on personality and social standing. Both Taita men and women prefer a lover who exhibits the proper cultural graces.

Love and Romance Among the Taita

My Taita informants distinguished between three kinds of love that are commonly found within their gender interactions outside of arranged marriages, from childhood through adult courtship rituals. Each kind has a different style of romantic expression. It must be noted that such emotions are considered by the Taita to have been present before European contact. Since contact occurred more than 140 years ago, it is difficult to corroborate my informants statements. It is important to note, however, that many older

Taita believe the introduction of English only provided convenient terms to express the emotions. I assume that myth and reality may cross somewhere back in time. The first kind of love is infatuation (what we might call puppy love), which is characterized by an irresponsible feeling of longing and deep attraction toward another person. It resembles in every way Western notions of passionate (or romantic) love. However, the Taita do not, as such, make this distinction. Moreover, it is the senior generation who insist that this type of love passion is nothing more than a misguided infatuation, "a kind of sickness." This kind of love tends to occur in the early stages of life (around ten to eleven years old), usually lasts only a few weeks or months, and then disappears forever.

A second notion of love closely resembles lust. This condition arises whenever someone desires another sexually. Although the Taita believe that relationships based entirely on sexual desire are a form of love, they acknowledge that this is not romantic love and seldom lasts for a long time.

For both men and women cultural restrictions in mate selection contribute to the production of erotic fantasies. Many young (eighteen- through twenty-four-year-old) Taita males, for example, experience a sexual desire for a woman (in their thirties through forties) just slightly younger than their mothers. To fulfill their sexual fantasy, some males engage prostitutes in this age group. Conversely, young females (fifteen through seventeen) prefer males who are their age mates (eighteen through twenty-two) but whom they will rarely marry.

The third kind of love is called romantic love, which is used to connote those relationships that combine passion and enduring affection. It differs from infatuation in being a more permanent affectionate bond. The Taita, at the beginning of the relationship, however, cannot determine whether it is driven by infatuation or genuine romantic sentiment. In this way the Taita notion of romantic love incorporates images of companionate love (or attachment love) and passionate love (or romantic love).

The Taita, however, never refer—at least in conversation—to this kind of love sentiment as companionship love but insist instead on calling it romantic love. Romantic love, the "love for life," or "love out of the heart," etc., is love that the younger Taita can often observe between a father and a "favorite wife." It is based upon deep admiration and intense affection for one another.

Many young informants believe it is "the best kind of love" and, as such, constitutes one of the primary life goals. Young males readily pointed out that this love can be a motive for fathers (i.e., any male relative who is in their father's generation) marrying a second, third, or fourth wife. Young females also spoke in envy over the "luck" of older siblings who married for love. Even when a couple involved cannot marry, they often continued their affair for years. Several parents informed me that they knew of many such affairs in the community. One important point is that love is considered a valid motive for entering into both a short- and a long-term relationship. Therefore, not every Taita marriage is organized around a concern with alliance building or economic necessity. Marriages can and do arise out of momentary infatuation and long-lasting romantic commitment.

Lovers and Other Strangers: Affairs and Marriage

Taita culture is organized around a patrilineal descent and residence system that honors, as an ideal, the larger lineage over the individual interests. The Taita are not atypical in this regard. According to David Maybury-Lewis,

> Many traditional societies recognize and value the kind of passion that *our* love stories are made of. They encourage it, but they contrive to keep it distinct from their formal marriage arrangements. They try to ensure that it does not destroy the lives of the lovesick or those around them, and above all, they try to prevent personal passion from disturbing the social order (1992:100).

Unmarried Taita are not allowed to carry their love interests too far. To do otherwise might undermine their commitment to the family. Taita men therefore strive primarily, but not always, to meet their familial obligations in the first marriage and thus fulfill their duties to the lineage. Once those duties are achieved, however, romantic passion can, and often does, become a primary consideration in selecting a new wife. This sentiment can arise both inside and outside of marriage. In fact, several Taita, who had arranged marriages, were romantically indifferent to their wife while passionately committed to their "outside lover." Many Taita admit to wanting, from time to time, to be involved with a particular person, but few admit to having done so. When these "affairs of the heart" did arise, however, they were unexpected and often directed toward someone unattainable. One informant remarked that "it can happen that your heart is lost to one you can never marry, but you love that person for your life." A middle-aged parent concurred, saying that "this notion is not a rare one." Many older men expressed their love for a woman who "belonged to another man." Some informants assured me that they had lovers elsewhere or that some of the children I had interviewed were the offspring of lovers who "played in the forest together." Such affairs of love and romance are not new to Africa or the Taita Hills.

David Maybury-Lewis, speaking of affairs among the Wodaabe of West Africa, notes the commonality and acceptance of them, and summarizes Wodaabe attitudes meant to help maintain social order: "What the eyes do not see did not happen, which means that rumors and suspicions have to be ignored" (1992:102). The Taita are extremely covert in their extramarital affairs and they have a somewhat elaborate set of rules similar to those found among the Wodaabe. Taita lovers, being discreet, seldom even hint at duplicity in public. Whenever they meet they act as if they are strangers. Or, to paraphrase Maybury-Lewis, "What people cannot imagine cannot be rumor or suspicion."

In sum, Taita seek to balance individual desires and family duty by insisting there are different motives for marriage.[2] They also strive to allow individual desires to be expressed without undermining the prevailing social order. The first and, perhaps, the second marriage may honor family obligations; thereafter a man's lust and/or love interest *can* constitute the primary motivation for taking a new bride. In this way, both the so-called lovesick that Maybury-Lewis discusses and the needs of "the social order" are fulfilled.

Old Ladies and Old Men Tell of Better Days

I came to know many older people (sixty to eighty years old) in my travels around the Taita Hills. Whenever I engaged in conversations about love and romance with younger people, older people noted that they had either experienced or knew someone who had been involved in a romantic encounter in their youth. What follows is a brief sample of Taita senior citizens' remembrances of love lost.

A woman, in her middle seventies, reported that she was infatuated with three or four men at different times during her early teenage years. Her father had, however, arranged a marriage for her with one of *his* peers. She had eight children. She recalled:

> A man from a highland village (nearer to her own age) was my lover. My husband would leave me for months at a time, and I would travel at night to a place we [she and her lover] would meet and "play in the forest" for plenty of time. My husband never caught me, and only one of my sisters (co-wives) knew of this. She would not reveal me because I had once caught her with her lover in the act.

Several old men remembered their affairs in sharp detail, as though they happened yesterday rather than some forty or fifty years earlier. One gentleman, nearly eighty years of age, described his fourth wife:

> She was the wife of my heart. We were almost similar in age. I loved her in the early days when she was married to another. Her family had arranged it that way. When she was widowed and I passed my stages and become an elder, I married her out of love. She and I had love. I would sit with her for hours on that hill (pointing to a hill behind his homestead). I could look at her and she at me—no words would pass, just a smile. We did this for several years before she died.

A woman, also in her seventies, stressed (through an interpreter) that "even when I was a young girl, women were having babies before marriage. And others had lovers in the forest after marriage. That which we speak of at the moment is not a new thing. It has always been here."

In this informal survey older people were quite open about their views on lust and love. Some felt it was acceptable for people to experiment with sex. Others thought it was rude and bad for people, especially girls. Young girls who become pregnant by lovers before marriage often reduced their bride price. Still, such "accidents" do not usually prevent the girl from entering into an arranged marriage. All of the older people I spoke with agreed that this is no longer as serious a situation as it was when they were young. Time, apparently, has changed the attitudes toward unwed mothers.

The Politics of Romance Among the Taita

In the literature on African polygynous systems, there is some mention of the favorite wife, but little is detailed as to what makes her "favorite." Is this status related to love, economic arrangement, family association, or clan politics? The Taita believe such a concept evolves around "love out of the heart." Some males indicated that a favorite wife could include some economic attachment to prime landholdings or business dealings; only a few men in the older generation conceded such economic considerations in the designation of favorite wife. Instead, as a rule, most Taita asserted that favorite status goes to the woman who is the man's true love, or, in some cases, to the woman whom the husband finds more sexually pleasing. Either love or sexuality could be the basis for the status, but most Taita men and women believed it indicated true love.

Another consideration must account for the role of the favorite wife within the context of the co-wife relationship. She must get along with the other women of the family with whom she shares a husband and a life. Co-wives usually try to maintain cooperative unions with one another. They attempt to secure the other wives as allies, attempting to set up clear working relationships while striving for peace and harmony within the larger family unit. This serves them well in times of emotional and physical difficulties (i.e., sickness, birth, or the death of a child). The wife who has married out of love may be the husband's favorite wife, and the husband may love her more than any of the others, but he cannot allow her to supplant the authority and status of the other wives, especially that of the first wife. Other members of the extended family will also not allow it. Such an obvious show of disrespect and breach of decorum toward the first wife, her family, those other wives who came before the favorite, and their families would challenge the social order prized by the Taita. It is important to note that the wives' families share in the favorite's honor or dishonor after marriage. For a wife to loose her honor, or status, within her husband's family is a loss of status and honor for her birth family as well. Since these other marriages were arranged and, in the course of daily life, formed alliances with other family groups, it is extremely vital to foster good relations with a wife's family. Loss of honor can also result in a loss of a business partnership.

It is often reported that a husband will not endeavor to replace one wife's status within his family, or her position in the extended family, with his favorite. Men seek to keep control over their polygynous families by maintaining as much harmony between wives as possible. A "wife out of love" would find it difficult to disrupt a family unit by manipulating her husband's feelings toward her for political gain inside the family. This is precisely where the Taita ideal of personality as part of female beauty comes into play, forestalling any serious wifely conflict. The favorite wife should be as pleasing as possible around the other wives to show her husband that she is indeed "beautiful."

Sometimes, however, co-wives just do not get along with one another. In such cases wives are kept in separate locations or homesteads rather than in the single compound that is the norm. In this instance the woman married out of love is often given special gifts of land, animals to tend and use for her needs, and other compensations for not being high in the family's female hierarchy.

However, a woman married out of love is not likely to cause disruption.

She knows she is at a slight disadvantage. The other wives know that the husband regards her as special and that he places her above them in romantic sentiment. It is to the favorite wife's advantage to hide her feelings and maintain a cooperative attitude toward co-wives. To experience constant attack from two or three other women, with whom one *must* cooperate on a daily basis, can be very damaging to her sensibilities as well as disrupt her status in the extended family. In spite of the harmonious ideal and pragmatic orientation to daily interaction, each co-wife pursues her own interests, with passionate love often being a very important concern.

The Taita have adopted a fail-safe system that serves to control, and thus minimize, the expression of this sentiment. Because the first wife has certain rights, privileges, and obligations that are never transferred to the other co-wives, she is able to maintain an active position within the family. Within the extended family group first wives are likely to be mother to all younger co-wives. Moreover, it is only after the first wife's economic needs are met that the other co-wives' economic needs can be discussed. Given the first wife's enormous fund of power, a favorite wife must move very cautiously.

Conclusion

The earliest missionary writings are unabashedly ethnocentric and focus more on the "lust of the flesh" than on exploring other human sentiments such as empathy, cooperation, and love. In time indigenous populations in Africa, especially the Taita, became the victims of erroneous observations and, thus, incorrect cultural interpretations. Some missionary writings reinforced the idea that the African was incapable of experiencing any other love emotion than lust. Thus, the ethnocentric assumptions that produced a Western racist ideology also contributed to strengthening the belief that love and romance were a European contribution to human history (cf. Jankowiak and Fisher 1992).

When Taita behavior is examined within the context of sexual encounters, it is apparent that they exhibit thoughts and concerns typically, though not necessarily of equal intensity, found among the average American teenager. Accordingly, Taita males expressed fear of rejection while Taita females giggled at the prospect of having an affair with a man *they* deemed "handsome" or "manly." In this way, lust, love, and romance are in the air on any weekend night in the hills of Taita, where people are seldom surprised when someone marries for love of the heart.

NOTES

The information that forms this paper was collected in 1981 over a twelve month period among the Taita of Kenya. The research was partially funded by National Science Foundation.

1. The Taita see personality as an intricate part of physical beauty. An ugly personality distracts from a pretty face or a charming body. Older men informed me how it was sometimes necessary to "beat a pleasing personality into a woman, especially a young woman who does not like the arrangements her family has made for her." Thus, a pleasing female personality is one that is of little or no trouble to a man. She is kind and thoughtful toward his relatives. She is respectful to him in public and serves him proper meals. She is pleasant for him to be around, and she acknowledges that he is the head of the household. Many Taita men repeatedly qualified their statement that they would never find such an ideal woman. In fact, I observed a few relationships where men were obviously attracted to women who did not, in any way, possess these attributes.

2. Kissing and fondling appear to be European-derived contributions to Taita culture. The older generation believes that both these methods of showing affection came to the Taita Hills with Europeans. I cannot refute this with any hard data, except to say that fondling seems quite common among East African peoples and, therefore, as a practice or a prelude to lovemaking, it may have its origins among the peoples of this region and was not therefore imported by Europeans.

REFERENCES

Clark, H. E. 1890. *The Story of Friends Mission in Madagascar.* London: Friends Missionary Society.

Fraser, D. 1928. *The New Africa.* New York: Missionary Education Movement of the United States and Canada.

George, K. 1958. "The Civilized West Looks at Primitive Africa: 1400–1800." *Isis* 49:62–72.

Hulstaert, G. 1938. *Le Marriage des Nkunde.* Bruxelles: Given Campenhout.

Jablow, A., and D. Hammond. 1977. *The Myth of Africa.* New York: Library of Social Science.

Jankowiak, W., and E. Fischer. 1992. "A Cross-Cultural Perspective on Romantic Love." *Ethnology* 31(2):149–155.

Johnson, H. H. 1911. *The Opening of Africa.* New York: University Books.

Kenyatta, J. 1953. *Facing Mount Kenya.* London: Seeker and Warburg.

Lovett, R. 1899. *History of the London Missionary Society.* London: Oxford University Press.

Lugard, F. D. 1904. *Uganda and Its People.* Edinburgh: Mansfield.

— 1922. *The Duel Mandate in British Tropical Africa.* Edinburgh: Blackwood.

MacDonald, A. J. M. 1916. *Trade, Politics, and Christianity in Africa and the East.* New York: Longman's Green.

Maybury-Lewis, D. 1992. *Millennium: Tribal Wisdom and the Modern World*. New York. 165
    Viking.

Mazrui, A. 1986. *The Africans: A Triple Heritage*. Boston: Little, Brown.

Noble, F. P. 1899. *The Redemption of Africa*. New York: Fleming H. Revell.

Parsons, E. 1906. *Christus Liberator: An Outline Study of Africa*. London: Macmillan.

Thomas, J. 1885. *Through Masai Land: Eastern Equatorial Africa*. London: Houghton,
    Mifflin.

Romantic Passion in the People's Republic of China

WILLIAM JANKOWIAK

The first time I saw her between her embroidered curtains she looked at me with eyes of love.

• SIXTEENTH-CENTURY CHINESE POEM

The predominant assumption among a number of scholars of love and sexuality in East Asia is that the Chinese are uninterested in love but not in the erotic. Denis de Rougement, for example, claimed that for "the Chinese the problem of love does not exist. [Their] needs are of the body, not satisfaction of the emotions" (1974:i). Other researchers have suggested that the Chinese have the ability to experience love as a tender attachment, but it is "largely associated with relationships between men rather than between the sexes" (Beach and Tesser 1988:331). Grant summed up the view of many non-China historians when he stated that "in traditional Oriental cultures, sexual love based on appreciation of the uniqueness of personality did not exist. . . . [As for the] Chinese, [their] lyrics do not sing of the one and only beloved that lives once and will never be found a second time" (Grant 1976:163). Concurring, Francis Hsu asserts that Chinese cultural tradition binds the individual emotionally into a web of dependency on others, thereby defusing the intensity of an individual's emotional experience. This dependency undermines the individual's proclivity to fantasize about a lover or the erotic. He further contends that the Chinese are situation-oriented, in contrast to Americans who are individually oriented (Hsu 1981). Hsu's views have received support from the research of Godwin Chu (1985), whose study of mate choice found that the Chinese do not *list* romance as a criterion for marriage. From this finding he concludes that Chinese males define themselves by their role relationships, which results in the creation of a "very little independent self" (Chu 1985:258). From these and related studies it has often been inferred that the Chinese are incapable of or are closed to feelings and desires that are independent of the social context or customary expectation. By this logic the social context circumscribes an individual's experience, and a simplistic one-to-one correspondence is assumed, implying that the internal life of the Chinese is one dimensional, inhibited, and heavily dependent on societal values.

These assumptions not only undermine the production of a romantic tradition but also ensure the muting of romantic attraction. By overlooking or underestimating the intensity and frequency of romantic attraction in Chinese society, the remarkable continuity of romantic love found in Chinese literature has been little appreciated, and the reality and the meaning behind its continuity and transformation have been underestimated, if not misconceived.

For my purpose romantic or passionate love will be defined as having three components: the idealization of the other, its occurrence within an erotic context, and the expectation of its enduring into the future (Lindholm 1988). Passionate love stands in sharp contrast to the companionship phase of love (sometimes referred to as attachment), which is characterized by the growth of a more peaceful, comfortable, and fulfilling kind of love relationship; it is a strong and enduring affection built upon long-term association (Hatfield 1988; Liebowitz 1983).

Romance, Literature, and the Individual Within Imperial China

There had always been in Imperial China two literary currents: that written in an elite literary language and that in the speech of everyday life. The former, embraced by the scholarly few, emphasized poetry, history, and moral philosophy; the latter, embraced by the uneducated, generally produced love stories told by professional storytellers, using colloquial language, in the marketplace and urban teahouses (Eberhard 1965; Li 1969; Waley 1948; Zheng 1986). In short, each literary genre highlighted and celebrated a different notion of personhood.

The typical Chinese love story of this second genre is characterized by interruptions or incongruities that are made manifest between conflicting forces within an individual's household (Li 1969). A general perusal of love stories from other historical eras reveals the personal anguish of people torn between filial duty and romantic desire. The T'ang dynasty (618–907), for example, produced numerous short tales known as *chuan qi* (strange stories), which were considered a "lower form of literature than the classical essays of contemporary scholars" (Zheng 1986:5). These describe real-life experiences of men and women involved in romantic entanglements (Lee 1984). In these stories one can see many of the attributes common to romantic infatuation. For example, in *The Wandering Soul*, Chen Xuanyou describes two people who, forbidden by the boy's father to marry, remain unwaveringly committed to each other and, in spite of considerable anxiety and agony, find their love withstanding the difficult passage of time. In *Ren the Fox Fairy* a fox transformed into a beautiful girl falls so passionately in love with her human lover that not even the threat of death can make her unfaithful to him. *Prince Huo's Daughter* highlights the love between the famous poet Li Yi and a singsong girl (i.e., who performed for men in tea houses) named Huo Xiayu. It is a tale of unrequited love and abandonment in which the girl, waiting in vain for Li Yi to return, falls ill and dies of a broken heart (Zheng 1986). These tales and others like them illustrate the pervasiveness of romantic love in China and its place in the Chinese mind.

The master-concubine relationship is yet another domain in which to examine the salience of romantic infatuation in daily life in Imperial China. Because only the wealthy men could afford to buy a concubine, this relationship was unique to that strata, and was sometimes characterized by greater emotional intensity than that between husband and wife. Levy notes that

> a man often chose his own concubine. Therefore there was more opportunity for the relationship to be based on patterns of romantic love than in the case of a wife chosen by someone else, and the emotional intensity of the husband-concubine relationship might not only be positive and great, but might exceed that of the husband and wife. (1968:201–202)

These stories and poems—indeed much of the entire literary tradition—reveal that the Chinese always knew of the pathos and power of romantic attraction and attachment and how they can lead to feelings of helpless passion, jealousy, yearning for exclusiveness, and unrequited suffering. The Chinese realized the conflict inherent in the struggle between individual desire and social obligation. Because the family was acutely aware of the destructive power of passion, and the threat it posed to their authority and personal interests, the family often went to extraordinary lengths to insure that its offspring would not haphazardly or impulsively fall in love. In addition to restricting, not always successfully, contact between members of the opposite sex (Furth 1987:3), some romantic tales served as morality tales designed to teach the younger generation that love was not an end in itself but a by-product of marriage, the formation of the family, and the continuance of society. Those individuals who violated this dictum were "branded shameless and immoral" (Wu 1987:27). In this way romantic love (the discourse of desire) became interweaved with ethics (the discourse of duty) (Nash 1986:205). From a reading Chinese popular literature it is evident, however, that the conflicts and tensions continued, despite the force of cautionary tales and societal pressure and, thus, from the Confucian perspective, the individual lessons had to be relearned. The consistency of this literature as a cautionary statement is evidence of the very persistence of the individual impulse toward the romantic and the erotic. The individual's socialization was never as complete as Confucian doctrine, family expectation, and contemporary public opinion suggest.

Love and Romance in Urban China

The idealization of romantic involvement in contemporary Chinese literature and film is remarkably similar to its treatment in Imperial China. Although Hsu has claimed that "the Western idea of romantic love has not had much of an impact on young adults in China" (1981:50), there have been, since 1976, over five hundred new magazines published in China, a large number of them focusing on the problems of romance, dating, and marriage. The other entertainment industries—television and film—have also increased the production of programs exploring romantic love in daily life. The contemporary love story differs from that written in Imperial China by disregarding the salience of the supernatural. However, in presenting love as an ideal and a virtue, they remain strikingly similar. The contemporary love tales, moreover, reflect the implicit value the Chinese place on the romantic experience and reveal, under the right circumstances, the proclivity to become preoccupied with love itself. It is not uncommon to hear Chinese discussing, savoring, and, at times, glorifying love's positive qualities. A woman's letter to the editor in the *China Daily* (November 18, 1982) captures the meaning that love holds for most Chinese. She wrote that "love is the only true friendship that can keep lasting understanding among couples." A thirty-three-year-old male informant believed that love is that "special feeling that only humans, and not animals, can have for one another."

Though the Chinese folk definition of love emphasizes companionship and enduring love, it is significant that the thematic treatment of romantic love in film and literature and the emphasis in personal accounts focus exclusively on the "attraction" phase of "falling in love" (*tan liang ai*). For instance, between May and August of 1987 I observed thirty-five different television programs depicting a variety of familiar love themes: the fate of lovers torn between parental demands and their own personal desires, love triangles in which two women love the same man (three weeks later the roles were reversed and two men loved the same woman), a young person who secretly is in love with someone but is afraid the other does not even recognize him, old friends who like one another but then discover they are in love, etc. Contemporary literature is no less wide-ranging in its treatment of love and romance within both urban and rural settings. Most popular magazine stories address men and women's anguish, loss, and exuberance over encountering, losing, and again finding true love. Significantly, it is a rare story or film that explores the attachment phase of love. The stuff of contemporary popular literature remains the fragileness of love, the magic of romance, and the uncertainty of commitment. The Chinese, like Americans, simply prefer love stories of conflict and anguish, crushes and broken hearts to those on the satisfactions and problems of maintaining a stable marital relationship. This fact is not lost on party officials, who feel that the younger generation's willingness to lose themselves in the love quest is silly and counterproductive to the interests of society and its own ideals. In 1981 a leading party official, Hu Yaobang, publicly proclaimed that, though the party was "not opposed to love, it was important to remember that other things were just as, and in many instances, more important than love" (*China Daily*, November 1981). Unsurprisingly, those "in love" continue to ignore the party's proclamation. The party's role today is analogous to Confucianism in the past: it counsels restraint and self-control in the face of the pull of romantic love.

Romantic Passion in Styles of Courtship

In urban China today there are two dating styles involving different conventions that can be called formal and informal and are complementary. Both are entered into with the intention of realizing either an immediate practical gain, enjoyment, or marriage. Formal dating (or courtship) differs from informal dating in its emphasis on normative rules, social judgment, and conventional standards for articulating romantic involvement. It is conducted according to rules that organize dating into a semiritualistic sequence of private and semipublic meetings characterized by incremental increases in the public expression of commitment, usually resulting in marriage. Informal dating, however, is pursued according to very practical rules, based on shrewd common sense and situational standards, which constitute solutions to particular problems that arise from dating in Chinese society. These rules are sometimes provisionally formed by the parties to avoid the pressure of social expectations or the disapproval of one's community. Informal dating may or may not culminate in marriage. Informal dating begins in secrecy, appears to be ad hoc or accidental, and is characterized by public denial of any intimate involvement. In general, informal dating is conducted by individuals who truly love one another but are restricted by prior obligations (e.g., already married, parental or work-unit disapproval, etc.) from publicly acknowledging or expressing their involvement. Within the formal style there can be what we call courtship (a relationship oriented toward marriage) or just plain going out with no stated intent to marry. In the case of formal dating, although an individual may use the services of an introduction agency or friendship networks to find a suitable mate, it should not be construed that this style is devoid of romantic excitement or aspirations. Once a person decides that a particular individual fits their ideal or comes close to most of their criteria, there is a pronounced tendency to fantasize about the other, which can often result in one becoming overwhelmed with romantic anticipation. Romantic passion may arise in either form of courtship and is characterized by emotional intensity (and a tendency to quick shifts within it), a kind of anxiety, expressions of romantic endearment, and the idealization of the other. The two styles differ in the domain of public expression but not necessarily the intensity of involvement. Attraction is the measure of the involvement.

Discussions with informants revealed that dating (i.e., the attraction phase), whether formal or informal, was remembered with mixed emotions. Some informants recalled it as a pleasant, enjoyable, albeit somewhat anxiety-filled experience that they did not want to relinquish; other informants were more ambivalent and expressed relief that it did not last forever. More women (sixteen out of twenty-eight) than men (nine out of twenty-nine) felt that this phase was enjoyable. The women who did not enjoy dating tended to have come from situations that they did not control: either they were involved with a married man or someone who was reluctant to make a commitment, both situations over which they had little real influence. In these instances the dating process was remembered as an acutely painful experience. Regardless of the form of dating, once the relationship had been successfully negotiated and the individual provided with the belief he or she had found the ideal mate or true love, the engaged individual tended to enter into a passionate experience. The vividness of the romantic experience was strong, often deeply memorable. For example, one thirty-three-year-old male intellectual fondly recalled the early stages of his informal courtship:

> At first it was terrible. I didn't know what to do. I thought my wife was the most beautiful girl I'd ever seen and that she wouldn't want me. I worried and worried about this. Then I asked her if she wanted to see me again. I truly believed she would refuse. But she did not. I was so happy for days and days I thought of nothing else but how much I loved her.

In romantic love the line separating anxiety and excitement is thin and easily crossed. A twenty-eight-year-old female worker, who had distantly admired her future husband for some time, readily recalled the initial phases of her formal courtship:

> After being introduced I was not disappointed but feared that I wasn't pretty enough for him. When he didn't call on me for several days, I sank into a deep depression that only lifted when he asked to see me again. After a few more encounters we were all but married. It was a wonderful time. Everything was easy and happy. Although I am satisfied with my marriage, we seem more busy and distant.

Another female worker, age twenty-four, remembered slowly responding to her future husband's overture for emotional involvement:

> He came to see me every other day and gave me a few small [i.e., inexpensive] but thoughtful gifts. At first I didn't have any excitement in my heart, but slowly I found myself starting to like him. After a month or so I found myself becoming excited in anticipation of his arrival. In fact, I even might have dreamed of him. When he asked me to be his girlfriend I was very happy. I knew that I loved him very much and that I wanted to marry him.

Previous marital experience does not appear to lessen the intensity of falling in love. Romance is romance, regardless. For divorced men and women wanting to remarry, their behavior and experience during a second courtship closely resembled that of their first. For example, a forty-four-year-old male confided to me that his girlfriend had "lost ten pounds because she is in love with me." He added that "she told me she can't sleep and misses me." When I was introduced to her she barely acknowledged my presence but stared at him and laughed at whatever he said, repeating in a very low singsong voice that he was "so intelligent and handsome." Her demeanor resembled that of a young unmarried girl who had just "fallen in love." Clearly, the courtship was a deep-felt, intensely emotional experience for her.

Not every romantic experience results in courtship. For example, a twenty-five-year-old woman explained how she came to develop a secret but intense infatuation for her former instructor:

> When I was eighteen years old, I knew a man who was thirty-eight. He helped me study. I was too young to start seeing men, so I had to keep my feelings secret. I remember that whenever we studied together I was acutely aware of his presence, especially his smell. He smelled like a man. When he talked, his saliva would hit me and I liked the sensation. I didn't think about having sex with him, but I was aware that I was very interested in him and that I wanted to be associated with him. I still think of him.

At the same time, courtship does not always invoke romantic attraction. For example, a forty-two-year-old, divorced male middle school teacher was courting a woman who was not particularly interested in him. He explained how he felt when he discovered that his "girlfriend" refused to become emotionally involved:

> I wanted this girl. She was thirty-four years old and kind of pretty. We had been writing for a few weeks and I asked her if she wanted to see me. After a few weeks she wrote back and asked me to come see her in Harbin (a city over one thousand miles to the northeast of Huhhot). I agreed. We spent the week together going different places. However, I knew she wasn't interested in me when she refused in the park to have her picture taken with me. What's more, every time she thought there was someone who might see her, she would raise her umbrella so that no one could see who was walking with me. I had hoped that our encounter would turn into something more significant. But I was cautious. I could tell she wasn't that interested. I think I am doomed to live alone and be sad.

A thirty-four-year-old female, who first met her husband when she was thirty-two, and desperate to marry, admitted that she never felt anything special for him. For her formal courtship was "a necessary path to marriage and to do what was expected of you." It did not by itself engender romantic passion or enduring love.

It is difficult to know with any certainty if premarital sex is more prevalent in urban China today than in the past. It is clear, however, that in the 1980s single Chinese women under the right circumstances do become sexually involved with lovers. They engage in premarital sex because it suggests an implicit obligation to marry, which is reinforced in the event of pregnancy and thus is not perceived as a serious problem; the inherent power of romantic involvement invokes equity and compels reciprocity. Those men whose primary interest is not marriage but seduction, during both formal and informal dating, manipulate these tacit factors in order to request or appeal for greater sexual intimacy. For example, one twenty-four-year-old male, who had seduced—at least—four women, explained that his strategy was simple and straightforward:

> I always use the direct approach. I tell them that I am available and want to settle down. However, my mother wants me to marry a hometown girl who I do not love. I therefore insist that if she agrees to go out with me that we do so secretly, as I have a number of people who know me, and I don't want them telling my mother that I am seeing another woman. After a few additional meetings they agree to go out with me, and when I tell them that I love them they seem to fall in love with me. After that it is relatively easy to go to bed with them.

Another married male, thirty-nine years old, who had seduced a number of divorced women and had gained an unfavorable reputation as philanderer, enjoyed discussing his "success" with women. He candidly admitted that "women, compared to men, tend to be more modest and guilty. So it is necessary to talk about love and true feelings, even when you only like them but do not love them." He felt that "divorced or married women were easier because they were no longer afraid of sex and were lonely for male companionship." He insisted that women enjoyed and, in many cases, demanded that he couch his request for sexual intimacy in terms of romantic endearment. Clearly, the informal style of dating is used not only to protect romance from social censure, but can be manipulated for sexual reasons as well. What is more, the manipulation can be mutual.

The seducer explicitly invokes the folk notion that romantic feelings are genuine and should be expressed through greater sexual intimacy, coupled with the cultural expectation that people who have sex together will marry, to justify himself and his desires and reassure women of his honorable intentions. Needless to say, women are not entirely fooled by this style. Their motives for becoming sexually or otherwise involved during informal rather than formal dating arise from either the preference to delay making a commitment, to become pregnant and force a reluctant man into marriage, or to obtain a specfic benefit that can only be achieved from a clandestine relationship. For example, a twenty-one-year-old female worker who had been attending a number of private dance parties told me that

> I enjoy men, but I am too young to marry and I do not want to make a commitment. However, I still want to be around men. The best men are married. Because I know they will not leave their wives and that they will be very nice to me, I am not afraid of them. Certainly I kiss and dance with them; however, I do not go to bed with them.

Another woman, a thirty-two-year-old clerk, remembered that she agreed to sleep with her boyfriend only because

> I was afraid that he would find someone else. I knew he was a good man, and I wanted him. I tried everything. I told him how much I loved him and how I knew we were meant to be happy. He was touched, and when he wanted to sleep with me how could I refuse? Besides, I thought, if I went to bed with him, that he would have to marry me, and he did.

A twenty-four-year-old woman admitted to sleeping with a number of different men because "I like the smell of men and I enjoy the things they say to me. I like to sit around and chat and hug and, yes, sometimes go to bed with them." When I asked her if she ever wanted to marry them, she replied,

> Well, of course. But I am an independent woman and I don't want just *any* man. I want a man who will be powerful and important and interesting. That kind of man you need to capture carefully. I think the men I sleep with will make a commitment, especially after they understand how much I am willing to love them.

Chinese men and women differ only in the basis for the idealization of the other, not, it seems, in the experience itself. The not uncommon expectation that romantic feelings and sexual intimacy will induce or lead to an emotional commitment can also lead to confusion, bitter disappointment, and, in some instances, as I will show, to tragedy. The degree and variety of the conflicting desires, understandings, and manipulations among both sexes is a measure of how prevalent informal dating is in Huhhot and how open-ended it can be despite family, community, and state.

Fragility of the Individual in the Courtship Process

The act of falling in love has negative (or destructive) as well as positive (or rewarding) aspects. Informants concentrated on the glory of love and romantic involvement; the other side of love—rejection—though acknowledged, is avoided in general conversation. However, the possibility of rejection by a lover is a very real option that everyone acknowledges. In many ways abandonment by a lover was seen as more devastating than divorce. Lindholm (1988) notes that suicide, from a lover's rejection or frustrated marriage plans, is an excellent marker for assessing the predominance of romantic idealization within a particular society. Nothing better illustrates the paramount importance of romantic idealization and involvement in contemporary China than to explore how the Chinese react to romantic rejection.

The fragility of the individual within a romantic context as well as the importance of the romantic ideal were aptly confirmed after seventy-three informants (across a range of economic, social, and ethnic backgrounds) admitted that they would feel more devastated and suicidal if the person they were engaged to (as opposed to their spouse) left them. Whenever informants recalled the experience of rejection or abandonment, the salience of romance was poignantly revealed. One thirty-five-year-old, noncollege-educated informant captured the intensity, anxiety, and essence of romantic involvement when he instructed me in the potential psychological terror that is often associated with the process of courtship:

> You do not understand Chinese customs. We aren't like Americans. We don't have opportunities to meet women like in America. Maybe you go to work where there are two unmarried women on your floor. You see them day after day. Maybe you become a little excited by them. If you are given an introduction and she agrees to see you again, you are almost engaged. This may be the first time you have thought about a woman. You become sexually excited when you see her. All those little dreams you have had about sex center on her. She is going to be your wife. You feel happy, anxious, and sexually aroused. During that time she is the center of your life. After you are married you have accomplished that goal. After sex, it is not as profound as before. If she died, you would be sad but you would not be devastated. However, if that girl leaves you when you are courting her, it can be terrible. You feel like everything in the world has been taken away from you.

When I asked, "Why is it that important?" he continued,

You just don't understand Chinese customs. It is not like America. You cannot run around. You must stay with one girl. That girl is the center of your life. She is special. When I was in Lanzhou I lived with four men. We annoyed each other. Then I met that dancer. She was pretty. She liked me. It was the first time I ever loved a girl. I wanted her. I desired her. I had to have her. When she left me for another man, I was crazy. I cried and cried, and I might have thought of killing myself.

Though the opportunities for romantic involvement may not be as plentiful, the effects are the same. A female informant, aged twenty-eight, summed up the feelings of her gender and age cohort by noting that because dating was a monumental experience it demanded that

you put everything into it. So that the other person becomes your life. For him to leave you when you are involved with him is crushing. It is an abandonment that is difficult to get over. When you are married you have obligations. The mystery is over. You aren't the same people.

The emotional investment, the sense of deep personal involvement in the dating phase is frequently enormous and excruciating.

The following case history movingly illustrates the felt absence of control and the risk of loss of identity in a state of preoccupation that marks a major characteristic of romantic involvement. A young college-educated woman whom I had known for over a year regularly confided to me and my research assistant her thoughts and anxieties about a host of concerns. After we had established a trusting friendship, she informed me that she might be becoming involved with a man. The following is from my field notes and captures the uncertainty and speed and terror that falling in love holds for many, if not all, Chinese.

4–3–83

I met a man named Chen in my hometown. He was very nice and we talked for sometime. The next day I left to return to Huhhot and he walked me to the train station.

4–9–83

I received a letter from Chen. This is the first letter he sent me. In the letter he told me something about his work and what he thought about the future. When I went home my first impression of him is that he is clever, honest, and a tremendous talker. When I asked my parents if I could continue seeing him, they said, "Of course."

4–14–83

> We don't know each other very well so we have to write more letters in order to improve our feelings. He asked me to bring some books for him but when I went to the store they were sold out. His subject is mathematics, but in his spare time I find he likes to read history and literature. His interests are wide.

5–2–83

> I received a letter today from my mother. She told me about Chen and said that I'm old enough to marry. I don't think so. Everyone in the family likes Chen. I don't know if I do or not. He is an honest boy. I've only known him for less than a month. . . . We will have to talk about a lot of things. If not, we must part immediately.

5–10–83

> I've been on my bed for most of the day. I didn't make a sound, but my heart is not calm. What am I thinking? Why am I so uncomfortable? Why am I just lying on the bed? I know why. I haven't received a letter from Chen in over a week.

5–16–83

> I'm so happy. I received a letter from him. Just like me——he is busy with his work.

6–3–83

> I returned home and we talked all the time. Now I can say we love each other. I never thought *love* was a great meaningful word. I only think it arouses dreams and romance, like in the novels. Now I believe in love. Sometimes I think I am a strange girl because I've met many boys before. When someone asked me to marry them, I felt angry and hated them, even if they had good jobs and were good-looking. Now I am attracted to Chen and love him deeply. How surprised I am! In the past my friends said I had no feelings. Now I can say I will give my boyfriend all my heart——my love and everything that belongs to me.

6–17–83

> Chen hasn't written to me. I think he has found someone else. He has refused to answer my letters for so long. I think he doesn't want to make friends with me. Maybe it is too hard for him to say that he doesn't love me. He should speak the truth. I'm not a little girl. I know how to act even if this is the first time I made friends with a boy. I think love is a terrible thing.

6–30–83

Chen still hasn't written. I had such wonderful dreams of the future. I now know that all is failure. I can't bear life. All my interests in life have disappeared. I find I am so poor, so sad. I know I shouldn't have such thoughts and I should study harder. But I think the future is dark.

The young woman's emotional torment is common to the romantic experience. It is a product of two factors—idealization and uncertainty—which later substantially contribute to a person's sense of illusion and deprivation. The idealization heightens the expectation and the pitch of intensity; experience is keener. The uncertainty drives the pitch of emotional intensity from one extreme to another, exaggerating the sense of deprivation or absence. In this sense the essence of romantic love is anxiety. Or, in the young woman's words, "I think love is a terrible thing." This uncomfortable state of arousal ultimately gives way to either a commitment to marry or an agreement to terminate the relationship. No longer caught in an existential crisis of doubt and uncertainty, anxiety ceases, as does the intensity of the romantic involvement. The triumph of romantic sentiment as a basis for marriage is not without its cost. What may be most significant about this diary is its lack of cultural specificity. If one was not told otherwise, one could easily imagine its author as American or European. From a historical viewpoint, in terms of emotional experience, the author could have been Prince Huo's daughter from the T'ang dynasty.

Attraction Phase: Desire and Marriage Expectations

Romantic love, which can be defined as the idealization of the other within an erotic context, is regarded as a unique and finite resource that, when experienced sufficiently, validates its authenticity and, as such, constitutes a proper reason for wanting to marry. This notion has enormous implications for the individual's ability to be satisfied with marriage and life in general.

Throughout much of China's postrevolutionary period marriage required parental approval (Whyte and Parish 1984). By the 1980s, however, that began to change. In China's largest cities a new generation had come of age and, through their ideas and actions, had expanded the customary notions of courtship, generating new expectations and demands for emotional satisfaction within marriage (Wu 1987). Part of this thinking suggested that if dating could provide some emotional excitement and satisfaction, marriage could do the same. In this way marriage is no longer seen as primarily a vehicle for procreation by many Huhhotians, but rather regarded as the primary institution for achieving happiness, contentment, and emotional security. As

I pointed out in the previous discussion of Chinese literature, the folk notion that love and romance *could be* combined within marriage is not a recent phenomenon. The two were not perceived as antagonistic or mutually exclusive, barring unfavorable circumstances. What is new is the state's legal endorsement of free choice and, thus, love as a basis for marriage and, more important, the eagerness with which that endorsement is being embraced by the younger generation of urbanites, who demand that love and marriage be synonymous or, at least, possible bedfellows.

The majority of Huhhotians assume that the loss of romantic intensity is an inevitable aspect of marriage. Typically, the intensity lessens following the birth of a child, which results in the couple's redefining their roles from lovers to parents. Other Huhhotians, especially the younger generation, do not believe that romance has to wane, and tend to deeply resent the dwindling of passionate love. The resentment is widespread. Honig and Hershatter report, for example, Shanghai and Tianjin women complaining that after "they were married, their relationship with their husband was robbed of its former glamour and romance" (Honig and Hershatter 1988:176).

Nevertheless, I found that regardless of one's place within the life cycle, the Chinese continue to speak favorably of, and believe in, romantic ideals, even if they no longer experience the passion. More significant, although the majority of married couples dismissed love per se as a simple illusion, their disillusionment rarely affected the younger generation's belief about either the value of love or the importance of remaining "in love."

Sex Differences in the Pursuit and Experience of Love

A chief ingredient of romantic love—anxiety—does not appear to vary by gender. I was not able to satisfactorily determine if the intensity of the romantic experience itself did or did not vary by gender. The cases presented above do not illustrate any significant gender difference in the experience of romantic involvement. It is, therefore, my impression that the quality of the romantic experience is not sex-linked. There are, however, noticeable differences in the content of men and women's romantic fantasies and the timing of romantic involvement. Men's romantic fantasies focused more on the idealization of female beauty and indicated only an incidental interest in the qualities of character. They assume that if a woman is beautiful, there will also be an affinity with the woman's personality. It is critical to note that Chinese men do value women as central symbols of love, security, and safety; however, their sexual and romantic fantasies do not express this value.

The male preference for beauty also affects the pace and growth of their involvement. Chinese men, like American men, fall in love more quickly than women. It was not uncommon for men to fall in love with a woman they had seen but never met. For example, one male informant noted this propensity in his own life, recalling a time, when he was twenty-four and eager to marry, that he would notice a pretty girl who worked in the same factory as he did but on a different shift:

> I would come to work early just to see her leave. I imagined she was the best woman in the world. I wanted her so bad. Finally, I got the nerve to talk to her, only to discover that she cursed and looked down on her parents. After that I did not like her.

A college-educated informant noted that "every time I see a pretty woman I think I might fall in love with her, but then I discover she isn't very intelligent. I feel disappointed and I am no longer interested in her."

Besides demonstrating that a fantasy based in appearance can be misleading, these anecdotes illustrate that, for men, lust is not attachment. When selecting a mate, men place great value on physical attraction; there are, however, other considerations. Women's education, social status, and personality weigh in equal importance in mate choice (but not in the domain of romantic fantasy). Although in fantasy and conversation men regard beauty as the most important attribute in mate selection, actual marital histories reveal that, all things being equal, compatible personalities and virtue were just as important and, in some instances, more important.

Analysis of twenty-two female fantasies concerning romantic attraction found that women tend to emphasize the potential qualities of the involvement. Their attitudes reveal more of an emphasis on doing together such things as traveling, discussing events, sharing feelings, and caring for a child.

Although female informants cited handsomeness as an important criterion in mate selection, it was obvious from informal conversations and observations of public interaction that this was a relatively unimportant factor. Women are more interested in understanding men's character. Women simply could not imagine themselves with an extremely handsome man whose character they truly despised. Since it obviously takes much longer to evaluate and rank character than it does physical beauty, women are slower in getting involved or making a final decision.

In summary, there are four major points discussed in this chapter. First, romantic love in China is not the product of Westernization nor an artifact

182   of Communist ideology. Even the brief survey of traditional Chinese literature indicates that while romance was seldom the basis for choosing a marriage partner, it existed well before the founding of the Han dynasty, and, in
some cases, actually thrived in the face of powerful parental opposition.
Second, a content analysis of contemporary Chinese literature and television
programs as well as personal accounts of romantic involvement reveals that,
though the Chinese define love as an enduring attachment, it is the attraction
phase of falling in love that holds the most interest. Moreover, the cultural
expression of romantic love is often mediated by formal and informal conventions of dating, strategies of seduction, family obligation, and the prevalent political ideology. Finally, the cool objectivity articulated whenever
Huhhotians list their respective mate selection criteria (e.g., for men physical
beauty, for women social status) quickly disappears when they discuss the
meaning and value they place in the ideal of love. For many romantic
involvement is regarded as one of life's truly authentic and deeply moving
experiences. It stands, as such, in direct opposition to the more instrumental
and pragmatic values found in their discussions of the ideal mate. The rec-
onciliation of these often competing values remains a rich and constant
source of public amusement, family anxiety, and personal pathos.

NOTE

*Partial funding for the research was provided by the University of California General
Research Grant, Sigma Xi, and CSCPRC, National Academy of Sciences. I am grateful
to the following scholars for their advice, encouragement, and thoughtful suggestions: Jim
Bell, Steve Harrell, Chuck Lindholm, Tie Liu, Tom Paladino, and Susan Pensak.*

REFERENCES

Beach, S., and A. Tesser. 1988. "Love in Marriage." In R. Sternberg and M. Barnes, eds.,
    The Psychology of Love. New Haven: Yale University Press.
Action, H., and Y. Lee. 1945. *Four Cautionary Tales*. New York: A. A. Wyn.
Chu, G. 1985. "The Changing Concept of Self in Contemporary China." In A. J. Marsella,
    G. DeVois, and F. L. K. Hsu, eds., *Culture and Self: Asian and Western Perspectives*,
    pp. 252–277. London: Tavistock.
Eberhard, W. 1965. *Folktales of China*. Chicago: University of Chicago Press.
Fisher, H. 1992. *Anatomy of Love: The Natural History of Monogamy, Adultery, and Divorce*.
    New York: Norton.

Furth, C. 1987. "Concepts of Pregnancy, Childbirth, and Infancy in Ch'ing Dynasty China." *Journal of Asian Studies* 46(1):7–35.

Grant, V. 1976. *Falling in Love.* New York: Springer.

Hatfield. E. 1988. "Passionate and Companionship Love." In R. Sternberg and M. Barnes, eds. *The Psychology of Love.* New Haven: Yale University Press.

Honig, E., and G. Hershatter. 1988. *Personal Voices: Chinese Women in the 1980s.* Stanford: Stanford University Press.

Hsu, F. 1981. *Americans and Chinese: Passage to Difference.* Honolulu: University Press of Hawaii.

Jankowiak, W. 1993. *Sex, Death, and Hierarchy in a Chinese City.* New York: Columbia University Press.

Lee, Y. 1984. *Fantasy and Realism in Chinese Fiction: T'ang Love Themes in Contrast.* San Francisco: Chinese Maternal Center.

Levy, M. 1968. *The Family Revolution in Modern China.* New York: Atheneum.

Li Yaochung. 1969. *Against Culture: Problematic Love in Early European and Chinese Narrative Fiction.* Ann Arbor: University Microfilm International.

Liebowitz, M. 1983. *The Chemistry of Love.* Boston: Little, Brown.

Lin Yutang. 1961. *Famous Chinese Short Stories.* New York: Washington Square Press.

Lindholm, C. 1988. "Lovers and Leaders: A Comparison of Social and Psychological Models of Romance and Charisma." *Social Science Information.* London: Sage.

Mann, S. 1987. "Widows in the Kinship, Class, and Community Structures of Qing Dynasty China." *Journal of Asian Studies* 46(1):37–56.

Nash, J. 1986. "Love and Obedience: Vietnamese Conceptions of Moral Conflict in American and Chinese Cultures." Paper given at the Southwest Conference for Asian Studies, Waco, Texas.

Rougemont, D. de. 1974. *Love in the Western World.* Trans. M. Belgion. Rev. ed. New York: Harper.

Waley, A. 1948. *Translations from the Chinese.* New York: Vintage.

Whyte, M., and W. Parish. 1984. *Urban Life in Contemporary China.* Chicago: University of Chicago Press.

Wu, Benxue. 1987. "The Urban Family in Flux." In *New Trends in Chinese Marriage and the Family.* Beijing: China International Book Trading.

Wu, Yenna. 1988. "Shrewish Wives." *Harvard Journal of Asiatic Studies* (December), 40(2):365–383.

Yutang, L. 1961. "Introduction." *Famous Chinese Short Stories.* New York: Washington Square Press.

Zhang Jie. 1987. *Love Must Not Be Forgotten.* Beijing: Panda.

Zheng Zhenduo. 1986. "Introduction." *Tang Dynasty Stories.* Beijing: Panda.

✗ PART THREE ✗

Cultural Expression: Family, Marriage, and the Politics of Romance

Passion as Politics: Romantic Love in an Australian Aboriginal Community

VICTORIA KATHERINE BURBANK

Introduction

Early in my first visit to the Aboriginal Australian community of Mangrove,[1] I was told that the "old men" thought adolescents went off to "love each other" because of the movies. The woman who told me this was not sure that she agreed with this formulation; now that the movies were shown less often, boys and girls were just the same, still going off to love each other. Nevertheless, in this essay I shall pursue the old men's hypothesis, arguing that Aboriginal constructions of "falling in love" serve as the ideology of adolescent resistance to arranged marriage.

In taking this theoretical course I am following the work of Lila Abu-Lughod and Catherine Lutz (1990). These authors advocate the "study of emotion as discourse" and the understanding of "emotional discourses as pragmatic acts and communicative performances" (1990:11). Their argument suggests that "showing how emotion discourses establish, assert, challenge, or reinforce power or status differences" (1990:14) is a useful analytic strategy. At the outset I want to note that my treatment of romantic love here also bears resemblance to those interpretations of Aboriginal women's "love magic" ceremonies as paradigmatic alternatives to the institutions of marriage and bestowal (e.g., Berndt 1950, 1965; Kaberry 1939; Merlan 1992). It must also acknowledge Fred Myers's (1979, 1986) conceptual linking of the "emotions" and the "political" in Aboriginal Australia.

Mangrove

The oldest Aboriginal people residing at Mangrove today were once nomadic hunters and gatherers who harvested the products of land and sea. Unlike their neighbors whose countries became pastoral holdings in the late 1800s, the history of these people does not, for the most part,[2] include the ecological and social disruption associated with the incursion of white men and their livestock into Aboriginal territory. Until the 1930s the distance of their land from centers of white population and its general unsuitability for farming or grazing protected them from white encroachment. After 1931 their protection from the most destructive forms of contact was assisted by the creation of the Arnhem Land Reserve (Cole 1982).

Since the late 1970s Mangrove has been a largely self-governed Aboriginal settlement. It began, however, in the early 1950s as a Protestant mission. According to journals, reports, and interviews, early mission goals were primarily evangelical. But the mission also had a charter to educate; it was to prepare Aboriginal people for "assimilation" into the larger society. As this goal was in concordance with Commonwealth policy, these efforts received government support; funds were given for the building and mainte-nance of the mission, its staff, and its Aboriginal wards (see also Cole 1982). The mission's assimilation policy efforts focused on education of the chil-dren, Christian conversion, and work programs designed, among other things, to teach the Western work ethic.

The Movies

The mission experience also included lessons about romantic love. The movies that so concerned the old men— largely products of Hollywood— were shown on a regular basis beginning in 1965. I made an annotated list of all that I saw at Mangrove during 1977, and though I focused on the models of Western women they presented—often as prostitutes or as the "romantic interest"— these notes provide some support for the old men's idea. Of course, what I might see in a Hollywood film and what an Aboriginal teenag-er might see are not necessarily the same. For example, following the screen-ing of *What's Up Doc?* in which Barbra Streisand relentlessly, but charming-ly, pursues the fiancé of a nagging woman, I was told that the "little children" didn't like the heroine: "She was greedy for that man, she took him away from that other [woman]." Nevertheless, adolescent interpretations also seem to support the old men's contention. I noted in my journal, for exam-ple, that the calls and whistles during love scenes were extreme. During a scene in a cowboy film in which a man and a woman drive together through a deserted countryside, the adolescent boys called out things like, "They're going to get married!" and "You're too young [to get married]!" (This second exclamation was a common reaction on the part of older people to the age at which young men were marrying or attempting to marry.) Indeed, the teenagers seemed to get the point before this Western moviegoer.

Romantic Love in Australia

When the old men say that young people run off together because of the movies, are they also saying that romantic love has no historical precedent at Mangrove? As the Australian ethnographer Ronald Berndt has written, it is easy to "underestimate this aspect" of Aboriginal social life because "so much is against it: the formal patterning of marriage preferences, infant and child betrothal, the narrow scope for individual initiative, the restraints written into the kinship system" (Berndt and Berndt 1964:160–161 in Berndt 1976:10).

At Mangrove arranged marriages of structurally defined partners were once effected via mother-in-law bestowal or child bestowal, and a premenarcheal marriage age for girls (Burbank 1988). Romantic love does indeed seem wholly incompatible with such a system.

Nevertheless, ideas about love do have a history at Mangrove that would seem to antedate Hollywood-introduced ideas about romance. It is important, however, when we look at this history to uncouple ideas of romantic love from ideas about marriage. Berndt's work on *The Love Songs of Arnhem Land* (1976) documents the elaboration of love and sexuality in song and ritual. Speaking of the area around Mangrove he says:

> [This song] cycle depicts what I have called the ritual face of love. . . . This particular face of love is both formalized and ritualized. Personal feelings are subordinated to ritual expediency: it is ritual which counts, and the sexual act assumes the role of a religious (ritual) performance. In this case, the sexual act *is* sanctified—and it is possible to speak of sacred love: but, again, not in reference to the person, and only in relation to the act. (1976:152)

There is, however, also a romantic and passionate tradition that elevates rather than subordinates personal feelings.[3] This is evident in the many tales of past love affairs and elopements:

> In olden times when a man's brother had lots of wives he couldn't go near them. The man would take his wives hunting. The brother would track them. When

they went back home, if flies went near that woman her husband would say, "You've been eating another man. You met another man." He would belt her, give her a hiding. He would ask that boy if he was with one of his wives, and if he said yes, they would fight. The old generation, the man wouldn't let his wife go and talk to another man, young man. . . . Old men were proper jealous before, but not now because of this mission. When the mission was new there used to be fights, young boys would throw spears from the other side.[4]

A romantic and passionate tradition that elevates personal feelings is also evident in the *jarrada*:

Sometimes a man says to a woman, "I'm going away for a little time." She lets him go. When he is gone he sees grass, sings a song, and throws a match on the grass. The smoke goes up curling. The woman sees the fire and her heart feels sorry, she thinks of him and she will go to meet the fire. She dreams about the man standing there beside her. The man comes back and she says, "You have taken my heart away from my husband." She says this in front of all the men. She will sit beside that man. People don't like to use this here now, but they used to use it before.

In the literature on Aboriginal Australia the term *jarrada* is more commonly used to refer to a complex of women's rituals that may include attempts to manipulate male/female relationships (see Burbank 1989 for an overview of this literature). One older woman who attempted to introduce *jarrada* of this kind at Mangrove told me that some of the older men told her to stop after a couple of performances. The ceremonies were too successful and young women were running off with inappropriate partners. Currently, women's attempts to entice men through supernatural means appear to be isolated, individual acts.

This is not to say, however, that the extra-Hollywood tradition of romantic love at Mangrove has an extra-Western locus. Across Aboriginal Australia there is evidence both for and against the idea of romantic love as a precontact experience. For example, in an analysis of designs typically found on "love magic objects" from Western Australia, Kim Akerman and Peter Bindon conclude that the associated rituals are "far older" than two hundred years (1986:25); while Ronald Berndt infers from the ethnographic record of fighting and elopement that "there were always persons willing to risk disruption and conflict in order to satisfy sexual desires and to pursue a passionate attachment outside the marriage bonds" (1976:15).

We should, however, also consider the possibility that love is an experience that has been accentuated by European expansion into the Australian continent. Specifically, the concept of love may express Aboriginal women's preoccupations with the perturbations and possibilities associated with their sexuality in the colonial and postcolonial periods. A reading of some who have asked about the effects of colonialism and welfare colonialism upon the position of Aboriginal women vis-à-vis Aboriginal men (e.g., Barwick 1974; Bell 1980, 1983; Hamilton 1975, 1981; Leacock 1978; Tonkinson 1990) suggests that women's freedom could be both undermined and accentuated in the changing social formation.

Take, for example, the possibility of sexual intercourse with whites. Whether sexual congress between white men and Aboriginal women was effected by force or choice, the legacy of this interaction in Australia is not a benign one (e.g., Hamilton 1989; McGrath 1980). Deborah Rose (in Burbank 1989) has suggested that insofar as Aboriginal women were compelled to provide the white intruders with sexual services, and bear the brunt of Aboriginal male hostility for doing so, conflict would characterize their attitudes toward their own sexuality and explain their interest in love magic not as a fanciful diversion but as a major preoccupation with European destruction of the Aboriginal way of life.

Nevertheless, some Aboriginal women may have perceived an advantage in their relations with white men (e.g., Rose 1992; Tonkinson 1990) and expressed their hopes for this advantage in terms of "love." For example, looking at women's ceremonies in an area of the Northern Territory where the pastoral industry had been a presence for sixty years, Catherine Berndt (1950:60) observed that "it is chiefly those women who consort with local 'white' men who stress the love magic interest at the expense of other features of the rituals" (1950:60):

> One young *naljiri* woman, for instance, named Badari, was infatuated with a "white" drover (now a station manager) who had shown her considerable attention. . . . She had a reputation, apparently well deserved, for ignoring or evading as much as she could of indigenous ritual and ceremony, and for sneering at the old people. . . . Moreover, she did not care for the dancing, even in the role of spectator, because of the dust that was raised by shuffling or stamping feet. "Too dirty," she would say, wrinkling her nose.

> But her drover sweetheart was away with a mob of cattle; and there had been some talk, partly to tease her, of his taking a "white" woman for wife. The local policeman had reminded the Wave Hill station manager that it was illegal for a "white" man to consort openly with an aboriginal woman: and Badari, knowing

this, had additional reason for anxiety. And so she turned for help to some of the *tjarada* ceremonies; there was no doubt in anyone's mind, including her own, as to the reason for her presence. Her dancing in the erotic sequences was particularly intense: and her faith received its justification when, a couple of weeks later, the drover returned to the station (Berndt 1950:59–60).

Whatever their source, it does seem that Aboriginal constructions of romantic love at Mangrove parallel ours (cf. Lutz 1985; Myers 1988). This is indicated by the ways they speak of love. For example, here a woman describes the results of what we might call love magic:

> The man that the girl has sung comes back, maybe he was hunting. He sees [the object that was enchanted] and he is gonna smile. . . . If that man is miles away, that girl can sing his heart and make that man turn away from that place. The man will dream of that girl naked, see her standing there naked. He just gets up and goes. He doesn't even talk. When the woman sees him, she knows.

And here a young woman speaks of the end of love: "Young girl and young boy—maybe the man got married to another girl and that young girl really loved him. That makes her shame; she won't ever cut across his pathway, she will never want to see him."

Romantic love is constructed by these and other speakers at Mangrove as an attraction based on the erotic idealization of a specific individual. This attraction incorporates ideas of commitment that today are expressed by some in terms of marriage. For example, here is the text of a bit of graffiti. I have changed the names: "Noah loves Suzette. Only for bloody sure. Till both have a kid and till both married for sure."

Note the parallels between this construction and a definition of romantic love used by William Jankowiak and Edward Fischer, who say:

> "By romantic love we mean any intense attraction that involves the idealization of the other, within an erotic context, with the expectation of enduring for some time into the future" (1992:150).

Discussion

Aboriginal adolescents may have long chafed against the restrictions of arranged marriage (e.g., Meggitt 1962; Hiatt 1965; Shapiro 1979). But it is probably only since settlement that a majority of Mangrove's adolescents have been able to successfully resist marriage to a partner not of their own choosing. Forbidding or otherwise discouraging polygyny, child betrothal, and a premanarcheal marriage age for girls, missionaries and other representatives of the Australian Commonwealth have worked to dismantle Aboriginal marriage practices. Imposed from without, however, these changes are not accepted by many in the adult community, particularly by those once held responsible for betrothing girls; thus the conflict between adolescent and adult over the choice of marriage partner (Burbank 1987; 1988).

I interpret the construction of romantic love at Mangrove as a paradigm of adolescent resistance in this conflict. Western agents have introduced the institutional means by which romantic love becomes more than what Abu-Lughod might call a "discourse of defiance" (1990:35). It becomes the ideological expression of actions whereby young lovers circumvent the arrangements of the senior generations and choose their own marriage partners. What once may have been only an ideology of subversion has become the idiom and means of changing power relations in marriage politics. Within the context of these changes, the old men's hypothesis that movies make the young people go off and love each other is validated.

NOTES

The essay is based on research supported by the Australian Institute of Aboriginal and Torres Strait Islander Studies and the National Institute of Mental Health. It is a pleasure to acknowledge William Jankowiak's enthusiastic belief in the importance of love as the spark for this paper.

1. Mangrove is a pseudonym for an Arnhem Land community whose Aboriginal population has grown over the years that I have been visiting it from about four hundred in 1977 to about six hundred in 1988. I spent eighteen months at Mangrove in 1977–1978, nine months in 1981, and seven months in 1988.

2. In the first few years of the twentieth century a cattle company used areas occupied by some of the clans represented at Mangrove today (Merlan 1978; Bauer 1964). It is claimed that some of the ancestors of people at Mangrove were killed in company-instigated slaughters of Aboriginal people (Cole 1982).

3. Although the Australian ethnographer L. Hiatt (1978) does not list love or similar emotions in his "Classification of the Emotions," there does appear to be a vocabulary for speaking about love and romance in the Australian language used by many people at Mangrove. For example, the linguist E. Hughes translates *rdamarrnguburr* as "like, love (ramarr 'thought', burr 'put-thoughts on')" (1971:45) and *ramarrarrgi* as "entice (lit. pull-with-thoughts, ramarr 'thought', rrg 'pull')" (1971:210). The linguist J. Heath translates *nganybanda* as "love" (1982:296). As a further example, he translates *wandha* as "obsessed with" and *wandha-mananung* as "lusty for women" (1982:200). Both linguists translate Australian words as "jealous," and "sexual affair" or "love affair"

4. While I attempted to write down people's words verbatim, this statement and all others from Aboriginal people should be regarded as an approximation of what was said. I have also translated and edited these statements.

REFERENCES

Abu-Lughod, L. 1990. "Shifting Politics in Bedouin Love Poetry," In C. Lutz and L. Abu-Lughod, eds., *Language and the Politics of Emotion*, pp. 24–45. Cambridge: Cambridge University Press.

Abu-Lughod, L., and C. Lutz. 1990. "Introduction: Emotion, Discourse, and the Politics of Everyday Life," In C. Lutz and L. Abu-Lughod, eds., *Language and the Politics of Emotion*, pp. 1–23. Cambridge: Cambridge University Press.

Akerman, K., and P. Bindon. 1986. "Love Magic and Style Changes Within One Class of Love Magic Objects." *Oceania* 57:22–32.

Bauer, F. 1964. *Historical Geography of White Settlement in Part of Northern Australia*. Vol. 2: *The Katherine-Darwin Region*. 2 vols. Canberra: Commonwealth Scientific and Industrial Research Organization.

Barwick, D. 1974. " 'And the Lubras Are Ladies Now,' " In F. Gale, ed., *Woman's Role in Aboriginal Society*, pp. 51–63. Canberra: Australian Institute of Aboriginal Studies.

Bell, D. 1980. "Desert Politics: Choices in the Marriage Market," In M. Etienne and E. Leacock, eds., *Women and Colonization: Anthropological Perspectives*, pp. 239–269. New York: Praeger.

—— 1983. *Daughters of the Dreaming*. Sydney: McPhee Gribble/George Allen and Unwin.

Berndt, C. 1950. *Women's Changing Ceremonies in Northern Australia*. Paris: Hermann et Cie.

—— 1965. "Women and the Secret Life," In R. Berndt and C. Berndt, eds., *Aboriginal Man in Australia*, pp. 236–282. Sydney: Angus and Robertson.

Berndt, R. 1976. *Love Songs of Arnhem Land*. Chicago: University of Chicago Press.

Burbank, V. 1987. "Premarital Sex Norms: Cultural Interpretations in an Australian Aboriginal Community." *Ethos* 15:226–234.

—— 1988. *Aboriginal Adolescence: Maidenhood in an Australian Community*. New Brunswick: Rutgers University Press.

—— 1989. "Gender and the Anthropology Curriculum: Aboriginal Australia." In S. Morgen, ed., *Critical Reviews of Gender in Anthropology: Implication for Research and Teaching*, pp. 116–131. Washington, D. C.: American Anthropological Association.

Cole, K. 1982. *A History of Numbulwar: The Story of an Aboriginal Community in Eastern Arnhem Land, 1952–1982*. Bendigo, Victoria: Keith Cole.

Hamilton, A. 1975. "Aboriginal Woman: The Means of Production." In J. Mercer, ed., *The Other Half: Women in Australian Society*, pp. 167–179. Harmondsworth: Penguin.

—— 1981. "A Complex Strategical Situation: Gender and Power in Aboriginal Australia," In N. Grieve and P. Grimshaw, eds., *Australian Women: Feminist Perspectives*, pp. 69–85. Melbourne: Oxford University Press.

—— 1989. "Bond-Slaves of Satan: Aboriginal Women and the Missionary Dilemma," In M. Jolly and M. MacIntyre, eds. *Family and Gender in the Pacific: Domestic Contradictions and the Colonial Impact*, pp. 236–258. Cambridge: Cambridge University Press.

Heath, J. 1982. *Nunggubuyu Dictionary*. Canberra: Australian Institute of Aboriginal Studies.

Hiatt, L. 1965. *Kinship and Conflict: A Study of an Aboriginal Community in Northern Arnhem Land.* Canberra: Australian National University Press.

— 1978. "Classification of the Emotions," In L. Hiatt, ed., *Australian Aboriginal Concepts*, pp. 182–187. Canberra: Australian Institute of Aboriginal Studies.

Hughes, E. 1971. *Nunggubuyu-English Dictionary.* Sydney: Oceania Linguistic Monographs, University of Sydney Press.

Jankowiak, W., and E. Fischer. 1992. "A Cross-Cultural Perspective on Romantic Love." *Ethnology* 31(2):149–155.

Kaberry, P. 1939. *Aboriginal Woman: Sacred and Profane.* London: George Routledge.

Leacock, E. 1978. "Women's Status in Egalitarian Society: Implications for Social Evolution." *Current Anthropology* 19:247–276.

Lutz, C. 1985. "Ethnopsychology Compared to What? Explaining Behavior and Consciousness Among the Ifaluk," In G. White and J. Kirkpatrick, eds., *Person, Self, and Experience: Exploring Pacific Ethnopsychologies*, pp. 35–79. Berkeley: University of California Press.

McGrath, A. 1980. " 'Spinifex Fairies': Aboriginal Workers in the Northern Territory, 1911–39," In E. Windschuttle, ed., *Women, Class, and History: Feminist Perspectives on Australia, 1788–1978*, pp. 237–267. Melbourne: Fontana/Collins.

Meggitt, M. 1962. *Desert People.* Melbourne: Angus and Robertson.

Merlan, F. 1978. "Making People Quiet in the Pastoral North: Reminiscences of Elsey Station." *Aboriginal History* 2:70–105.

— 1992. "Male-Female Separation and Forms of Society in Aboriginal Australia." *Cultural Anthropology* 7:169–193.

Myers, F. 1979. "Emotions and the Self: A Theory of Personhood and Political Order among Pintupi Aborigines." *Ethos* 9:343–370.

— 1986. *Pintupi Country, Pintupi Self: Sentiment, Place, and Politics Among Western Desert Aborigines.* Washington: Smithsonian Institution Press.

— 1988. "The Logic and Meaning of Anger Among Pintupi Aborigines." *Man* 23:589–610.

Rose, D. 1992. *Dingo Makes Us Human: Life and Land in an Aboriginal Australian Culture.* Cambridge: Cambridge University Press.

Shapiro, W. 1979. *Social Organization in Aboriginal Australia.* New York: St. Martins.

Tonkinson, R. 1990. "The Changing Status of Aboriginal Women: 'Free Agents' at Jigalong." In R. Tonkinson and M. Howard, eds., *Going It Alone? Prospects for Aboriginal Autonomy: Essays in Honor of Ronald and Catherine Berndt.*, pp. 125–147. Canberra: Aboriginal Studies Press.

A Good Spouse Is Hard to Find: Marriage, Spouse Exchange, and Infatuation Among the Copper Inuit

PAMELA R. STERN AND RICHARD G. CONDON

His eyebrows wishing to meet
His eyebrows wishing to meet properly,
Wishing to meet, meet.
His armpit, its odor.
His eyebrows wishing to meet properly,
Wishing to meet, meet.
Its odor.
His eyebrows wishing to meet properly,
His eyebrows wishing to meet,
Wishing to meet, meet.
His armpit, its odor,
His eyebrows.

• DANCE SONG PERFORMED BY JENNIE KANAYUK,
A COPPER INUIT GIRL

Introduction

Early accounts of arctic explorers, traders, and missionaries have created a stereotype of the Inuit as promiscuous and lusty in their sexual liaisons. The typical scenario is that of an Inuit man who displays his generosity to strangers by offering the sexual favors of his wife or daughters. The stereotype of sexual liberalism is as enduring an image of Inuit culture as snowhouses, raw-meat eating, and female infanticide. The fact that this stereotype has taken such a firm hold on the Western imagination probably says more about our own sexual voyeurism than about the true nature and function of Inuit marriage and spouse exchange.

As is so often the case with simple stereotypes, there exists a parallel but opposite myth. The contrasting myth presents the archetypal Inuit male consumed with fear and jealousy lest another man abduct his wife. Indeed, the precontact practice of selective female infanticide did result in a scarcity of women and thus a skewing of the sex ratio. The result was that competition between males for wives, occasionally leading to murder, was commonplace in some areas. With both stereotypes women are presented as mere pawns of their men, giving freely of their bodies with a minimum of emotional attachment.

The reality of Inuit pairbonding and spouse exchange, however, is much more complex, although some facets of the stereotypes may ring true. We cannot deny the existence of spouse exchange (which some have inappropriately called wife exchange or wife lending), nor can we fail to recognize the importance of male competition for females. As is true of all societies, the sexual mores of the Inuit were mitigated by a host of demographic, social, and economic realities. That Inuit husbands would be concerned over the potential loss of their wives to a competitor while at the same time accepting their sexual liaisons with other men highlights one of the paradoxes of Inuit culture. Such an apparent paradox begs the question "What is the nature of Inuit marriage and to what extent is it based upon affection between partners versus a simple marriage for convenience?"

There is a great deal of evidence in the ethnographic literature to suggest that Inuit husbands and wives had strong affective ties to one another, although the high value Inuit placed upon emotional restraint could mask the expression of these feelings to the naive outside observer. While sexual attraction and infatuation could serve as the basis for pairbonding, it was unlikely that this was the rule. The demands of the harsh arctic ecosystem resulted in both high mobility and low population density. The scarcity of suitable marriage partners and the demand that young men and women make a rapid transition from childhood to adult responsibilities effectively limited opportunities for courting behavior or individual choice in pairbonding. In short, a good spouse was hard to find.

Traditional Inuit marriage, however arranged, had a particularly interesting feature—institutionalized spouse exchange. Many scholarly treatments of traditional Inuit marriage and sexual relations have attempted to make sense of this practice (see Balikci 1970; Burch 1970; Burch and Correl 1972; Damas 1971; and Guemple 1979). To Westerners accustomed to thinking of extramarital sexual activity as necessarily illicit, the widespread acceptance of socially sanctioned extramarital sexual activity—apparently devoid of jealousy—is difficult to comprehend. For example, Diamond Jenness, who spent three years in extremely intimate contact with the Copper Inuit, recorded the following confession in his diary:

> There was an interesting insight into the customs of these Eskimos last night. After "supper" Itoqunna disappeared and Niq entered the house. . . . She took Itoqunna's place and a little later turned in to bed. Itoqunna, I believe slept with Niq's husband Akhiatak—an exchange of wives for the night–very likely in connection with the change from the summer hunting of caribou on land to the winter's sealing on the ice. In the morning Niq turned out, mended the trousers of Haviuyaq's father, who sleeps in the other part of the house, and generally took the place of Itoqunna. A little later Itoqunna came in, said not a word but went into the other part of the house, trimmed the lamp, and appeared to wait for Niq to depart, which she did quietly a few minutes later. No words passed between the two women, but when Itoqunna entered, Haviuyaq laughingly asked me "Where is Itoqunna?"–alluding to my question of the night before, whereupon everyone laughed. I do not know if everyone exchanged wives last night, though Haviuyaq asked me if I still wanted to sleep alone. The custom is, of course, well known among savages from books, but strangely enough it shook my nerves more than anything else I have seen in the Arctic. . . . I have not dared enquire yet whether it was in connection with the sealing–though I feel rather ashamed of my weakness in this respect as an ethnologist. (Jenness 1991:350)

Jenness recorded several other instances of spouse exchange between the two couples mentioned above, including an extended trip by Ahkiatak into the territory of Itoqunna's relatives. Although Itoqunna was married to Haviuyaq, she accompanied Ahkiatak in order to visit her kin *and* to assure Ahkiatak's welcome among strangers. Niq and Haviuyaq remained behind together. Upon completion of the trip each returned to his or her own spouse (Jenness 1970:85–86; Jenness 1991:357, 370).

These and other anecdotal accounts of Inuit sexual activity often leave the faulty impression that Inuit husbands and wives lacked the strong emotional attachments to each other that might be characterized in our culture as romantic love or infatuation.[1] In fact, some researchers have even suggested that the Inuit lack emotional attachment altogether (Lubart 1970). This argument is often supported by referencing high separation rates for Inuit men and women, either as a result of divorce or accidental death (see Burch 1970 and Heinrich 1972 for discussions of divorce among North Alaskan Inupiat). Thus, in this view, the rigors of life were so great for the Inuit that emotional attachments must necessarily be shallow, as concerns of the stomach must inevitably supersede concerns of the heart.

In attempting to understand Inuit spouse exchange, many researchers have sought purely economic explanations. These include the cementing of

social ties between families already engaged in some kind of trading or hunting partnership (McElroy 1979), the extension of kinship networks (Damas
1971), and the creation of alliances between families of different regions
(Burch 1970; Burch and Correl 1972. Whether an Inuit male seeks to solidify a hunting partnership through spouse exchange or desires safe passage
through a strange territory by bringing along an exchange spouse who orig-
inates from that area, it is the alliance function of spouse exchange that takes
precedence in most scholarly discussions. Burch (1970) emphasizes that
spouse exchange must be viewed as an integral part of Inuit marriage in
which most married couples engaged at some point in their lives. Diamond
Jenness (1970:86), alone, considers lust and power in addition to the standard
alliance explanations of spouse exchange.

Unfortunately, purely materialist explanations of Inuit marriage and
spouse exchange serve to oversimplify the complex sexual, psychological,
economic, and political motivations of Inuit couples in establishing spouse
exchange relationships. Indeed, the personal motivations for creating such
alliances may have varied from one circumstance to another and from one
spouse to another. Who is to say that infatuation with another's spouse was
not a critical motivating factor for many exchange relationships, even those
that may have resulted in some kind of formal alliance?

Admittedly, it is difficult for outsiders to understand the emotional relationships and motivations of Inuit husbands and wives. At least two of the
researchers in the best position to interpret the Inuit marital relationship,
Diamond Jenness and Jean Briggs, have readily admitted that there is little
that they understand fully (Briggs 1974:272; Jenness 1991). It has been our
experience that Inuit are exceedingly reluctant to openly discuss any sort of
emotional experience, even though they may be quite candid in their sexual
joking. It is far easier to describe peoples' behaviors than to ascribe, with any
degree of accuracy, the motivations to those behaviors. As a result, like
Briggs and Jenness, we are left to interpret emotional states and motivations
primarily from observable behavior and hope that our interpretations bear
some resemblance to reality.

The authors have spent in excess of fifty-seven person months between
1978 and 1993 engaged in ethnographic fieldwork in the Copper Inuit community of Holman in the Central Canadian Arctic. During this period we
have investigated a number of topics including adolescent development,
health, and nutrition, reactions to extreme seasonal variation, and the impacts
of rapid social change. Since 1987 we have been engaged in detailed oral his-

tory interviewing and genealogical data collection from community elders. Overall, our involvement in this community has entailed fairly intimate participation in and observation of community life. For this reason we feel reasonably qualified to make some observations regarding Inuit marriage and the kinds of changes it has undergone since the arrival of Euro-Canadian traders, missionaries, and government functionaries. Our data pertaining to the precontact era are mostly derived from the observations of researchers such as Diamond Jenness and Knud Rasmussen, while our data on the post-contact period (contact-traditional horizon, in the words of Helm and Damas 1963) come primarily from life history interviews conducted with Inuit elders. Lastly, information regarding courtship and marriage patterns since the late 1970s are based entirely upon our own extensive fieldwork.

The Inuit couples we know in Holman are no more homogeneous than our married friends and colleagues here in the South (who we admit are no more a representative sample than our Inuit informants). There are couples who seem to be happy with each other and couples whose relationships are clearly strained. There are couples who fight and couples who do not, couples who work and relax side by side and couples who spend little time together. Some of our Inuit friends have marriages that were arranged by parents against their wills, but have nonetheless come to value and appreciate their spouses. Other couples boast of having chosen one another without parental intervention. And still others admit to having married over the objections of their parents.

The circumstances leading to these marriages are as varied as the personalities involved in them. There is no doubt that precontact pairbonding and the spouse exchange relationships that eventually developed from those marriages were similarly varied. While traditional pairbonding was heavily influenced by the availability and economic competence of the potential partners, there was certainly room for infatuation based upon personality and physical appearance. While the amount of "room" for romance was probably small, Inuit society has always been characterized by a high degree of negotiability and flexibility. It is this flexibility that allowed for the expression of individual choice in all domains of Inuit life. In short, Inuit men and women could have passions. These passions could result in a young girl rejecting a marriage partner selected by her parents, they could lead a man to kidnap another man's wife, and they could motivate a woman to urge her husband to enter a spouse exchange relationship with an enticing trading partner. Far from being automatons oriented toward the brutish and some-

times tedious tasks of finding food and shelter, Inuit had individual personalities with varied agendas, or, to put it more simply, they were human.

In the text that follows we will try to discuss some of the changes that have
occurred in Copper Inuit marriage and spouse exchange practices over the
past sixty to seventy years. Because we consider the Copper Inuit to be distinct from other Inuit groups, either to the east or west, we will make no
attempt to generalize our observations to the entire Eskimo culture area.

Fieldsite

The residents of Holman are primarily descendants of the northernmost
groups of Copper Inuit who occupied the western coast of Victoria Island:
the Kanghiryuarmiut of Prince Albert Sound and the Kanghiryuatjagmiut of
Minto Inlet. There are also a small number of "western" Inuit families from
the Mackenzie Delta whose ancestors entered Copper Inuit territory in the
1930s and 1940s for the purposes of trading, trapping, and wage employment. The Victoria Island Copper Inuit were among the last groups to come
into prolonged and direct contact with traders, missionaries, and government
officials, and, hence, were the most recent group to experience the extreme
changes in economic, social, and religious activities demanded by the outsiders. In our view the postcontact experience of these northern Copper Inuit
differs from that of other Canadian and Alaskan Inuit in one major respect:
the majority of the most dramatic acculturative changes have occurred within the memory of Holman's oldest residents.

No aspect of Copper Inuit life was left unchanged after contact with
Euro-Canadians. Traders, missionaries, and the Royal Canadian Mounted
Police (RCMP), each with their own agendas, entered Copper Inuit territory at virtually the same moment. Each group demanded changes in Inuit
social organization and ideology. In addition, Euro-Canadians were a vector
for a host of lethal diseases that, by themselves, would have been enough to
change Inuit life forever.

During our 1982–83 fieldwork we came to the startling conclusion that
divorce did not exist in Holman. Our genealogical, life history, and household census data indicated that from the 1940s onward couples who had
established a coresidence *never* separated. A check with informants confirmed that there had, indeed, been two "divorces"[2] within their memories.
All other marriages were not necessarily harmonious but, once established,
did not end in divorce. While Roman Catholic and Anglican missionaries
had successfully eliminated institutionalized spouse exchange, they were

unable to affect basic attitudes regarding sexuality and sexual behavior. "Extramarital" sexual activity continued to be common, but without the reciprocity required of formal spouse exchange, leading at least one Holman elder, Albert Palvik, to assert that promiscuity never existed before the arrival of whites. Oddly enough, in their attempt to guide the Inuit from a "heathen" existence to a Christian life, the missionaries may have inadvertently contributed to an increase in illicit sexual activity by eliminating a culturally approved and open system of spouse exchange. Palvik's assertion of the recent origin of promiscuity certainly makes sense from an emic perspective. An extremely large number of children are reported by Holman residents to have resulted from extramarital affairs. This is testimony, at least to the community's belief, that sexual fidelity is not the key ingredient to a successful marriage.[3]

Upon returning to Holman in 1988 for another extended research visit, we documented a number of significant social, economic, and physical changes in the community. In addition to experiencing an increase in population, the community had a new multimillion dollar school building equipped with a large gymnasium. School attendance had improved so dramatically that truancy was no longer a problem. Television programming, which first became available in 1981, had increased from a single station (CBC North) to five channels, including an NBC station from Detroit, offering people an even bigger window to the outside world. Wage labor had become the primary economic activity and, consequently, store-bought food comprised a large percentage of most families' diets. People increasingly looked to the South rather than to the land for their leisure diversions, and many (especially younger) families chose to vacation in Yellowknife or Edmonton. Finally, in the process of updating our household census records, we discovered that there had been a number of divorces and separations.

While it is perhaps too soon to determine if Holman is undergoing a major shift in its marriage patterns, more recent data collected in 1992–1993 suggest that young adults, at least, are following a more Euro-Canadian style of pairbonding. Not only are many young adults deciding to delay pairbonding to a later age, but a large number of those who do form a domestic unit with a spouse often separate after a few years. Interestingly, this observation seems to conform to the nearly universal pattern of marriage and divorce identified by Fisher (1987, 1992). While we agree with Fisher's general observations, we feel that the biological/evolutionary case presented by her is insufficient to fully explain this behavioral change in Holman, nor does it account for the very different patterns of marriage operating in the pre-contact and postcontact periods. Fisher does, however, point out that economic, social, and historical factors can and do alter even those human behaviors that appear to be most strongly rooted in biology. As a result, we feel that it is important to identify these social and historical factors, an exercise that is best achieved by examining changes in marriage institutions within individual societies over a long period of time. In the remainder of this essay we hope to accomplish this task for Copper Inuit society by describing marriage (and extramarital) patterns for three historical periods: 1) contact to circa 1935, 2) circa 1935 to 1985, and 3) 1985 to the present. We make no claim that these are distinct historical periods with firmly delimited boundaries; they are simply convenient markers for discussing somewhat gradual but nevertheless distinct changes in Copper Inuit pairbonding.

Copper Inuit Marriage and Divorce: Contact to 1935

At the beginning of this century, when the first Euro-Canadian explorers, traders, and missionaries arrived in the Central Arctic, Copper Inuit marriage was an extremely informal affair. While it is clear that children were prepared for adult roles that were synonymous with marriage, no elaborate ceremonies existed to mark either the transition from childhood to adulthood or the establishment of a pairbond. Nevertheless, marriage was clearly a significant marker of adulthood and was necessary, in the words of elder Sam Oliktoak, "in order to have a full life." In fact, an idiomatic expression meaning "a lonely man" translates literally as "one who is without a woman" (Rassmussen 1932:319).

Social and economic conventions mandated highly distinct but equally crucial roles for men and women. This mutual dependency, for both economic and reproductive purposes, necessitated that nearly all adults be married. There was little incentive and certainly no advantage to staying single. As has often been noted in the anthropological literature, the Copper Inuit region of the Central Arctic is an extremely harsh, unproductive environment. A spate of poor hunting luck or an accident could, and frequently did, result in starvation. Marriage for women signified security; for men, hunting success was synonymous with marriage. This is expressed most clearly in the following Copper Inuit dance song:

How here telling me to find subsistence.
Caribou when they take to the water despite my wish to secure them.
Only one its way, this one,

Of Marau to the lands, to the place possessing caribou down thither.
How here telling me to find subsistence.
Seals, they will not come to me, although one wishes to secure them.
Only one its way, this one,
Of Qoingnannaq to the lands, to the place possessing seals down thither.
A more abundant place than this one though being hard to find . . .
To a place with seal-holes, a place with seals; when there are no seals one is always
   idle.
How here telling me to find subsistence.
Women, those, they will not marry me although I wish to get them.
Only one its road, this one,
Of Tamarsuin to the lands, though wishing to go.
A more abundant place than this though being hard to find . . .
To a place with women, to a place with people; when there are no women one
   always dreams of them. (Roberts and Jenness 1925:451)

To some extent, it was probably easier to find "subsistence" than to find suitable marriage partners. Given the practice of female infanticide, there were
a large number of bachelors in precontact Copper Inuit society. Extremely
low population density throughout the region meant that as a youngster
approached marriageable age there might be few or no suitable mates.
Children of both sexes were betrothed at birth, but these commitments were
rarely honored (Jenness 1970:158). Families were highly individualistic in
their travels, and encountering a potential spouse for a son or daughter was
often serendipitous. Consequently, individuals could not afford to be too
choosy with respect to the selection of a mate. Most first marriages were
arranged by parents, although it was not unusual for a young woman or man
to reject the parents' choice of mate. But, given the absence of any sizeable
adolescent peer group to function as a playing field for courting and sexual
experimentation, parents were generally in a better position to locate potential spouses for their offspring. In spite of arranged marriage, it is clear that
some couples were clearly infatuated with one another:

> Instances of genuine affection are not at all uncommon, even before a child is
> born to cement the union. Avranna and Milukkattak might often be seen
> stretched out on the bed-skins in their hut pressing noses and caressing each
> other, wholly oblivious to the presence of other natives around them.
> Milukkattak would go out hunting with him, and sealing too at times, so that they
> might not be separated for a single hour. (Jenness 1970:160)

Other couples were not as emotionally involved and simply tolerated each other. The value traditional Inuit placed on tolerance, nondemandingness and noninterference (see Condon 1992; Honigmann and Honigmann 1965) undoubtedly pervaded the marital relationship as well. In many cases couples who were incompatible did not stay married more than a few days or weeks. The economic necessity of marriage encouraged flexibility. These included temporary unions between brothers and sisters (which occasionally involved sexual intercourse) as well as polygyny and, less commonly, polyandry.

Marriage for females generally occurred right around menarche, while for males it was delayed until they demonstrated the necessary hunting and survival skills *and* could locate a suitable mate. The first months or years of a marriage were really a trial period for the couple. If the man planned to take his wife to another region, he was expected to provide a modest brideprice to the woman's family. If, however, the couple planned to stay in the same vicinity, it was common for the young man to move into his in-law's household and to work with his father-in-law as a kind of brideservice. This one- to two-year period provided an opportunity for the couple to determine their compatibility and to mature into their adult roles before embarking out on their own. Divorce was common during the trial marriage period; both the man or woman could abandon the partnership at any time. The only requirement was that the brideprice, if one was paid, be returned. Many traditional unions were long and enduring, ending only with death. Both Jenness (1970:160) and Rassmussen (1932:51) report that divorce was exceeding rare after the birth of a child. Nevertheless, high accidental death rates, especially for males, and often large age differences between husbands and wives meant that most people married several times over the course of a lifetime. Young widows had fewer problems in remarrying than young widowers. Men as well as middle-aged and elderly widows, however, might have a long wait for another spouse if they remarried at all (Jenness 1970:163).

Despite the extreme hardships of a single life, individuals who found themselves in intolerable marriages took steps to remedy the situation. In the words of Frank Kuptana,

> After my father, Iqalukpik, died, my mother remarried . . . [but] she got tired and fed up with her second husband, Urhuraq, and feeling sorry for the way he treated me. So she left Minto Inlet because her husband would beat her up. . . . My mother started her trip away from Minto when the land had no more snow, so that her husband couldn't go and track her down. My mother and I reached people

near Read Island [three hundred miles to the south]. . . . Me and my mom never saw my [stepfather and his people] again. Well, they weren't able to track us down. He must have looked for us, but they never did find us. My mother must have known that there were people down around Read Island, so that's where we ran off to. . . . There were quite a few people there. My mother and I were adopted by Kanayoks and those people looked after us. Then my mother married Qunmuktuk. . . . That man, Qunmuktuk, was a very nice man. He sure was good to me. He showed me a lot of affection. . . . That's how I remember him.

Although compatibility rather than infatuation was undoubtedly the critical element in pairbonding, Jenness (1970:163) reports that jealousy was a perennial source of conflict between husbands and wives, although one that rarely led to divorce. Given the Inuit emphasis on cooperation, and the value placed upon the avoidance of conflict within local groups, such jealousy may have been highly controlled. It is within this context that we must consider the practice of spouse exchange. Burch (cited in Briggs 1974) reports that, for North Alaska, spouse exchange relationships, rather than marriages, were often made on the basis of infatuation. It is reasonable to conclude that while most marriages were arranged on the basis of convenience, availability, compatibility, and potential alliances, spouse exchange relationships had the potential to be based upon more amorous concerns for *all* parties involved. Seen in this light, spouse exchange may be viewed not only as a technique for alliance formation, and the ultimate extension of the Inuit tendency to share everything in their possession, but also as a method to diffuse sexual tension and jealousy. It was also a legitimate avenue for the expression of sexual attraction. Spouse exchange provided a reciprocal and egalitarian method for extramarital sex that neither threatened the critical marriage bond nor led to its dissolution. In fact, the occasional temporary exchange of partners might very well have resulted in a strengthening of the marriage bond. Why leave your husband for another when you can have your husband and share someone else's too?

In discussing the spouse exchange event cited at the beginning of this chapter, Jenness (1991:352) observed that Itoqunna and Haviuyaq showed each other a great deal of affection "despite the temporary change in marital relations the other night." The woman Itoqunna is the focus of many of Jenness's observations of spouse exchange. She is also the subject of an improvised dance song dealing with infatuation. According to Jenness, the singer, Aquluk, observed Itoqunna gaze longingly across the room at the husband of a third woman (all three couples were present). When Itoqunna realized that she was being observed she looked down in embarrassment.

> Her husband, she feeling love for him,
> The woman she was smiling.
> Her husband when she felt love for him,
> Her husband, I began to gaze at her.
> Wishing to come—when she felt love for him,
> The woman, she looked down ashamed.
> Wishing to come,
> Myself [I], bending down
> To the drum, to the drum-stick,
> Myself, bending down [on account of their weight].
>   (Roberts and Jenness 1925:442)

Rasmussen (1932:140–144) also transcribed two songs in which a man expressed his desire and longing for the wives of other men. During at least one of the performances, the man claimed embarrassment when he discovered that the objects of his desire were present.

While many benefits may have resulted from spouse exchange relationships, it is quite likely that the practice served to prevent conflicts stemming from illicit sexual liaisons. If infatuation is a natural tendency of the human condition—and we suspect that it is—then legitimizing extramarital sex in a controlled fashion may have ensured the relative stability of the marital union and prevented sexual conflict and jealousy from undermining essential cooperative relationships within both households and local groups.

The Disappearance of Divorce, 1935–1985

The arrival of traders, missionaries, and the Royal Canadian Mounted Police (RCMP) led to dramatic changes in Copper Inuit marriage patterns. By the late 1920s introduced diseases, especially influenza and tuberculosis, are estimated to have decreased the Copper Inuit population at least one-third to as much as half (Usher 1965:67–8). This population decline probably made finding a spouse an even more difficult endeavor than had been the case previously.[4] Genealogical data supplied by our informants indicate that illness, rather than starvation or injury, had become the most common cause of death of both adults and children. These data indicate that large numbers of men and women died leaving no offspring.

The Inuit concept of marriage also changed after contact with whites. As the RCMP report of 1932 shows, people were easily converted to

Christianity (both Anglican and Roman Catholic):

> The influence of the missionaries is very noticeable and at the camps visited the natives would show me their hymn books. The Minto Inlet natives held a service while I was their [*sic*], which consisted of singing six hymns. They observe sunday [*sic*] very closely and will not do a thing, spending most of the day singing hymns even if the camp is out of meat. (RCMP annual report, January 1935:5)

The preceding statement indicates a pattern typical of many Inuit camps throughout the Canadian Arctic after conversion to Christianity. Many Inuit believed that the decrees of the missionaries had the force of law as well as the force of the spiritual realm. As a result, they modified their behavior accordingly to avoid conflict. While precontact marriage involved only the consent of the parties involved and a period of trial marriage, missionaries were highly successful in pushing the Christian view of marriage as a sacrament that required a ceremony and a certificate. The marriage certificate that was issued became a tangible reminder that the missionaries had official backing. In the community of Holman today many couples frame and display their wedding certificates on their livingroom walls. In our conversations with elders regarding marriage, those who had lost their marriage certificates took pains to point that out. "My marriage certificates are all gone. My daughter was cleaning the house. She had put the box and the papers out to dry and they blew away. That's when my wife and I were out hunting seals in Prince Albert Sound" (Albert Palvik, cited in Condon fieldnotes, 1989).

As a result of missionary work the institution of marriage took on new meaning for the parties involved. Linguistic evidence from Holman supports this view. Traditionally, according to elders Mabel and Morris Nigiyok, people used a single Inuinaqtun term (*teteutimiulittut*) for a couple living together regardless of the length or permanence of the union. With the arrival of missionaries and the availability of Christian marriage ceremonies, a new term (*kattitiktut*) was applied to couples who were married by a minister and the former term was applied only to couples who were not formally married.

Conversations with Holman elders also indicate that after the missionaries arrived people's definition of marriage changed. Consider the following exchange between our research assistant, Julia Ogina, and an elder, Frank Kuptana:

JULIA: When did you get married?

FRANK: When I was becoming an adult. After I quit trapping with Iqutaqs and it was time for me to get a wife. Fred Kahak asked me to travel with them so I could marry Avilingak's (Kahak's wife) sister, Qiuvikhaq.

JULIA: Where did they take you after Kahak asked for you?

FRANK: I returned to Read Island and lived there for a while with Kahaks and Iqutaqs. They went to Read Island to visit and trade. That's when they asked me to come along and marry Qiuvikhaq. That's when they came to Read Island from Naluayok and when they were returning. That's when I went with them.

JULIA: When did you guys get married?

FRANK: We were married long ago by a minister called Mr. Webster.

JULIA: Where did you guys get married?

FRANK: We were married I think at Read Island. That man, Mr. Webster, used to travel a lot. He married a lot of people back then.

The new concept of marriage as representing a permanent and less casual commitment was undoubtedly reinforced by an incident that occurred around Minto Inlet in April 1935. The previous winter a young Copper Inuit woman and a Mackenzie Delta man had been living together in a traditional marriage arrangement. Although she had become pregnant, she was abandoned by her husband and returned to her parents' home. Fortuitously for the woman's family, this occurred immediately prior to the annual patrol of the Coppermine-based RCMP officer. The woman's father complained to Constable Albert "Frenchie" Chartrand, who convened a hearing to settle the dispute. After each family stated its case, Constable Chartrand decreed that the marriage was dissolved, but that the young man was required to turn over to the woman's family one-half of his trapping income for that year. The Hudson's Bay Company clerk, George Burnham, who recorded this incident (Burnham 1986:116), felt that Chartrand's ruling was acceptable to "all parties involved," but half of a year's trapping income must have seemed like an extremely heavy fine to people previously accustomed to walking away from unsuccessful marriages.

Throughout the 1930s to the 1950s, Holman Inuit resided in seminomadic hunting and trapping camps. Trading posts were moved around the region in accordance with administrative decisions made in Ottawa, London, and elsewhere. Often, as the trading posts moved so did the people. This was especially true as people became increasingly dependent upon southern trade items. The Christian holidays of Christmas and Easter became major ingathering periods at the trading posts that provided opportunities for matchmaking and marriage. At other times of the year Anglican and Catholic missionaries (sometimes, but not always, accompanied by RCMP) traveled by dogteam from their bases in Coppermine to outlying camps. The performance of baptisms and marriage ceremonies were a critical feature of these circuits. Often nuptials were performed for couples who had lived together for many years, but, undoubtedly, the forceful presence of the missionaries and other whites led to legal marriages between new couples who might not have remained together (see Matthiasson 1992:81–82 for an example of this from Baffin Island). The RCMP and the missionaries were often feared, and their decrees were generally respected. The former had the ability to admonish and arrest, while the latter had the force of a powerful deity *and* government laws behind their admonitions.

In 1939 both the Hudson's Bay Company and the Roman Catholic Mission established permanent locations at the site of the current community of Holman. Throughout the 1940s and the 1950s people used Holman much as they had the other trading posts: as a place to socialize, to seek medical attention and welfare rations as well as a place to exchange fox furs for imported goods. Few families settled there permanently before the early 1960s, when the federal government embarked on a housing program intended to entice people into the new town. It was during this period that the Anglican Church finally provided a year-round missionary in Holman. However, largely due to the efforts of earlier Anglican missionaries (especially the Reverend Harold Webster), nearly all of Holman's residents were already Anglican. The Roman Catholics, on the other hand, had been successful in converting only a handful of Copper Inuit. Competition between the two churches continued and, to some extent, accelerated after the arrival of the full-time Anglican missionary. The missionaries kept score in this competition by comparing performances of sacraments such as baptism, funerals, communion, and marriage.

Through the mid-1970s a formal marriage ceremony was viewed as an essential aspect of pairbonding, and nearly all young couples submitted to either a Roman Catholic or Anglican ceremony. The missionaries were also quite active in repressing the traditional practice of spouse exchange, although we have been unable to determine how long it took for these formal exchanges to drop out of use. More problematic for the missionaries during this period were premarital and extramarital sexual relations. The latter seemed to increase in response to the disappearance of spouse exchange as a legitimate social practice.

Even after most families moved into the settlement (population concentration was completed by the late 1960s), parents continued to be heavily involved in spouse selection, but not necessarily premarital sexuality. Most, although not all, of our middle-aged informants reported that their marriages were arranged by parents or, at the very least, that their parents had significant input. One of our informant couples, currently in their mid-forties, claims to have been the first couple to have an unarranged marriage and a southern-style ceremony complete with a white wedding gown and tiered cake. The wedding occurred in 1972. Though they appear to have been trendsetters, they did not live together prior to the wedding and their first child was born *after* the ceremony.

As in the precontact and immediate postcontact periods, nearly everyone married and eventually had children. During the early settlement period, however, especially after the construction of public housing in the early 1960s, there was a slight increase in the numbers of both never married and widowed women with children. Without the physical and economic security of the settlement, most of these women would probably have been remarried several times. The creation of the settlement and its associated system of public housing and social assistance allowed these women to remain relatively independent. The absence of a spouse (either by choice or by circumstance) did not, however, limit a woman's opportunity for a full sexual and reproductive life.

The concentration of people into the settlement also led to a new demographic phenomenon for the Copper Inuit and one that had significant implications for pairbonding and sexuality—an adolescent peer group. This process has been described in detail by Condon (1987, 1990). Improvements in medical care in the 1950s and 1960s led to a drop in infant mortality and a dramatic increase in the number of live births. By the late 1970s this birth cohort had reached their teenage years, essentially constituting the first large, adolescent peer group to exist in Copper Inuit society. This group of young Inuit was profoundly influenced by formal schooling, mass media exposure, and a settlement existence that provided both safety and security. Freed from the responsibilities and duties characterizing the childhoods of their parents and grandparents, these children and adolescents had relatively little to do other than spend their nonschool time engaged in impromptu sports and sexual liaisons. Most critically, the amount of time spent with and learning from parents declined dramatically as the peer group attained paramount importance.

For many of these new adolescents pairbonding decisions were made without the imput of parents and were motivated by new criteria. Marriage was no longer an absolute economic necessity for either men or women, but it remained an important marker of adult status and, thus, was desirable. Men and women, for the most part, continued to maintain distinct, but complementary, roles. Men remained the hunters and, therefore, the providers of high-quality meat. Women maintained the household, cooked, sewed, and, quite frequently, earned the cash income that supported male hunting activities. Single women (and their children) had less reliable access to land foods than did married women and were often dependent upon gifts of fresh meat and fish from relatives.

Availability of housing also played a significant role in pairbonding. From the earliest days of the settlement until the mid-1980s Holman suffered from a shortage of housing. Young couples wishing to establish a separate household from parents often had to wait years for an available unit, a requirement that was unnecessary in the presettlement era when a new house could be easily fashioned from snow or skins.

By the mid- to late 1970s, church weddings ceased to be a critical element in the pairbonding process, indicating a departure from the experience of the preceding generation. Not only were young people selecting partners on their own, but they were generally living together for several years and having children long before the formal marriage ceremony. The typical pattern was as follows. A young couple would start to see one another on a regular basis. This frequently entailed sexual relations, but on an extremely clandestine basis. The secretive nature of premarital sexuality was not due to any fear that parents would disapprove but reflected a concern that parental knowledge of such activities would lead to subtle pressures for the couple to establish a more permanent union. Once the young couple decided upon their compatibility, they would get "shacked up" (to use the local expression). This entailed either the young man or the young woman moving into the other's bedroom in the parents' home. When a housing unit became available, the young couple would set up a neolocal residence. Frequently— only after several years of marriage and at least one or two children—the couple would decide to have a formal church wedding. Prior to the formal ceremony the couple nevertheless considered themselves and were considered by others to be husband and wife.

For the teenagers and young adults of the 1970s and early 1980s, semisecretive, premarital sexual activity and subsequent bedroom pairbonding must have served the same purpose as trial marriages had during the traditional period. Undoubtedly, sexual gratification was the purpose of many teenage sexual liaisons. However, as a young person matured a (generally) exclusive sexual relationship, based on compatibility and affection, replaced the more promiscuous activities of youth. Since nearly all potential marriage partners were individuals known since birth (now that the population was concentrated in the same location), "dating" in order to get to know one another was unnecessary. Parentally arranged marriage was also unnecessary since young people were no longer plagued by the scarcity and scattering of nuptial resources. Boys and girls reported that they frequently had little to talk about and as a result generally spent their time together in sexual play, including intercourse: "Sometimes [when I want to have sex,] I just call up a girl and ask her to come over. After we have had tea for a while and talked a bit, I might say, 'Hey, you want to fool around?' And then we do it" (eighteen-year-old male quoted in Condon 1987:144–5). Most of the teens we interviewed in 1983, both boys and girls, cited personality rather than physical characteristics as desirable qualities in a potential spouse, even though physical attraction was clearly important for sexual partners. And, as in the previous period, compatibility rather than infatuation appeared to be the most important factor in the choice of a spouse.

The Current Situation: 1985–Present

Prior to the mid-1980s it was extremely rare to see couples, of any age, openly display any signs of affection in public. Hand holding, kissing, and hugging in public were considered inappropriate. Affection between courting couples and life-long partners was expressed in different and often more subtle ways: with a glance of the eye, an eyebrow flash, or the simple making of a cup of tea for a partner. We have interacted with older couples who obviously hold great affection for one another, although it was rarely expressed overtly. Beginning in the mid-1980s we noticed a distinct change in the public presentation of affection. Couples, both young and old, were observed walking hand in hand, hugging at the community hall, and kissing one another goodbye at the start of the workday. We suspect that these changes have been brought about, in part, by exposure to southern mass media, particularly television, with its ubiquitous displays of both positive and negative emotions.

Many of the courtship and marriage practices that developed in the 1970s have continued to the present. For nearly all couples formal marriage ceremonies are delayed until the couple has been together for several years.

Most have one or two children at the time of their wedding. Several of our younger informant couples have mentioned sexual fidelity as a desirable characteristic, but we are uncertain if their views and behaviors in this regard differ greatly from those of their parents.

One consequence of the fact that Holman young adults are now making their own marriage decisions is that many are delaying the age of pairbonding, and an increasing number of men and women seek spouses from the neighboring, and larger, community of Coppermine. Young singles from both communities make frequent visits back and forth during holidays, usually staying with relatives, while searching for possible mates. While intracommunity marriages have always been common, there has been a dramatic increase since the mid-1980s. Some of our young informants admitted that Coppermine Inuit are more exciting as partners because they do not suffer the stigma of familiarity. It also seems likely that, given the short courtship periods that these intracommunity relationships necessarily have, infatuation is a critical ingredient in pairbonding. It may also contribute to the current fragility of marriages.

In addition to an increase in both the average age of marriage and the number of intracommunity marriages, one of the most noticeable changes has been an increase in the number of single-parent households.[5] In 1987 we updated our household census and discovered a large number of separations and legal divorces—the first that we have been able to document for the settlement period. This was even more evident by 1992. Most of the couples affected were young people who had been together for short periods of time (less than two years), and many had at least one child. To some extent these relationships were clearly trial marriages, much like those of the precontact period. The difference was that while traditional trial marriages stabilized after the birth of the first child, this appears not to be the case in the modern period. While attitudinal changes brought about as a result of extensive exposure to southern television programming may be partly responsible, we suspect that economic conditions are a more critical factor. Unlike the precontact period, the essential economic interdependency of males and females in Copper Inuit society no longer exists. Several factors seem to be at work here. As the people have become more and more involved in the wage-labor and social welfare economy of Northern Canada, women find no particular economic advantage to marriage. During the early settlement era (and just prior), most of the cash needs of a family were generated by fur trapping—a male activity. Women contributed to the family economy, but often by supporting male subsistence hunting and trapping. Prior to the mid-1980s, there were very few wage-labor jobs in Holman that were sufficient to support a family not also reliant on hunting and trapping. Holman's incorporation as a hamlet in 1984 enabled a much larger number of people to find both skilled and unskilled wage-labor employment. The new jobs went to both men and women.[6] At the same time southern antifur sentiments, coupled with high equipment and fuel costs, destroyed fur trapping as a viable economic strategy. As a result, the presence of two adults in a household no longer ensures greater financial security. Finally, the presence of extended kin living nearby, rather than being spread out as they were during the traditional era, provides single mothers with access to desirable land foods and to babysitters.

Attainment of adult status, which was once synonymous with marriage, now can be achieved in other ways. In the traditional period marriage enabled young people to separate from their parents. It was this separation, and not the marriage, that established a person as adult. Within the settlement era housing shortages served the same purpose. Until very recently young people could not get a house apart from parents before they established their intention to marry by getting "shacked up." Even then, there was often a delay. A construction boom in the 1980s created a housing surplus that enabled older adolescents to move out of their parents' homes. As a result, a number of new households were formed by siblings in their late teens and early twenties, giving these youngsters a degree of social independence and autonomy not possible in their parent's homes. The surplus in housing may have also contributed to the reappearance of divorce. Having a place to go must clearly figure into any decision to leave a spouse. As Holman's population grows, however, it is unlikely that the current housing situation will continue. In fact, the Housing Corporation of the Northwest Territories recently announced plans to curtail new construction in Holman.

From the perspective of many young women in the community today, their lives are better as single mothers than as wives in marriages that are less than ideal. The increase in alcohol and drug abuse throughout the Canadian Arctic has unfortunately contributed to a growing tide of spousal assault. Repeated spousal abuse is an oft-cited reason for separations and divorce, and the changes in household composition we have noted are not surprising.

Although most of our data regarding separation and divorce come from unsystematic and informal interviews, both authors are quite familiar with many of these individuals and are therefore able to suggest motivations. A woman's motivations for leaving an abusive husband should be fairly obvious, especially when economic conditions allow. We suspect that these young women do not remarry right away (if at all) in part because of raised expectations concerning ideal marriage relations *and* recognition that their lives and those of their children are better in single-parent households. Both of these factors may also account for why many other young women now choose not to marry, but, nonetheless, decide to have children. The sexual lives of single women do not seem to be hampered by their choice to remain single. They often engage in a series of short-term relationships based upon infatuation or physical attraction rather than any concern for the compatibility that might lead to marriage. In short, just as in the traditional period, a good spouse is still hard to find.

Conclusion

Copper Inuit marriage customs have undergone some distinct changes as the Copper Inuit have adapted to the demands and realities of ever increasing integration into global society. Yet, a number of aspects of Inuit marriage have held steady. First and foremost among these is a quality that can be said to characterize Inuit culture overall, that is, its flexibility. Just as traditional Inuit were willing to accommodate a variety of marriage types in order to adjust to particular environmental and social circumstances, so their descendants modified their marriage practices, first to satisfy the demands of powerful outsiders and, more recently, to cope with changing economic and social conditions. Many Inuit continue to choose their spouses on the basis of compatibility rather than infatuation. While this may contribute to extramarital affairs, to our knowledge infatuation with someone other than an Inuk's spouse has not resulted in the dissolution of a single contemporary Holman marriage.

During the traditional period extremely low population density severely limited people's choices of potential mates. Consequently, they had few opportunities to develop unrealistic expectations of their marriages. As the attitudes of Euro-Canadian culture infiltrate Copper Inuit culture, either explicitly through mass media or surreptitiously through economic changes, there are greater opportunities to regret a marriage decision. Despite an increase in the numbers of single adults, the majority of Holman's young people continue to court and form pairbonds. Perhaps the only unfortunate consequence of having choices regarding mate selection is the opportunity to question the choice made.

NOTES

The Copper Inuit poem quoted in the epigraph that precedes this essay is from Roberts and Jenness (1925:468).

1. Throughout this essay we will use the word *infatuation* in the place of the term *romantic love*. While both terms bear the stigma of wide popular use, which lends them a Western cultural bias, we believe that is it possible to more narrowly define *infatuation*. We accept Fisher's (1992) construction of the term. In that sense infatuation refers to the uncontrollable, anxious, ecstatic, and often short-lived neurochemical reaction a person has for someone to whom he or she is sexually attracted. The attraction, however, extends beyond the mere sexual.

2. Neither of theses were divorces in the legal/official sense. One involved a woman who was legally married running away from her husband to become the co-wife of another man. The separation occurred within the first few months of the marriage. The second case involved what is often referred to in the anthropological literature as a trial marriage. It, too, lasted less than a year.

3. It is important to note that the 1940s and 1950s coincided with the first TB surveys conducted in the Holman region. A number of men and women were evacuated to Charles Camsell hospital in Edmonton where many remained for years undergoing treatment. It is not surprising that the spouses left behind continued what could be called normal sexual lives, but with partners other than their spouses.

4. Indeed, it is quite possible that the marriage practices documented by the earliest anthropologists and explorers, especially in the Netsilik regions to the east (e.g., scarcity of marriage partners, competition over women, and high frequencies of bachelorhood), may have been considerably amplified by these dramatic population changes.

5. Not surprisingly, these single-parent households were primarily those headed by women. While most resulted from divorce or separation, a growing number were headed by women who had never married or lived with the fathers of their children.

6. There remains a shortage of full-time, wage-labor jobs in Holman and other Inuit communities. Most families continue to get by with a combination of social assistance, wage labor, and reciprocity.

REFERENCES

Balikci, A. 1970. *The Netsilik Eskimo*. Garden City, N.Y.: Natural History Press.

Briggs, J. L. 1974. "Eskimo Women: Makers of Men." In C. J. Matthiasson, ed., *Many Sisters*, pp. 261–304. New York: Free.

Burch, E. S., Jr. 1970. "Marriage and Divorce Among the North Alaskan Eskimos." In P. Bohannon, ed., *Divorce and After*, pp. 152–181. Garden City, N.Y.: Doubleday.

Burch, E. S., Jr., and T. C. Correl. 1972. "Alliance and Conflict: Inter-regional Relations in North Alaska." In D. L. Guemple, ed., *Alliance in Eskimo Society*, pp. 17–39. Seattle: University of Washington Press.

Burnham, G. 1986. *The White Road*. Interlake Graphics, Inc.

218   Condon, R. G. 1987. *Inuit Youth*. New Brunswick: Rutgers University Press.

— 1992. "Changing Patterns of Conflict Management and Aggression Among Inuit Youth
in the Canadian Arctic: Longitudinal Ethnographic Observations" *Native Studies
Review* 8(2):1–15.

Damas, David. 1971. "The Problem of the Eskimo Family." In K. Ishwaran, ed., *Canadian
Family: A Book of Readings*, pp. 54–78. Toronto: Holt, Rinehart and Winston of
Canada.

Fisher, Helen. 1987. "The Four-Year Itch." *Natural History* 96(10):22–33.

— 1992. *The Anatomy of Love: The Natural History of Monogamy, Adultery, and Divorce*.
New York: Norton.

Guemple, D. L. 1979. "Inuit Spouse-Exchange." Ann Arbor: University Microfilms
International.

Heinrich, A. C. 1972. "Divorce as an Alliance Mechanism Among Eskimos" In D. L.
Guemple, ed., *Alliance in Eskimo Society*, pp. 79–88. Seattle: University of
Washington Press.

Helm, J., and D. Damas. 1963. "The Contact-Traditional All-Native Community of the
Canadian North: The Upper MacKenzie 'Bush' Athapaskans and the Igluligmuit."
Anthropologica 5(1):9–21.

Honigmann, J., and I. Honigmann. 1965. *Eskimo Townsmen*. Ottawa: Canadian Research
Centre for Anthropology.

Jenness, D. 1970. *The Life of the Copper Eskimos*. New York: Johnson Reprint.

Jenness, S., ed. 1991. *Arctic Odyssey: The Diary of Diamond Jenness 1913–1916*. Hull,
Quebec: Canadian Museum of Civilization.

Lubart, J. M. 1970. *Psychodynamic Problems of Adaptation: MacKenzie Delta Eskimos*.
Ottawa: Department of Indian Affairs and Northern Development.

McElroy, A. 1979. "The Negotiation of Sex-Role Identity in Eastern Arctic Culture
Change." *Occasional Papers in Anthropology* 1:73–81.

Matthiasson, J. S. 1992. *Living on the Land*. Peterborough, Ontario: Broadview.

Rasmussen, Knud. 1932. *Intellectual Life of the Copper Eskimos*. Report of the Fifth Thule
Expedition, 1921–24, vol. 9. Ottawa.

Roberts, H. H., and D. Jenness. 1925. *Eskimo Songs*. Report of the Canadian Arctic
Expedition, 1913–18, vol. 14. Ottawa.

Royal Canadian Mounted Police. 1935. "RCMP Patrol Report, Coppermine Detachment."
Ottawa: Public Archives of Canada.

Usher, P. J. 1965. *Economic Basis and Resource Use of the Coppermine-Holman Region,
N.W.T.* Ottawa: Department of Northern Affairs and National Resources.

Possessed by Love: Gender and Romance in Morocco

DOUGLAS A. DAVIS AND SUSAN SCHAEFER DAVIS

We in the West hear little about romantic love in other parts of the world, and this has led many people to believe it does not exist in non-Western cultures or that it is a recent innovation, following on the heels of the global spread of Western media. In what follows we will explore this question from the viewpoint of Arab Muslim culture in general and Morocco during the last decade in particular. We begin with the Arab poetic tradition that influenced European notions of courtly love and then examine the ideas of current Muslim authors on the position and influence of Islam on love, sexuality, and couple relationships. Finally, we look for evidence of these ideas in current experiences of love for Moroccan young people living at a time when marriages arranged solely by parents are being replaced by those desired by the couple and approved by parents. In these matches, and the relationships preceding them, young men are more likely to feel love so strongly as to be "possessed," while young women always have a practical eye open, even when strongly drawn to a suitor.

Western Views of Love and Romance

Most Americans today plan to "fall in love" and to choose a spouse on this basis. In Morocco, and in most of the world's cultural history, this has not been the primary basis for marriage; instead, marriage was an alliance between families, and the couple involved were meant to get along but did not need to be in love. Yet the idea of love existed and is becoming more important for young people in many parts of the world. Just what is being in love, and is it similar in different cultures?

Although the topic of romantic love has been neglected by social scientists until recently, there are several important general discussions of this topic. In a 1992 book Helen Fisher uses a natural history approach to analyze the occurrence of love (as well as monogamy, adultery, and divorce) in various cultures. Fisher describes being in love or infatuation as being "awash in ecstasy or apprehension . . . obsessed, longing for the next encounter . . . etherized by bliss" (1992:37). She goes on to argue that "above all, there was the feeling of helplessness, the sense that this passion was irrational, involuntary, unplanned, uncontrollable" (1992:40). Obstacles to the relationship seem to make the passion more intense. Finally, she concludes that this feeling must be universal among humans. She is supported in this by the research of two anthropologists, William Jankowiak, the editor of this book, and his colleague Edward Fischer (1992). They looked at data from 168 cultures worldwide, and found that 87 percent of them showed evidence that romantic love existed.

Tennov (1979) cites some evidence on the European attitude toward limerence or romantic love in the Middle Ages that resonates with the attitudes expressed in Islam and the Islamic culture of Morocco. She cites a thirteenth-century handbook for witch hunters, the *Malleus Maleficarum* (Witches' hammer) by Kramer and Sprenger, prepared at the request of a pope. The authors claim that "all witchcraft comes from carnal lust, which is in women insatiable (Kramer and Sprenger 1971:122). As we will see below, some Muslim scholars feel that Islam mandates separation of the sexes based on a similar fear of women's seductive capacity. Thus, being in love with a woman was said to be the cause of all evil, and the beloved woman controlled a man's actions by bewitching him (Tennov 1979:236). *The Art of Courtly Love*, a tenth-/eleventh-century work by Andreas Capellanus, also sees men who are in love as enslaved by women, and while the author excuses the men, he blames and condemns the women. His statement on women and love is echoed by one of the young Moroccan men we will quote below:

"The mutual love which you seek in women you cannot find, for no woman ever loved a man or could bind herself to a lover in the mutual bonds of love. For a woman's desire is to get rich through love, but not to give her lover the solaces that please him" (Capellanus 1941:200).

Tennov notes that these attitudes supported a change from matrilineal to patrilineal descent, with an accompanying control by males. She asserts males blamed females for a limerence or infatuation that tied them to women, concluding, "Limerence may have been a persistent thorn in the movement to control women's reproductive capacities" (1979:240). We suggest that a similar ambivalence about women's role in male romantic affections characterizes modern Moroccan society.

Love and Lust in Arab Islam

The position of Islam on love and sexuality, at least in the western part of the Arab world, is convincingly summarized by a Tunisian author, Abdelwahab Bouhdiba (1985 [1975]). Bouhdiba argues that Islam is prolove and tolerant of sexuality when sanctioned by marriage: "Unity is attained by the affirmation of Eros. . . . God himself is a being in love with his own creatures. From the thing to the Supreme Being, love exists as a guarantee of unity" (Bouhdiba 1985 [1975]:212). Sexual pleasure in marriage is thought of as both a privilege and a duty. Congugal bliss is described as a foretaste of paradise and a proof of God's love. On the other hand, Islamic accounts of love and sexuality often conclude that this divine model is seldom attained by human beings, and Bouhdiba suggests that "one must probably be a prophet oneself . . . if one is to grasp, conceive of and above all achieve this essential unity" (1985 [1975]:212). The rhetoric of love and erotic passion sanctioned by the religion has often led, according to Bouhdiba, to the unleashing of excessive libidinal force, and to the subjugation of women as the objects of male lust:

> By confining woman to pleasure, one turns her into a plaything, a doll. By doing so one limits love to the ludic and one reduces the wife to the rank of woman-object, whose sole function is the satisfaction of her husband's sexual pleasure. Marital affection is reduced to mere pleasure, whereas in principle pleasure is only one element of it among others. But by stressing the child-bearing role of women, one valorizes the mother. (Bouhdiba 1985 [1975]:214)

Bouhdiba contends that the privileged yet closely circumscribed role of the mother in the Arab Muslim household, as well as the sharply gendered roles prescribed for adults, have created a cult of the mother that is the central dynamic in Muslim child rearing and a cause of modal personality styles in "Arabo-Muslim" societies (1985 [1975]:214). The corollaries of this basic personality structure include unequal responsibility for control of one's passions, with the male allowed freer rein even as the female is blamed in instances of fornication, a mother-child bond that is the strongest tie in the society, and sharply contradictory expectations by the males reared in such households of women as both idealized nurturers and sex objects. The mother-centered Arab household confronts the male child with a world of women he must eventually renounce, and many of the connotations of this early immersion in a society of mother, aunts, and sisters have erotic implications. The boy is taken to the *hammam* (public steam bath) by his mother, and Bouhdiba asserts that this and other experiences of physical intimacy with women leave a legacy of charged images that are evoked in the context of adult sexual activity, so that "the Arab woman is the queen of the unconscious even more than she is queen of the home or of night" (Bouhdiba 1985 [1975]:220–221). It is this primal, ambivalent femaleness, we believe, that the adult male faces in the *jinniya* 'Aisha Qandisha, who possesses men and makes them her sexual slaves. Behind the idealized image of the pious and pure mother/sister is an antithetical fantasy of a fallen woman—lustful, seductive, and dangerous:

> Arab man is still obsessed by the anti-wife whom he seeks in every possible form: dancer, film star, singer, prostitute, passing tourist, neighbour, etc. The dissociation of the ludic and the serious examined above still continues, then, and acts as a stumbling block to the sexual emancipation not only of women but also of men. (Bouhdiba 1985 [1975]:243)

The contemporary societies of North Africa, in Bouhdiba's view, are experiencing a sexual and religious crisis, as women seek to move beyond the traditional roles assigned them and men resist this change:

> Today Arab woman is striving to renounce the illusory kingdom of the mothers and is aspiring to an affirmative, positive rule, rather than a mythopoeic one. . . . She is determined to affirm her ability to give. . . . I give love, therefore I am. . . . And yet there is a curious ambiguity inherent in the concept of female emancipation, as if the partners could be dissociated from the question, as if one could emancipate oneself alone! As if Arab man were not alienated by his own masculinity! (1985 [1975]:239)

The Moroccan sociologist Fatima Mernissi has written several important works on gender differences in contemporary Moroccan society and the relation of these to Muslim history and modern political and economic conditions. In an argument similar to Bouhdiba's she asserts that gender politics are rooted in Islam and deeply revealing of the political issues facing North African society today:

> The conservative wave against women in the Muslim world, far from being a regressive trend, is on the contrary a defense mechanism against profound changes in both sex roles and the touchy subject of sexual identity. The most accurate interpretation of this relapse into "archaic behaviors," such as conservatism on the part of men and resort to magic and superstitious rituals on the part of women, is as anxiety-reducing mechanisms in a world of shifting, volatile sexual identity. (Mernissi 1987 [1975]:xxvii–xxviii)

Mernissi argues that, in contrast to Muslim praise of legitimate sexual pleasure, conjugal intimacy threatens the believer's single-minded devotion to God; hence the loving couple is dangerous to religious society. While Bouhdiba asserted that the true basis of Islam is a unity through love (whether attainable or not), Mernissi concludes that "the entire Muslim social structure can be seen as an attack on, and a defence against, the disruptive power of female sexuality" (1987 [1975]:44). Mernissi develops this argument from the concept of *fitna*, or "chaos" (lit., temptation, enchantment), frequently applied to fornication, which she contends is embodied in women's erotic potential, so that society maintains its equilibrium only by controlling women's behavior. From the time of the Prophet on, Mernissi argues, males have felt the need to veil and seclude women and to surround sexual activity with rule in order to keep men safe from the seductive potential of women. The emphasis on *female* sexuality as the force that drives erotic relations for both partners in heterosexual encounters accords well with our reading of the role of magic and possession in love affairs. The male is anxious about his powerful longings for physical intimacy and the loss of autonomy it implies, and he projects desire onto the female, casting her as the agent of unrestrainable lust.

The Arab Poetics of Love: Layla and Majnun

In an influential work on the origins of Western European romantic discourse, Rougement argued that the seminal tradition of courtly lyrical poetry in twelfth-century France owed its origins to the confluence of Persian Manicheanism and Middle Eastern Sufi rhetoric transmitted by Muslim Spain (Rougement 1956 [1940]:102–107). These Eastern sources of romantic imagery and practice drew on Arabian models in the *qasidas* (odes) of Imru' al-Qays and other oral poets of the late pre-Islamic period (Sells 1989), and this native Arab romanticism is a wellspring of passionate language for modern society, with sources at least as deep as those of Western Europe. A thousand years before Romeo was moved by the radiance from Juliet's window, the oral poets of Arabia rhapsodized about the qualities of the remembered beloved.

The most persistent and evocative of the early Arabic romantic stories has probably been that of the star-crossed lovers, Layla and Qays/Majnun, whose unconsummated passion has inspired both the scholarly and the popular imagination of the Arab world for many centuries. The legend of Layla and Majnun probably has pre-Islamic roots. The earliest recorded version is that of Ibn Qutayba (d. 889), and a variety of anecdotes attributed to the love-crazed poet were recorded in the ninth and tenth centuries A.D. (Khairallah 1980:49). The early sources attribute to Majnun a variety of poetic fragments also credited to other poets, including all those that mention a female beloved named Layla (from the Arabic root *l-y-l*, night) (Khairallah 1980:53). Arab and Western scholars are divided on whether there was an actual Qays bin al-Mulawwah, of the Beni 'Amir tribe, who lived in the seventh Christian (first Muslim) century. In any case, the verses attributed to him passed from the oral tradition to a more or less stable text when they were compiled a century later by Abu Bakr al-Walibi—himself perhaps a merely legendary figure (Khairallah 1980:60–61). By A.D. 1245 a written corpus of Qays/Majnun's poetry existed, and this and other versions are widely read today. In later centuries the story of Majnun and Layla was adopted and expanded by the Persian Sufi poets Jami and Nizami; it has retained a fond place in the popular imagination of both Arab and non-Arab Muslims. The modern Egyptian poet Ahmad Shawqi (d. 1932) wrote a verse tragedy "Majnun and Layla," and an immensely popular version in song was created by the Egyptian composer-singer Abdel Wahab that is still widely played and sung on Arabic radio stations.

The story itself, as recounted by Ibn Qutayba, has two children, Qays and Layla, of neighboring clans, growing up together in the proud herding culture of Arabia. The two meet as children and, each being perfect in beauty and grace, fall immediately in love:

> I fell in love with Layla when she was a heedless child, when no sign of her bosom has yet appeared to playmates.
> Two children guarding the flocks. Would that we never had grown up, nor had the flocks grown old! (Khairallah 1980:136)

Qays begins to compose poetry to Layla, but she is unwilling to respond in public to his praise of her beauty, and her family is shamed by this broadcasting of love. Qays becomes as one possessed by *jnun*, the usually invisible beings who share the earth with humans, and he is thereafter known as "Majnun," possessed. He tears off his clothes and lives alone in the desert with his poetry, and he will converse only with those who ask him of Layla. All attempts to mediate between the two families and arrange a marriage fail, and Qays/Majnun spends his life as a wandering mendicant, communing not with the real but with the imagined Layla:

> You kept me close until you put a spell on me and with words that bring the mountain-goats down to the plains.
> When I had no way out, you shunned me,
> But you left what you left within my breast. (Khairallah 1980:136)

Majnun's poetry is itself the source of his estrangement from Layla, in the sense that her parents object to the notoriety it brings them through her—and Layla herself is described as complaining of Majnun's poetic divulgence of the secret of their love (Khairallah 1980:65). Khairallah argues that in the Arabic tradition from which the Majnun corpus springs, "Love and madness are pretexts for poetry" (1980:66). Majnun's love torment may therefore be seen as drawing on his poetic gift, since a talent for poetry is associated with a tendency to powerful cathartic emotion and with possession by a creative daemon. Madness is also a metaphor for passion, however, and it may be "feigned in order to claim inspiration and total bewitchment by the muse of love and poetry" (1980:66). Not only is the actual Layla of the legend portrayed as the natural stimulus for Majnun's passion, but her name is used in incantatory verses reminiscent of Sufi *dikr*, in which chanted repetitions of evocative syllables induced a meditative trance analogous to that of the Prophet Mohammed when he received each part of the Quran. The powerful need to divulge the message received in poetic form through such cathartic experience has remained a feature of popular practice in many parts of the Arab world, and a recourse to poetry for expression of the strongest and most personal feelings is characteristic of many traditional Arab men and women (cf. Abu-Lughod 1986).

The love of Majnun for Layla is fated, inexorable, transforming, and undying, and it is compared to a magical spell under which he labors and by which he is inspired:

> She's Magic; yet for magic one finds a talisman, and I can never find someone to break her spell. (Khairallah 1980:74)

Majnun's passion for Layla has been represented in each era of Arab and

Persian writing. For the thirteenth-century philosopher Ibn 'Arabi, as for other Sufi writers, Majnun's love is represented as ultimately transcending the real, physical Layla to attain a mystical union with her idealized form (Khairallah 1980:78). From the earliest of the verses ascribed to him, Khairallah argues, it is "difficult to draw a demarcation line in Majnun's poetry between the erotic and the mystical, or between the profane and the sacred" (1980:81). For a thousand years this tragic love story has inspired Arabic speakers, and millions can quote a stanza or two of Majnun's poetry, such as his reaction to finding himself one night at the camp of Layla's people:

> I pass by the house, the dwelling of Layla
>   and I kiss this wall and that wall.
> It's not love of the dwelling that impassions my heart
>   but of she who dwells in the dwelling.

The examples we present below of love and romantic longing come from a society geographically and temporally distant from the Arabia of Qays and Layla, but one in which romantic love is still extolled and men are still possessed and obsessed as a consequence of passion.

Zawiya, the community in which we have heard most of the examples of passion and obsessive love that follow, is an Arabic-speaking town of roughly twelve thousand in the Gharb, an agricultural region of northern Morocco. We have been interested in Zawiya for over twenty-five years, and one or both of us has visited every year or two. In 1982 we spent a year in Zawiya as part of the Harvard Adolescence Project, conducting fieldwork on adolescence (cf. Davis and Davis 1989). We observed family dynamics and child-rearing practices and interviewed over one hundred young residents of Zawiya about a variety of topics, including love, marriage, and sexuality. In 1984 Susan returned and recorded open-ended interviews with twenty adolesents; in 1989–90 she recorded young adults in Zawiya and in Rabat (the Moroccan capital) describing their beliefs and experiences concerning love and marriage.

The Demon Lover: 'Aisha Qandisha

One sort of love possession seen in Morocco is of a less poetic sort than experienced by Majnun, but its sufferers are described with the same epithet—*majnun*, possessed by *jnun*. Experience of the *jnun* is pervasive in Morocco. Crapanzano, whose work on the ethnopsychiatry of possession in Morocco is the best in English, has presented several examples of possession by the most distinctive of these beings, the *jinniya* (singular female of *jnun*) 'Aisha Qandisha (Crapanzano 1973, 1975, 1977, 1980). Capable of appearing in visible human form, she is the most commonly named of the *jnun*, who are most often referred to generically. Males are the usual victims of Lalla (Lady) 'Aisha, as she will often be called to avoid the risk of explicitly naming her. She dwells near wells and watercourses and may appear either as a seductive and attractive woman or as a hideous hag. If the victim does not notice her cow or goat feet and plunge an iron knife into the ground, he will be struck (*mdrub*) and inhabited by her (*mskun*). He is then likely to become impotent or to lose interest in human women, and he may suffer a variety of physical or psychological effects unless and until his possession is brought under control by the intervention of one of the popular Moroccan curing groups. Although there are many of these in all parts of Morocco, the Hamadsha (cf. Crapanzano 1973) are the group particularly concerned with possession by 'Aisha Qandisha. Members of the Hamadsha are found in most neighborhoods of northern Morocco. They are likely to have themselves been possessed by 'Aisha Qandisha or other *jnun* before joining the group, and they have learned to alleviate the effects of possession by means of distinctive trance-inducing musical performances and sacrificial rituals. Several of the accounts we have heard in Zawiya of males overwhelmed by sexual or romantic problems were attributed to possession by 'Aisha Qandisha or other of the *jnun*, and many of these have been successfully treated by Hamadsha performances.

In a detailed account of Hamadsha history and practice recounted for Douglas in 1982, a Hamadsha member from Zawiya attributed the central role of 'Aisha Qandisha in Hamadsha belief and curing to the fact that the *jinniya* had fallen in love with one of the patron saints of the Hamadsha, Sidi (saint) 'Ahmed Dhughi, several hundred years ago. Sidi Ahmed was inspired to play the flute and drum of the Hamadsha, and women heard him and fell instantly in love. The attitude of the Hamadsha toward 'Aisha Qandisha is ambivalent. On the one hand she is seen as the source of the suffering they and their clients experience and which draws them to the Hamadsha music and trance. Yet many of the terms used to refer to her connote respect or deference, and this does not in every case seem to be a mere attempt to evade her wrath. Just as the *jnun* number among themselves Muslims and unbelievers, those influenced by 'Aisha Qandisha and other *jnun* may be seen as good and pious people, spoken of as struck by "clean" 'Aisha, or as derelict, violent persons transgressing against Islam, and hence stuck by "dirty" 'Aisha (cf. Davis, unpublished).

Crapanzano notes that the language of possession offers the sufferer a collective symbolism for experiences of problems of sexuality, marriage, or family responsibility. Males who are unable to carry out expected roles of suitor, husband, or family provider may undergo an experience of possession by 'Aisha Qandisha, whose emotional demands and jealous interference with relations with human women externalize the apparent psychological conflict. Both Crapanzano's published accounts of possession by 'Aisha Qandisha and those we have heard frequently involve possession after a failed love affair, an estrangement from a spouse, or the death of a family member.

Tajj: An Example of Love-Obsession

Milder forms of suffering caused by failed or unrequited love are often attributed not to the *jnun* explicitly but to magical influence, as in a case recounted to Douglas in 1982. The young man described, N., was a friend of our friend and research assistant, Hamid Elasri. The first meeting with him occurred on one of the long nighttime walks around Kabar, a small city near Zawiya, during the Ramadan fast—a time when many people stay awake much of the night, after breaking the daylong fast with a heavy meal, and walk about town visiting with friends. N. called out to Hamid, and they had a brief conversation on a street corner, agreeing to meet to talk later in the evening. Hamid gave the following account of N.'s troubles:

> N., who was about twenty-four years old in 1982, had been engaged [*khotba*] to a girl for several years. They were both elementary teachers in a nearby large city. He wanted to break the engagement, but he was both worried about the dowry money he would have to repay and afraid of the magic [*suhur*] he believed her family had put on him. He believed they put something in his food which caused him to be obsessed [*tajj*] with the girl. He also became impotent, and he found himself giving a lot of money to her family. What money he had left he was increasingly spending for wine to try to forget her. The girl's family were apparently pressing him to turn over his entire salary to them. He told his father about this, who took him to a *fqi*—a man with Quranic and practical religious training. The latter, who examined his hand [*muhalla*] and wrote something there as a means of telling the subject's current situation and future, said N. had indeed been the victim of magic, and performed some counterspells.

Like other accounts of which we heard concerning infatuation, there is an assumption here that the feelings of love are overwhelming and pathological, and that they imply supernatural influence. Blame for the male's inability to deal with his love reasonably, or to put it aside, is laid on the female beloved (and her family). N.'s father intervenes on his behalf, calling on the white magical powers of a *fqi* to counter the black magic of the girl's family. A few days later Hamid and Douglas met N. in another town, and he said he was en route to visit relatives. Hamid assumed, however, that N. was in fact going to visit a nearby beach resort, where we had just seen the brother of his fiancée, but that he had been ashamed to admit this evidence of how obsessed he still was. The following week, near the end of Ramadan, Douglas had occasion to talk with N., whom we met on another nighttime walk. He asked about Douglas's interest in Moroccan psychology, and pointedly asked what he thought about the problems that arise when a man and woman in the same line of work marry, as is the case with him and his fiancée as newly trained primary teachers. N.'s problem had not resolved itself when we left Morocco at the end of the year.

N.'s inability to reconcile himself to marriage to his fiancée, despite his obsession with her, is a more extreme form of a male love dilemma of which Douglas heard repeatedly. The male finds a young woman toward whom he is powerfully drawn sexually and emotionally, but there are powerful obstacles—often in the form of family opposition or limited economic resources—in the way of a marriage. Gradually the man grows suspicious or hostile toward the woman, and he begins to expect or experience physical and emotional symptoms he attributes to magical influence. Moroccan popular culture is permeated with the concepts of magical influence and poisoning, although suspected instances are treated with circumspection by the concerned parties out of fear of the uncanny.

Romance, Love, and Marriage in Morocco

Many changes are occurring in Morocco today. While the population was mainly rural in the 1960s, it is now about equally rural and urban. Public education barely existed before Morocco became independent from France in 1956, while today all children should attend at least primary school. Although this goal is still being pursued in remote rural areas, nearly all children in cities do attend. Many young people attend high school, while few parents did; in the mixed classes young people have a chance to meet. Marriages in earlier generations were mainly alliances arranged between families to which the young people were supposed to agree. Today many of the young, especially males, select a potential mate and request their parents' approval. Girls too may have someone in mind, but it is not culturally acceptable for them to make such suggestions.

These trends were apparent in the semirural town of Zawiya. When we asked one hundred adolescents who should select a marriage partner, 64 percent of the girls and 55 percent of the boys said the parents should choose. Older youth, and those with more years of education, were more likely to want to make the choice themselves. Among a smaller number of their older siblings about half chose their own spouse, but only one-fourth of the adolescents said they wanted to do so (Davis and Davis 1989:126).

When we pressed him for estimates about the frequency of pure love marriages, Hamid suggested that very few in his experience marry exclusively for love. The most common pattern is marriage through family arrangement, followed by marriage when forced by legal or family pressure after the girl became pregnant.

This conversation grew out of Hamid's recounting of the story of A., a Zawiya friend whom he and Douglas were planning to visit at a beach resort where he was vacationing away from his estranged wife. He had married a beautiful local young woman who had been previously married off by her family to an older Moroccan man in France. The first husband divorced her a year later, when she hadn't produced a child. She became pregnant by A., and her family pressured his family to arrange a wedding. After the marriage A.'s mother increasingly put down the bride, who would become angry, catching A. in the middle. A. was in the process of divorcing the wife because he couldn't fight his mother. He still loved the wife, who bore his child after they separated.

Hamid and Douglas found A. at the beach resort, and spent an evening with him listening to Arabic and Western music and talking about life and love. A. was intensely preoccupied with his wife, and he had spent much of his vacation week at the resort listening to romantic music and dreaming about her. He was fond of Elvis Presley's song "Buttercup," with its vivid imagery of the palpitations of passion:

> When I'm near a girl that I love the best
> My heart beats so it scares me to death.
> I'm proud to say that she's my buttercup
> I'm in love, I'm all shook up.

The Arabic song to which A. was especially devoted at this time was a poignant piece by the popular female singer Fathet Warda. Its refrain, a drawn out "You have no thought [of me]," [*ma'andiksh shi fikara*], seemed to A. to capture his wife's lack of feeling for him and made him realize how he longed for her. A few months later A. and his wife were reconciled.

Zawiya Attitudes Toward Marriage

To better understand young people's feelings about who should choose a spouse, we devised a marriage dilemma that Susan discussed late in 1982 with twelve young women and three young men who were especially comfortable talking to her. She said there was a couple who loved each other and wanted to get married, but the parents were opposed. She had to stress that they were *really* in love, because there is an expectation that a young man may declare his love just to convince a girl to spend time with him; this is a semirural setting where people disapprove of dating. When she asked what the couple should do, eight said that they should follow the parents' wishes, and six that they should pursue what the couple wants, but in a way to reach a compromise and make it socially acceptable, including entreating relatives to convince the parents. Only one young man, aged eighteen and in high school, said that the couple's wishes were clearly more important than those of the parents.

> If that boy gets married to the girl he likes, they will certainly live happily. Because money is not happiness; happiness is something the heart feels. The boy must have the feeling that the girl likes him. This is why I say that if the boy is hooked on a girl and he truly loves her, he should go and propose to marry her no matter what she's like. It is not the father who should choose for the son a girl he doesn't like. It is the son who should decide what he likes. . . . It is not the father who is getting married.

A more typical response was that of a young woman of nineteen who had attended primary school.

> She should follow her parents' decision. Parents come first. . . . If she goes against their wishes it will be her own responsibility. She'd be ungrateful [lit., cursed by them]—very much so. If she marries him against their will, she'll face a catastrophe—an accident or something—or even death, some kind of death. They may have an accident or something—she shouldn't. Her parents told her not to marry him: she shouldn't marry him, period. . . . Since she has grown up, [her parents] have taken good care of her: they clothe her, give her money, provide for her needs. Whatever she asks for they provide, and then at the end they give an opinion and she rejects it. This is not possible; it is not admissible that she doesn't accept that advice.

Like many others, she notes the respect due to parents and fears negative consequences of disobedience. Others said more specifically that if they married against parental wishes they would have no support in marital disputes and nowhere to return in case of divorce.

This young woman's response reflects both a social conformity and a practicality in matters of the heart that we found in most young women, single and married, semirural and urban. We have noted elsewhere that young women in Morocco develop a sense of socially responsible behavior (*'aql*) sooner than their male counterparts (Davis and Davis 1989:49), and this is reflected in their attitudes toward romance. While Douglas heard several tales of young men's infatuations and longing, Susan heard very little to suggest that young women had similar experiences. They did have romantic encounters, and did care for the young men, but not as totally and intensely as the young men—or, it was not apparent in the way they spoke. Furthermore, they nearly always had a practical eye open to the consequences of their relationships, which *could* be social censure but that they *hoped* would be marriage.

Young Women's Personal Experiences of Love

When girls discussed magical influences on them related to love, they usually mentioned a spell cast to keep them from marrying, not something done by a male who wanted to possess them. Only a few young women talked about love in a way approaching the kind of intensity described in early and current Arabic songs and poetry and that Douglas encountered in young men. One case was that of Amina, a Zawiya woman in her twenties with a primary education. "A girl has to go through a period of intense attachment (*rabta*). The girl feels a great love for a boy. They start talking, kidding around. She starts learning new things [from him]. They exchange thoughts. The girl starts to become aware of things" (lit., awakens).

Amina notes that it is all right for couples to have such interactions now, though discreetly, and how things have changed. "In the past it wasn't right. It was shameful for a boy to talk to a girl. A boy would have one week to ask for a girl's hand and marry her ten or fifteen days later. He only gets a good look at her when she moves into his house."

Amina describes her own experience of romance:

A boy will tell you, "I trust you. I care for you. . . . If I don't see you for just half a day I go crazy; it seems to me I haven't seen you for a year." And at that time the boy does have feelings. He cares for you. Truly. Powerfully. But he doesn't have any money [to marry], and you just keep sacrificing yourself for him, talking to him, laughing with him. And you lose your value [reputation]—and your family's. Okay, people see you together, but you say, "They don't matter to me. Because even if I'm standing with him, he'll marry me, God willing."

And finally, he doesn't marry you—how do you feel? It feels like a calamity, like a "psychological complex." You feel angry at home, and you're always upset, because you don't trust anyone, even your parents. You sacrificed yourself for that boy, talking to him even in public. (Davis and Davis 1989:123)

Notice that Amina repeats the boy's intense statements, but not her own. She clearly felt strongly about him, both risking her reputation to be seen with him in public and evidenced by her condition after they broke off. But is the core of her concern lost love or a lost opportunity for marriage? Which was it that motivated her to take the risks of which she was clearly aware?

Another young woman reports romantic experiences that are close to what Douglas heard from young men, but still with somewhat less intensity and, certainly, an awareness of the consequences of her actions. When we spoke Jamila was married and in her twenties. She had grown up in a small town but now lived with her husband in the city where she had attended the university.

Jamila describes a typical way of couples getting together, something she first experienced around fifteen:

There were guys who followed me, but I did not feel anything toward them. Nothing. I had no reaction to them. They were classmates, but I never thought of having a relationship with any of them. And when anyone wrote me a letter telling me about his feelings toward me, I thought it was humiliating; I thought he just wanted to make fun of me and take advantage of me. I got mad at him and wouldn't talk to him anymore.

At sixteen, one young man who had been just a friend became something more. She found herself

wishing to be near Karim. I used to hope to meet him all the time, and I started to wanting to kiss and hug him. That was because when I was near him I used to feel very relaxed; I felt a great pleasure at being near him. Also, when I was going out with him, I tried everything possible to meet him. When he told me to meet him at night, I would go out at night, even when it was dark. . . . I used to tell [my mother] that I was going to study with Naima.

Yes, he taught me a bit of courage.

When we were together, he told me about a movie he had seen or a book he had read. Sometimes he kissed me, but when he wanted to sleep with me I couldn't accept. I wouldn't let him. I never had sex with Karim. . . . I used to tell myself, "If I sleep with him, I will stop liking him." That was my idea; I don't know why. . . . I used to have worries. I knew there was the possibility of getting pregnant. The other possibility was that he would lose control and then I would lose my virginity.

While she gives practical reasons for avoiding sex, a bit later Jamila describes the ideal of platonic love.

Emotions are strong in youth. I think that if I had slept with Karim, I wouldn't have remained so attached to him. . . . That's called platonic love. In platonic love, however, there are no kisses, no sexual relations, nothing. One loves a girl and they know they love each other, but they don't meet. Our love was, in a way, ideal. If we had slept together, we probably wouldn't have stayed—I personally still feel attached to him and still think about him. I don't know about his feelings.

The relationship finally ended after about four years. Yet even in the midst of it Jamila was not entirely carried away. "I also used to tell myself that because of the problems with Karim and his family, I was certainly not going to remain with him a long time. Despite my love for him, our relationship was doomed to end. I was always afraid of the future. . . . There was no hope."

Partly because of this, and for other practical reasons, in spite of her love she refuses Karim's offer to take things into their own hands and elope.

Once he suggested I run away with him. . . . I said no. I didn't want to do that. I told myself that even if I had run away with him, I would have had to go home sometime, and they would have refused to take me. I was worried that it would hurt my father and be embarrassing to him. My family gave me a certan freedom to go wherever I wanted to. They didn't ask me for anything as long as I passed my exams at the end of the year. They also used to buy me whatever I wanted. So in the end, I just couldn't leave. It didn't make sense. . . . But any day I wanted to meet [Karim], I did.

Other young women described marrying their husbands because they loved them, but in a matter-of-fact rather than passionate way. Qasmiya is a small-town woman in her twenties, married for three years. She describes the process of her marriage to a husband she cares for. It provides a good example of the results many traditional young women (she has a primary education) hope for when they venture to interact with men in an environment where dating is not accepted.

> I met him one day when I went out to the country. . . . He was working. He said "Hey, girl," and I said "Yes." He said, "Would you knit me a sweater?" and I replied, "When you are ready, I'll knit for you." One day I was passing by and he was on his way to visit his friend, our neighbor's son. . . . He asked his friend, "Does this girl live here?" and the other said yes. He asked, "Can I speak with you?" I answered, "If it is something serious, I will speak with you, but if you are going to take advantage of me and then abandon me . . . " I spoke with him over about fifteen days, and then he came: he brought his family and came to propose officially. He proposed quickly, I mean, we didn't wait long. . . . When I spoke with him, I found what I wanted. I talked with my mother. I told her there is a guy who wants to come and propose to me. I told my mother because it is not proper to tell my father such a thing. I told my sister first . . . and she told my mother. . . . I said, "I haven't been talking to him, but they are coming to propose," and his sisters and family came and my parents agreed. . . . When I spoke with him, I knew that he is good. He has a white heart; he is not nasty. From his warmth I knew that he is good. He buys me clothes, gets things [presents] for me. . . . My husband takes good care of me; I mean, we assist each other. He loves me. . . . I mean, I show my pride in him to my girlfriends and he shows his pride in me to his boyfriends.

Another young matron says she married her husband because she loved him, but her description is hardly rhapsodic; her concern with the practical is evident. She was in her twenties and had completed some college, and been married and living in a medium-sized town for about three years when we spoke. She had met her husband in his office.

> At the beginning, I was not sure that he was a good man. I married him because I loved him, that's all. You cannot know if he's good. I used to speak with him on the phone . . . because in [a small town] I couldn't meet him—impossible. Someone could see us and tell my father or something or tell my family. . . . He is serious. Before marriage I wasn't sure about that. I couldn't know, because you have to live with someone; it's life that lets you know if a person is good. I found out that he is serious from what people say and from what I see. Since I don't work, I rely on him for many things.

An urban young woman near thirty said she had been through two "shocks," or crises, before she married her current husband at twenty-six.

Although she didn't go into detail, the crises involved men she didn't marry. She met her husband through relatives, and married him after three months. She was currently working and taking university courses, and had two small children.

> I had decided to marry him, and to convince my parents if it was necessary. . . . I had experienced a shock in my life, and it affected me. I said "I might find a husband or I might not." I got sort of a complex. . . . [One] was frivolous: he used to date many girls and lie, and my husband was not like that. So I was attracted to him and said, "Anyway, he won't lie to me or take advantage of me."

> Marriage for me must be founded on love; one cannot marry someone without love—impossible. Then one has children and they become everything to you; you have to raise them. That is marriage for me, happiness. There are ups and downs, of course, but with love you can surpass them, you can make sacrifices.

Farida, an urban teacher and graduate student of thirty who is still single, discussed her problems in finding the right man and her family's reactions.

> Everybody in my family is upset; my mother wasn't, but now she is. There is a problem: it's really unbelievable. . . . I'm a little concerned, but not in the same way as my family. I'm concerned because I cannot find a perfect match. I've been meeting young men, but I haven't been satisfied. . . .

> At the beginning I say, "This is the man of my life," but when we talk and become more intimate I get another picture of him. I dislike every one for a different reason. I don't want to marry for marriage's sake, just to have children and a family. I want someone who shares my studies, my interests. I want something besides marriage and home, something that would link us more. . . . I may be wrong, because everybody says that you can't find a perfect match. . . .

> They say in my family "You must marry a rich man, someone who has a car." . . . In my family they don't insist on his youth or good looks. No, what is important is that he has money.

Although Farida disapproves of marriages based on material concerns, she says the family has much influence with such demands. She describes a friend of hers who loved a young man and had a good relationship, but he was not rich. In the end the girl decided she wanted a more comfortable life, and did not marry him.

Susan encountered a similar view in a discussion with a male Moroccan social scientist in his early thirties. She said that she thought marriage in Morocco was changing, and that while in the past it was an alliance between families based largely on economic considerations, today romantic love between the partners was more involved. He said no, it was almost the opposite. In the past, money wasn't that important, but today, if a young man didn't wear a suit and have a car, a young woman wouldn't consider him, even if she cared for him.

Conclusion

Thus the experience of romance in Morocco differs for males and females. Both sexes today hope to marry someone with whom they are compatible (*mutafehemin*; lit., they understand each other). But females rarely seem to experience the same intensity of romantic passion as males. This may be partly because they are less likely to report such feelings to anyone but their best friend, given the still functioning ideal of female purity. However, their socialization to behave responsibly from an early age, the myraid warnings of sexual dangers, and the practical importance of forming a stable marriage all encourage young women *not* to rely on only their feelings. Young men as children are more likely to be given whatever they want, and expect similar indulgence in adulthood. The involvement of families in marriage decisions serves to temper some of their impulses, and the objects, the young women themselves, are perhaps the best insurance against terrible mistakes.

REFERENCES

Abu-Lughod, L. 1986. *Veiled Sentiments: Honor and Poetry in a Bedouin Society.* Berkeley: University of California Press.

Bouhdiba, A. 1985 [1975]. *Sexuality in Islam.* Trans. A. Sheridan. London: Routledge and Kegan Paul.

Capellanus, A. 1941. *The Art of Courtly Love.* Trans. V. V. Parry. New York: Columbia University Press.

Crapanzano, V. 1973. *The Hamadsha: A Study in Moroccan Ethnopsychiatry.* Berkeley: University of California Press.

—— 1975. "Saints, *Jnun*, and Dreams." *Psychiatry*, no. 38, pp. 145–159.

—— 1977. "Mohammed and Dawia: Possession in Morocco." In V. Crapanzano and V. Garrison, eds., *Case Studies in Spirit Possession.* New York: Wiley.

—— 1980. *Tuhami: Portrait of a Moroccan.* Chicago: University of Chicago Press.

Davis, D. A. N.d. " 'Qasm': Hamadsha History and Practice." Unpublished manuscript.

Davis, S. S. 1983. *Patience and Power: Women's Lives in a Moroccan Village.* Rochester, Vt.: Schenkman.

238 Davis, S. S. and D. A. Davis. 1989. *Adolescence in a Moroccan Town: Making Social Sense.* New Brunswick: Rutgers University Press..

— 1993. *Sexual Values in a Moroccan Town.* In W. J. Lonner and R. S. Malpass, eds., *Psychology and Culture.* Needham Heights: Allyn and Bacon.

— 1993. "Dilemmas of Adolescence: Courtship, Sex, and Marriage in a Moroccan Town." In D. L. Bowen and E. Early, eds., *Everyday Life in the Muslim Middle East.* Bloomington: Indiana University Press.

— N.d. "Love Conquers All? Changing Gender Relations in a Moroccan Town." In E. J. Fernea, ed., *Childhood in the Muslim World,* forthcoming.

Fisher, H. 1992. *Anatomy of Love: The Natural History of Monogamy, Adultery, and Divorce.* New York: Norton.

Jankowiak, W. R., and E. F. Fischer. 1992. "A Cross-Cultural Perspective on Romantic Love." *Ethnology* 31(2):149–155.

Khairallah, A. E. 1980. *Love, Madness, and Poetry: An Interpretation of the Magnun Legend.* Beirut, Lebanon: Orient-Institut der Deutschen Morgenländischen Gesellschaft.

Kramer, H., and J. Sprenger. 1971. *Malleus Maleficarum.* Trans. M. Summers. London: Arrow.

Mernissi, F. 1987 [1975]. *Beyond the Veil: Male-Female Relations in a Modern Muslim Society.* Rev. ed. Bloomington: Indiana University Press.

— 1982. "Virginity and Patriarchy." In A. Al-Hibri, ed., *Women in Islam.* New York: Pergamon.

Rougemont, D. de. 1956 [1940]. *Love in the Western World.* New York: Pantheon.

Sells, M. A. 1989. *Desert Tracings: Six Classical Arabian Odes by Alqama, Shanfara, Labid, 'Antara, Al'Asha, and Dhu al-Rumma.* Middletown: Wesleyan.

Tennov, D. 1979. *Love and Limerence: The Experience of Being in Love.* New York: Stein and Day.

Wehr, H. 1966. *A Dictionary of Modern Literary Arabic.* Ithaca: Cornell University Press.

The Language of Love in Northeast Brazil

L. A. REBHUN

There are three kinds of marriages: those based on economic interests, on intelligence, and on sentiment . . . and it's the third that is the worst of all because sentiment, it stays diminishing and diminishing until it goes away and there is no more reason to stay together. . . . It is only intelligence which lasts, that the man and the girl recognize that they need to stay together because it is only together that they will build a home and have children. And it is building a home and having children together that the two love.

- SIXTY-THREE-YEAR-OLD NORTHEAST
  BRAZILIAN MAN

Love is a major theme in the lives of Northeast Brazilians, from the family love that sustains them both emotionally and economically to the passionate love that threads through the rhythms of their music, dance, and poetry. During two years of anthropological fieldwork among lower-working-class women and men (December 1988 to December 1990) in Caruaru (pop. two hundred thousand) in the Northeast Brazilian state of Pernambuco, I learned a number of distinct terms for different types of love.

The relations among these varying definitions is complex, affected by changes in economic system, family structure, gender role, and the organization of social class. Love (*amor*) is a gloss for a wide variety of sentiments, attitudes, beliefs, and affiliations. It is used to characterize family relationships, each of which is bounded by economic, emotional, role-based, and historical dynamics as well as the emotions involved in sexual relations. In addition, like all sentiments, the experiences glossed by the word *amor* are often transitory, shifting, and contradictory. People do not always know what they feel, they change their minds, fool themselves, and make mistakes. And the situation gets even murkier when they try to figure out what others feel. The heart, as a Brazilian popular expression puts it, is unknown country (*terra desconhecida*).

Personal sentiments occur in the context of and in response to larger social patterns, among these marriage and courtship. Historians Peter and Carol Stearns have proposed a distinction between what they call "emotionology" and emotional experience, which is useful in examining this context. While emotional experience is individual and psychological, emotionology is the study of broader cultural patterns that reflect, shape, and enforce socially defined emotional norms. These include cultural styles of courtship and patterns of marriage as well as class, gender, ethnic, and religious factors (Stearns and Stearns 1985:825). Emotionology focuses on broad cultural configurations in the context of which individuals have personal emotional experiences. Its subject matter is strongly affected by economic, technological, and social change.

The Stearns point out that the relationship between emotionology and emotional experience is neither rigid nor invariable (1985:827). People do not always feel what they or others believe they ought to, though they may try, and individuals vary not only in their personal temperaments but also in the opportunities or misfortunes that chance sends their way. Some are more able or willing to try to feel or at least behave as they are expected to no matter what the emotional cost, while others are more determined or able to act upon their personal sentiments.

People speak of love even in arranged marriages because by creating legal kinship, marriage endows erstwhile strangers with affective obligations. Gender and economic relations, emotion roles, and sexuality come together in marriage under the gloss of love. Many of the difficulties my informants faced in their personal lives derived from contradictions between the dynamics of sexuality and marriage, and those of love, as well as from misunderstandings based on the various contradictory definitions of love in the culture.

Love is especially problematic in this regard, not only because the word is used to describe so many disparate sentiments. It has been used both as a conservative cultural ideal utilized by those who wish to enforce monogamy, parental authority, and female subordination to men and paradoxically as a form of youthful rebellion against parental authority.

A consideration of every aspect of love is beyond the scope of this chapter; here I will confine myself to concepts of sexual and marital love. Sexuality, love, and marriage are not the same things, but they are often conflated both in the way my Brazilian informants discussed them and in their presentation in academic writings. Like most academic writers, Brazilians are heir to a shared European tradition that includes a rich history of social, religious, and economic aspects of loving relations. While some theorists posit that love in the sense of deep personal regard is of relatively recent, upper-class origin, coterminous with the rise of modern industrial civilization, the invention of private property, and the Romantic movement of early modern Europe (following Stone 1977), others trace its present forms to social and religious ideas of great antiquity and wide class and geographic distribution (MacFarlane 1987). Still others state that love has always had multiple, complex, and competing definitions throughout European history and that what has happened is not the invention of a totally new sentiment in the modern era but rather a shift from an association of love with sharing, economic interdependence, and loyalty to a definition of love as pure feeling expressed in the domestic sphere and related to the tender sensibilities of women (Gillis 1988; Cancian 1985, 1986).

According to historian John Gillis, what has changed about love and marriage over the course of European history is not whether couples had the capacity or inclination for positive affect toward one another but rather the details of the script of the role of lover, the importance of love as a prior condition for marriage, and the propriety of particular actions as declarations of love. While this shift has responded to the changing economic and political systems described by Stone and his followers, the existence of love as a sentiment is not created ex nihilo by the economic shifts; it is molded rather than generated by them (Gillis 1988:102–103). This same process is evident in my informants' statements about and definitions of love.

The contemporary language of love in Northeast Brazil has been affected by the history of love and marriage in that region. The specific history of Northeast Brazil includes not only events unique to the region, like particular patterns of conquest and slavery, but also by the broader European economic and social changes that found their echo in this Portuguese colony.

The History of Love and Marriage in Northeast Brazil

Marriage is not necessarily an outcome of sexual love nor love a part of marriage. As in Europe, only very recently has the idea that deep love precedes marriage been widespread in Northeast Brazil. In this region marriage is heavily marked by class. Historically, only the upper class married, partly because legal marriage was expensive and also because it was only necessary when rights over property were an issue (Nazzari 1991:74–75). In the lower classes, while legal marriage was an ideal, consensual unions were the norm

(Bruschini 1990:63). Prior to the nineteenth century the Brazilian family was the central social institution (de Azevedo 1968:291) and the primary purpose of marriage was to create economic and social ties between spouses' families. Therefore selection of spouses was largely controlled by parents, and the personal opinions of the future mates were not socially important. Spouses were expected to treat one another with respect and to develop the same kind of mutual economic interdependence and affection that ideally exists among relatives, but love was not absolutely necessary for the marriage to be considered successful.

Until 1880 Northeast Brazil was dominated by large, slave labor plantations. Slave owners commonly used female slaves sexually, as well as employing them as wet nurses and nannies (Freyre 1983:278). Upper-class white women's sexuality was seen as a commodity associated with inheritance and confined to marriage, while male sexuality was both a biological imperative expressing power and a source of pleasure (Bruschini 1990:62). Lower-class women's sexuality belonged to powerful men to use as they pleased. This led to an emotional isolation of the upper-class wife, who was confined to producing heirs, serving as a conduit for the transmission of inheritance and being an ornament for her husband's honor, while the physical and emotional needs of her family were relegated to slaves (de Alameida 1986:702–703). Even after the abolition of slavery upper-class men used their power to attract or coerce lower-class women into affairs. Some of these affairs may have included an element of mutual attraction, but they occurred in the context of a power structure that saw female volition as irrelevant to sexual relations, so love was not necessarily a part of them.

In addition to affairs with lower-class women, upper-class men might feel strong attractions for women of their own class whom they were unable to marry because their families pushed them toward another spouse. Many women also were married against their will to virtual strangers, breaking up nascent attractions they had formed toward cousins or other young men with whom they were allowed to have social contact. As in Europe, the frustrated passions of these thwarted infatuations were seen as both tragic and glorious. From the eighteenth to the early twentieth century Brazilian literary and popular representations portrayed romantic passion as a tragic extraconjugal passion, necessarily frustrated and doomed to a melancholy end (Leite and Massaini 1989:72). It was characterized by separation and obstacles, with moments of ecstatic reunion, whereas the marital relation was seen as calmly routine, if affectionate (Trigo 1989:90). Whereas marriage was public, passionate love was clandestine: a transcendent, irrational, tragic, and glorious ardor (Leite and Massaini 1989:76). This was similar to eighteenth-century European concepts in which marital love was seen as a social duty while couples in clandestine love affairs were believed to be able to reach the purest heights of spiritual and physical union (Borscheid 1986:158).

In the later twentieth century Brazil experienced a massive population movement into cities (Perlman 1976:5; de Araujo 1987:167) and an increasingly capitalist economy. No longer a unit of production, the family took its role in a consumer economy in which men could support their wives on their earnings instead of depending on inheritance or dowries (Nazzari 1991:148). As the economy depended less on inherited wealth, parents lost economic power over their children and could no longer easily compel marriages (Nazzari 1991:148). Marriage was redefined as an amorous union between an individual man and an individual woman who married on the basis of personal desire (Trigo 1989:90), and young people began to choose their own spouses.

However, these economic changes affected men and women differently. Unlike scholars of Europe who see capitalism as leading to a general ability of young people to choose spouses, my Brazilian evidence shows that modernization frees young men more than young women. In rural areas of the South and in Brazil's impoverished Northeast region, capitalization was never complete, and the economy remained a mixed economy in which cash and reciprocal exchange coexist. Rural workers today receive cash wages in return for their labor, but they also continue to receive *parceiros*, or shares of the crop (Gnaccarini 1989:159), or to be paid in boxes of staple foods. The traditional system of patronage, in which labor and loyalty are owed to a landowner who gives economic support and protection in return, remains strong. And while individuals can find wage labor, integration into a family or the pseudo family of a social network remains essential for economic survival partly because hyperinflation has rendered cash nearly worthless and partly because access to goods and services still follows lines of personal contact.

The ability to leave the family or defy parents because of the independence of wage labor remains a largely male liberty. Unmarried girls or women cannot live alone not only because the state of being unchaperoned would reflect badly on family honor but also because a woman not clearly protected by a father, brother, or son is considered fair sexual game. Women living alone are subject to sexual harrassment that includes both verbal and physical assaults. Girls living with families help their mothers or other female relatives with household labor. Marriage does not change a woman's daily routine very much, except that it adds sex to her domestic obligations and changes her residence.

Many young couples live with the parents of the groom or, less commonly, the bride, until they are able to afford their own house. In such cases the young woman goes from working for her father to working for her husband, under the supervision of her mother-in-law. Marriage is still economically important because it brings a wife-worker into the family and creates child-workers, and because it creates social and material alliances between families (Gnaccarini 1989:159), useful in a society in which so much economic exchange and opportunity follows the lines of personal relationships in networks. In the lower classes marriage often takes the form of *amaziamento*, or living together, which is treated much the same as legal marriage in daily life and has a similar economic role.

In the family ties of affinity and consanguinity are reinforced by economic cooperation, and the poorer the family, the more compulsory the cooperation to ensure family survival. Usually, sons and daughters who work outside the home give all or most of their earnings to their father, who redistributes them among family members or uses them to buy food for the entire family (de Oliveira 1985:114). The ability of young women to work outside the home increased in the 1950s, when the urban market in domestic labor grew rapidly. As women increasingly realized that they could be paid for doing laundry, washing dishes, and child care, they came to see their domestic labor as a commodity, and daughters began to resent even more the requirement that they work in their fathers' home. In a trend starting in the 1960s and growing to this day, daughters see doing domestic labor at home, or turning over earnings from labor outside the home, as voluntary, whereas parents continue to see it as compulsory. This leads to great tensions within the family (de Oliveira 1985:116).

Since colonial times young people have rebelled against parental schemes to manipulate the distribution of their domestic labor, dowries, and alliances through marriage by eloping. The practice of elopement, called both *fuga* (flight, escape) and *rapto* (kidnapping, theft), is widespread and of great antiquity. Usually *rapto* is consensual, although there are cases where a bride is kidnapped against her will and then forced to marry her abductor-rapist to preserve family honor. More commonly, couples use consensual *rapto* to force parents to recognize an inconvenient romance.

However, there are also many young women who elope with the first man who gives them an opportunity. Frequently women told me that they had eloped with men they had known very briefly—a few days, even a few hours. These young women, who may be as young as twelve or fourteen years of age, flee partly to escape what they see as their parents' oppressive demands for their labor and partly because of their romanticized ideas of liberty and love with their new spouse. They chafe at the tight chaperonage imposed by their fathers or brothers, which may include violence or threats of violence. In some cases they are fleeing sexual or other physical abuse at home. But most of these young women are badly mistaken about the consequences of their actions because their new husbands treat them little better than their fathers did, and sometimes treat them worse.

> I had never seen this man. . . . And when we saw each other, I don't know what it was that happened, if it was love at first sight or what it was. . . . After one week I eloped with him . . . I didn't know him, it was, like, a sudden thing. . . . It was horrible for me . . . it was like a prison because I didn't even know the guy. . . . I found out . . . I had eloped with a married man separated from his wife . . . a violent man, who drinks and chases women. . . . My mother's dream and my father's was that we girls would leave in a wedding dress from home, like poor people, but well married, with legal papers. But I had to go do this thing, and have children with him besides! (twenty-three-year-old woman)

Young women's mistaken ideas about love are important motivations in their elopements. Their romanticized visions, influenced by both popular culture in the form of television and magazine soap operas and traditional folklore in the form of folktales and aphorisms, lead them to believe in love as a union of souls in tender intimacy and to expect devotion and protection from male suitors. This vision is far from reality.

> I always thought that this enchanted prince would come for me, fall in love, and go live together in a castle. And I would stay in the castle, and him out in the world fighting the dragons to protect me. But as it turned out, who has to fight the dragons is me, here in this [sarcastically] castle of mine, him out there in the world chasing sluts (*raparigas*) on the street. I think what I married is not the prince but the frog. (thirty-five-year-old housewife)

Ideas of what constitutes love have changed over time in response to economic and social change. In the developing class society of the nineteenth century, such traditional feminine virtues as self-sacrifice, submission, dedication, and abdication of personal desire were increasingly seen as proofs of love (Trigo 1989:90), and love as the glue holding marriage, family, and society itself together. What had once been the virtues of mothers were now proofs of the love of brides. The more chaperoned, virginal, submissive, and self-sacrificing a woman, the more loving she was considered and the higher the status of her family.

From the beginning of the colonial enterprise theologians had been concerned with promoting Christian forms of marriage in Spanish and Portuguese New World colonies. Much of the activity of religious courts in Brazil revolved around adjudicating cases of rape, elopement, and defloration according to the guidelines of the sixteenth-century Council of Trent during its reformulation of Catholic doctrine (Lavrin 1989:4–5). In the 1880s ideas of hygiene combined with rising capitalization to create a new view of the nature of the family that was then codified into law. Brazilian hygienists promoted the love-based, monogamous nuclear family as conducive to social order and a marker of economic and moral progress (Costa 1989:171).

As love became the stated basis of and raison d'être of marriage, the definition of marital love increasingly merged with concepts of extramarital passion. This caused a shift in prevailing notions of the nature and course of passionate love, because tying it to marriage necessitated that it be stable, permanent, and have a happy outcome. Marital love was increasingly seen as like maternal and familial love, concepts deeply influenced by Christian religious belief, especially the theological idea of *agapé*, or benevolent, selfless love. However, marriage's basis in love was more a manner of speaking than a social reality.

To say that love had become the basis of marriage does not mean that all couples married for love, nor that marriages suddenly became more amorous than they had been in the past. It means simply that love became the idiom in which marriage was discussed. Where before a couple would speak of having married for family reasons, now they spoke of having married for love, although the economic underpinnings of the marital relationship remained strong motivators for forming and sustaining the relationship (cf. Borscheid 1986:168). In addition, the definition of love, what kinds of sentiments and expressions constituted "true love (*amor verdadeira*)," changed. Love became part of emotionology but did not necessarily strongly impact personal emotional experience.

Whatever affections people may have felt for one another occurred in the context of these events. Not everyone was able to act on their feelings, but

the high incidence of cases of elopement and complaints of sexual misbe-
havior in religious courts is evidence that many tried. These court cases show
that young lovers resisted arranged marriages and often maintained life-long
covert courtships despite having been married to others (de Azevedo 1986:7).
Other couples were able to force the issue by elopement, cohabitation, or ille-
gitimate pregnancy (Kuznesof and Oppenheimer 1985:217).

In today's Brazil consensual union remains the norm in the lower classes
and legal marriage the norm in the upper classes (Ribiero 1982). Religious
marriage is not legally binding, but it carries higher status than civil marriage. Lower-class people emulate the stereotypical upper-class white family
in their unions. To the extent that a couple can hold a formal religious wedding party, marry legally, and confine the wife to the home as a housewife,
they can gain status. To the extent that they cohabit without legal or religious
marriage and the woman works outside the home, they loose status. Many
couples describe their relationship as marriage and refer to one another as
husband (*marido*) and wife (*esposa*), even when the union is not legalized in a
bid for honorable legitimacy. The language of love in present-day Brazil
reflects these historical and class influences on marriage.

The development of a discourse on love marriage does not mean that sexual relationships in general are any happier today than they were in the past.
Because the two genders have different expectations of the marital relationship, and because they rarely discuss emotional issues openly, misunderstandings and disappointment are rife. This, combined with the different
economic and sexual interests of the two genders, leads to widespread disillusion, and is a factor in the frequent breakup of marriages and less formal
alliances.

> People confuse love and liberty. The way I was raised, the children divided their
> earnings with their parents and paid the rent, but today the kids think they know
> everything and that their earnings are their own. . . . Too many marriages are
> based on lies, that she promises him or he promises her what he or she will not
> really do. . . . Sometimes it is not really a promise, it is that she thinks that he
> promised or he thinks that she promised, but the other one has a different idea.
> Then each one ends up feeling betrayed, but there was no real promise to start.
> Just a lot of hope and a little delusion. (sixty-three-year-old man)

My informants had differing definitions of love and opinions about its frequency, course, and outcome. They used a number of terms to describe loving relations including *amor verdadeira* (true love), *amor da mãe* (mother

love), *consideração* (consideration), *amor* (love), *paixão* (passion, infatuation), and *lóvi* (modern love) or *amor da novela* (soap opera love). In the next sections, I review this language of love.

Mother Love

Some kinds of love are considered true, while others are false illusions. The phrases "*abaixo de Deus, mãe* (under God, mother)" and "*amor só da mãe* (love [is] only of mother)" are commonly spoken as well as written on truck bumpers and mud flaps, T-shirts, stickers, and stationery. Veneration of mothers as devoted, self-sacrificing, and semidivine has a long history in Mediterranean Portugal and its daughter culture, Brazil (de Aragão 1983). Ideally, a mother is a woman's best friend and a man's most devoted admirer.

> We have lots of aquaintances (*colegas*), but as a true friend we only have our mother. You can trust your mother in everything. You can confide in her. She will help you. You can depend on her. Without my mother I would not have survived until now, not only when I was a baby and she raised me, but now, advising me on how to manage my husband, helping me raise my children, nursing me when I am sick, lending me money when I am broke. (thirty-two-year-old housewife)

Few mothers actually live up to the ideal of self-abnegating love venerated in religious imagery of Christ's sorrowing virgin Mother, but most try to raise their children to believe that they do. There is a strongly felt competition between mothers and wives or girlfriends for men's love. "My mother always told me that I only have one mother, one mother who loves me truly. I can always find some slut (*rapariga*) there on the street, but I can never replace my mother" (thirty-four-year-old married man). Historically, the mother-son bond was stronger than the husband-wife bond, and it was the location of romanticized love. Today women who are disappointed in the weakness of their husbands' love still turn to their sons for the veneration and companionship their husbands cannot give them. "I raised my boys almost alone because my husband was young, beautiful, a lover of women, and a truck driver. When I saw how he really was, I dedicated myself to my sons. . . . I love them and they love me" (thirty-four-year-old housewife)

In turn, men are often disappointed when their wives fail to give them the uncomplaining devotion they expect from their mothers. A full examination of mother love is beyond the scope of this chapter, but mother love is important in any consideration of sexual love, because it is the yardstick by which the "trueness" of all other kinds of love are measured.

Companionate Love

Northeast Brazilians are in general a gregarious people, loving company, fearing loneliness. They frequently used the term *saudade*, which does not translate directly into any single English word but refers to the mingled sadness and pleasure of remembering people, places, or events now distant in time or space; like a mixture of the English *nostalgia, homesickness,* and *to miss.* Most of my informants had never been alone in their lives, and felt intense *saudade* for people not present. They lived in a crowded style, partly because of poverty and also because they enjoyed the social and physical contact of shared meals, beds, and living space. Many quoted the proverb *Amor 'ta na convivência* (Love is in familiarity), stating that association itself constitutes love.

Here, love is the accumulation of presence; the kind of becoming-used-to that leads to *saudade* when the loved one is gone. Certainly, ideal relations among kin and friends are characterized by *convivência* and *saudade*. In marriage this kind of love includes respect and friendship within the performance of traditional gender roles. For the man these include the provision and maintenance of the house, provision of food, and protection of the family from physical or social harm. Wives kept house, cooked, bore and raised children, and upheld family honor through chastity. While men were not required to be sexually faithful, it was polite to be discrete about extramarital affairs. Courtesy was the rule between husband and wife. One elderly man summed it up this way:

> A woman is like a cow. If you want the cow's milk, you can't beat her, yell at her, no. You have to treat her with tenderness and care for her to give you her milk. With a woman it is the same thing. . . . You have to choose a good woman, respectable, and treat her well. That way it will work out.

In this view loving couples cohabit within a framework of trust and mutual cooperation: "Love is trusting in that person, having refuge, being honest with that person, making a home together, working together, raising children together, supporting each other" (twenty-five-year-old housewife). In addition, the physical labor the partners perform as part of their gender roles not only reflects but constitutes their love.

> Because I cook my husband's food, because I wash his clothes, because I clean his house, because I do his service [have sex with him], because I bear his children, because the people say, "O amor e a fé nas obras se vem" [Love and faith you see in actions], in these actions that I do, in my work, is the love. And he works in the

factory, and he brings the money home, and he pays the costs of the household, and thus he shows his love for me. (thirty-year-old housewife)

The proverb quoted by this housewife makes the religious underpinnings of companionate love explicit: love is a form of keeping faith with the beloved.

This definition of love is what Cancian in her analysis of the contemporary United States has called the masculine style (1986: 692). It is generally more typical of definitions in precapitalist Europe. Both academic writers and my informants identify it as an old-fashioned, rural style of thinking about marriage, although age and rurality did not in fact predict which individuals used this definition in Caruaru. It was as common among young urban people as among older, rural people in this small city. It is possible that the situation is different in larger, more cosmopolitan urban centers.

Many informants described their marriages in terms of *obrigaço* (obligation) and *consideração* (consideration) (cf. Robben 1989:577). Married couples have obligations to fulfill to one another, the husband to provide and support a house, the wife to do housework and raise children. They can simply perform these obligations dutifully, but they can also add little flourishes of *consideração*, or actions beyond strict responsibility. While *consideração* is not strictly necessary in a marriage, its lack is seen as bad treatment. One male informant described it like this:

> When a couple does not have *consideração*, they treat each other badly. What a man does bad to a woman is to not value her, not listen to her, he betrays her [sexually], he doesn't let her take part in decisions, he only communicates them to her, he mistreats her even physically. What women do bad to men is to try to dominate him, to impede him from having her physically, to try to manipulate the man.

While everyone has obligations and is free to act with consideration, obligation and consideration operate differently for men and for women. Men are forgiven for lacking consideration: they can even get out of some obligations without too much social consequence. But women are held to their obligations and expected to show consideration as well, because they are responsible for nurturing and worrying about others and are expected to be obedient and submissive.

For many women true love requires renouncing one's own interests in favor of those of the beloved. "For me, love is the renunciation of I (*a renuncia de eu*). When you like another person, when you love, understand, you give yourself totally to that person, you forget yourself and remember to love the other person" (eighteen-year-old woman). Here, love between

women and men has taken on some of the qualities of mother love: self-abnegating, suffering, generous. While several women spoke to me of their obligation to self-abnegation in love, not a single man saw self-abnegation as
something he was required to do. This attitude contributes to women's cynical idea that men are incapable of true love.

Women's personal identities are submerged in their families and social
networks to a much greater extent than men's, and they are expected to sustain the emotional relationships that hold networks and families together.
While most men and some women said that supporting a wife economically
is sufficient proof of love, most women wanted *consideração* in the form of
emotional intimacy as well, what Cancian calls the "feminized" style of love
(1986:693). "I feel needy. . . . He gives me material things that I don't need. I
need more like a friendly word from him, I wish that he was more my friend
than my husband, but he isn't like that" (thirty-two-year-old housewife).
Sometimes men and women differ in their ideas on what constitutes *consideração*. For example, women stated that talking over problems together was
part of *consideração* and a sign of affection. "What upsets me is that he's a
cold, shut-up man, has a problem and doesn't talk . . . that is to say, he does-
n't have confidence in me. He doesn't love me" (thirty-year-old housewife).
However, men may think that sparing their wives worry over personal problems is considerate, and not understand their wives' discontent.

Style of Courtship and Style of Love

Brazilian folk sayings such as "There is no sin below the equator" reveal a
self image as hot-blooded, passionate Latins (Parker 1991). In the Northeast
this self-image of passion sharply conflicts with a stringent code of sexual
morality in which a family's honor is embodied in the chastity of its women.
Historically, girls were closely chaperoned and then married off as early as
possible, often before or shortly after the first menstruation, to avoid any
possibility of loss of virginity before marriage. Marriage at fourteen or fifteen years of age remains common for girls, especially in rural and recently
rural areas. Men, given greater latitude to act out sexually, married when they
had proved adulthood by earning enough to buy and furnish a house. They
were generally forgiven sexual indiscretions both before and after marriage.
The polygynous tendency of Brazilian men continues to this day, and many
men have long-term residential relationships with more than one woman at
the same time. In addition, they may frequent prostitutes or pick up an occasional woman for a brief physical relationship.

Love, says the proverb, is born in a glance and matures in a smile. Because of chaperonage many couples shared little more than glances and smiles for the duration of their courtships. Couples now in their mid-thirties and older, and young couples in rural areas, describe a heavily supervised courtship, entered into only with the girl's father's permission.

> My father-in-law told me that marriage is a serious commitment and asked me how I would get a house. . . . We arrived at an accord about her age and how the courtship would be. . . . It was once a week on Saturday or Sunday that we met . . . everyone together conversing in the living room, very serious conversations, about the future like the old-time people used to talk—different from today. Then her father would tell a ghost story, which was the signal for me to leave. I would get on my bicycle and leave, just "raining" [peddling furiously]. (fifty-year-old man)

Today, while people still practice the traditional chaperoned courtship in rural areas, sexual mores have loosened in the cities. But still, in small cities like Caruaru, only couples who are officially engaged go out on dates alone; other courting couples go out in groups with their siblings and cousins. Glances, smiles, and occasional stolen moments remain a major part of courtship, shaping concepts of love. Young women's social lives are still policed by their fathers and brothers, and there is occasional violence over courtships the family does not want. Chastity as honor remains important. Sometimes parents use dishonor to force a marriage, as in the "sledgehammer wedding" (*casamento na marra*) in which a man is forced by threat of violence to marry a woman he has sexually dishonored. Alternately, couples may force their parents to agree to a marriage by making the woman's lack of virginity publically known, shaming the parents.

The conflict between the stable, companionate love underlying mature marriage and the tumultuous emotions of sexual attraction are reflected in the distinction made between *amor* (love) and *paixão* (passion, infatuation). There was a great difference of opinion on the nature and distinction of these two sentiments.

Amor vs Paixão

The emotions aroused by marriage, cohabitation, and short-term physical relations are viewed as both similar and distinct. Informants state that the difference between what they call *amor* and *paixão* is deeply confusing. They debate which, if either, is true love and struggle to fit these concepts to their experiences. People can't always tell what they really feel, except that it is powerful.

> Really, it doesn't make sense. Sometimes we only know that we like someone when it ends. Sometimes we think we hate someone and it turns out we love them and didn't know it, or we didn't want to admit it. And *amor* is so good and yet people are so scared of it, because it can really hurt a person. But the thing is, sometimes we are so afraid of being hurt that we go push the other person away and get hurt just so as not to get hurt. I told you, no sense! (twenty-five-year-old man)

Ideally, *amor* is distinguished from *paixão* by duration and selflessness.

> Now, *amor* and *paixão*, they walk together, but before the end of the road, *paixão*, it stops walking. But *amor* goes the whole distance, no matter how difficult the road, *amor* walks with you, and if you fall, *amor* carries you. (twenty-six-year-old man)

Informants saw *paixão* as characterized by more idealization than *amor*, and as therefore less satisfying.

> *Paixão* is that fantasy, that you see the person and start to imagine how they are. But with time the impression changes and one becomes disillusioned, and goes looking for another person to idealize, always thinking, "This is her! This is the only one!" But it never is, because it is imaginary. (twenty-eight-year-old male)

But the subjective experience of *amor* and *paixão* are very similar, especially in the early stages of a relationship, when the two sentiments are nearly indistinguishable.

> *Paixão* is a temporary sentiment. It doesn't last forever. It is only something that we beautify [*embeleza*] about someone. We idealize them, but that is temporary. At times *paixão* is the deceiver because it seems like *amor*. But *paixão* is quick, it is also very greedy; it only wants for itself. *Paixão* is where jealousy exists. *Amor* does not have jealousy, it lasts forever. It is certain. But *paixão* is unsure, and uncertainty is what breeds jealousy. The people say, "Bem ama quem nunca esquece" [Whoever loves well never forgets]. That is, love never forgets, it endures. (nineteen-year-old male)

Even when informants tried to distinguish their descriptions of the two, they ended up saying very similar things about *amor* and *paixão*.

> *Amor* is when you feel a desire to always be with her, you breathe her, eat her, drink her, you are always thinking of her, you don't manage to live without her.

There are moments when you will adore staying with her, and there will be moments when you will hate to stay with her. And about *paixão*, you feel an attraction as if it were a rocket: I want to hug you, to squeeze you, to kiss you. But this is not love, it's horniness [*tesão*], a very strong sexual attraction for a person. (twenty-five-year-old male)

Lovers must ask themselves constantly whether what they are feeling is true love or merely *paixão*:

> Sometimes I stay thinking, could it be that what we feel is really love? We become infatuated thinking it is love, but from one hour to the next all that ends. Except that what we feel does not end, but the relationship ends, we stay with that stored inside of us, hurting, injuring us. I don't understand it. Is it only love if the two both love? Sometimes I think back about some old girlfriend and I remember some little thing about her with great pleasure, still all this time later. Does that mean I loved her? Or did I just love that one little thing and the rest was *paixão*? (thirty-two-year-old man)

While men were more likely to puzzle over *amor* and *paixão*, women also experienced them as different, seeing *paixão* as youthful and *amor* as enduring and mature. Many women stated that their feelings toward their husbands had changed over the course of the marriage. "I like him, I love him. I won't say it's that LOOO-OOO-OOVE of before, love of a bride . . . but if, God defend me, if I became a widow, I wouldn't want another man, I'm his wife until the end" (forty-seven-year-old seamstress) Other women saw this change as not only due to the maturation of *paixão* but also to their own personal maturation.

Paradoxically, whereas those who believe in the companionate love concept regard cohabitation as constitive of love, those who see love as *paixão* regard it as destructive of love. "It is so difficult, so very difficult to live with a person. It's like a drop of water dripping, dripping, and eventually you can't stand it any more. There is no love capable of surviving cohabitation" (thirty-two-year-old woman). To this woman cohabitation destroys the idealization necessary for love. But for other informants that very idealization is not love but *paixão*, and its fading is part of the development of true love.

While both men and women spoke of the distinction between *amor* and *paixão*, men were much more confused about how to distinguish them. In addition, many men stated that it is possible to feel true *amor* for more than one woman at a time, whereas women emphatically rejected this idea, seeing *amor* as monogamous. Other men said that their infidelities did not threaten their marriages precisely because what the husband felt for the "other woman" [*a outra*] was *paixão*, whereas what he felt for his wife was *amor*.

For many women this male attitude is part of men's inability to love truly, like women do.

> Love between men and women? Is that what you asked me, my daughter? I can't tell you what means a thing that does not exist. You hear? It doesn't exist. It's a lie. It's deception. It's just a word men use to get women into bed and women use to get men to pay their bills. That's all. (sixty-year-old farmer's wife)

While some informants had strong opinions on how to distinguish *amor* and *paixão*, others were unsure of the differences or used the words interchangeably. Brazilian social scientists attribute this to the development of what they call *amor-paixão*, or the modern conflation of sexual passion with marital love.

Lóvi

While watching the extremely popular prime-time Brazilian soap operas (*telenovelas*), I was sometimes startled to see fictional couples look deeply into each others' eyes and declare, "*Ai lóvi iú.*" This English phrase is also written on T-shirts, notebooks, truck bumpers, and stickers of all kinds. *Lóvi*, also called *amor da novela* (soap opera love), or, in academic writing, *amor-paixão*, is generally considered a U.S. import, although it might more accurately be described as a natural outcome of economic and social changes in Brazil rather than as a foreignism.

Lóvi is characterized by mutual economic and emotional interdependence, expressed in verbal tenderness and declarations of love, and constitutes as much a merging of souls as of bodies. It contains a number of suppositions on the basis of which couples interpret the strength of their relationships (Botas 1987:54–55). The configuration of *amor-paixão* is a mixture of the various types of love, combining the romantization of *paixão* with the merging of souls and self-abnegating devotion promised by Christian theological *agapé*, and adding the veneration of marriage as the basis of stable society promoted by the hygienic movement.

Amor-paixão or *lóvi* fits urban life styles because it emphasizes the importance of the couple as a social unit, the primacy of personal emotional experience, and the dependence of women on men. The companionate love of *obrigação* and *consideração* fit a system in which men and women were economically, socially, and personally interdependent, since neither could live without the work performed by the other. But *lóvi* emphasizes the expressive side of love while downplaying its economic and instrumental aspects. The emphasis on *lóvi* as the basis of marriage conceals the economic interdependence of the sexes (cf. Cancian 1985: 258) and furthers the process of redefining obligations as voluntary forms of consideration. Since consideration is more obligatory for women than for men, it has the effect of rendering male obligations voluntary while keeping women obligated to perform not only duties but favors. *Lóvi* takes its place as a tactic in the struggle for control between men and women.

Lóvi's emphasis on emotional intimacy is very difficult for men, raised to act powerful and independent, to accept. In addition, its insistence on monogamy conflicts with men's felt need to prove their virility and independence from female control by promiscuity. Some men reject *lóvi* outright as feminine frippery. Others are torn between traditional *machista* views of sexual relations and the modern expectation of a more equal sharing:

> I like women who please me, stroke me, do things for me. . . . But generally they are very empty people, and I don't manage to stay with them. . . . I try to be open minded but it is impossible to liberate yourself from the remnants of machismo . . . so we always want there to exist women who live as functions of us, but this doesn't satisfy us. It's impossible, the situation. (twenty-five-year-old man)

Other men like the idealization and tenderness of *lóvi* but find it hard to take seriously enough to commit permanently to one woman. A common saying goes, "Ser carinhoso é fácil, dificil é ser sincera" (It is easy to be tender, difficult is to be sincere). Other men want to enjoy the union of *lóvi* but find it difficult to attain, either because they do not know how, or because the problems of daily life interfere.

> The human being is incomplete, and the man completes the woman, and the woman the man. A couple shouldn't lack anything. But for the two to get along well you have to understand the others' problems in detail, each point. There are times when you don't have a head to get a hold of even your own problems, much less those of others. (thirty-four-year-old man)

Problems in communication between the genders, disappointment with ruptured love affairs, the disillusion of long acquaintance all combine to leave many feeling very cynical indeed about love.

Love as Suffering

Love would be fraught with difficulties enough, even if social and economic pressures and gender differences were absent. Attractions are not always mutual or of equal strength, partners may not be sufficiently mature, empathic, or generous to know their own hearts, much less their partners', or appeal may be based simply on sexual attraction, lacking sufficient depth to survive the fading of the fires. If these personal difficulties were not enough to derail romances, conflicting economic and social pressures on lovers and the different perspectives of the two genders combine with cultural difficulties to ruin romances.

Disillusionment and traditional expectations of suffering on behalf of loved ones combine in many informants' description of love as a form of suffering. Brazilian proverbs declare, "A mulher brasileira é feito de amor" (The Brazilian woman is made of love), "Ser mulher é sofrir" (To be a woman is to suffer), and "Amar é sofrir" (To love is to suffer). Love can cause suffering by being unrequited or failing to endure:

> I don't know. I only know that love is a sadness that goes away The heart still cries. But we have to have it, don't we? We have to suffer it. It doesn't do any good to run away from it, because it will come after us, hurting. . . . Now all I ask my sweet Jesus is to send me strength to raise my children. And don't send any more men my way . . . because never does anyone know the heart of another! Never! (forty-year-old marketwoman)

Love can be painful simply because it is such a powerful passion it overcomes the ability of the lover to ignore it:

> I think that love is a little thing, a little teeny tiny beastie [*bichinho bem pequenininho*], you know? That gnaws away a lot there inside and goes on gnawing, gnawing. That if we aren't careful he kills us. . . . There is only one love—that true love we kill and die for. (forty-year-old housewife)

Or love can be painful, because it calls upon the lover to sacrifice self for beloved. For men love causes suffering when it is unrequited.

> I think all men carry with them the memory of that one girl who did not want them. . . . Men suffer with love because always there is the girl you can't have. The one who you love desperately, and she does not love you. And you end up with a broken heart. Just because men don't cry all the time like women do doesn't mean they don't get broken hearts too. (twenty-eight-year-old man)

For women unrequited love is also painful. Even more painful is the disillusion brought on by women's interpretation of men's behavior toward them.

> They say men suffer from the women they can't have. Well, my daughter, women suffer from the men they *do* have. It is much better to have a broken heart and live your life dreaming of how it might have been than it is to get your heart's desire, marry, and find out that it is hopeless, what you thought was love is not love at all. (fifty-eight-year-old woman)

In this view, far from being a sublime and beautiful experience, love is a powerful but painful experience that calls upon people to make sacrifices, endure pain, and suffer disillusion and rejection.

My informants describe love as an alluring but frightening mix of passions that while seeming to sweep over an overwhelmed ego from outside also reach deep within, dragging up everything so carefully hidden from oneself—frightening not only for the chance of rejection but perhaps more for the possibility of success. In a culture where suffering is both one's lot in life and one's defense against it, the prospect of enduring happiness is frighteningly unfamiliar and destablizing.

While many are disillusioned with love, some believe that love is worth all the pain.

> The question of love doesn't have to be useful, love is good in itself. Love is so good, so good that even loving a person and she doesn't love you, even hurting, hurting you don't want it to end, because love is good, is delicious, is a sentiment that God left for the world. (thirty-year-old-male mechanic)

The search for love brings its own rewards, and some thrive on the excitement of love's emotional ups and downs. For some, sequential bouts with *paixão* and broken hearts give life the energy that makes it worth living.

> Have you ever been in love [*apaixonada*]? I have been so many times, and been hurt so many times. And when it ends it is the worst pain in the world. But even so, all the pain is worth it for those few minutes. Because love is the most delicious dish there is to eat in the world, it is what makes life worth living, those moments of love. (twenty-one-year-old female secretary)

Love, with all its drama, is after all more interesting than any other story people might make of their lives, and in its pursuit they can reach not only for what is best in human character but also taste of what is worst.

The primacy of *lóvi* in contemporary public discourse does not mark the introduction of a completely new sentiment. Rather it indicates a shift in emphasis from companionate to passionate love as appropriate within marriage as well as a shift from mothers to wives as primary love objects for men. In addition, the economic dynamics of marriage continue to change to a system in which the couple rather than the extended family is the basic social unit. These shifts are ongoing, and people's current opinions on their experiences reflect the rapid changes they have experienced over their lifetimes.

Social and economic change has made it easier for young people to act on their feelings in the formation of marriages. However, economic considerations and traditional gender roles remain important forces in the shape of marital relations. Men remain freer than women to satisfy their physical and emotional desires, and both sexes must negotiate complex situations as they try to figure out what they feel, how they can act, and what the consequences of their actions may turn out to be. The choices they make are not necessarily the best or most rational ones. Frequently they mistake each others' or their own motivations and miscalculate the consequences of their actions. While many are disillusioned by their experiences, others hold on to the hope that one day they will achieve true love and perfect union.

> I think that there still exist people in the middle of a thousand, there are two or three who still love truly. And we all watch them, and envy them, and try to be like them, and cause ourselves and those we love so much pain trying so hard to love, and failing because we are human, we err, we are imperfect, and love is a sublime thing that comes from God and can get so lost inside of us. And yet every once in a while there it is, a flower blooming in a desert, surviving against all the odds. (twenty-seven-year-old woman)

Love-marriage is an idealistic thing, an attempt to wrest a small measure of happiness from a too often indifferent world. While frequently destroyed by the inequities of social arrangements and the human weaknesses of its participants, it remains an attempt at a noble endeavor. And while my informants may lament their failures in love, nursing their hurts and snarling their angers, in the end they still strive for love. In their own way they achieve it.

NOTE

The research upon which this essay is based was supported by grants from the Fulbright Foundation-International Institute of Education, the Lowie Foundation, the Tinker Foundation, the Social Science Research Council, the National Science Foundation, the National Institutes of Mental Health, and a Hannum-Warner Travel Fellowship from

Mount Holyoke College, and was facilitated by affiliation with the Universidade Federál de Pernambuco, Departamento de Antropologia. This essay benefited from comments by Donna Goldstein and Molly Lee and could not have been written without the support of my parents, Mildred and Lionel Rebhun, and the cooperation of my Brazilian informants, to whom I owe many thanks.

REFERENCES

de Alameida, A. M. 1986. "Sexualidade e Casamento Na Colonização Portuguesa No Brasil." *Analise Social* 22(92–930:697–705.

de Aragão, L. T. 1983. "Em Nome da Mãe Posição estrutural e disposiç&es sociais que envolvem a categoria mãe na civilização mediterrânea e na sociedade brasileira." *Perspectivas Antropológicas da Mulher, no. 3.* Rio de Janeiro: Zohar.

de Araujo, T. B. 1987. "Nordeste: Diferenciais Demográficas Regionais e Seus Determinantes." *Cadernos de Estudios Sociais* 3(3):167–192.

de Azevedo, T. 1986. *As Regras do Namoro à Antiga.* São Paulo: Editora Atica.

Borscheid, P. 1986. "Romantic Love or Material Interest: Choosing Partners in Nineteenth-Century Germany" *Journal of Family History* 11(2):157–168.

Botas, P. C. L. 1987. "Casamento: O Crepúsculo da Paixão." In Moacir Costa, ed., *Homem Mulher Crises e Conquistas.* São Paulo: Melhoramentos de São Paulo.

Bruschini, M. C. A. 1990. *Mulher, Casa e Família Cotidiano nas camadas médias paulistanas.* São Paulo: Editora Revista dos Tribunais, Ediç&es Vértice.

Cancian, F. M. 1985. "Gender Politics: Love and Politics in the Private and Public Spheres." In A. S. Rossi, ed., *Gender and the Life Course.* pp. 253–264. New York: Aldine Publishing Company.

— 1986. "The Feminization of Love." *Signs: A Journal of Women in Culture and Society* 11(4):692–709.

Costa, J. F. 1989. *Ordem Médica e Norma Familiar.* Rio de Janeiro: Graal.

Freyre, G. 1983. *Casa-Grande e Senzala: Formação da Família Brasileira sob o regime da Economia Patriarcal.* 22d ed. Rio de Janeiro: Livraria José Olympio Editora.

Gillis, J. R. 1988. "From Ritual to Romance: Toward an Alternative History of Love." In C. Z. Stearns and P. N. Stearns, eds., *Emotion and Social Change Toward a New Psychohistory.* pp. 87–122. New York: Holms and Meier.

Gnaccarini, J. C. 1989. "O Rapto das Donzelas." *Tempo Social Revista Sociológico USP São Paulo* 1(1):149–168.

Kuznesof, E., and R. Oppenheimer. 1985. "The Family and Society in Nineteenth-Century Latin America: A Historiographical Introduction" *Journal of Family History* 10(3):215–234.

Lavrin, A. 1989. "Introduction: The Scenario, the Actors, and the Issues." In L. Asunción, ed., *Sexuality and Marriage in Colonial Latin America,* pp. 1–46. Lincoln: University of Nebraska Press.

Leite, M. M., and M. I. Massaini. 1989. "Representações do Amor e da Família." In M. A. D'Inção, ed., *Amor e Familia No Brasil,* pp. 72–87. São Paulo: Editora Contexto.

MacFarlane, A. 1987. *The Culture of Capitalism.* Cambridge: Basil Blackwell.

Nazzari, M. 1991. *Disappearance of the Dowry Women, Families, and Social Change in São*

Paulo, Brazil, 1600–1900. Stanford: Stanford University Press.

de Oliveira, M. C. F. A. 1985. "O Casamento e as Estratégias de Sobrevivência da Família Operária na Agricultura Paulista." *Revista Brasileira de Estudios de População* 2(1):105–142.

Parker, R. 1991. *Bodies Pleasures and Passions Sexual Culture in Contemporary Brazil*. Boston: Beacon.

Perlman, J. 1976. *The Myth of Marginality*. Berkeley: University of California Press.

Ribiero, R. 1982. "O Amaziamento e Outros Aspectos da Família No Recife." In R. Ribiero, ed., *Antropologia da Religião e Outros Estudios*, pp. 59–70. Recife: Editora Massangana-Fundação Joachim Nabuco.

Robben, A. C. M. G. 1989. "Habits of the Home: Spatial Hegemony and the Structuration of House and Society in Brazil." *American Anthropologist* 91(3):570–588.

Stearns, P. N., and C. Z. Stearns. 1985. "Emotionology: Clarifying the History of Emotions and Emotion Standards." *American Historical Review* 90(4):813–836.

Stone, L. 1977. *The Family Sex and Marriage in England, 1500–1800*. New York: Harper Colophon.

Trigo, M. H. B. 1989. "Amor e Casamento No Seculo XX." In M. A. D'Inção, ed., *Amor e Família No Brasil*. pp. 88–94. São Paulo: Editora Contexto.

Putting Romance Into Systems of Sexuality: Changing Smart-Rules in a Trinidadian Village

KEVIN K. BIRTH AND MORRIS FREILICH

Romance is a complex cultural model that structures sexual relationships. As such it is one of many possible cultural models, and it coexists and even competes with them. In Eastern Trinidad in the 1950s the predominant cultural model that applied to sexual relationships was based on an idiom of exchange, or what we call "sex and begging." Men see sex and begging as a game in which sexual conquests must be broadcast to achieve prestige. Sexual conquest is obtained through a set of rules involving begging sex from women. Women see sex and begging as a system in which they obtain male company, sexual satisfaction, and gifts through acquiescence to begging, but they must keep sexual encounters relatively secret to remain desirable targets for begging. In this system men involved with sex and begging present themselves as inferior to women: "beggars" pleading to be accepted as lovers. Unlike "sex and romance," sex and begging involves little sentimentality. In sex and begging gifts offered (invariably by men to women) are more like exchanges for pleasures received than presents to someone admired and loved.

Our essay shows a system that went from sex and begging to something close to sex and romance. We identify some of the major variables that led to changes, such as contradictory goals of the men and the women, and factors that impinge from outside, such as American television, movies, radio, and novels. In addition, we explore the impact of these changes on male systems of domination.

Our ethnographic data come from Eastern Trinidad, from a rural community we call Anamat.[1] Our data make a diachronic analysis very feasible because they came from two projects done in Anamat more than thirty years apart. Research done by Freilich (1957–1958) provides baseline data and research done by Birth (1989–1991) provides comparative data, showing changes.

Due to the difficulties inherent in gender relationships in Trinidad, it is very difficult for male anthropologists to obtain the same quality of data from women as from men (Angrosino 1986). To that extent, we had to rely heavily on a few female informants. Despite our best efforts, it is possible that some data are skewed in favor of a Trinidadian male perspective. We must add, however, first that we received no contradictory information concerning any given love affair irrespective of whether our informants were male or female, second that significant changes have taken place in Trinidad, and that our informants, both male and female, related these changes to changing images of romance.

Freilich's data show sexual relationships as a system where men beg sex from women, the sex and begging system. We focus first on the major factors that made sex and begging viable for a short time; second, we examine some of the instabilities in the system that triggered changes. Next we describe elements of the sex and romance system and attempt to account for changes in the relationship of romance, male domination, and sexual relationships.

Sex and Begging: Anamat, Eastern Trinidad, 1957–1958

Anamat was a dispersed settlement community spread over six or so square miles of land in one of the mountain ranges of Trinidad.[2] The village was extremely isolated—a function of poor roads, no telephones, and a lack of direct public transportation to larger towns.

Anamat had only a brief experience with plantation agriculture. It was settled in the late nineteenth century, and the period of plantation dominance ended because of the combination of worldwide economic depression and devastating crop diseases in the 1930s.[3] By the 1950s agriculture in Anamat consisted predominantly of small-scale farming. At that time the peasants of Anamat possessed landholdings ranging from ten to thirty acres. Cocoa and coffee were the major cash crops and citrus fruits and bananas were subsidiary cash crops. Most of the peasants had full title to the land they worked. Some engaged in gardening, which sometimes involved cultivating state-owned land in order to provide a regular supply of food. Land was typically controlled by men, although a few women engaged in gardening (Freilich 1960).

Status, Prestige, and Sex

Anamatian peasants valued economic independence. They felt fortunate and proud that they could always provide for themselves. Economically independent villagers were considered socially superior to those whose livelihood partially or totally depended on the whims of other people. Since land was owned and worked by men, few women were economically independent. Hence, in general, a woman's social status and her economic survival was dependent on men.

Economic independence enabled men to engage in multiple love affairs. Economic well-being was often a necessary condition for initiating and maintaining love affairs, i.e., for successfully begging. For purposes of initiating such relationships, economic independence gave men "fooling power," meaning that the promises made by men to initiate a love affair were taken seriously by women. Having a wife[4] limited a man's fooling power because his promises to leave the wife for the lover were generally not taken seriously. Consequently, the category of men with the most fooling power were those men who were unmarried and economically independent.

In addition, the sex and begging system in Anamat included a male classification of sexual relationships based, in part, on an economic idiom. Men classified the sex act into two categories: "breed" and "brush." To breed referred to a situation where a man had sexual rights over a woman and used them to sire children. Minimal prestige was obtained from breeding because, as the locals put it, "he was only using what he already owned." On the other hand, a "brush" was a sex act where the male had no publicly recognized sexual rights over a woman. To get a brush, a male approached a woman as a humble supplicant: he had to "beg for a brush." A man's fooling power played an important role in the success of begging. Since fooling power was based on economic status, the likelihood of successfully begging was also based on economic status. Thus, both breed and brush implied a view of women's sexuality as a commodity that could be owned and obtained through promises of providing goods and services.

A conception of sex and romance was not absent from Anamatians' discussions of sexual relationships, but the situations to which it is was applied were limited. With regard to sex acts and their relation to romance, men could follow either "proper-rules," designating the correct or honorable way of acting, or "smart-rules," designating practical or personally satisfying acts (cf. Freilich 1980, 1991). Those who followed proper-rules established breeding relationships through church-sanctioned, legal marriage. To get a bride a man had to write a "demand" letter to a woman's parents.[5] The demand letter expressed the suitor's great admiration, attraction, and love for their daughter, requested permission to become a frequent visitor in their home, and declared that the writer's intentions were honorable: he wished to marry their daughter in a church, to make her his legal wife. Embedded within the "proper" were English moral standards (Rodman 1971) and a conception of romance. Yet the image of romance found in cultural conceptions of the proper was not articulated outside the domain of the moral standards explicitly linked to England, the upper class, and the Church.

While much lip service was paid to the importance of the proper, it was rarely pursued. Most Creoles followed guidelines that led to common-law marriages, unions considered best according to local smart-rules. These smart-rules were an integral part of the sex and begging system in Anamat. Indeed, even those who eventually went the legal marriage route usually began married life by living in a common-law marriage, and no demand letter was ever involved. Any woman brought into a house as a sexual partner had the status of a wife, although a distinction was made between categories of wife: a woman who goes to live with Mr. Jones was referred to directly and indirectly as "Ma Jones," i.e., the common-law wife of Jones. A legally married woman was given the higher status of "Mistress Jones."

Women who accepted common-law marriage—most of the Creole women of the community—did so because of its valuable consequences. First, most women believed this provided a relationship that was more respectable than that of an "outside woman"—a woman involved in a love affair. Second, they saw common-law marriage as a step toward legal marriage. Third, common-law marriage was seen as the best means available to women for economic survival.

Once a common-law marriage was established, the man was expected to provide economic support for his wife and children—even for his wife's young children sired by other men. The woman was expected to provide the husband with meals, a clean house, good companionship, and sexual services. Marriages lasted only as long as a couple felt they had "good cooperation," and each party to the union was understood to be capable of judging when and if cooperation existed. When a union dissolved the wife and *her* children (children were understood to belong to the mother) left the relationship to reside either in her mother's house or in the house of a new husband. Occasionally a woman rented a room in the village while looking for a new husband. The man might live alone for awhile in his house or quickly have another woman move in with him.

The fragility of conjugal ties was an important entailment of the sex and begging system. Due to the importance for men of successfully begging to obtain prestige, men changed spouses several times during their lives and, by implication, women changed spouses several times as well. The average Anamatian peasant had lived with three spouses; 45 percent of the group had lived with three or more spouses.

Number of Spouses of Peasant Household Heads, Anamat, Trinidad, 1957–1958

Number of Heads of Households	Number of Spouses
1	0
6	1
10	2
6	3
4	4
1	5
1	6
2	9

Creole peasants never considered a given union a life-time relationship. Even those who lived with a spouse for many years considered marriage a "now-for-now" affair. A marriage's present conditions took precedence over past satisfactions and future possibilities. If, at present, there was "no cooperation," then the relationship dissolved. Usually, after a relationship ended, men quickly "begged" another woman and began to live with her. In fact, most men were successfully begging sex from outside women in addition to their common-law wife.

Sex and begging was guided by an "information pool" created by men who shared local sex information. Members of this information sharing unit (ISU), knew about recent experiences of given males—about their conquests and about their rejections.[6] They also shared a conception of sexual relationships in which the ability to supply women with goods and services made a man a desirable sexual partner.[7] This knowledge provided additional smart-rules: they knew that the probability of successful begging is higher 1) with women who were currently husbandless, 2) with lower-class women, who had greater need for the goods and services, and 3) with women whose husbands stray frequently, as against women whose husbands rarely stray.[8]

In addition to sexual desire men were motivated by the pursuit of prestige. Their ISUs provided rules for evaluating sexual conquests and establishing prestige derived from such conquests. Men who obtained great amounts of prestige were called "famous." To be famous a man had to be a "hot boy": one always ready to grab an opportunity to beg, who was almost always successful at begging, and who developed a reputation for being able to physically perform after successful begging. To be successful a man needed a good memory and a creative imagination. That is, he had to remember promises made, to whom, and when. Moreover, when necessary he had to provide artful and believable explanations as to why previous promises made were not fulfilled.

Consequently, the smart-rules shared by men indicate that a man's economic status was an important factor in his ability to beg but not the sole factor in his success. Despite these other factors men still viewed sex as a situation in which women "give" sex in expectation of something tangible in return.

The smart-rules shared by women's ISUs emphasized making women prestigious sexual conquests for men. To do so, women sought respectability (see Wilson 1969). Class ideology was closely tied to the idea of respectability, so that it was assumed economically well-off men would legally marry only respectable women. Consequently, respectability did not guarantee obtaining an economically well-off husband, but lack of respectability barred women from marrying such a man. In addition, the more respectable the woman, the more desirable a sexual partner she was and, consequently, the more likely she would be begged for often.

This proper-rule of respectability often came into conflict with a belief in gender equality in which women should be entitled to behave as men. Since their husbands did not abandon sexual affairs after establishing a common-law relationship, sooner or later most women came to believe that extramarital sex was permissible, even desirable. However, these beliefs were linked to a basic proviso—a proviso regularly broken by men. Namely, that such affairs must be kept secret. It was through secrecy that women attempted to maintain a semblance of respectability.

Women were also guided by an information pool concerning sexual relationships in the village. This pool of information, while less formalized than the smart-rules, was yet a valuable source of data. It consisted largely of secrets one woman told a friend or two—information that the friend was never to reveal to anyone but that she told to her friend, etc. Women with access to the sexual information pool

1. knew that some men regularly and widely broadcast sexual conquests
2. knew which men spent a lot on lovers and which were miserly
3. knew men's reputation as lovers

Affairs had a dual quality for women. Sexual experiences provided women with valued goods, but there was the possibility that 1) husbands would discover the outside sex affairs of their wives, and 2) sex-affairs would produce pregnancy. Women tried to maximize peace at home while continuing to have sexual affairs. Put otherwise, they tried to play a "secret sex game."

For men, sexual encounters were avenues to social applause. All they had to do was to broadcast actual (or at times fictitious) conquests. They did this with much relish. As noted, the sex-fame game was played well by hot boys, frequent beggars for sex. To beg frequently and keep some minimal level of credibility regarding promises made required giving some gifts to several lovers. Successful hot boys therefore had to keep their sex expenses low so that 'funds' for many affairs were available. Hot boys received fame from peers both for the number of their conquests and for their fooling power.

The richer the peasant, the more he could participate in the sex and begging system: the more his promises were believed and the more affairs he actually had. The poorer the woman, the more often she would be successfully begged. The sex-fame game thereby served as a distribution-of-goods mechanism within the community.[9] Marriage, for Anamatian peasants, was a now-for-now affair and the sex-fame game facilitated serial polygamy (Freilich 1961). However, the sex-fame game had a disruptive effect on the stability of marital relations.

Viewed as a system in a general state of equilibrium, the sex and begging system had two flaws. The major flaw was that the fame goal of men was inconsistent with the secrecy goal of women. Indeed, most community members knew the secret sex life of most other community members. A minor flaw was that women wanted men to keep the promises made while men had to break promises. Men who kept all their promises revealed themselves as pygmies in fooling power.

The sex and begging system placed women in the dilemma of whether to participate or not. It was difficult for women to avoid the system, since men did not ask women (the equivalent of), "Do you want to participate?" Men enjoyed the beggar role and came (for among other reasons) to prove their begging ability. As one man boasted, "I beg and beg and beg. Finally they give in. A man must know how to beg so well that the women never refuse!"

The outcome of this system, then, was asymmetrical relationships between men and women with regard to sex. In the system women were not valued as individuals but as means of enhancing male prestige. They were not seen as active participants but as passive targets of male begging. To all appearances, the system looked like an exchange between men and women in which men provided economic goods and stability for prestige-enhancing sex. Even women's attempts to present themselves as respectable were related to attracting a man of high economic standing. Indeed, the more respectable the woman, the more she enhanced her lover's prestige.

The asymmetry between men and women, then, was based on economic asymmetry, and reinforced by a system whereby men obtained sex from begging and women attempted to ensure economic and social survival by attracting it. This system relied on men motivated by a desire for prestige, women motivated by desires for economic stability and respectability, and a fiction of secrecy that allowed the pursuits of prestige and respectability to coexist. Romance was viewed as part of a domain of upper-class relationships characterized by English values. It entered into the lives of those in Anamat through the tradition of demand letters, which involved proper-rules for obtaining a wife. Very few followed such proper-rules, however.

Sex and Romance: Anamat, Eastern Trinidad, 1989–1991

Thirty-five years ago a sex and romance system played an insignificant role in Anamatian sexual affairs. Instead, sexual relationships were seen in terms of fun, fame, and gift giving: women gave sex to a man who was a good beggar and able to reciprocate in goods, services, and even money. Anamat has changed, and some factors that supported this sex and begging system no longer exist. In particular, 1) economic development has increased female economic autonomy, 2) the fiction of secrecy has become harder to maintain, and 3) the threat of AIDS has entered to interfere with the sex-fame game. In addition, through mass media Trinidad has been inundated with American presentations of a sex and romance system as the desirable way to structure sexual relationships.

Given these changes, it is not surprising that a new set of smart-rules, rules heavily influenced by the presentation of romance found in American mass culture, have developed. These rules are rooted in the growing economic independence of women in Anamat. Anamatian women can now

270 more successfully resist male sexual domination, and in doing so they have managed to influence their mates to consider and sometimes to adhere to a model of romantic love found in sex and romance systems. In short, sexual life has greatly changed. From a woman's perspective there is a reduction of pain from the sex and begging system. From a man's perspective there is a reduction of glamour and excitement surrounding fame from successful begging. For both, the system of sexual relationships is increasingly viewed in terms of romance. While this system has yet to become entirely a system of sex and romance, it has changed considerably from the sex and begging system in the 1950s.

Changes: Economics, Aids, and Mass Media

During the last thirty-five years the pattern of economic development in Anamat followed that of the rest of Trinidad. Explosive growth in the 1970s due to sky-rocketing oil revenues was followed by a severe recession caused by decreasing prices of oil in the 1980s. During the 1970s many women were able to establish economic independence from men, mostly by becoming involved in the service sector. In the recession of the 1980s many men lost their jobs—most of these men had worked in the construction and manufacturing sectors, which were those hardest hit by the recession. Despite deteriorating economic conditions, many women retained their jobs because the service sector proved more resilient, although their incomes decreased. This brought about a situation in which some unemployed men became dependent upon their girlfriends or wives for money.

In addition, the increased accessibility of transportation and the availability of electricity for roadside houses motivated many families to move from their land to rented lots along the road. This changed the distribution of houses from that of a settlement haphazardly dispersed to a settlement strung along several miles of road. As the concentration of homes increased, and electric lighting illuminated the village at night, the fiction of secrecy became impossible to maintain. Due to these factors women are less dependent on exchanging sex for economic well-being. Consequently, women are resisting and rejecting the system of exchange that turned their bodies into commodities.

Into this situation has entered two new factors: 1) AIDS, which has changed many Anamatians' views concerning sexual intercourse, and 2) American television programs, which has changed many Anamatians' views concerning the place of romance in sexual relationships. Anamatians have become aware of the threat of AIDS in the last decade. Understandably, this has prompted some to change their sexual behavior, and it has become a factor in choosing sexual partners. Men have devised a new category of women, "AIDS-ting"[10]—a promiscuous woman thought likely to be infected with the HIV virus. Having sex with an AIDS-ting not only threatens a man's life later but damages his reputation now.

Television programs, particularly American soap operas, have provided a new source of ideas concerning sexual relationships. The plots of soap operas all involve romance, betrayal, and marriage, and they emphasize a sex and romance system. Women, the primary audience of these shows, become involved in following the shows—parallelling the behaviors of the American romance readers studied by Radway (1984). Radway notes that romance readers accept the model of a monogamous, sexually exclusive marriage but protest the failure of marriage to satisfy their emotional needs—by vicarious participation in the lives of the heroines, readers of romance novels partially compensate for these failures (Radway 1984:213). Modleski (1982) adds that American soaps serve to reinforce women's faith in the family despite the "weakness and unreliability of men" (1982:23). In addition, Modleski argues that soap operas displace blame away from men onto a "villainess" character. Because of the villainess "the spectator has the satisfaction of seeing men suffer the same anxieties and guilt that women usually experience and seeing them receive similar kinds of punishment for their transgressions" (1982:96).

Trinidadian women emphasize such themes in their discussions of the soap operas they watch. In addition, because of the variety of characters, both good and bad, in soap operas, women find a great deal of material to use in talking about their own and others' relationships without making direct reference to them.

As in American media presentations of gender roles, the importance of romance in defining a woman's value is emphasized. Anamatian women work hard to make themselves attractive to potential mates and husbands. While beauty enhances the prestige accorded a male conquest, it also poses a risk to a man's prestige, viz., that the man's partner might attract the interest of other men. If a man's partner acquiesces to the begging of other men, then the husband loses prestige. Indeed, this has become a common theme in Trinidad's weekly newspapers. The frequent presentation of such scenarios in television programs enhances this fear in men. Women feel that if they are attractive enough and seductive enough, their mates will respond with relative fidelity (only "slipping" as opposed to "skylarking") and, eventually, legal marriage.

Men view attractiveness in a sexual partner as enhancing their prestige, but because of behaviors of the villainess in soap operas, beauty in a mate also becomes a source of anxiety, particularly in breeding relationships where men are expected to control their mate's sexuality.

Many Trinidadian men are avid viewers of daytime soap operas or nighttime soap operalike dramas such as *Dallas*. The discussions that soap operas generate among men concern the ways in which male characters' authority and autonomy are threatened by women characters, in particular the villainess character. Men express fear that women watching the shows will get "wrong ideas" and mimic the behavior of the villainess.

Two different interpretations arise from soap operas, then. Women interpret soap operas as portrayals of relationships surviving despite the weaknesses of men and the existence of bad women who prey upon male weakness and men interpret soap operas as series of threats to men's reputations by women.

Many men, particularly young adults, still try to beg, but doing so involves a conceptualization of sexual relationships in terms of exchange, a conception now rejected by most women in favor of romance. Consequently, to successfully beg in order to obtain the prestige associated with sexual conquest, men must make promises based on the idiom of romance rather than the idiom of exchange. These promises of fidelity, loyalty, and long-term commitment conflict with attempting to participate in multiple love affairs inherent in the sex and begging system, and if promises are broken women no longer have their economic survival threatened when they terminate a relationship. In fact, common-law unions are no longer based exclusively on the idea of "good cooperation" in the management of domestic affairs but now include components from the cultural model of romance—components emphasizing commitment and loyalty.

While many young adult men still view the association between sex and romance in terms of the sex and begging system, many —particularly as they enter middle age—are willing to fulfill the promises made in the idiom of romance, and, in a sense, become converts to (what we call) the sex and romance system. Due to women's economic independence and the presentation of women as potentially unreliable in soap operas, men express insecurity about women, and particularly about their ability to sexually satisfy their partners. They worry about impotence and suggest that "a prick can dead, but a cunt can never dead."

Explaining the Decline of Sex and Begging

In the system of sex and begging men clearly benefited at women's expense. To a great extent this was because of the dependence of women on men for economic survival. In the cultural construction of sexual relationships according to romance that is now prevalent, women have more power to influence the outcome of sexual relationships to their benefit. The ascendancy of a system of romance was facilitated by economic development, which, in turn, provided women with greater economic independence from men than what they experienced in the 1950s. Yet changes in economic conditions only serve as a necessary, not a sufficient, explanation of the redefinition of sexual relationships. As Appadurai (1990) has pointed out, the world system, which is frequently treated as a purely economic system, also includes a "world system of images" (1990:4). In particular, American "mass-culture" has diffused worldwide (Bauman 1992), often creating havoc on traditional ideologies. We argue that American media presentations of romance have provided women with a means to redefine sexual relationships in a context where they are gaining economic independence from men.

Historically, in Trinidadian villages of the type discussed above, sex and romance systems as a form of formal discourse or as a desired life goal rarely played a role in public representations of sexual relationships. Instead, a sex and begging system, in which men begged for sex to enhance prestige and women gave sex to obtain economic security predominated. Conceptions of romance existed, as idealized courtship rules imply (see Herskovits and Herskovits 1947; Freilich 1960), but these conceptions of romance were associated with legal, church-sanctioned marriage—a type of marriage associated with the urban middle and upper classes. Because of the realities of rural and lower-class life, men did not desire the permanency and long-term costs implied by legal marriage and women made survival a greater priority than romance.[11] This system was widespread throughout the Caribbean,[12] and it has led some to suggest that romance played little or no role in Caribbean sexual relations (Henry and Wilson 1975).

The results of development, increased economic independence of women, and AIDS now make man's pursuit of reputation through sexual conquest based upon promiscuity far more risky. In addition, soap operas have become fertile ground from which new ideas of gender relationships emerge. When applied to cultural systems of sexual relationships, the ideas from soap operas foster security in women and insecurity in men who hold to the old view of sex as an exchange. Women increasingly define men as weak and liable to have an occasional extramarital affair, and men increasingly see their wives (common law or legal) as potential threats to their reputations if they become unhappy. Women seek to limit their husbands temptation to have affairs through expressions of romance and passion. On the other hand, on the basis of concern about their wives mimicking behavior on soap operas, men seek to prevent their wives from being unfaithful by increased expressions of passion and romance toward their wives as well as upholding promises of long-term commitments.

Consequently, the changes in Anamat from a sex and begging system to a sex and romance system cannot be attributed simply to economic changes, from which changes in sexual ideology emerge, but must also be attributed to a complex interaction of cultural and material influences in the context of sexuality.

Finally, it must be noted that the relationship of romance to increasing gender equality in Trinidad differs from American systems of romance where cultural models reinforce women's subservience to men (see Holland and Eisenhart 1990). Consequently, we do not suggest that romance results in gender asymmetry or symmetry. On the contrary, we suggest that romance must be viewed in terms of its relationship to specific cultural contexts. While romance might have a universal definition involving passion and commitment (Jankowiak and Fischer 1992), local implications of such conceptions vary. Indeed, this is one of the fascinating aspects of studying romance. So while sex and romance seems liberating for Anamatian women when compared to sex and begging, this does not necessarily signal the end of male domination. Since romance can facilitate male domination by encouraging women to view themselves as dependent on men, this possibility is not untenable for Trinidad. The extent to which this will develop, and what shape it may take in a region noted for strong female roles in the family and marketplace, is yet to be seen, however.

NOTES

We would like to thank Alexander Bolyanatz and Elizabeth Throop for reading early drafts of this paper. We are also indebted to William Jankowiak for his insightful comments on the specifics of this paper and the topic of romance in general.

1. A pseudonym.
2. Data presented in this section was collected by Morris Freilich and was originally

presented as part of a doctoral dissertation (Columbia University, 1960).

3. See Brereton 1981; Gilbert 1931; Shephard 1936.

4. Unless otherwise stated, references to marriage include both legal and common-law unions.

5. See Herskovits and Herskovits (1947:85) for an example of such a letter.

6. We here follow the insightful analysis made by philosopher W. W. Sharrock: a collectivity "owns" a corpus of knowledge. Irrespective of the subject or "culture" being investigated. Hence it is mandatory for social scientists to link shared-knowledge to agency. In Sharrock's words (1974:45) it is necessary to identify and interpret "the relationship between a collectivity's corpus of knowledge and the activities of its members." Sharrock's ideas have been developed by Freilich to include an ISU, an information-sharing unit that "owns" knowledge much like an inter not unlike a gene-pool (cf. Freilich 1993).

7. This should not be confused with being desirable sexually. Women expressed preferences for having sex with men who were sexually skilled, but a sexual partner who provided goods and services was also desired. Optimally, women preferred a combination of both in their partners, and such men had the greatest success in begging.

8. Freilich's data indicates that no husband in the village was (and in Western terms) totally "faithful." So the distinction here is one of frequency of begging; not between husbands who stray and husbands who don't stray.

9. Rodman (1971) argued that the Trinidadian sexual system—with its multiple, sequential relationships—serves to increase the economic resiliency of lower class Trinidadians.

10. Men commonly refer to both women and the sexual act as "tings," i.e., things.

11. Herskovits and Herskovits 1947; Freilich 1960, 1968, 1980; Freilich and Coser 1972; Rodman 1971.

12. Clarke 1957; Henriques 1953; Otterbein 1965; Smith 1962, 1966; Smith 1956, 1988.

REFERENCES

Angrosino, M. 1986. "Son and Lover: The Anthropologists as Non-Threatening Male." In T. Whitehead and M. Conaway, eds., *Self, Sex, and Gender in Cross-Cultural Field Work*, pp. 64–83. Urbana: University of Illinois Press.

Appadurai, A. 1990. "Disjuncture and Difference in the Global Cultural Economy." *Public Culture* 2(2):1–24.

Bauman, R., ed. 1992. *Folklore, Cultural Performances, and Popular Entertainments*. New York: Oxford University Press.

Brereton, B. 1981. *A History of Modern Trinidad*. Kingston: Heineman.

Clarke, E. 1957. *My Mother Who Fathered Me: A Study of the Family in Three Selected Communities in Jamaica*. London: George Allen and Unwin.

Freilich, M. 1960. "Cultural Diversity Among Trinidadian Peasants." Ph.D. diss., Department of Anthropology, Columbia University.

—— 1961. "Serial Polygyny, Negro Peasants, and Model Analysis." *American Anthropologist* 63:955–975.

—— 1968. "Sex, Secrets, and Systems." In Stanford Gerber, ed., *The Family in the Caribbean*, pp. 47–62. Rio Piedras: Institute of Caribbean Studies.

— 1980. "Smart-Sex and Proper-Sex." *Central Issues in Anthropology* 2(2):37–51.

— 1991. "Smart-Sex and Proper-Sex: A Journey Through Deviance." In M. Freilich, D. Raybeck, and J. Savishinsky, eds., *Deviance: Anthropological Perspectives*. New York: Bergin and Garvey.

— 1993. "New Knowledge, Old Knowledge, and Information-Sharing Units." Paper presented at the Annual Meetings of the American Anthropological Association, Washington, D.C.

Freilich, M., and Coser, L. 1972. "Structured Imbalances of Gratification: The Case of the Caribbean Mating System." *British Journal of Sociology* 23(1):1–19.

Gilbert, S. M. 1931. *The Cocoa Industry of Trinidad*. Council paper no. 4. Port of Spain: Government Printing Office.

Henriques, F. 1953. *Family and Colour in Jamaica*. London: Eyre and Spottiswoode.

Henry, F., and P. Wilson. 1975. "The Status of Women in Caribbean Societies: An Overview of Their Social, Economic, and Sexual Roles." *Social and Economic Studies* 24(2):165–198.

Herskovits, M., and F. Herskovits. 1947. *Trinidad Village*. New York: Knopf.

Holland, D., and M. Eisenhart. 1990. *Educated in Romance*. Chicago: University of Chicago Press.

Jankowiak, W., and E. Fischer. 1992. "A Cross-Cultural Perspective on Romantic Love." *Ethnology* 31(2):149–155.

Modleski, T. 1982. *Loving with a Vengeance: Mass-Produced Fantasies for Women*. Hamden, Conn.: Archon.

Otterbein, K. F. 1965. "Caribbean Family Organization: A Comparative Analysis." *American Anthropologist* 67(1):66–79.

Radway, J. 1984 *Reading the Romance*. Chapel Hill: University of North Carolina Press.

Rodman, H. 1971. *Lower-Class Families: The Culture of Poverty in Negro Trinidad*. Oxford: Oxford University Press.

Sharrock, W. W. 1974. "On Owning Knowledge." In R. Turner, ed., *Ethnomethodology*, pp. 45–53. Penguin.

Shephard, C. Y. 1936. *The Cocoa Industry of Trinidad: A Financial Survey of Estates During the Seven Years 1923–24 to 1929–30*. Series 2. Port of Spain: Government Printing Office.

Smith, M. G. 1962. *West Indian Family Structure*. Seattle: University of Washington Press.

— 1966. "Introduction" in Edith Clarke, *My Mother Who Fathered Me*. London: George Allen and Unwin.

Smith, R. T. 1956. *The Negro Family in British Guiana*. London: Routledge and Kegan Paul.

— 1988. *Kinship and Class in the West Indies: A Genealogical Study of Jamaica and Guyana*. Cambridge: Cambridge University Press.

Wilson, P. 1969. "Reputation and Respectability: A Suggestion for Caribbean Ethnography." *Man* 4(1):70–84.

The Balance of Duty and Desire in an American Polygamous Community

WILLIAM JANKOWIAK AND EMILIE ALLEN

> *In 1852 Orson Pratt in defense of celestial marriage rhetorically*
> *asked: "Can a man love more than one wife with all his heart?"*
> *Yes, was the reply, he can love each one God gives him with all*
> *his heart; and if he have 100, he can love them with the same*
> *intensity he could love one.*
>
> • ORSON PRATT, *The Seer*

> *In 1993 a polygamous wife commented about her marriage,*
> *"The worst mistake I ever did was getting married on*
> *Superbowl weekend. We go to celebrate our anniversary and it's*
> *all day in a motel in front of the TV."*

Introduction

Desire unleashed, undisciplined, and unregulated poses a threat to the values that bind a community together. This is especially true for romantic passion, a complex emotion that can, and often does, disrupt social relations. It is romantic passion's ability to provoke reflective and nonreflective behavior that makes it such a turbulent and complex human emotion. As other contributors to this collection have illustrated, this ability to engender new social relations, often in the face of negative sanctions, makes it such a volatile catalyst of resistance to cultural convention and communal harmony.

This theme is especially prevalent for the contemporary polygamists of Mormon Fundamentalism. Because the early church guidelines concerning the practice of plural marriage were not clear-cut, "Mormons, as free agents, were left to find out for themselves how to conduct their affairs" (Bradley 1993:3). As a result each family creates, to some degree, its individual synthesis of the need for communal harmony and the opportunity for personal fulfillment. In this way, compared to other polygamous cultures, the fundamentalist family ethos, is often more novel, idiosyncratic, and thus unpredictable (Foster 1991; Young 1954).

We will argue that the primary reason for the cultural variation in family organization arises from striving to balance often competing notions of love, sexual passion, and religious duty. This is especially dramatic with romantic passion, which often serves as the catalyst, however momentary, for men and women to question and reexamine cultural assumptions upon which they base and continue to construct their lives.

We hope to make this statement clearer by focusing on the relationship between fundamentalist Mormon theological notions of salvation, agency, and the pursuit of fulfillment. We intend to explore how these ideals form part of a unified cultural system that not only fosters the polygynous family form but also accounts, in large part, for the behavioral variation found within that form. Specifically, we will examine romantic passion as a fondly remembered, deeply troubling, and socially disrupting phenomenon. Because of romantic passion's volatile nature, it serves as a lighting rod for the issues that unite and divide the polygamous family. An analysis of the interplay between the experience of romantic passion, the hope for family harmony, and the longing for religious salvation in Angel Park, a small township located in the intermountainate region of the western United States, will provide a key to comprehending what Paul Bohannan calls "America's unique experiment in family living" (1985:81).

Theology, Mainstream Culture, and American Politics

The origins of Mormonism (or the Church of Jesus Christ of Latter Day Saints [LDS]) rest squarely in the frontier American experience, a powerful experience that shaped and continuously modified the earlier doctrines brought from Europe. It is a religion organized around tenets derived from three books: the Bible, the Book of Mormon, and The Doctrine and Covenants. The latter two books are revealed as holy scripture, the words of God revealed directly to Joseph Smith (Musser 1944).

Unlike mainstream Mormons who reject polygyny in this life, but not in the next, fundamentalist Mormons believe that the principle of celestial, or plural, marriage is the essence of their religion. It is only by practicing plural marriage here on earth that the highest exaltation in the Celestial Kingdom of God be attained. Accordingly, it is held that the great purpose of this life is to prepare for the coming of the Celestial Kingdom, a belief that supports the fundamentalists' conviction that they are God's chosen people born to create the polygamous family, God's ideal family form (see Baur 1988).

The fundamentalists believe that heaven is organized in a hierarchy whereby some people are nearer to God than others. An individual's celestial rank is determined by the virtuous deeds performed in this life, with the greatest virtue assigned to men who create and, to a lesser extent, maintain a large plural family. Through hard work and the assistance of his co-wives, a man elevates his own and, by extension, his family's spiritual rank in the Heavenly Kingdom.

Women can only achieve salvation, however, through joining the institution of the celestial or plural marriage as a sister-wife (i.e., a co-wife). Paul Bohannan (1985) points out that since "a woman in the next life shared the social position of her husband, it was in her interest to advance her husband's interests which meant that she should bear a large number of children (1985: 81). In this fundamental doctrine the family unit therefore extends beyond the grave into an eternal world, with the marriage contract "sealing" a man and woman together "for time and eternity" in the Heavenly Kingdom.[2]

Given the unusualness of the community's family system, it is easy to overlook the commonalities that fundamentalist Mormons share with mainstream American culture. Forged out of nineteenth-century American frontier experience, fundamentalist Mormonism embraces American culture values that range from frugality to personal autonomy.

Although the residents of Angel Park feel that certain aspects of the larger culture are immoral (e.g., MTV and R-rated movies), most members of the community participate as interested spectators and, at times, disgruntled critics of national and international events. Several polygynous families have even appeared on various talk shows to defend their religiously based lifestyle. Contemporary fundamentalists are thus not like the Amish, who disapprove of, and strive to withdraw from, mainstream America culture. For the fundamentalist Mormons life is to be enjoyed, and they do not hesitate to partake of some of life's many pleasures (e.g., drinking coffee and alcohol, touring local and national attractions, and feasting at Las Vegas's all-you-can-eat $4.99 buffets). Common dinner topics range from religious issues, secular philosophy, the entertainment value of Jurassic Park, Clinton's open marriage and its reflection on changes in American culture, to what herbs one should eat to prevent sickness.

Angel Park is not isolationist by choice. Fundamentalist Mormons never rejected mainstream culture as much as they feared to provoke its wrath. As a middle-aged man explains, "We follow the law of the land except when it contradicts with God's law of plural marriage." Nonetheless, for most of its eighty-year existence the community has repeatedly encountered social harassment and political persecution.

From 1882 on, federal and state governments sought to disenfranchise the Mormons in Utah. As a result, many polygynists went into hiding, fleeing into remote areas of Utah, Idaho, Arizona, and into Mexico. By 1897 almost two hundred Mormons were sent to prison for practicing polygyny (Bohannan 1985:81). However, despite the arrests and the opposition from Americans outside the community, several church leaders, including some of the founders of the Angel Park community, believed that the church would be compromising fundamental religious principles and therefore refused to cease forming plural marriages. Their refusal has resulted in more than two generations of strife between Angel Park and the mainstream Mormon Church, which after 1890, officially prohibited polygamy.

Thus began an ongoing antagonistic and sometimes bitter conflict between Mormon Fundamentalists, the mainstream Mormon Church, and state and federal governments. From the 1930s until the 1950s Angel Park was the site of numerous governmental raids, the last and largest of which took place in 1953, resulting in the arrest of 39 men and 86 women and their 263 children placed in foster homes for up to two years (Bradley 1993:110; Van Wagoner 1991). An unintended consequence of the raids was to "strengthen everyone's conviction and dedication to maintain their life-style. Outside pressure had in effect turned everyone into a community of believers" (Bradley 1993:110).

Since the late 1960s there has emerged a greater tolerance, albeit a reluctant one, between the States of Arizona, Utah, and the polygamous community. Although the state remains adamant in its insistence that the polygamous life style is illegal, it has tacitly adopted a "live and let live" posture toward Angel Park. Given American mainstream culture's tolerance toward cohabitation, alternative child-rearing practices, and other related social experiments in family living, the polygamist community is culturally and politically tolerated, a position that has been reinforced by the 1987 Supreme Court ruling that found children could not be taken from their mother solely on the basis of living in a polygamous household. The court ruled that documentation of child abuse, and not unorthodox family form, was the primary basis for police intervention. Today some community members are openly proud that, after decades of persecution, their religiously inspired way of life has finally received legal protection.

Angel Park: The Religious Community

Angel Park is a sectarian religious community that forms one of five polygamous communities found in western North America and northern Mexico. Each community is separately governed and maintains only nominal, if any, contact with the others. The population of Angel Park is approximately 6,000, with around 470 families ranging in size from two to over forty family members, accounting, in all, for less than one-tenth of the estimated, depending upon sources, between 21,000 to 50,000 Americans affiliated with a polygamous life style (Kilbride 1994; Quinn 1991).

On the whole, Angel Park is a town that, on first appearance, appears quaint and rather ordinary. Like other small American rural communities, its main roads are paved while its side streets are not. The town has one grocery store, a health food store, a post office, police station, volunteer fire department, an elementary and high school, a dentist (who is non-Mormon), two gas stations, a small motel, auto shops, a sewing factory, a large mortgage company, three restaurants (two for locals and the other more upscale, for tourists on their way to the Grand Canyon), and a petting zoo. The houses are large, with many in various stages of completion or renovation.

Angel Park is a community of practioners who live, or expect to live, or want to live, in a plural marriage. Unlike nineteenth-century Mormonism, where an estimated 10 to 20 percent of the families were polygamous (Foster 1992), more than 40 percent of the families in Angel Park are polygamous. Individuals who do not plan to create a plural family usually move to another community. This ensures that the community is constantly replenishing itself with outsiders (mostly women) committed to living "the principle" (i.e., plural marriage).

Because of its location, Angel Park's economy cannot support all of its residents, who thus work in a variety of jobs outside the community as janitors, masseuses, caretakers, nurses, school teachers, mechanics, long distance truck drivers, and construction workers.

Politically, Angel Park, like other small rural Mormon communities, is a closed system organized around a male theocratically oriented system (Cannon 1992). Few town officials are selected without proper religious credentials (Parker, Smith, and Ginat 1975:693). Recent disagreements within the community, however, have resulted in it splitting into two rival religious branches that have formed two separate communities organized around their own church and school. This split has generated additional problems for the members who have chosen to leave. Because families merely lease the land and do not own it, the church leadership is able to evict "undesirable" members from their homes by terminating their leases. This fact provides the church leadership with an enormous fund of political power and a practical means to reward its followers while expelling those who fail to conform. In the past expulsion was reserved only for the marginally deviant: today it is being used to evict the entire membership of the rival faction. The disagreement has become a legal matter tied up in state courts for over five years. In this and every other way, Angel Park has remained, throughout its history, both demographically and culturally a theologically governed religious community.[4]

Arranged Marriage, True Love, and the Priesthood Council

The Mormon conception of true love closely resembles that of nineteenth-century Victorian England, which Seidman tells us was "essentially spiritual, not physical or carnal in origin and essence" (Seidman 1991:45). In practice, however, sexual love in fundamentalist Mormon society, as it was in Victorian society, is often highly eroticized. Sexual pleasure is an appropriate desire provided it is the by-product of spousal affection and hence marital love. Angel Park fundamentalists, while disapproving of premarital sex, believe firmly that sexual pleasure should be an enjoyable aspect of every marriage.

Mormon cosmology holds that, before birth, everyone lives with God as a spirit. In this preexistence state men and women were promised to one another, for time and eternity. Individuals must therefore strive to find their "true love" and, in a sense, remarry. Failure to strive in such a way can potentially lead to an awkward situation whereby one's earthly spouse will differ from one's heavenly spouse. To ensure that death will not result in the separation of the spouses, it is imperative that the couple follow God's will. To this end, the priesthood's council members, as God's representatives, are eagerly sought in matters of the heart. One of the council's most important functions is to help community members find their celestial mates. The priesthood council is continuously involved in ongoing dialogues within itself and the community in its effort to sort out individual matters of the heart and, ultimately, marital placement.

It should not be inferred that romantic passion is a prerequisite for marriage. To date we have found that more than half of the marriages in Angel Park are not based on romantic love. In these marriages individuals, particularly teenage women, followed the matrimonial recommendations of their parents and the priesthood council. These marriages seldom have intergenerational conflict or personal turmoil. Not deeply emotionally involved with a spouse, the individual enters marriage expecting, as in many cultures, that in time "love will come." As a twenty-seven-year-old woman, who on the eve of her tenth wedding anniversary, said, "During the first three years of my marriage I did not even like my husband, but now I can say I truly love him." Hers is not an atypical opinion.

Nevertheless, dilemmas do arise. There are times when parents disapprove of a daughter's (though seldom a son's) choice or, more important, the priesthood council considers the relationship inappropriate. When this occurs, individuals must reconcile their romantic feelings with their deep-seated religious beliefs, which include the priesthood council's importance in guiding the community and its members to salvation and eternal happiness. This is never an easy task. Many couples, in the face of such resistance, break up and marry whomever the priesthood council recommends. Other couples, whose love is more deeply felt, often prefer to resist the council's recommendation. There are numerous precedents of individuals asserting that their romantic experience is authentic and, thus, sanctioned by God. Because Mormon theology is derived, in part, from nineteenth-century transcendentalism, it holds that God's will can be known through acts of private introspection and personal revelation. Accordingly, it honors individual conviction, and this religious tenet gives romantically entangled couples solid ground on which to argue that the council might be mistaken in its judgment. Although an individual's testimony of being divinely inspired is never directly challenged, the common response is to wonder whether God or the Devil is the real source of the inspiration. Still, the notion of "agency," or personal choice, serves as an effective counterpoint to the community's formal organization, its male-centered priesthood council.

Although it is understood that the priesthood council's duty is to assist, guide, and instruct the community in its collective and personal endeavor to achieve salvation, it is equally understood that personal visions are of profound religious significance and must be taken very seriously. To this end individuals seek to understand God's will through the aid of visions and dreams. Given these religious and secular values, it is accepted that the individual has the right to agree or disagree with any recommended marriage proposal.

Marriage negotiations are just that—negotiations that take place between the priesthood council and the couple, with the woman serving as both the object and the arbitrator of the negotiations. If the bride to be cannot be persuaded to change her mind, the council will often, albeit reluctantly, support her marital choice. For, as one informant said, "who can deny God and God's love" (i.e., choice)? However, in those instances where either the parents or the council refuse to sanction the marriage, the individual will either recognize and submit to the council's authority or the couple will elope and marry outside the community, returning, once a suitable time has elapsed, as a duly legitimized couple.

A twenty-seven-year-old man, who eloped with his wife, told us that "my wife's parents liked me until they found out that I wanted to marry their daughter. Her father wanted her to marry someone else. But we loved each other and knew we were meant to be together. My wife was only sixteen and I was twenty when we left the community and married. A few months later we returned and were accepted back into the family." In this instance, the disagreement was between the girl's parents and the boy and not the council, which had taken no strong position in the matter.

Another example of intergenerational antagonism is found in the tale of a young woman who, at the age of fifteen, refused her parents and the priesthood council's insistence that she marry a sixty-two-year-old man. She recalls that

> he was so sure that I would agree that he immediately began to build a new house for me, while keeping his first wife in an old trailer. After six years of waiting and pleading he finally got the hint and accepted the fact that I never would marry him. I wanted to marry someone who I love, and I did.

In this way marriages in Angel Park are often quasi-arranged, but only with the tacit support of some members of the younger generation who were not able to find someone on their own and so had no difficulty acceding to the wishes of their parents or the priesthood council's marital recommendations.

Romantic Experience: Male-Female Commonality

Fundamentalist polygamists customarily use the quality of affection, and not duty, to assess and measure the overall quality of their family life. For analytical purposes we have distinguished the range of feeling that men and women characteristically express concerning their experience with love. Angel Park residents are similar to those found in nineteenth-century Mormon polygamist love letters, which are typically filled with romantic yearnings, emotional turmoil, and heartrending disclosures. At a biopsychological level these contemporary romantic yearnings and emotional longings

resemble those found not only in mainstream America but also those reported in other cultures around the world. It is important to remember that most
people, at some point in their lives, experience some of these emotional highs
and lows, and often with the same spouse.

The accounts presented below illustrate the importance of romantic love
as a desirable personal emotional state, at the same time reflecting a deep-
seated ambivalence. For women romantic love's presence or absence—much
more than role equity—constitutes the primary measure of the quality of
their relationship. Its primacy is movingly revealed in the following personal accounts of what happens when a husband's love is lost.

In one case a husband told one of his wives that he no longer loved her.
Sinking into a deep despondency, she took rat poison, crying that she no
longer wanted to live. Although she became very sick, she survived. Instead
of growing more sensitive and supportive, her husband was horrified and
refused to talk to her. Another example of the power of love can be seen, by
negative inference, in the habitual cynicism of many mature women who
often privately counsel engaged women not to fall in love with their husbands. A bitter romantic experience makes for a repeated warning among
Mormon wives. One woman told a prospective bride, "If you do fall in love,
he will hurt you." In this instance, the young bride confessed that it was too
late, as she had "already fallen in love."

The ambivalent attitude held toward romantic love is further illustrated
by the following episode. One Sunday afternoon after church a young girl
announced her engagement by showing her new wedding ring to her friends.
When asked if her husband had any other wives, she said, "No, I am the
first." An older sister-in-law, who was a second wife, overhearing the comment replied, "She is the first wife. She is the one who gets to go through all
the heartache."

Fundamentalist women are not the only gender, however, that fears emotional vulnerability, although men maintain a more stoic, if not cynical, posture toward romantic love. Many men dismissed the emotion altogether,
stressing that it was, at bottom, an illusion and not the best basis for a marriage. More in-depth probing, however, found that two-thirds of the men
interviewed had been romantically rejected as young men in high school.
The experience was so distressing that they became determined never to
become emotionally involved again. For example, when I asked one man if,
on his wedding day, he was in love with any of his three wives, he indicated
that he was not, but acknowledged that, when in high school, he had fallen in

love with two women who rejected his overtures. He admitted that "it hurt so much I decided never again to let myself experience that feeling." His attitude sounds a familiar male chord in Angel Park. Men's anxiety over the possibility of losing emotional intimacy and being abandoned is a propensity revealed in the following account.

A middle-aged women recalls the anxiety of her beloved husband and his words on their wedding night: "Have you ever wanted something your whole life and, when you finally have it, you feel that it is going to be taken away from you?" "No," she replied, "I guess I have not lived long enough to desire something that much." Then he told her he was "so afraid of losing me because he loved me so much." That night she promised never to leave him. Twenty years later her husband, bedridden from old age, could no longer control his bowel movements. Whenever she grew weary of the tedious duties involved in bathing, feeding, and cleaning him, she remembered her wedding night promise never to leave him. She asserted that "I stayed with him because in the end I realized that I love him. I know right now he is preparing a place for me on the other side and, when I die, he will come and take me back with him, but only if I am worthy."

Mormon fundamentalist men's reaction to the loss of love, whether through death, divorce, or abandonment, resembles their American mainstream male counterparts, who tend to slowly recover from emotional separation. Men's capability for extended sadness, due to the absence of romantic love, is revealed in the following account.

A middle-aged woman unexpectedly met the son of a former high school classmate who had asked to marry her years ago. Much to her surprise she discovered that the man had, for more than twenty years, harbored a love crush he only recently revealed to his young son who, upon meeting her, blurted out, "So you are the woman that my father always talks about. He was so crushed when you married that older man."

Another example of men's propensity to quietly endure emotional loss is found in the torment of a man whose second wife left him to join another polygamous community. The man did not want to discuss the incident for fear of emotionally retrieving it. However his son told us that "my father was depressed for months. He lost the woman he loved." Another wife revealed that her husband was devastated when his third wife left the family, remarking that "when Sam's third wife left him for another man who had been secretly courting her, it affected his health. He cried for three straight weeks and simply deteriorated into an invalid. We buried him six months later."

Polygamist men and women, when discussing the benefits of arranged marriages, often mention the avoidance of emotional entanglements as its chief one. What is significant is that no one takes these discussions seriously. Everyone knows that each man and woman will have to reconcile, in their own way, the desired, feared, and often deeply troubling emotional experience that is romantic love.

Gender Differences: The Search for True Love

Because marriage is a reality that confronts women at an earlier age than men, women more than men are preoccupied with finding a "true love." It is a goal that is considered and discussed with a genuine intensity and singleness of purpose. For young men, however, marriage remains a kind of abstraction that will not involve them until later in life. At this point of their lives (sixteen to seventeen years old) many young women realize that they do not want to live in a plural marriage and decide to leave the community. For women who decide to remain, however, they must confront the dueling demands of romance, marital happiness, and family harmony.

Unlike polygamist men who can and, often do, find romantic passion by taking an additional wife, women's opportunities are more restricted. They can marry only one man at a time. Although more than 8 percent of women in Angel Park will divorce over the course of their lives, it is not the preferred solution to a loveless marriage. It is far better to choose wisely and form a good marriage and thus "add to the Lord's flock." To this end prayer, visionary dreams, and one's own inner promptings are evaluated in an attempt to understand God's will—processes that are not unlike the approach taken by American Puritans to spiritual problems. The validity of dreams as a vehicle of truth is so strong that they are often the critical guide used in making important decisions. A middle-aged woman, for example, who had recently terminated a short but difficult marriage and was temperamentally hesitant to become emotionally involved again, changed her mind when she, by chance, met a man who resembled a man that she had dreamed about as a young girl. She recalls that "I dreamt of a man with blue eyes and curly blond hair. Neither of my first two husbands had blue eyes or curly hair. When I saw him standing with blond hair and blue eyes, I knew he was the man in my dreams and I wanted to immediately marry him. It did not matter what others might think, he was my true love."

Another woman prayed for a sign of whom she would marry. After several weeks of intense prayer she had a vision that revealed her "promised love," a married man whom she had never spoken to. Immediately she sought out a member of the priesthood council for confirmation as to the authencity of her vision. He informed her that it was a good sign. A few days later he approached the man and suggested that her vision was God's sign that he take another wife. Although he did not know the woman very well, he agreed. The woman was filled with anticipation and excitement over being united with her true love. The man, however, took a reserved, almost emotionally guarded, attitude toward his new bride. For him marriage was more of a duty—in this case, a duty derived from a true visionary dream.

Younger men are consistently concerned more than older mature men with finding their true love. This is not unusual. Without the financial backing of their families, young men are economically unable to compete with the more established mature males. The only resources they have, being unmarried, are those not immediately available to older married men: access and the opportunity to offer exclusive attention to a particular woman. Because most male-female relationships begin in high school, many young men are able to form substantial emotional bonds. Although lacking economic means of support, a young man can often convince a woman that she would be happier marrying him than a middle-aged man with several wives. The pattern is that if the young woman falls in love with the young man, she will probably marry him. On the other hand, if he is unsuccessful in attracting a high school sweetheart, he will ultimately leave the community to find a wife.

There is always a shortage of eligible women in every polygamous society, and Angel Park is no exception. The community is, therefore, always seeking ways to attract outsiders to convert to their religion and embrace their lifestyle. The primary boosters are men who, on their own accord, seek to marry women outside the community who will convert to their religion. To this end men invoke religious scripture and secular ideals of harmonious love to justify the life they have to offer. Many women find these courtship persuasions intriguing and, provided they also enjoy the man's personality, often decide to marry the man and adopt his lifestyle. In these instances it is not religious doctrine per se that is attractive, though it is a useful support, as much as it is the man himself and his alternative lifestyle.

Polygamous wives are drawn from three backgrounds: widows, divorcées, and youths who are open to a polygamous lifestyle. Their motivations range from deeply felt emotional and/or religious commitment to the pragmatic need for support of themselves and their children. Regardless of motivation, polygamist men are willing to marry them as to do so increases the size of their earthly family and thus their celestial rank in the heavenly kingdom. Despite this, it is young nubile women who are preferred over middle-aged mature women. The reasons rest on reproductive pragmatics and male erotic aesthetics. Men want to have sex and children and they prefer to have both with young women.

As in other cultures, physical attraction is the hook that pulls men into the relationship (Buss 1994). Angel Park women are acutely aware that men find younger women more attractive than older women. Some wives relate stories of their husbands going, in their words, "crazy and chasing young girls." As a mature woman explained, "My husband went through a mid-life crisis and began chasing a young fourteen year old around. During the courtship my husband would spend his money on her, instead of giving it to me and the children. I hated that young girl for the neglect she caused my family." Another middle-aged woman, when asked what the difference was between men and women, replied, "Men and women." She added that "men desire young girls and women friendship." Although women emphasize lust as the primary motivation for men's involvement with a younger wife, men report, however, that it is not sexual desire per se that "drives a man crazy" as much as it is the anticipation and enjoyment of being with an attractive woman, which seems to invoke romantic idealization. As one man noted, "I was obsessed with her in ways that I did not understand. She became my life." Youth is the catalyst that provokes male idealization, transforming lust into passionate love.

Men justify their interest in building a plural family entirely on the premise of religious tenets. They are hesitant to admit that they find erotic pleasure in sexual variety. It is, however, a pleasure often acknowledged in moments of private humor and spontaneous (and sometimes drunken) asides. This is not a recent occurrence. Kimball Young, writing about polygamous life in the 1930s, observed that "older men got a thrill out of courting a younger woman" (1954:282). Most men in Angel Park would concur, although some more loudly than others. They are adamant in their insistence, however, that their primary motive for entering into a plural marriage is one of religious conscientiousness. This notion is not self-deception. It is the fundamental reason why men and women strive to live "the principle" and, hence, create God's model human family system.

Politics of Romance: Inside a Polygamous Family

Angel Park is a community organized around a set of religious standards and secular principles that emphasize the pursuit of salvation through the avoidance of sin, selfishness, and arrogance. Within the family the religious principles are centered on the notion we call harmonious or familial love. Harmonious love is somewhat akin to communitas in being unbounded in its potential for forging, strengthening, and sustaining affectionate bonds. Because it encourages respect, empathy, helpfulness, and lasting affection, harmonious love often serves as the principal means to bind and unite the polygamous family. Its nondyadic focus stands in sharp contrast to romantic love, a tolerated but seldom glorified emotional experience. Although harmonious love is fervently stressed as the preferred ideal, it is vulnerable, as we have seen, to personal desires.

Angel Park distinguishes between two types of families: "united polygamy" (i.e, living together in one house) and "divided polygamy" (i.e., living in separate homes). The cultural ideal is to live together in one large house, but the reality is that more than 60 percent of the Angel Park's polygamous families live in separate households.

Social relations in the Mormon polygamous family, unlike other polygamous societies, revolve around personal sentiment as much as duty. There is a twin pull of almost equal force. Whenever a conflict arises an individual response is unpredictable and thus threatening to the social order: will he or she uphold family harmony or seek to satisfy personal gratification? This is especially so of romantic love, which, more than any other emotional experience, not only overwhelms a person's judgment but also can reorder his or her priorities for an uncertain period of time.

There is a continuum in both men's and women's involvement in plural marriage that ranges from shared equality to outright favoritism. Men, as the symbolic center of the family, must balance each wife's emotional and economic interests. Conscious of the impact of favoritism on the family harmony, men strive to modify some of its harmful impact. To this end most husbands are diligent in spending quality time (e.g., dinners and trips), if not equal time, with each co-wife. In this regard, women intently study and assess their husband's actions and are quick to note acts that suggest favoritism. If a husband can avoid pursuing his interests and struggle or, in their words, "sacrifice" in order to uphold the religious principles, the household ambience will be relatively harmonious and content.

The most delicate and potentially dangerous situations arise whenever a new wife enters the family. This is the most unstable time in a fundamentalist household and often tests a woman's religious convictions and, in turn, her willingness to participate in a plural marriage. During this liminal state the new wife usually receives the husband's undivided attention, and co-wives do not complain about their husband spending a lot of time with the new wife. It is understood that the honeymoon intimacy will continue once the couple returns from their trip. However, if the intimacy continues beyond a few weeks, it will engender a round of questions and doubts and, ultimately, generate intense jealousy among the co-wives.

Mormon polygamous wives who are not the central focus of their husband's attention and love, like their counterparts in other cultures (see chapter 9), deeply resent the favorite wife. If the favoritism persists, a wife will assume that her husband has grown emotionally distant and is no longer interested in her. Whenever this happens a wife will respond in one of three ways: 1) seek to rekindle romantic their husband's waning interest 2) resign herself to the loss of affection and seek emotional fulfillment exclusively in her children, or 3) divorce and seek love in another marriage. Clearly, for all concerned, it is imperative that the husband and his wives avoid favoritism and work together to sustain a harmonious family ambience.

As we have seen, it is romantic passion's volatility that makes it a feared, resented, and admired emotional experience. For the fundamentalists of Angel Park it tests the faith and commitment of long term co-wives as well as newlyweds' religious faith. For example, in the case of a new wife, her emotions and expectations are often challenged by the reality of sharing a spouse. The adjustment is never easy. A young woman, who had recently taken a new sister-wife, told us that "sometimes I want to always be with my husband, but I know that it is selfish so I encourage him to see his other wife." Not every wife is as generous or as noble. Some are confused, experiencing doubt and distress. A young woman told us that "I did not think my husband's second marriage would bother me—I was ready to live the principle. But I stayed awake at nights, unable to sleep. I felt so alone and abandoned." Other co-wives cease believing in the spiritual nobility of harmonious love and focus entirely on getting their fair share of emotional attention. This attitude is exemplified in the following account of a new wife's surprise and eventual resignation that her co-wife did not believe in, nor did she want to work to create, a "united polygamous" family. She reported,

> Right before I married my husband, he, his first wife, and myself went for a walk. My husband had his arms around both of us as we walked down the street. As we walked I put my arm around my husband's waist, just below the first wife's arm who was already holding on to him. Latter that evening the first wife told me,

"When I felt you arm around our husband's waist it made my blood boil." I was shocked at her comment because I thought she wanted to live the principle and create a harmonious large family. [Pause] This marriage has been a challenge from that day forward, because the first wife refuses to accept God's law" [i.e., polygyny].

An uneasy and perennial tension exists between a woman's desire to receive exaltation by participating in the plural marriage and her fear of losing her husband's interest and attention. This accounts for the continuous evaluation of every potential marital prospect. Wives are keen to discover shortcomings in a potential wife and become annoyed and, at times, paranoid whenever their husband is considering another wife. How unsettling this transition can be is illustrated by the following account. A woman had been staying with a polygynous family for a short period of time. Although she assured everyone that she was not interested in plural marriage, the wives of the family were leery of her true intentions. After the visit the woman explained to a co-wife that she had a boyfriend and only wanted to stay with them for a short vacation, whereupon the wife immediately reported the conversation to her husband and then watched, in delight, his surprise and disappointment. Another example of the tension between religious conviction and pragmatic interest is found in the various ways that co-wives often seek to discourage a prospective wife from joining the family. These can range from ignoring her presence whenever she visits to asking her assistance in performing a particularly odious domestic chore. After a young woman who was being courted had spent the entire night talking with her potential husband, the next morning a co-wife requested that she wash the family's Sunday dinner dishes, a task that meant washing by hand more than one hundred dishes and taking more than an hour and a half. The point that the co-wife wanted to communicate to the potential wife was that plural marriage did not involve stimulating discussion of love, religious philosophy, and family harmony.

If polygamist women are emotionally vulnerable, particularly to psychological abandonment, so are men. If a polygamist husband becomes too attached, he knows that he will disrupt family bonds and do damage to his reputation within the community for being unable to manage his family. The burden of this management falls heavily on the man. A man knows that if the family has the reputation of being disharmonious he will lose honor and social standing in the community, which can result in difficulty in attracting a future wife.

A man is dependent on his wife's (or wives') assistance in attracting another spouse. For even if the priesthood council recommends a marriage partner, the woman still must decide. Her decision is often based on three factors: 1) the quality of family harmony (actual and potential) represented in the cooperation between co-wives, 2) the intensity of affection held for the husband, 3) the number of wives, especially young wives, in the family. It is a cultural given that it is often in a young woman's short-term interest to marry a middle-aged man with mature wives. This is a powerful motivation and requires assessment.

Mature wives are not powerless. They are respected, valued, and loved not because of seniority but rather for either the quality of marriage or their access to valuable resources (e.g., a deceased husband's retirement funds, social security benefits, or some other forms of inheritance or income). This wealth, while not considerable, is often sufficient to assist a man in attracting another wife. With this supplementary source of income a man can buy a used car or build a home for his new wife. If a wife withholds her income it can undermine her husband's ability to attract another wife. A polygamist husband depends on his co-wife's (or co-wives') assistance to sustain a friendly household environment and to provide economic aid in helping him build his heavenly kingdom.

It is a dilemma for men and women. They embrace the polygamous principle and its call for plurality, while simultaneously seeking to hold onto, or rekindle, the romantic passion once felt toward a particular spouse. The tensions that erupt around this dilemma are the source of drama found in daily life at Angel Park. The reality is that the majority of Angel Park's polygamous families seldom achieve genuine long-lasting harmony, but remain, at best, a house of competing interests that periodically rupture the fragile balance that unites a man, his wives, and children together in their religiously inspired and unified cultural system. In seeking to fulfill God's law and create the polygamous family, the residents of Angel Park endure "sacrifices" that they believe will ultimately enable them to achieve salvation. The domestic tensions serve to build character, which, in the eyes of the Lord, will make them worthy to enter his Heavenly Kingdom.

In summary, nineteenth-century Mormons strove to achieve a spiritual community based on the institution of plural, or celestial, marriage, which exalts harmonious love as the center of family life. This ideal stands in sharp contrast to romantic love, which Angel Park has neither rejected nor encouraged, but recognized. Furthermore, the competing nineteenth-century

294   notions of agency and collectivism contribute to ongoing tensions within Angel Park, often pulling the individual in opposite directions.

Since this community honors the individual's freedom to determine which emotional orientation—harmonious or romantic love—is the more important, there is tremendous variation in response. In this way romantic love constitutes both an authentic, creative force and a potentially disruptive emotion. As such, it is an experience that challenges collective religious conviction and the individual will to participate in America's most unique experiment in family living.

NOTES

The data that forms much of this research is part of a larger ongoing research project that began in 1992. The work is partially supported by a minigrant from the Nevada National Endowment for the Humanities and a UNLV Research Grants and Fellowships Award. We would like to thank Paul Bohannan, Hans Baur, Jim Bell, Janet Cannon, Philip Kilbride, Lee Munroe, Thomas Paladino, Susan Pensak, and Michael Quinn for their encouragement, suggestions, and comments.

1. Polygyny has been studied primarily from a structural perspective that seeks to understand its evolution as a form of adaptation to certain ecological restraints. With the notable exceptions of Young (1954) and Bohannan (1985), analysis of an individual's experiences in a polygamous household is, for the most part, overlooked.

2. In the early 1970s Parker, Smith, and Ginat (1975) found that every family in "Weston," a polygamist community in northern Utah, was polygamous.

3. Girls marry earlier than boys, usually after graduating from high school. Boys must wait until they have a job that provides sufficient funds with which to start a family. The dress code is one of modesty. Women wear long-sleeved ankle-length dresses and long hair; men's hair is kept short and diligently groomed.

4. Although many nineteenth century Mormons argued that sexual intercourse was for procreation and not personal enjoyment, this is not always the case. Sexuality is not an embarrassing topic in Angel Park. Although modesty is stressed, men and women are not sexual prudes. Given the frequency of childbirth, reproduction and sexuality are simply taken as a natural aspect of life.

REFERENCES

Baur, H. 1988. *Utopia in the Desert.* New York: SUNY.

Bohannan, P. 1985. *All The Happy Families.* New York: McGraw Hill.

Bradley, M. 1993. *Kidnapped From that Land.* Provo: University of Utah Press.

Buss, D. 1994. *The Evolution of Desire*. New York: Basic.

Cancian, F. 1987. *Love in America*. New York: Cambridge University Press.

Cannon, J. 1992. "My Sister, My Wife: An Examination of Sororal Polygyny in a Contemporary Mormon Fundamentalist Sect." *Syzygy* 1:4:315–320.

Foster, L. 1991. *Women, Family, and Utopia*. Syracuse: Syracuse University Press.

Kilbridge, P. 1994. *Plural Marriage for Our Times*. Westport, Conn.: Bergin and Garvey.

Musser, J. 1944. *Celestial or Plural Marriage*. Salt Lake City: Truth.

Parker, S., J. Smith, and J. Ginat. 1975. "Father Absence and Cross-Sex Identity: The Puberty Rites Controversy Revisited." *American Ethnology* 2(4):687–706.

Quinn, M. 1991. "Plural Marriage and Mormon Fundamentalism." In M. Marty and R. Appleby, eds., *Fundamentalisms and Society*. Chicago: University of Chicago Press.

Seidman, S. 1991. *Romantic Longings*. London: Blackwell.

Van Wagoner, R. 1991. *Mormon Polygamy: A History*. Salt Lake City: Signature.

Young, K. 1954. *Isn't One Wife Enough?* New York: Holt, Rinehart and Winston.

Contributors

EMILIE ALLEN is a graduate student in the Anthropology Department at the University of California, Los Angeles. She has conducted field research in Belize and among a Mormon polygamous community in the Southwest. Presently she is working on a life history of a polygamous wife and editing a book on changes in the American family.

JIM BELL is an Associate Professor of Anthropology at California State University, Los Angeles. He received his Ph.D. in 1986 from University of California, Santa Barbara. He is an ethnographic filmmaker and the author of numerous articles. Presently, he is working on a book that explores the presence of racism before European contact.

KEVIN K. BIRTH is Assistant Professor of Anthropology at Queens College, City University of New York. He received his Ph.D. in 1993 from the University of California at San Diego. His primary research is on cultural representations of time in Trinidad. He is also collaborating with Morris Freilich on studying social change in Eastern Trinidad. He has published on the relationship of British anthropology and psychoanalysis as well as on calypso and the 1990 attempted coup d'état in Trinidad and Tobago.

VICTORIA KATHERINE BURBANK is an Associate Professor at the University of Western Australia. She was educated at Rutgers University, where she received her Ph.D. in 1980, and at Harvard University, where she was a Postdoctoral Research Fellow between 1980 and 1983. Her publications include *Aboriginal Adolescence* (Rutgers University Press, 1988) and *Fighting Women* (University of California Press, 1994).

JAMES S. CHISHOLM is an Associate Professor in the Department of Anatomy and Human Biology at the University of Western Australia. He has done research at the Institute of Child Health of the University of London, on a Navajo reservation, at the Laboratory of Comparative Human Development at Harvard University, and in Arnhem Land. He received his Ph.D. in Anthropology from Rutgers University and has taught at the University of New Mexico and the University of California, Davis, where he is currently on leave from his position as Associate Professor. His research interests lie in the fields of psychological anthropology and evolutionary ecology.

RICHARD CONDON is an Associate Professor of Anthropology at the University of Arkansas and editor of the international journal *Arctic Anthropology*. He received his Ph.D. from the University of Pittsburgh in 1981 and held positions at Harvard College, Bowdoin College, and the University of Alaska before joining the faculty at Arkansas. Since 1978 he has been conducting fieldwork in the Copper Inuit community of Holman located in the Central Canadian Arctic. He has published numerous articles and two books: *Inuit Behavior and Seasonal Change* (UMI Press, 1983) and *Inuit Youth: Growth and Change in the Canadian Arctic* (Rutgers University Press, 1987).

JAN CLANTON COLLINS is a Jungian analyst and licensed marriage and family counselor. She received her training at the C. G. Jung Institute in New York and Los Angeles and is well known as a leader of training seminars for psychotherapists. She is a training analyst in the Inter-Regional Society of Jungian Analysts, and is the author of articles linking psychological and anthropological approaches to healing and analytical psychology. Dr. Collins (with Professor Gregor) is presently completing a book on the nature of loving relationships in successful marriages.

DOUGLAS DAVIS is a Professor of Psychology at Haverford College, where he teaches courses in personality and culture. he received his Ph.D. in Psychology from the University of Michigan. With Susan Davis he is the author of *Adolescence in a Moroccan Town.*

SUSAN DAVIS earned her Ph.D. in anthropology at the University of Michigan, Ann Arbor, and works as an independent scholar and a consultant on international development. She has written books on adolescence and women in Morocco, and articles on those topics and on women, water, and development.

HELEN FISHER is Research Associate in the Department of Anthropology at Rutgers University. Her books include *Anatomy of Love* (1992, 1994) and *The Sex Contract* (1982, 1983). Among her other publications are articles in *The New York Times Book Review* (1994), *The Journal of NIH Research* (1994), *Psychology Today* (1993), *The American Journal of Physical Anthropology* (1989), and *Natural History* (1987). She has been on the college lecture circuit since 1983, and in 1985 she received the American Anthropological Association's Distinguished Service Award for her work in disseminating anthropological data and ideas to the lay public.

MORRIS FREILICH is a Professor of Anthropology at Northeastern University. He received his Ph.D. in anthropology from Columbia University in 1960. He has done research with Mohawk Indians, Trinidadian peasant farmers, hospitalized mental patients, and Hasidic Jews in the United States and Israel. He has edited several books, including *Marginal Natives: Anthropologists at Work*, *The Relevance of Culture*, and *Deviance: Anthropological Perspectives*. Among his many articles are "Myth, Method, and Madness," "Toward a Model of Social Structure," and "The Natural Triad in Kinship and Complex Societies."

THOMAS GREGOR is Professor and Chair of Anthropology at Vanderbilt University. He is the author of numerous scientific publications, including his most recent book, *Anxious Pleasures: The Sexual Lives of an Amazonian People* (University of Chicago Press). Professor Gregor's scientific specializations include gender and sexuality and psychological anthropology. Professor Gregor (with Dr. Collins) is presently completing a book on the nature of loving relationships in successful marriages.

HELEN HARRIS is a graduate student in the Department of Anthropology at the University of California, Santa Barbara. She is currently completing her dissertation on the significance of romantic love for understanding human behavior and daily life in the Mangaian culture.

WILLIAM JANKOWIAK is an Associate Professor of Anthropology at the University of Nevada, Las Vegas. He received his Ph.D. from University of California, Santa Barbara in 1986. He has conducted extensive field research in China, Inner Mongolia, and North America. He is the author of numerous scientific publications, including his most recent book, *Sex, Death, and Hierarchy in a*

Chinese City (Columbia University Press), the first in-depth study of urban life in the People's Republic of China. Presently he is working on a book about contemporary American polygamy.

CHARLES LINDHOLM is a University Professor and member of the Department of Anthropology at Boston University. His research is on passionate relationships of identification and on complex societies with egalitarian ideologies. His most recent book is *Charisma*. He is presently writing about the history and culture of the Middle East.

LEONARD PLOTNICOV is Professor of Anthropology at the University of Pittsburgh and Editor in Chief of *Ethnology*, an international journal of social and cultural anthropology. His several books on Africa include *Strangers to the City* and *Social Stratification in Africa*.

L. A. REBHUN is a Visiting Assistant Professor of Medical Anthropology at Case Western Reserve University. She has done research on the connections between family and health in Northeast Brazil. Her publication of "'Nerves' and Emotional Play in Northeast Brazil" in the *Medical Anthropology Quarterly* won the Society for Medical Anthropology's W. H. R. Rivers Prize for 1991. She is currently working on a book about gender, economy, and love in Northeast Brazil.

HELEN A. REGIS is graduate student at Tulane University presently competing her Ph.D. thesis, "Pluralism in Practice: Everyday Medicine in a Fulbe Village." When in New Orleans she works with the Social Aide and Pleasure Clubs that sponsor numerous parades held throughout the year in the city's predominately Black neighborhoods.

PAMELA R. STERN is a research associate with the Department of Anthropology at the University of Arkansas. She received her M.A. degree from the University of Pittsburgh in 1983. Since 1980 she has conducted research in the Canadian Arctic on gender roles and gender socialization as well as on the process of medical acculturation. Her most recent publication (with husband/colleague Richard Condon) is "Gender Role Preference, Gender Identity, and Gender Socialization Among Inuit Youth" in *Ethos: Journal of the Society for Psychological Anthropology*. When she is not in the field Pamela works as a professional caterer specializing in exotic deserts.

Designer: Teresa Bonner
Text: Fournier
Compositor: Columbia University Press
Printer: Edwards Brothers
Binder: Edwards Brothers

Index

CPSIA information can be obtained
at www.ICGtesting.com
Printed in the USA
LVOW13s1603180718
584181LV00010BA/305/P